Criminal Justice: Introduction and Guidelines

Criminal Justice: Introduction and Guidelines

(a revision of **Law Enforcement and Criminal Justice: An Introduction**)

Paul B. Weston

California State University
Sacramento, California

Kenneth M. Wells

Public Defender
Sacramento County, California
McGeorge School of Law
University of the Pacific

Goodyear Publishing Company, Inc.
Pacific Palisades, California

Library of Congress Cataloging in Publication Data

Weston, Paul B
  Criminal justice.
First ed. published in 1972 under title: Law enforce-
    ment & criminal justice: an introduction.
    Includes bibliographies and index.
  1. Criminal justice, Administration of—United States.
    I. Wells, Kenneth M., joint author. II. Title.
    KF9223.W43 1976   345'.73'05   74–19946
                        ISBN 0–87620–169–9

Library of Congress Catalog Card Number: 74–19946
                        ISBN: 0–87620–169–9
                                    Y–1699–1
Current Printing (Last Number):
  10 9 8 7 6 5 4 3 2 1
Printed in the United States of America

Contents

List of Illustrations

Preface

It is common in community life in America for all citizens to expect certain fundamental freedoms and rights: the services of police officers who are paid to maintain order, detect crime and arrest offenders; the due process of law from state and federal law enforcement agents; and judicial review to protect all citizens from injustice. Additionally, the control of crime now extends from its prevention to the rehabilitation of convicted criminals.

The origin and aim of the criminal law and legal process is the place of beginning in this text. Then, role, theories, and practices of the agents and agencies of criminal justice are reviewed in alignment with the book's theme of criminal justice as a system to maintain domestic tranquility and control crime. Lastly, this is an open-end text. The past and the present are viewed as frames of reference for new horizons in law enforcement and criminal justice.

This is an introduction to the people and the procedures comprising America's methodology for protecting the citizen and community against crime, and to change the behavior of lawbreakers. It is a detailing of the components of an interlocking system of legislators, the judiciary, and agents of the executive branch of government—and of the criminal offender and his victim or victims.

Part One, *Introduction to Crime and Criminal Behavior*, is oriented to criminology, the causes of crime, and the universe of criminals. The emphasis in these four chapters is upon both the victim and the offender as persons and the interactions that often lead to crime.

In Part Two, *American Police,* the first two chapters relate the history of police in America and the police mission and role. The remaining chapters concern the functional organization of police: The General Field Force, Criminal Investigation, and Crime Prevention.

Part Three, *Individual Rights,* contains three chapters about individual rights, fair trial, and the due process of law. Taken together, these chapters examine the constitutional rights of the individual and how they have been threatened, safeguarded, and limited.

Part Four, *The Courts,* goes into the conflict between individual rights and government, examining the concept of fair trial before an impartial jury for all persons accused of crime, and discussing plea negotiations as conviction without a trial and prejudicial publicity as a block to the opportunity for a fair trial.

Part Five, *Corrections,* is concerned with juvenile justice, crime and punishment, and corrections and rehabilitation. This part covers disposition of juvenile offenders, the individualization of treatment in corrections, new standards proposed by the National Advisory Commission on Criminal Justice Standards and Goals to guide sentencing judges in selecting alternatives to imprisonment, and procedural due process for prisoners and parolees.

Part Six, *The Criminal Justice System,* begins with a chapter on organized crime as a threat to police, courts, and corrections in its capability to corrupt public officers. The chapters that conclude the book are an overview of emerging standards for police and corrections officials in developing career advancement plans as a core area of manpower development, and of the criminal justice system, its agents, and its agencies.

The seven new chapters that have been added to this revision are included in the foregoing explanation of the chapter organization. These new chapters are:

VII. The General Field Force
VIII. Criminal Investigation
IX. Crime Prevention
XII. The Burger Court and Individual Rights
XVIII. Sentencing Offenders—The Least Drastic Alternative
XIX. Procedural Due Process for Prisoners and Parolees
XXI. Careers in Criminal Justice Agencies

This text has been footnoted to guide and encourage further study. There is a list of selected references at the end of each chapter which can guide study and help in the development of a personal library.

Throughout the revision new material has been added and obsolete material deleted as warranted by changes in case law, current practices, standards, and new perspectives.

Paul B. Weston
Kenneth M. Wells

Part I

Introduction to Crime and Criminal Behavior

Chapter I

Law and the Legal System

Systems of law and systems for the determination of guilt do not spring forth full grown. Our present system of justice is the product of centuries, and perhaps millenia, of trial and error. In addition to the experience of history, the complexity of civilization must determine the methods by which men determine codes of conduct and execute sanctions for disobedience of those codes.

Making the Law

There is a trend to reliance on the criminal law to control human behavior that threatens the security of persons and property. However, legal controls require respect as well as obedience for true viability. Where did the criminal law come from? What means or authority causes obedience to the law?

We can speculate that when man began living in family units there was a need for interpersonal problem solving. The particular code of conduct was determined on the basis of day-to-day disputes and the arbitrary and changing decisions of the one in authority. The natural choice for the role of lawmaker was the family authority figure, usually the father, or the oldest member of the family. Because of longer experience, the oldest member may have been considered the wisest. Respect, awe, fear, or a combination of the three resulted in obedience to that person's decisions.

We may also reason that as families grew into communities of families, one or more of the experienced or stronger members became

3

the leader or leaders, and settled disputes and determined the codes of conduct for the community.

As populations grew and were joined together to form nations, the codes of conduct were established by the authority of physical force, the gods, or both. The sanctions for disobedience were either penalty in this world, or damnation in the next. The authority or leader had to be sufficiently powerful to physically force obedience or speak and act as a god's representative, or even as a god himself.

One of the many illustrations of the early codes of conduct and the basis for obedience is found in the story of Moses.[1] After Moses led his people out of Egypt they began to disobey him. It was then that God told Moses he would come in a cloud and speak to the people on Moses' behalf. Having done so, He called Moses to the top of Mount Sinai where He gave him the commandments and ordinances with this admonition:

> For I, the Lord, your God am a jealous God, visiting the iniquity of the fathers upon the children to the third and the fourth generations of those who hate Me, and showing steadfast love to the thousandth generation of them that love Me and keep My commandments.[2]

These commandments and ordinances covered most of the major present-day crimes. For instance:

> Murder: You shall not kill.[3] Whoever strikes a man so that he die shall be put to death. But if he did not lie in wait for him, but God let him fall into his hand, then I will appoint a place for you to which he may flee. But if a man wilfully attacks another to kill him treacherously, you shall take him from my altar, that he may die.[4]

> Adultery: You shall not commit adultery.[5]

> Theft: You shall not steal.[6]

> Protection of Property: If a thief is found breaking in and is struck so he dies there shall be no blood guilt for him.[7]

> Perjury: You shall not bear false witness against your neighbor.[8]

> Kidnapping: Whoever steals a man, whether he sells him or is found in possession of him, shall be put to death.[9]

1. Exodus.
2. Exod. 20:4.
3. Exod. 20:13.
4. Exod. 21:12.
5. Exod. 20:14.
6. Exod. 20:15.
7. Exod. 22:2.
8. Exod. 20:16.
9. Exod. 21:16.

Arson: When a fire breaks out and catches in thorns so that the stacked grain or the standing grain or the field is consumed, he that kindled it shall make full restitution.[10]

Embezzlement: For every breach of trust, whether it is for ox, for ass, for sheep, for clothing, or for any kind of lost thing, of which one says, "This is it," the case of both parties shall come before God; he who God shall condemn shall pay double to his neighbor.[11]

Rape: If a man seduces a virgin who is not betrothed, and lies with her, he shall give the marriage present for her, and make her his wife. If her father utterly refuses to give her to him, he shall pay money equivalent to the marriage present for virgins.[12]

Sodomy: Whoever lies with a beast shall be put to death.[13]

These and similar regulations formed the code of conduct for the people of Israel by the direct authority of God through Moses. Because of the subsequent spread of the Judeo-Christian ethic, it is the foundation upon which our present system of criminal justice is based.

Violating the peace of an individual often led to blood feuds and *wergeld,* but in later years vengeance was subordinated to *composition.** Violating the king's peace was an offense punishable by *outlawry.* The outlaw was declared an enemy of the community—no one could harbor or aid him—and killing the offender was lawful. In extending the concept of king's peace and in making decisions about outlawry, the community began to codify the antisocial and unfair deeds and the measure of their punishments. In Anglo-Saxon England this marked the transition from private law to public law.

In the English, or common law** system, which we have to a large degree inherited, the tribunal hearing the original factual circumstances in disputes or accusations decided whether the acts were violations of the basic code of conduct or acts which should be added to those deemed criminal. These decisions adding crimes to existing law were written down and records were kept, so that when a similar factual circumstance occurred, the deciding tribunal could apply to the precedent of the

10. Exod. 22:6.
11. Exod. 22:9.
12. Exod. 22:16.
13. Exod. 22:19.
*Composition and *wergeld* are similar; *composition* was the sum of money paid by an aggressor to the victim or his family as satisfaction for a wrong or personal injury, usually by mutual agreement; *wergeld* was the "price" of a homicide or other violent crime. It was paid by the aggressor, but the payment was apportioned between the victim (or the family), the community, and the king.
**"Judge-made" law: within the English legal system, the principles and rules of action derived solely from ancient usages and customs, or from judgments and decrees of courts enforcing such usages and customs. Collaterally, the doctrine of *stare decisis* is the policy of courts to stand by precedents.

former case for guidance. In this way, each new case and decision added to the basic code of conduct. This mountain of law created by court decision followed the early colonists from England and remained the primary method of determining what was a crime.

Following the American Revolution and the experiences of federal and state legislative governments, more and more states compiled the body of law into codes, criminal and civil, which now have become the only source of the *substantive law** and subject to interpretation only by courts of competent jurisdiction.

Statutory law is not essentially different from common law. The common law (or *adjudicative law*) results from decisions in real-life criminal proceedings; statutory law is the enactment of legislation prior to any actual trial for its violation, and as such postdates some expressed need for such legislative action. On the one hand, the court waits for the situation to develop in controversy; on the other hand, the legislative action is a response to a developing situation. In the common law, the judicial decision arrayed the rule of the law together with the reason for the decision. Statutes and their provisions of law normally contain nothing more than the essential elements of law. They are assertive, rather than explanatory.[14]

The major problem of statutory law is the proper application of statutory language to individual events alleged to be crimes. The author of a legislative act may not intend the meaning expressed in the legislation. A statute defining a crime is subject to reasonable interpretation on the basis that statutory law is not what the lawmakers intended to say, but rather what they succeeded in saying.[15] What the law *is* may vary because of the meaning of the words used in the law and inferences drawn from its structure and general content.

Courts do not have unlimited power to assess meaning to the words of a law in a *criminal code* or *penal law* (the codification of statutory law), but one of the roles of the courts in the American legal system is the appropriate application of statutory laws to cases before the courts. Judicial interpretations and applications of statutory laws are crucial to the development of justice under statutory law. When such judicial action is founded on principles and policies related to the ultimate purpose of establishing sound foundations for a tolerable and durable social order, then statutory law develops coherence and intelligibility. The quality of rational interpretation then becomes a quality which is characteristic of the body of *unwritten* laws (the common law).[16]

*That part of the body of law creating, defining, and regulating rights.
14. Lon L. Fuller, *The Anatomy of the Law* (New York: Praeger Publishers, 1968), pp. 84–91.
15. Ibid., pp. 13–18.
16. Henry M. Hart, Jr., "The Aims of the Criminal Law," *Law and Contemporary Problems* 23, no. 3 (Summer 1958): 401–42.

Law and its making, by court decision or legislative action, has been characterized as an order directed to the citizens of a community by its government, and the words *command* and *duty* are particularly useful in understanding the making of laws, the sanctions for their enforcement, and the nature of voluntary compliance. In 1832, John Austin discussed these two terms as follows:

> *Command:* A command is distinguished from other significations of desire, not by the style in which the desire is signified, but by the power and the purpose of the party commanding to inflict an evil or pain in case the desire be disregarded. If you cannot or will not harm me in case I comply not with your wish, the expression of your wish is not a command.
>
> *Duty:* Being liable to evil from you if I comply not with a wish you signify, I am *bound* or *obliged* by your command, or I lie under a duty to obey it. If, in spite of that evil in prospect, I comply not with the wish which you signify, I am said to disobey your command, or to violate the duty it imposes.
>
> *Command* and *Duty:* Wherever a command has been signified, a duty is imposed.[17]

The Law of Crimes

The concept of criminal law as a command and a duty carries over to the purpose of law—to prevent or reduce the incidence of behavior that is viewed as antisocial. This is a utilitarian objective. The retributive view of law has long been rejected for the view of law as a device for deterrence—to modify the future behavior of offenders and others who might be tempted to commit criminal acts.

A *crime* is an act committed or omitted in violation of a law forbidding or commanding it, and for which a punishment is assigned on conviction. The penalties for crime may be death, imprisonment, fine, removal from public office, or disqualification to hold public office. A *capital crime* is one for which the punishment may be death; a *felony* is a serious crime for which the offender may be sentenced to state prison for more than one year; and a *misdemeanor* is a lesser offense for which the punishment should not exceed one year. Some jurisdictions add a *minor offense* or *infraction*, which is less than a misdemeanor and usually associated with vehicle and traffic violations. The seriousness of a criminal offense has always been related to the penalty assigned for its violation, and the punishment is contained in the judgment and sentence of the trial judge

17. John Austin, *The Province of Jurisprudence Determined and the Uses of the Study of Jurisprudence* (New York: Noonday Press, 1954, reprint ed.; originally published in 1832, 1863), p. 14.

after a verdict of guilty. In most areas, the sentence imposed determines whether the crime is a felony or misdemeanor.

Clearly written statutory criminal law with its sanctions (penalties) assigned according to the seriousness of the offense is a fair warning against criminal behavior, and a means of securing voluntary compliance. The criminal law tends to group or categorize crimes and criminals in relation to the nature of the offense and the punishment established by law. Distinctions as to the act done that was criminal led to the legal typology of misdemeanors and felonies. This division based on the gravity of the offense was also linked to punishment.

Severe punishment, death and lengthy sentences of imprisonment, lead to a category of *serious offenses*. These are the traditional crimes of violence, of death, and of injury to the victim. The FBI in its role of recorder and reporter of offenses known to police, has placed five serious crimes in its Index of Crimes. These are: murder, non-negligent manslaughter, forcible rape, robbery, and aggravated assault.

Crimes based upon the moral code change as the times change. Many victimless crimes, based on moral concepts rather than the concept of injury, are being modified or done away with completely. Homosexual acts have been accepted, prohibited, or ignored depending upon the historical period of time. Presently in most law codes a homosexual act is a crime. However, in many jurisdictions it is either being ignored by enforcement officers or has been repealed by the legislatures. The whole subject of obscenity as a crime is being reevaluated in the light of the right of an adult to choose what he reads, sees, and hears as long as there is no injury to another. Until recently abortion was a crime in most western countries, but many jurisdictions are now drastically revising their abortion laws, or eliminating abortion as a crime.[18]

Until now legislation concerning drunkenness, sexual variations, gambling, and blue laws has established as crimes acts which are popular with many citizens of any community. This overreach of the criminal law has contributed to our criminal population and made any typology of offenders more difficult. An array of various types of criminals and a study of their characteristics would be much simpler if the criminal law returned to its origins and attempted, as its function, no more than the protection of "the king's peace," and of persons and property. When a particular form of behavior (gambling, prostitution, etc.) is forbidden by law, participants are led into contacts with the criminal subculture and other criminal activities. The popularity of forbidden goods and services has led to the development of career criminals and profit-motivated criminogenic organizations, and to the growth of criminality. Many customer-victims

18. See People v. Barksdale, 8 Cal. 3d (1972); and _California Penal Code_, Section 274; _California Health and Safety Code_, Section 25950, _et. seq._

resort to a variety of crimes in order to secure funds for the high-priced forbidden goods and services.[19]

Special interest groups also influence state legislatures in creating new crime areas, and increasing or decreasing the punishment for existing ones. The crime of theft illustrates the power of special interests to try to protect their particular product against criminals. *Grand theft,* a felony in California,[20] is the unlawful taking of money, real property, labor, or personal property exceeding a value of $200. *Petty theft,* a misdemeanor in California, is any unlawful taking of property valued at $200 or less. However, if the property is domestic fowls, avocados, olives, citrus or deciduous fruits, nuts or artichokes, then grand theft is the unlawful taking of such property exceeding a value of $50. If the property is an automobile, firearm, horse, mare, gelding, any bovine animal, any caprine animal, mule, jack, jenny, sheep, lamb, hog, sow, boar, gilt, barrow or pig, it is a grand theft regardless of the value. A separate section of the law on thievery makes dog stealing a grand theft if the value of the animal is in excess of $200.[21] An additional section makes dog stealing for the purpose of sale, medical research or other commercial uses, a grand theft without regard to the value of the dog.[22]

Actions previously lawful are frequently made criminal by legislative acts which are the result of the ever-increasing complexity of our civilization. We often add to our basic moral-criminal offenses and special interest offenses. These are the offenses which have to do with health, safety, government, and welfare of the individual. These new laws regulate the manufacture, sale, and use of products: drugs, explosives, fireworks, swimming pools, atomic energy development, paints, cosmetics, foods (human and pet consumption), bakeries, canneries, housing, and many others. They also regulate the actions of persons or business organizations to license lawyers, doctors, hospitals, bars, restaurants, and the like. In addition they protect or combat disease: communicable disease control, sanitation, garbage disposal, sewer control, cemeteries and undertakers.[23] In California alone, laws fill over 50 volumes of codes which cover every conceivable relationship of man to man, man to machine, man to activity, and man to animal.

Criminal law is also affected by the political reality of lawmakers responding to the public mood. Certain crimes have a scare value by which the vocal and visible activity of legislators gains votes, and actions to increase penalties are considered good politics. Narcotic and dangerous

19. Norval Morris and Gordon Hawkins, *The Honest Politician's Guide to Crime Control* (Chicago and London: University of Chicago Press, 1969), pp. 2–24.
20. *California Penal Code,* Section 484 to 486.
21. Ibid., Section 487.
22. Ibid., Section 487.
23. *California Health and Safety Code.*

drug abuse offenses are an excellent example of political reasons for a particular punishment at a particular time.

Marihuana, in the 1960s and 1970s, is and will be the subject of moral, social, and political concern. This concern is quite visible in the history of the law prohibiting its possession, use, and sale. The possession of marihuana was not a public offense in the state of California until 1929, at which time the legislature enacted a statute making the possession of marihuana a crime punishable as a misdemeanor (a maximum of six months in the county jail). By 1945, the punishment for possession of marihuana was imprisonment in the county jail for six months to one year, or in the state prison for not more than six years. The punishment for possession of marihuana was then the same as for the possession of hard drugs (opium, heroin, and cocaine).[24]

In 1959, the maximum penalty for possession of marihuana had increased to ten years in a state prison. In 1961, after a great deal of public agitation about the use of marihuana, there was a basic change in the offense and its punishment. The Health and Safety Code was amended to punish possession by *deleting* that portion of the section on the illegal possession of marihuana which authorized the judge to sentence a first offender to imprisonment in the county jail for not more than one year (a misdemeanor). In its place the following mandatory punishment was specified: ". . . shall be punished by imprisonment in the state prison for not less than one year nor more than ten years, and shall not be eligible for release upon completion of sentence, or on parole, or on any other basis until he has served not less than one year in prison."[25]

In addition, the above section of law provided that persons who had been previously convicted of a narcotic-type felony shall be punished by imprisonment in state prison for not less than two years and no more than twenty years; and must serve, in prison, at least two years. Furthermore, that if the person had been twice previously convicted of a narcotic-type felony, the punishment for possession of marihuana was imprisonment for five years to life with a minimum of five years spent in prison.

For the next seven years a conflict raged between those who claimed marihuana was a dangerous drug and those who argued it was no worse than alcohol. During those years, the great majority of persons convicted of marihuana offenses were young people in college or high school—persons who had no connection with crime other than their experiments with marihuana. In 1968, the law was again amended by the legislature to reinsert the option of the judiciary to sentence first offenders to the county jail (a misdemeanor). The punishment for the second and third offense remained the same.

The use of drug or narcotic laws as a political tool is also evident in

24. *California Health and Safety Code,* Section 11713.
25. Ibid., Section 11530.

the evolution of punishment for the unlawful possession of dangerous drugs.* In 1945, the offense was codified with the punishment of a fine of $50 to $500, or imprisonment in the county jail not to exceed six months (a misdemeanor). In 1949, the minimum fine was raised to $100.[26]

In 1965, after the rise of the hippie culture which made the abuse of dangerous drugs a visible and growing problem among college-age men and women as well as children in the high schools and junior high schools, the law was amended and recodified to provide for: ". . . a fine of not more than $1,000 or by imprisonment in the county jail not exceeding one year . . . ."[27] Additionally, the penalty section of this law specified that if the person had been convicted of a similar drug or narcotic offense he should be punished by imprisonment "in the state prison for not less than one year or more than five years (a felony) or . . . in the county jail for not more than one year."

In 1968, as the abuse of dangerous drugs grew, and as the public reacted adversely to the hippies' activities associated with drug use, it became good vote-getting strategy for lawmakers to get tougher on drug users. The law was amended to drop the alternate punishment of a fine and add, for the first conviction, the alternate imprisonment of from one year to ten years in state prison. In addition, for the person who had been previously convicted of a similar offense, the alternative county jail sentence (a misdemeanor) was deleted and the sole punishment was imprisonment in state prison from two years to twenty years, and it was also specified that a minimum of two years had to be served *in* the prison.

As a constrast to the above punishments, examine the following review of the punishments specified in California law for the commission of the basic crimes:

1. Murder second degree, five years to life

2. Manslaughter, not exceeding fifteen years

3. Robbery, five years to life (first degree), one year to life (second degree)

4. Burglary, five years to life (first degree), one year to fifteen years (a felony), or county jail (a misdemeanor, second degree)

5. Theft, one year to ten years (a felony), or county jail (a misdemeanor—petty theft, $200 or less).

Narcotic or dangerous drug abuse, in California and many other states, became punishable by equal or greater penalties than those offenses which left injured or dead victims at crime scenes. Any review of

---

*Hypnotic drugs, barbituric acid derivatives, amphetamines, lysergic acid, (LSD) and others.
26. *California Health and Safety Code*, Section 29026.
27. Ibid., Section 11910.

criminal law must recognize not only the relationship of the specified penalty for crimes in determining the grade of crime, but must also be aware of political realities as lawmakers respond to many influences in their enactment of new criminal laws, or in amending the laws relating to crimes.

The appellate courts, with their right to limit legislative excesses through the constitutional prohibition against "cruel and unusual punishments,"[28] may, in cases brought to them, adjust punishment made law by the legislature.

> In 1972 the California Penal Code provided: Every person who willfully and lewdly exposes his person, or the private parts thereof, in any public place, or in any place where there are present other persons to be offended or annoyed thereby is guilty of a misdemeanor.

> Upon the second and each subsequent conviction under subdivision 1 of this section, or upon a first conviction under subdivision 1 of this section, after a previous conviction under Section 288 of this code (lewd or lascivious acts upon a child), every person so convicted is guilty of a felony, and is punishable by imprisonment in state prison for not less than one year.[29]

Upon a second conviction of indecent exposure the defendant could be punished by a one-year-to-life indeterminate term in state prison.

In deciding the invalidity of this punishment when given to a twice convicted "exposer" the Court said:

> The provision of Penal Code #314, making a second offense of indecent exposure a felony rather than a misdemeanor and in effect imposing a sentence of life imprisonment on one suffering a second conviction, inflicts a penalty so disproportionate to the crime as to violate the prohibition of California Constitution, Article I, #6, against cruel or unusual punishments. The traditional legal treatment of indecent exposure as a social nuisance conforms to the view adopted by modern psychiatric science, and though the offense is not a victimless crime, any harm it may cause appears minimal; such second offense punishment is greater than that prescribed by California law for far more serious crimes, and far more severe than that provided in other recidivist statutes, penalizing conduct that is indisputably more serious; and review of the statutes of sister states reveals their virtually unanimous judgment that indecent exposure, no matter how often it may occur, can be adequately and appropriately controlled by the imposition of a short jail sentence and/or a small fine."[30]

Again in 1974 in a narcotics case the California Supreme Court applied the cruel and unusual punishment clause of the California Con-

---

28. U.S., *Constitution*, Amend. 8; California, *Constitution*, Art. I, Sec. 6.
29. *California Penal Code*, Section 314.
30. In re Lynch, 8 Cal. 3d 410 (1972).

stitution: The defendant was convicted of furnishing heroin and admitted a previous conviction of illegal possession of heroin.[31] Pursuant to the requirements of the section at that time, the defendant's sentence was ten years to life imprisonment, and further, the Code required that the entire minimum of ten years must be served before such convicted person would be eligible for release or parole. Without the special provision he would have been eligible for parole after serving one-third of his minimum sentence. The Court here commented:

> The provisions of Health and Safety Code, #11352, and of former Health and Safety Code, #11501, precluding consideration of parole for a narcotics repeat offender for a minimum of 10 years in the case of a second offender, and 15 years for a third offender, constitute both cruel and unusual punishment under California Constitution Article I, #6. The provisions are cruel in terms of the additional punishment imposed without regard to the character of either the offender or the offense, and unusually excessive when compared with punishments imposed in other jurisdictions on the same class of offenders. Punishment may violate California Constitution, Article I, #6, if, although not cruel or unusual in its method, it is so disproportionate to the crime for which it is inflicted that it shocks the conscience and offends fundamental notions of human dignity.

> It is the legislative branch's function to define crimes and prescribe punishments and, in the first instance, such questions are for its judgment alone. The legislative power is limited, however, by California Constitution Article I, #6, relating to cruel or unusual punishment. The cruel or unusual punishment clause of California Constitution Article I, #6, like other provisions of the Declaration of Rights, operates to restrain legislative and executive action and to protect fundamental individual and minority rights against encroachment by the majority.

> Where a defendant under an indeterminate sentence challenges the sentence as cruel or unusual under the California Constitution, the test is whether the maximum term of imprisonment permitted by the statute punishing his offense exceeds the constitutional limit, regardless of whether a lesser term may be fixed in his particular case by the Adult Authority.[32]

The Determination of Guilt

Guilt is the opposite of innocence. It is the basis of a person's confession to a crime: *I am guilty*. It is the jury verdict when a defendant is convicted of one or more charges in the accusatory pleading (*indictment* or *information**): *guilty*. In the American legal system, guilt in a criminal

31. *California Health and Safety Code*, Section 11501.
32. In re Foss, 10 Cal. 3d 910 (1974).
*In many states a prosecutor may use either method to bring a case to trial. The indictment originates with a grand jury hearing; the information, with a preliminary hearing in court.

proceeding is personal. Crimes always are committed by persons—and in a limited sense by corporations—but not by states. There is a doctrine of legal responsibility of corporations and states which imposes a collective liability, but a criminal act is difficult or impossible to justify on some legalism which transfers responsibility from the perpetrator to some collective organization.

Very early in man's development he chose one or more of his tribe to be the judge in disputes or accusations, and to determine where the truth lay. Those chosen as judges were the oldest (most experienced), the wisest, or the individuals who were deemed the agents or representatives of God or the gods.

The ancient books of the Bible illustrate the indirect intervention of God to settle disputes.[33] The well-known incident of the judgment of King Solomon in determining who was the mother of a child illustrates, as decision maker, the supportive nature of divine intervention:

> And all Israel heard of the judgment which the King had rendered and they stood in awe of the King because they perceived that the wisdom of God was in him, to render Justice.[34]

Divine intervention was sought as a resource for determining guilt or innocence in criminal proceedings by tribal leaders in Africa, and the medieval governing groups in England during the eighth through the twelfth centuries. In England, they used the *ordeal* to determine whether an accusation was true or false. The ordeal involved either a hot iron, boiling water, fire, or cold water. The process sought the direct intervention of God for a minor miracle to show guilt or innocence. Later, in the wager of battle, there was some trust in the belief that the innocent antagonist was to receive divine assistance.

The ordeal of the hot iron required that a fire be kindled within the church. The accused was seated in front of the fire and all those interested and the clergy surrounded him. The iron bar was laid on the fire and heated. After a prayer for God's assistance, the accused lifted the iron bar and carried it nine yards from the fire. When he laid down the iron he was taken to the vestry by the priest. His hands were wrapped in linen cloths. After three days, the cloths were removed. If an infected stripe was found in the mark of the iron he was considered guilty. If the wound was clean he was deemed innocent.

In India the ordeal of fire was quite similar; the accused was required to walk barefoot on the fire. Of course, innocent persons would be uninjured by the ordeal.[35]

---

33. Num. 27:1–11; 36:1–13; Joshua 17:1–6.
34. 1 Kings 3:28.
35. Henry Charles Lea, *Superstition and Force*, 4th ed. (Philadelphia: Lea Bros. & Co., 1892), p. 303.

The ordeal of boiling water was involved in an incident in Africa. There was a theft in the camp and the Barotse tribesmen asked permission to try a boiling water test to identify the thief. Some 60 natives, men, women, and children, lined up and the test and its purpose were explained to them. No one disagreed to the test. A fire was built and a large pot of water placed on it. When the water came to a boil, a smaller pot of cold water was placed next to it. Then each of the 60 "suspects" walked up to the pots. The ritual was to immerse the right arm into the cold water, then place it in the boiling water. When each of the natives had taken the test, he was told to return at the same time the next day. In theory, the individual who had lost some skin or showed blisters would be guilty. When the natives returned the next day, each passed by and showed his arm. Only one of the 60 showed any sign of a burn, and he confessed.[36]

The ordeal of cold water (*judicium acquae frigidae*) required, after suitable prayer, that the accused be lowered into pure water. If he sank, that is, the water accepted him, he was innocent. If he floated, that is, the water rejected him, he was guilty. It was believed that the pure element would not receive into its bosom anyone stained by a crime.[37]

As late as 1594, Jacob Rickius, a learned jurist, who as judge in the court of Bonn had ample opportunity to consider the value of the ordeal of cold water, vividly described the usefulness of the ordeal when a judge was confronted by a serious crime and worthless evidence. His elaborate discussion of all the arguments in favor of the ordeal may be condensed into this observation: (1) use the ordeal when the offense is so difficult to prove that there is no other certain evidence than the ordeal; (2) without it, courts would be destitute of absolute proof—which would be an admission of the superiority of the Devil over God—an unacceptable conclusion. Judge Rickius concluded that he never administered the ordeal when the evidence was sufficient for conviction, nor when there was insufficient proof to justify the use of torture.[38]

Trial by battle was performed either by the parties involved or their champions. It was thought that God would not allow the wrongdoer to triumph over the party in the right. Therefore, the winner of the fight was the victor in the lawsuit. Vestiges of this concept existed in England until 1819, when the English Parliament acted to abolish this last form of nonlegal trial. A system of *waging the law* and *trial by jury* began the nonviolent legal process to determine the guilt or innocence of persons accused of crime.

36. Margaret Carson Hubbard, *African Gamble* (New York: G. P. Putnam's Sons, 1937), p. 129.
37. Lea, *Superstition and Force*, p. 318.
38. John H. Wigmore. *A Kaleidoscope of Justice* (Washington, D.C.: Washington Law Book Co., 1941), p. 16.

To *wage the law* was to produce in the court the number of witnesses demanded by the judge to declare the accused guiltless. When the accused produced a sufficient number of friends to testify in his behalf, he was acquitted. Friends of an accused who testified in support of his oath were called *compurgators* and, in effect, they would swear to the credibility of the accused. These "oath helpers" did not testify to any personal knowledge of the crime as an event, but only to their belief in the accused's story given under oath. Exoneration of criminal charges by compurgation was a valued right of English citizens, and it was not wholly abolished until 1833.[39]

Waging the law is no doubt the origin of one of our present rules of evidence: that the accused may produce character witnesses to testify to various qualities of the defendant which may bear on his guilt or innocence. For instance, in California this rule is stated as follows:

> Evidence of the defendant's character as to those traits which ordinarily would be involved in the commission of a crime such as that charged in this case is relevant to the question of the defendant's guilt or innocence because it may be reasoned that a person of good character as to such traits would not be likely to commit the crime of which the defendant is charged. Evidence of good character may be sufficient to raise a reasonable doubt whether the defendant is guilty, which doubt otherwise would not exist.[40]

While there is no presumption that the defendant is of good character, when evidence is introduced of good reputation regarding the traits involved in the crime charged, a California judge must instruct a jury that character evidence (waging the law) of itself may be sufficient to raise a reasonable doubt as to whether or not a defendant is guilty.[41]

Originally the trial jury was a jury of witnesses. The jury was made up of the witnesses in the case, and their verdict was the summary of their knowledge of the crime and its surrounding circumstances. Trial by jury probably originated with early Spanish kings as a form of inquest or inquiry; it was introduced into England by the Norman invaders.

Apparently, at one time there was a belief among the agents of criminal justice that the jurors should be chosen for their knowledge of the defendant and his crime. This is one step removed from a jury of witnesses. The following tale illustrates this belief: William of the Palace was accused of stealing from the king's treasury. When arraigned in court, he demanded a trial by jury. The sheriff was asked by the court if he had a jury. The sheriff replied:

---

39. Marcus Gleisser, *Juries and Justice* (New York: A. S. Barnes & Co., 1968), pp. 31–33.
40. *California Evidence Code*, Sections 1100–1102.
41. *California Jury Instructions—Criminal*, rev. ed. (St. Paul, Minn.: West Publishing Co., 1958), pp. 60–61.

I am proud to say it will be an excellent jury for the Crown. I myself have picked and chosen every man on the panel. I have spoken to them all, and there is not one whom I have not examined carefully, not only as to his knowledge of the offense wherewith the prisoner stands charged; but of all the circumstances from which guilt can be collected, suspected, or inferred. All the jurors are acquainted with him, eight out of the twelve have often been known to declare, upon their troth, that they were sure one day he would come to the gallows, and the remainder are fully of the opinion that he deserves the halter. My Lord, I should ill have performed my duty, if I had allowed my bailiff to summon the jury at hap-hazard, and without previously ascertaining the extent of their testimony. Some, perhaps, know more and some less, but the least informed of them have taken great pains to go up and down in every hole and corner of Westminster, they and their wives; and to learn all they could hear, concerning the prisoner's past and present life. Never had any culprit a better chance of having a fair trial.[42]

The present form of the trial jury dates back to the time of the Tudors. The modern jury now provides a court with 12 persons who have no discernible bias against the defendant or the prosecutor, or preconceived beliefs as to the outcome of the particular case at hand. A few states use six-person juries. Florida's "six-man" jury law has been upheld by the U.S. Supreme Court in *Williams* v. *Florida,* 399 U.S. 78 (1970). The functions of a modern jury include: (1) the determination of the credibility of witnesses, (2) the weighing of the evidence, and (3) the drawing of justifiable inferences from proven facts.

The Admissibility of Evidence

As we have already discussed, the ordeals did not require any formal evidence other than the accusation in order to put the accused to the test. In practice, however, the accused was put to the ordeal only after he had been accused under the prosecutor's oath and the oaths of others, or a public reputation of guilt, or after capture while in fresh pursuit with *hue and cry.* *

In waging the law, the evidence admitted at trial was relevant only to the good or bad reputation of the accused and he was judged on that alone. The ancient right of compurgation was based on the concept that a guilty person's friends would know whether the accused was guilty, and if he could find a meaningful number of them to uniformly testify to his plea of innocence and his credibility as a witness he was likely to be innocent.

42. Wigmore, *A Kaleidoscope of Justice,* pp. 24–25.
*In old English law: a loud outcry with which felons were pursued (all who heard were bound to join the pursuit).

During the time when jurors were chosen because of their knowledge of the crime or the accused, there were no rules concerning what could be told to and discussed by the jurors in order to decide the issue of guilt or innocence. The only rule of evidence at this time prevented the accused from testifying in his own defense.

It was not until persons without knowledge as to the facts of the crime and the activities of the accused were selected as jurors, that rules developed for presenting evidence to the jury. The rules were few to begin with and became more complex as a concept of fairness became more and more important to the ideal of justice. The system now practiced in the United States is deeply concerned with fairness to the accused and with the eventual ascertainment of the truth. Justice in our present system is equated with fairness, and truth is the desired result of the equity of the system. Thus rules of evidence have developed to maintain and insure that the government acts justly toward each of its individual citizens who may be suspected of, accused of, or tried for the commission of a crime.

In fact, ongoing rules for the admissibility of evidence stress the doctrine of fair trial, and enhance it by the concept of *due process* for the purpose of avoiding the conviction of the innocent and preserving the basic sense of security of citizens in a democratic society. Fairness and legality of the methods by which law is enforced are of increasing concern to the American judiciary and is a major theme of twentieth-century judicial policy.

The essence of this theme in modern judicial policy was stated in the dissenting opinion of Supreme Court Justice Louis D. Brandeis in the 1928 case of *Olmstead* v. *United States:*[43]

> The protection guaranteed by the Amendments is much broader in scope. The makers of our Constitution undertook to secure conditions favorable to the pursuit of happiness. They recognized the significance of man's spiritual nature, of his feelings and of his intellect. They knew that only a part of the pain, pleasure and satisfactions of life are to be found in material things. They sought to protect Americans in their beliefs, their thoughts, their emotions, and their sensations. They conferred, as against the Government, the right to be let alone—the most comprehensive of rights and the right most valued by civilized men. To protect that right, every unjustifiable intrusion by the Government upon the privacy of the individual, whatever the means employed, must be deemed a violation of the Fourth Amendment. And the use, as evidence in a criminal proceeding, of facts ascertained by such intrusion must be deemed a violation of the Fifth.
>
> Experience should teach us to be most on our guard to protect liberty when the Government's purposes are beneficent. Men born to freedom are natur-

43. Olmstead v. United States, 277 U.S. 438 (1928), pp. 471–85.

ally alert to repel invasion of their liberty by evil-minded rulers. The greatest dangers to liberty lurk in insidious encroachment by men of zeal, well-meaning but without understanding.

And if this Court should permit the Government, by means of its officers' crimes, to effect its purpose of punishing the defendants, there would seem to be present all the elements of a ratification. If so, the Government itself would become a lawbreaker.

Will this Court by sustaining the judgment below sanction such conduct on the part of the Executive? The governing principle has long been settled. It is that a court will not redress a wrong when he who invokes its aid has unclean hands. The maxim of unclean hands comes from courts of equity. But the principle prevails also in courts of law. Its common application is in civil actions between private parties. Where the Government is the actor, the reasons for applying it are even more persuasive. Where the remedies invoked are those of the criminal law, the reasons are compelling.

The court's aid is denied only when he who seeks it has violated the law in connection with the very transaction as to which he seeks legal redress. Then aid is denied despite the defendant's wrong. It is denied in order to maintain respect for law; in order to promote confidence in the administration of justice; in order to preserve the judicial process from contamination. The rule is one, not of action, but of inaction. It is sometimes spoken of as a rule of substantive law. But it extends to matters of procedure as well.

But the objection that the plaintiff comes with unclean hands will be taken by the court itself. It will be taken despite the wish to the contrary of all the parties to the litigation. The court protects itself.

Decency, security, and liberty alike demand that government officials shall be subjected to the same rules of conduct that are commands to the citizen. In a government of laws, existence of the government will be imperilled if it fails to observe the law scrupulously. Our Government is the potent, the omnipresent teacher. For good or for ill, it teaches the whole people by its example. Crime is contagious. If the Government becomes a lawbreaker, it breeds contempt for law; it invites anarchy. To declare that in the administration of the criminal law the end justifies the means—to declare that the Government may commit crimes in order to secure the conviction of a private criminal—would bring terrible retribution. Against that pernicious doctrine this Court should resolutely set its face.

Courts are attempting to insure fair trials for persons accused of crimes. Judicial control over the admissibility of evidence has been a significant factor in the development of the law almost from the year of Justice Brandeis' opinion cited above. The prosecutor and police have had many practices declared unconstitutional and evidence secured in such circumstances excluded upon timely application by the defense for legal relief from the use of unlawfully secured evidence. Initially, the concern of the judiciary was the Fourth Amendment right to privacy and then it was extended to the Fifth Amendment privilege against self-incrimination. Recently it has been concerned with the right to counsel, not only at trial, but also during any critical stage of the pretrial period.

Selected References

Books

Fuller, Lon L. *The Anatomy of the Law.* New York: Praeger Publishers, 1968.

Gleiser, Marcus. *Juries and Justice.* New York: A. S. Barnes & Co., 1968.

Wigmore, John H. *A Kaleidoscope of Justice.* Washington, D.C.: Washington Law Book Co., 1941.

Periodicals

Hart, Henry M., Jr. "The Aims of the Criminal Law." *Law and Contemporary Problems* 23, no. 3 (Summer 1958): 401–42.

Cases

Olmstead v. United States, 277 U.S. 438 (1928)

In re Foss, 10 Cal. 3d 910 (1974).

In re Lynch, 8 Cal. 3d 410 (1972).

Williams v. Florida, 399 U.S. 78 (1970).

Chapter II

Crime: The Offender–
Victim Relationship

The amount of crime in the United States is unknown. While there is
some uniformity to police reports of known crimes, it is a tiresome detailing of figures against a broad population base. There are statistics without
adequate data on the numbers of crimes that occur and remain undis-
covered by or unreported to the police. While definite data on all crimes
will never be known (murder and other secret crimes do not always out),
there is a projection potential in field surveys of victims as to their knowledge of crimes. There appears to be a possibility of estimating the total
incidence of any crime within a community for a given period of time by
developing the "loss" between data from field surveys of crime victims
and the number of offenses known to police. For instance, one extensive
survey of crime victims indicates that less than half of the thefts under $50
(petty thefts) are reported; and only slightly over half of the burglaries are
known to police (37 percent of 473 cases; and 58 percent of 313 cases).[1]
Surely, such data afford reasonable projection figures.

The availability of victims for crimes (individuals, business, and other
organizations), is the major socio-environmental factor contributing to the
total amount of crime in America. The person intent on committing a
crime must find an available victim. Except for insurance frauds and
other crimes with fictitious victims, crime is a strange partnership be-

1. Phillip H. Ennis, *Criminal Victimization in the United States* (Chicago, Ill.: National
Opinion Research Center, University of Chicago, 1967; A report to the President's Commission on Law Enforcement and Administration of Justice), pp. 41–42. *See* U.S., Department of Justice, Law Enforcement Assistance Administration, *Crime in the Nation's Five
Largest Cities: Advance Report* (Washington, D.C.: U.S. Government Printing Office,
1974).

tween victim and offender, with the victim providing the opportunity for the crime and the offender capitalizing on the circumstances. Victim distribution ranges from victim-precipitated crimes to pure chance in victim selection.

In crimes against the person, the availability of victims is a result of residence, employment, and daily living patterns. Among the common major crimes, only rape limits its victims by sex; and crimes against children limit the victims by age. Otherwise, male adult victims predominate. There is a greater percentage of men working at night—a favorite time period for many crimes—and in high-crime areas. Additionally, many more men than women visit entertainment areas and roam about unescorted.

In major crimes against property, the availability of victims involves the type of structure or establishment (residence, store, and other commercial occupancies). Victims in these crimes are the householder, the retail store owner-operator, or the person or firm with property in commercial buildings. In auto thefts and theft from motor vehicles, the victim may be the owner of the vehicle or the person or firm owning the material stolen.[2]

One criminologist, Hans von Hentig, classified victims as persons who were weak, mentally inadequate, and those who precipitated crime by their travels in high-crime areas, through dissolute living or by their own aggressiveness. Hentig's major categories in this classification are:

1. Children
2. Females
3. The aged
4. Dull normals and mental defectives
5. Acquisitive persons (the larceny-in-their-soul victims of frauds)
6. Wanton women
7. Tormentors (aggressiveness leads to disputes, altercations, assaults).[3]

Victim Distribution: The Place of Occurrence

Whenever a crime happens there is a *place of occurrence*. Penal codes and police records systems use the place at which a crime occurs to

2. U.S., The President's Commission on Law Enforcement and Administration of Justice, "Measurement of the Nature and Amount of Crime," by Albert J. Reis, Jr., in *Studies in Crime and Law Enforcement in Major Metropolitan Areas*, vol. 1 (Washington, D.C.: 1967), pp. 43, 65–77.
3. Hans von Hentig, *The Criminal and His Victim: Studies in the Sociology of Crime* (1948; reprint ed., Hamden, Conn.: Archon Books, Shoe String Press, 1967), pp. 404–50.

determine the seriousness of the offense. Bank robberies are often a federal offense, while liquor store robberies are violations of state law; the burning or burglarizing of a residence is a more serious degree of crime than setting fire to a factory or breaking and entering a store. Police record keeping uses the place of occurrence for subdividing the records of many crimes such as taxicab robberies, street robberies, residential burglaries, and commercial burglaries.

The place of occurrence is a key factor in the availability of a victim of crime. If no one is present in a street or public place, or in a home, store, or other occupancy, the murderer, rapist, or robber is without a victim. If there is nothing of value in a premises entered by thieves, there can be no stealing; if there is no unlawful taking away of another's property, there is no victim. Therefore, the place where the crime takes place supplies the victim of a crime.

The locations at which victims of crime are available to offenders is indicated from the following index headings used by many police departments in their records systems and in their analysis of crime patterns:

Street	Residence (except public housing)
Park	Railroad property or bus station
Taxicab	Bar and tavern
Automobile	Drug store
Truck	Supermarket
School property	Gas station
Public housing	Bank
Airports	Other businesses

A study of criminal victimization in the United States for the U.S. Department of Justice reveals the place of occurrence of crimes in relation to the victim's residence, and whether they happened in a public place or building, or a private building or place. Citizens were queried in this study until persons were located who had been victims of crime in the year prior to these interviews. Facts about five crimes were probed; these were the crimes likely to have individual victims (as opposed to businesses or organizations as victims) and usually coming to the attention of police: (1) robbery, (2) aggravated assault, (3) rape (force), (4) grand larceny, and (5) auto theft. In a grand total of slightly over 2,000 such crimes discussed with their victims by interviewers, 29 percent occurred near* the victim's home, 23 percent were inside the residence of the victim, and 10 percent in other private buildings or places; 24 percent occurred in public buildings or places; and 14 percent took place in taxicabs and places not specified. Since over half of these reported crimes occur-

*Contiguous yard, sidewalk, driveway.

red in or near the victim's home, it is apparent that residence is an important factor in determining who is to be a victim of crime.[4]

A Washington, D.C. survey of crime victims also provided data that victimization is related to the home: (1) close to 75 percent of all crimes reported by victims to survey interviewers happened in the home neighborhood of the victim; (2) approximately 60 percent happened on the residence block of the victim; and (3) fully 50 percent of the victims termed the place of occurrence as home. The only other location reported with any frequency was the victim's place of employment.[5]

In armed robbery the reward factor is of secondary concern because the safety of the robber or robbers is the primary determinant in the selection of the victim. Banks, loan companies, and supermarkets offer the greatest reward in the amount of money likely to be on the premises at the time of the robbery, but these places are usually crowded. The normal robber, or robbery group of from two to four persons, cannot control more than two to four persons effectively during a robbery. The basic safety factor in robbery lies in the offender's control of victims, and it is this factor which accounts for the popularity of liquor stores as targets for robbery. A robber or robbery group often cruise the streets of a neighborhood, examining liquor stores and how many people are in them, and walk right in and rob the selected victim when the odds are that no more than the clerk or owner and one or two customers will be present. The rewards in any one of these liquor store robberies are not large, but one robber or robbery group often invades and robs two or three places a night.[6]

The Agent-Victim

Most criminals with rational motivation for crime (as opposed to the traditional motivation of kleptomaniacs* or pyromaniacs**) seek a perfect set-up. This requires a cooperating, if not consenting, victim. The term *agent-victim* originated in studies of the styles of robbery. It was found that robbers recognize a basic security in victims who cooperate. For this reason, targets are selected for attack and looting that are

4. Ennis, *Criminal Victimization in the United States*, pp. 37–40.
5. U.S., President's Commission on Law Enforcement and Administration of Justice, Bureau of Social Science Research, *Report on a Pilot Study in the District of Columbia on Victimization and Attitudes Toward Law Enforcement, Field Survey I*, prepared by Albert J. Biderman, Louise A. Johnson, Jennie McIntyre, and Adriane Weir. (Washington, D.C.: Government Printing Office, 1967), p. 62.
6. Werner J. Einstadter, "The Social Organization of Armed Robbery," *Social Problems* 17, no. 1 (Summer 1969): 64–83.
*Thieves who steal because of a so-called compulsion, and not for gain.
**Fire setters, other than those who set fraud or revenge fires, or blazes to conceal another crime.

owned by corporations or large organizations, or in which the owner-operator is covered by insurance. The employee who becomes the victim in these robberies is viewed as an *agent-victim:* a person with no personal loss as a result of the robbery. The concept of the agent-victim includes the rationale that no employee is going to fight or resist when the money demanded by the robbers does not belong to him. This is also true, to an undetermined lesser extent, when the money may belong to the victim but the victim is covered by insurance (a lesser extent because a series of losses usually results in the cancellation of such insurance).[7]

This concept of the agent-victim contributing to the perfect set-up in robberies is in direct opposition to victim-precipitated crimes. The agent-victim's expected cooperation by-passes any possible provocation or contribution to the crime as an event. While resistance to robbery attempts cannot be construed as victim-precipitated crime, robbers do justify the use of force against their victims by claiming self-defense when the victim resists the armed robbery.[8]

Victim Distribution: The Opportunity Factor

The distribution of victims of crime among various social groups is not a factor of race, creed, or national origin, but of opportunity for the offender to commit a crime. Where people live and work, and the nature of occupancies in a neighborhood are the most valid criteria for determining who or what place will be the victim of crime. While thousands of words have been written on the white to nonwhite ratio of victims, it is meaningless unless some proof is developed that either group is more likely to be a victim of crime than the other—over and beyond the factor of residence, place of employment and type of occupancy. If a person lives or works—or plays—in a high-crime area, whether white or nonwhite, he or she is more likely to be a victim of crime because he or she *is there*, not because of the color of his or her skin. If a store or other place of business has cash or property of value, it is more likely to be stolen if the occupancy is in a high-crime area solely on the basis of accessibility. Merchants in such areas have been robbed as often as five times in a week, and thieves have returned for nocturnal looting to stores and warehouses in these areas with an equal frequency. It is the accessibility of cash or valuable property that identifies these victims. They are *targets of opportunity*, and they are not selected because the merchant or businessmen happens to be white or nonwhite.

7. Einstadter, "The Social Organization of Armed Robbery," pp. 64–83.
8. Gerald D. Wolcott, "A Typology of Armed Robbers" (M.A. thesis, Sacramento State College, 1968), p. 48.

One study of the habit patterns of armed robbers revealed that the most common premises attacked were grocery stores, off-premises liquor stores, bars, and gasoline stations. When these armed robberies were unplanned—the criminals cruising a neighborhood for a target of opportunity—the favorite premises attacked were liquor stores.[9]

Age and sex are factors in determining who will become victims of crime, but such factors are relevant only to crimes against the person (murder, non-negligent manslaughter, aggravated assault, child molestation, and rape).

The Genovese case in Forest Hills, New York, is a classic example of this type of crime and the manner in which chance determined the victim's identity; and the opportunity factor provided the offender with a victim for the necessary doer-sufferer relationship. Twenty-eight-year-old Catherine (Kitty) Genovese lived alone in a small apartment on the second floor of a two-story building with ground-floor business occupancies. She worked as a hostess in a bar-restaurant in New York's theater district. Kitty Genovese's work day ended at about 2:00 A.M. on March 31, 1964. She drove home, parking in a parking lot at the end of her apartment house, arriving about 3:00 A.M. Kitty's attacker caught up with her between the parking lot and her home. The first stabbing of Kitty was on the street. Her assailant slashed and stabbed and ran away. Kitty staggered about 50 yards and fell on the sidewalk outside her home. Her attacker came back, stabbed her again, and fled in a car. Kitty walked and fell to the stairway leading up to her second story apartment. The attacker returned and searched the area for his victim. He found Kitty on the stairs, a few feet from the door of her home and he killed her. Kitty's killer was arrested and convicted of this murder; police investigators reported he had never met his victim prior to the attack. (The screams of Kitty Genovese did not go unheard during this chance encounter and attack. Other residents turned on their lights, went to their windows, and shouted at the attacker—but no one of the 38 witnesses called police to destroy the 35 minutes of opportunity for this crime).[10]

A 1967 study of the offender-victim relationship by sex, age, race and place of occurrence in major crimes against the person (homicide, aggravated assault, and forcible rape) and robbery, authorized by the National Commission on the Causes and Prevention of Violence, revealed patterns based on a study of police records in 17 cities. This nationwide survey supports the data of more local studies as to the place of occurrence, and relates data as to sex, race and age. In this survey, the leading combinations for the five crimes studied were: *Homicide:* male offender, male victim; black offender, black victim; 26-year-old and older offenders, same age group victims; and the general place of occurrence was outside, more

9. Wolcott, "A Typology of Armed Robbers," pp. 31–32.
10. A. M. Rosenthal, *Thirty-Eight Witnesses* (New York: McGraw-Hill Book Co., 1964).

specifically, alley and street. (Note: The place of 39 percent of these homicides was in the residence category.) *Aggravated Assault:* male offender, male victim; black offender, black victim; 26-year-old and upward offenders, same age group victims; and the place of occurrence was outside, in the alley and street area. *Rape* (force): offender-victim relationship classic male-female; offender and victim, black; victim and offender in 18-25 age group; and the residence was the place of occurrence, with the bedroom appropriately predominating as the specific place for rape. *Armed Robbery:* offender-victim relationship male-male; black-white; 18-25 age group offender, 26-year-old and upward victim; and these crimes took place outside, with alley and street as the specific place. *Unarmed Robbery:* male offender, male victim; black offender, white victim; victim and offender in 0-17 age group; and the place of occurrence was the residence area, with the specific locale designated as basement, hall, elevator or garage.

Victim Distribution: Victim-precipitated Crime

Victim-precipitated crime refers to criminal acts in which the victim is either the direct or a contributory cause of the crime, setting in motion the chain of circumstances spelling out the crime. When the victim is an active partner in the circumstances leading to the event classified as a crime, his contribution to the dynamics of the situation justifies investigation of his role. It is because so many victims can describe these precrime circumstances that police investigators probe the background of the victim-offender relationship in all crimes. The classic avenues of inquiry are usually structured by the following queries:

1. Did the victim know the offender? Is there any relationship?
2. Was the victim armed?
3. Is the victim known to be aggressive?
4. Has the victim been "field interrogated?" Are there any "connect-ups" with the victim and reports of other crimes?[11]

A previous relationship of victim and offender doesn't suggest a victim's active participation in the precrime circumstances, but it does reveal a potential for contributing to the crime event. Children may make an unknowing contribution to crime against them by relatives and friends. Women contribute to a crime because some of their interrelationships suddenly move from normal to abnormal. A previous relation-

11. Paul B. Weston and Kenneth M. Wells, *Criminal Investigation: Basic Perspectives*, 2d. ed. (Englewood Cliffs, N.J.: Prentice-Hall, 1973), p. 97.

ship often leads offenders to victims, such as children or women, the dull normals and mental defectives,[12] and the aged.

Friendships of the victim and the offender may also make an overt contribution to the dynamics of a crime when the victim is depressed, emotionally disturbed, or lonesome. These persons seek new friends and liaisons among chance drinking partners, prostitutes, homosexual pick-ups, and hitchhikers. These are the *night-people* victims of crime, and their provocative conduct and circle of acquaintances among hustlers, pimps, bartenders, and taxi drivers is the stage setting for sex crimes, crimes of violence, and crimes against property.

When a victim is armed at the time of a crime (carrying something for self-protection), or is known to be aggressive, there is a direct provocation for crime. To qualify as a crime determinant, however, an act is required beyond that of simply being in an area or place not likely to be frequented without arms or self-confidence. The necessary act is aggressiveness, or a combative response to threat, real or implied.

When a victim has a history of being field interrogated or stopped and frisked by police, it can be indicative of a predisposition to frequent high-crime areas or to be a night person, both invitations to crime. When a person has been victimized previously, the facts of the earlier crime or crimes may reveal a relationship between the victim and one or more offenders. When a victim or his car is connected to a previous crime it may also reveal a course of conduct inviting crime.

It is in the fields of homicide and other crimes of violence that the most valid evidence of victims within the foregoing relationships acting provocatively to cause a crime are found. The crime-provoking function of the victim in such crimes has been thoroughly supported by major research. In a study of 588 criminal homicides in Philadelphia, 150 (26 percent) of these killings were classified as "V.P.": victim-precipitated. Many of these V.P. homicides in which the killer was provoked into the fatal attack showed a husband and wife relationship between victim and offender; or male victims killed by female offenders who had some previous relationship.[13]

In Chicago, a study of the patterns of murder collected sufficient data about 311 killings to divide these homicides into VP and non-VP categories. A total of 118 of these 311 killings (37.9 percent) were classed as victim-precipitated. The relationship between victim and offender in these 118 homicides was found to be family or friend in 59 cases (50 percent).[14]

12. Von Hentig, *The Criminal and His Victim*, pp. 415–19.
13. Marvin E. Wolfgang, *Patterns in Criminal Homicide* (Philadelphia: University of Pennsylvania Press, 1958), pp. 254–60.
14. Harwin L. Voss and John R. Hepburn, "Patterns in Criminal Homicide in Chicago," *Journal of Criminal Law, Criminology and Police Science* 59, no. 4 (December 1968); 499–508.

In a British study of crimes of violence in London, a survey of previous association between victims and offenders discovered many instances in which the victim was not free of some culpability in the crime committed. At least, this three-year study reveals that the majority of violent crimes in London during the survey years (1950, 1957, 1960) were not unprovoked attacks by offenders who were complete strangers to their victims. It was found that 27 percent of the victims had a previous family relationship or an interrelationship (sweetheart, friend or rival, fellow employee, club member, or neighbor) of some duration; and 20 percent had a previous business or casual relationship.[15] A subsequent study in America, based on interviews with victims of crime, validates the foregoing report. About 45 percent of all serious crimes against the person (homicide, forcible rape, robbery, and aggravated assault) were committed by someone familiar to the victim.[16]

In the 1967 survey authorized by the National Commission on the Causes and Prevention of Violence of five major crimes against the person, the collected data supports the concept of a previous relationship between offenders and their victims. Among the relationships predominating in this report were:

Homicide: Acquaintances; and family members other than husband, wife, or child

Aggravated Assault: Acquaintances; husband and wife; close friends, including mistresses and homosexual partners

Rape: Acquaintances; and family members other than husband and wife or child

Armed Robbery: Little or no relationships found (less than 1 percent usually); strangers predominated (78.6 percent)

Unarmed Robbery: No relationship between offender and victim at family or other intimate levels; acquaintances and neighbors to a slight extent; strangers were the primary victim.

Victim Distribution: Hardening the Target

Victims of crime are not unaware of its threat. Many possible victims of crime change their habits or *harden the target* so as to make themselves less available to persons intent on the commission of a crime. In a recent survey of things done to protect themselves against crime, several habit changes were reported by residents in Boston and Chicago. These

15. F. H. McClintock, *Crimes of Violence* (London: Macmillan & Co., 1963), pp. 36–39.
16. Ennis, *Criminal Victimization in the United States*, p. 30.

changes were: (1) staying off the streets at night; (2) using private vehicles or taxicabs for nighttime transportation; and (3) not talking to strangers.[17] Additionally, the respondents in this study also reported hardening the target by the following means: (1) carrying a firearm, knife or club when out on the street; (2) placing locks on doors, and locks or bars on windows of their home or store; (3) lighting up the exterior area around a residence or place of business; and (4) keeping a dog or weapon in a residence or store for protection against intruders. (See Chapter IX, Crime Prevention.)

The Complainant

The victim is legally an aggrieved party: a *complainant*. This is a person whose legal rights have been invaded by the criminal act which is the subject of the report (complaint) to police. Modern criminal jurisprudence affords little recognition to victims of crime. The community and its agents of justice discharge any moral obligation to victims of crime by the apprehension and prosecution of the offender.

The role of victim in modern criminal proceedings is primarily as a focus for the essential elements of the crime charged. However, trial procedures sometimes establish the complainant as an accuser, and to be a victim participating in a criminal procedure is sometimes a disturbing experience. This is especially true if a person is unfamiliar with the role of the defense counsel and the court's objective to protect the rights of an accused person. The U.S. Supreme Court in the 1933 case of *Snyder* v. *Massachusetts*,[18] commented on the need in criminal proceedings of some balance between offender and victim: "But justice, though due the accused, is due to the accuser also."

Not all victims promptly report a crime to police and cooperate in prosecution. The seriousness of the crime, in terms of personal injury or the value of the property stolen, is a factor in reporting. Aggravated assaults are reported more frequently than ordinary assaults; and the victim of a grand larceny (substantial loss) is more likely to report the theft than the victim of a petty theft. Crimes are not reported for the following reasons:

1. Identification with the offender as opposed to police
2. A belief the act was not a crime

---

17. U.S., The President's Commission on Law Enforcement and Administration of Justice, "Public Perceptions and Recollections About Crime, Law Enforcement and Criminal Justice," by Albert J. Reis, Jr. in *Studies in Crime and Law Enforcement in Major Metropolitan Areas*, vol. 1 (Washington, D.C.: Government Printing Office, 1967), pp. 102–14.
18. Snyder v. Massachusetts, 291 U.S. 97 (1933).

3. Fear of physical harm—reprisal by offender or friends and associates of offender
4. Economic loss through usually increased insurance rates
5. Unwillingness to get involved (because of adverse publicity)
6. Loss of faith in police effectiveness.[19]

Of course, in cases of crimes without victims (abortion, homosexuality, prostitution, illegal gambling, and drug abuse) and some frauds there is a refusal to report crimes to police, which makes it difficult for police to discover the crime. The girl who seeks an abortion, the two consenting adults of the same sex, the whore and her customer, the person who bets on the outcome of some game of chance, and the user of dangerous and addicting drugs, do not report their criminal acts. They do not view themselves as victims of a crime. Moreover, there is the doctrine of *volenti non fit injuria* which holds that a person who consents to an act cannot receive an injury.

Frauds are often based on the exploitation of an inherent dishonesty in the victim; and the victim's silence is guaranteed by his belief that he is involved in a criminal act. There is a general ignorance among fraud victims as to their criminal responsibility—a state of mind useful to criminals seeking to silence the victims of various frauds.[20]

Restitution and Compensation for Crime Victims

Restitution for victims of crime has an ancient origin. It is an act of restoration of property to the rightful owner, or of giving the equivalent in cash or merchandise. It is also the making of a payment to the victim or his family as an equivalent for death or injury.

Originally, restitution was a form of personal reparation by the offender or his kin to the victim or the victim's family. It stemmed from the primitive blood-feud (a sort of private war) and was a settlement between the family of the murder victim and the offender and his family. Later, the government participated in the arrangements. The amount of money paid by the offender as compensation (or satisfaction) for an offense varied with the status of the victim (royalty, nobility, clergy, freedman, slave), and the money was apportioned between the sovereign (loss of a subject), the Hundred or earlier community in which the victim resided (loss of a member), and the victim's family (loss of a relative).

19. Ennis, *Criminal Victimization in the United States*, pp. 41–44.
20. A *confidence game* or *con game* is any type of fraud or swindle in which the mark (victim) is allowed to profit by dishonest means, then is induced to make a large investment and is fleeced. *See* David W. Maurer, *The Big Con—The Story of the Confidence Man and the Confidence Game* (Indianapolis and New York: Bobbs-Merrill Co., 1940).

Courts may allow restitution in an agreement between victim and of-fender to *compromise* a minor criminal action. This type of settlement re-quires a situation in which the victim has a cause for civil action arising from the crime, and the victim acknowledges that restitution has been made (satisfaction for the injury). If the court has no reason in its discre-tion or in the public interest (i.e., the crime was committed riotously; was against a public officer; or the offender's intent was to commit a felony) to deny the restitution as an effective settlement, then it is allowed.

Courts may also order restitution as part of the sentence of a con-victed offender. These cases usually involve vandalism, malicious mis-chief, arson, or larceny. It is financial restitution for the costs of damage done to property, or a reasonable amount related to the current market value of stolen property.

In contemporary law, there is a strong belief that restitution is more properly a civil action for damages against an offender by the victim or his family. Any schedule of payments for injuries are in the area of *torts*— private or civil wrongs for which a civil action can be justified. However, victims without funds cannot hire attorneys to pursue their claims in court. In addition, most criminal offenders are without assets, and court judgments against them are worthless.

Probably a combination of indigent offenders and victims led to the concept of compensation for victims of crime. In 1964, Great Britain and New Zealand enacted similar legislation to relieve the poor victim of the costs of his injury and loss of income during the resultant disability period, if any. Such law making is within the obligation of a government to its citizens. Modern government accepts responsibility for the protec-tion of citizens against criminals by its vast budgets for law enforcement and criminal justice. Failure to afford such protection makes the govern-ment (as representative of the whole community) to some extent liable for injuries to innocent victims—and there is some rationale for spreading the costs of treatment for injured victims to the whole community.[21]

There must be some level of maximum compensation: a ceiling on payments in any scheme for reimbursing victims of violent crime. How-ever, when payments are keyed to wages (wage earners) and the value of lost services (housewife), the victim's inability to sustain the cost of treatment without help develops a welfare level compensation. This is unfair. It requires victims to exhaust minimal financial resources to qual-ify for victim's compensation.

State victim-compensation systems should be administered to refer claims to an attorney in the community in which the crime occurs. He would investigate and determine the award to the victim within the wages-services and out-of-pocket expenses framework, but without re-

21. David J. Bentel, "Selected Problems of Public Compensation to Victims of Crime," *Issues in Criminology* 3, no. 2 (Spring 1968): 217–31.

gard for the victim's ability to pay. Compensation would be immediate for out-of-pocket costs, and weekly or monthly for lost wages or sevices.[22]

Compensation for victims of crime should be extended to provide funds to cover injuries received by innocent bystanders or citizens who have rushed to the defense of a crime victim. This may overcome the existing reluctance of many citizens to get involved in an ongoing crime.

Restitution for the victims of crime by the government raises a rather different but important question in regard to innocent defendants being classed as victims. Should a defendant, having been found innocent, be reimbursed for his legal expenses, damages due to loss of wages or job loss while incarcerated, and the traumatic effect of jail life? Perhaps the jury or judge who acquits, or the judge who dismisses, might determine whether the defendant did or did not cause the victim's injury and was in fact sufficiently innocent of the charges to merit government reimbursement. In such instances, the innocent defendant may not be a crime victim, but he is a "victim" of the criminal justice process.

Selected References

Books

Ennis, Phillip H. *Criminal Victimization in the United States*. Chicago, Ill.: National Opinion Research Center, University of Chicago, 1967; a report to the President's Commission on Law Enforcement and Administration of Justice.

von Hentig, Hans. *The Criminal and His Victim: Studies in the Sociology of Crime*. 1948; reprint ed., Hamden, Conn.: Archon Books, Shoe String Press, 1967.

Wolfgang, Marvin E. *Patterns in Criminal Homicide*. Philadelphia: University of Pennsylvania Press, 1958.

Periodicals

Bentel, David J. "Selected Problems of Public Compensation to Victims of Crime." *Issues in Criminology* 3, no. 2 (Spring 1968): 217–31.

Childres, Robert. "The Victims." *Harper's*, April 1964, pp. 159–62.

Einstadter, Werner J. "The Social Organization of Armed Robbery." *Social Problems* 17, no. 1 (Summer 1969): 64–83.

Cases

Snyder v. Massachusetts, 291 U.S. 97 (1933).

22. Robert Childres, "The Victims," *Harper's*, April 1964, pp. 159–62.

Chapter III

Crime and Criminals

As communities organized for social control through law and its enforcement, the agents of criminal justice began to classify criminals into legal typologies. As the problem of crime developed over the centuries, scientists and scholars developed classification systems to *type* criminals for a better understanding of the one-time offender, the professional criminal, and the recidivist or repeating offender whose life history is primarily a criminal career.

Criminal or offender typologies categorize criminal behavior into *sets* (which can be identified by certain specific offender characteristics), and then use these individual categories: (1) to study the universe of criminal behavior and relate it to the known causative factors of such behavior, or to develop new theories of criminal behavior; and (2) to study individual offenders and classify them within the sets of a typology for an improved insight into the causative factors of their behavior for the purpose of treatment and rehabilitation.

There is a de facto division of criminals by police and other agents of criminal justice. It is a classification system with two major groups: (1) the professional criminal, whose criminality is a means of making a living, and (2) the accidental or occasional offender, whose criminality is a one-act aberration from his normal life style and pattern of behavior (despite the fact that the antisocial act may be repeated from time to time).

There is a legal division of criminals aligned with the seriousness of criminal acts or the grades of crime: misdemeanants and felons. This, however, his a very broad classification and of little scientific use in any attempt to secure greater knowledge about offenders. In addition, it is a classification based solely on the "thing done." A typology of offenders must be based on facts about the offender as a person. The nature and circumstances of the act that makes the behavior criminal is useful data in typing the offender, but no more so than other significant data.

For the purpose of these typologies the data base for studying offenders is the life history and criminal record of the individual, no less. In some of the offender typologies, life-history data is supplemented by interviews with the offender. The standardization of terminology used to describe criminal acts contributes a uniformity necessary to construct typologies and also to determine the appropriate category within a typology for a particular offender. Offender interviews add a new and significant dimension to our understanding. Not only do they afford an opportunity to observe the offender and ascertain how he sees himself in relation to others, but they offer a chance for reviewing reported factual information about his crimes.

The Professional vs. the Occasional Offender

The *"pro"* vs. the one-time offender is a useful classification of criminals for police and other agents of criminal justice. It is directly related to the police apprehension process, to some of the judicial and legal concepts of sentencing, and to the work of probation, parole, and corrections generally. The professional criminal tends to concentrate on crimes in which there is a consenting victim; or the offender is unseen by, or unknown to, the victim. He is a two-to-seven-time offender; and is not usually an appropriate candidate for probation or release on parole after a short term of imprisonment. The accidental or occasional offender is usually identified by his victim or by his knowledge of, or access to, the victim of a crime or the place of occurrence. He is generally a first, or less serious offender; and is eligible for probation or parole after a short term of imprisonment.

Gabriel Tarde, a noted French criminologist, suggested a classification of criminals which would stress the identification of criminals whose major source of income came from crimes. He believed these individuals were criminals because of habit, and his measure of the professional criminal was whether the favored criminal activity was viewed as a trade. Criminals because of opportunity (accidental or occasional offenders) were to be classified separately as violators of personal rights because of vengeance, or violators of property rights in order to supplement a legal income at some honest trade.[1]

1. Gabriel Tarde, *Penal Philosophy* (Boston: Little, Brown and Co., 1912), pp. 265–68.

The first extensive classification along these lines was made by chief of detectives Thomas Byrnes in New York City.[2] Byrnes classified professional criminals only to show the trade of crime, rather than the acts of an occasional offender. These criminals were described by Byrnes as "clever in their own peculiar line," and as "intelligent and thoughtful rogues" who profited from their criminal activities.

In this classification of 204 professional criminals, a total of 11 categories were listed. The titles given each distinguishable group of criminals—whose photographs and criminal records were listed by Byrnes—in this contemporary classification are:

1. Bank burglars
2. Bank sneak thieves (daytime thefts by trick, speed, and stealth)
3. Forgers
4. Hotel and boardinghouse thieves
5. Sneak and house thieves
6. Store and safe burglars
7. Shoplifters and pickpockets
8. Confidence and bunco men (general swindling)
9. Receivers of stolen goods
10. Sawdust men (swindles involving the sale of alleged counterfeit money or bonds)
11. Dishonest horse dealers.[3]

A review of the case histories of these offenders reveals a mixed pattern of arrests in many instances, but in the majority of the criminal histories listed the offenders have a single pattern of arrests for the same kinds of crime.

In 1939, Dr. Arthur N. Foxe established a similar classification of criminals,[4] in which the professional criminals of Chief Byrnes' listing are grouped as repetitive criminals, and the occasional offender is subdivided into *situational* and *physical* categories.

In this typology of crime and criminals, the deeds of the repetitive criminal are listed as burglary, forgery, robbery, sexual crimes, swindling, and picking pockets. Dr. Foxe comments on this type of individual

---

2. Thomas Byrnes, *1886—Professional Criminals in America* (1886; reprint ed., New York: Chelsea House Publishers, 1969). Publication was approved by the New York Board of Police in 1886.
3. Ibid., pp. 1–51.
4. Arthur N. Foxe, "An Additional Classification of Criminals," *Journal of Criminal Law and Criminology* 30 (July-August 1939): 232–236. (*Police Science* had not been added to the title of this periodical at that time.)

as follows: "His lack of maturation makes him commit the same crime with appalling consistency in his twenties, thirties, forties, and even fifties."[5]

Dr. Foxe rejects the term *accidental offender* since there is no evidence the thing done by the occasional offender is an accident. Foxe's occasional criminal is a person who has had a satisfactory adjustment to his life situation until some circumstance or series of events destroys that adjustment. These offenders may not be personally responsible for the events leading to the crime (victim-precipitated, possibly), but under the stress of certain circumstances they become criminals. Dr. Foxe's subdivision of the occasional lawbreaker is as follows:

1. Situational:
   a. Economic factor (problems)
   b. Life crisis (related to role of fiancée, father, spouse—such as frustration in love or infidelity of spouse—or reaction to an insult or a hostile act)
2. Physical:
   a. Alcoholic episode*
   b. Venereal and other ego-destroying illness or injury (blow to vanity, pride, or capacity)
   c. Curable or incurable mental disease, syphilis, and the like.[6]

Professional Criminals in the Ghetto— The Hustler and the Drug Seller

Hustling is a form of criminal activity which not only has a distinguishable behavior pattern, but which also has some conflict relationship between the offender and the community. This is the activity and life-style of the hustler or the *cat*.

Hustling was once a deviant rather than criminal occupation limited to poolroom hustling.[7] The poolroom hustler made his living by betting and deceit. He would convince a stranger to play pool and wager small sums, but the hustler initially concealed his own skill at the game. When the wagered amounts were increased, the hustler used his skill to win back the money he had lost and the sums bet by the victim in anticipation

5. Arthur N. Foxe, *Studies in Criminology* (New York: Nervous and Mental Disease Monographs, 1948), p. 105.
*Drug abuse episodes would be similar, although not common around 1939.
6. Ibid., p. 107.
7. Ned Polsky, *Hustlers, Beats and Others* (Chicago: Aldine Publishing Co., 1967), pp. 41–116.

of further winnings. The decline in poolrooms since the first quarter of the century has led to economic disaster for the poolroom hustler.

The new breed of hustlers is still related to night hours, unsupervised occupations, and the thrill of working for part or all of the "action" rather than weekly or monthly wages. However, they now operate in ghetto areas and their hustle is diversified, profitable, criminal behavior: shoplifting, receiving stolen property, pimping, numbers running (gambling agent), and selling narcotics or dangerous drugs.

Hustlers, in a strange shift from the all-man world of the traditional poolroom before mid-century, began to use—or misuse—women. Hustlers exploit women. Many attractive young females support a hustler in some luxury, by shoplifting and prostitution. Hustlers supervise the basic arrangements and operations, and the women dutifully hand over the proceeds. Additionally, the hustler sees himself as an operator with a scheme to avoid arrest because of an angle. His angle is to remain aloof from contact with stolen merchandise or the criminal conduct of prostitutes. Police find it difficult to gain probable cause for an arrest without evidence of active participation in crime.

Since it is the concentration of minority group members in a slum area that makes a ghetto, and since most such areas in the U.S. are now predominantly black, it is not surprising that many young black males have become hustlers. Since petty crime and street and tavern solicitation for prostitution have always been identified as a source of income in low-rent areas, it is not surprising that many of these black ghetto residents have seized this illegal opportunity for economic enrichment.

The black hustler is best characterized in a study made of the Negro numbers man. The *numbers game* is a lottery in which the player bets small sums (ten cents to a dollar) and the outcome is determined by chance. In some areas, a specific procedure has been established for computing the day's winning number from the total payoffs reported in the day's pari-mutuel betting at a major horse-racing track. Numbers men were interviewed in this study and they admitted to the "fast-dollar" philosophy of the "angle boy," and observed that they did not think their work was in violation of the lottery laws (as a real criminal activity). These agents of a numbers ring (or bank) said their adolescent behavior was in the role of sport or big spender, and their chief adult recreation *(kick)* centered on betting on horses and sports events. However, both the juvenile police-encounter record and the adult arrest history of these numbers men were usually related to disorderly acts or gambling; there was no evidence of stealing or violence.[8]

A modern variation on the black hustler in ghetto areas or urban population centers is the *cat*. Usually a drug user, each cat has his hustle

8. Julian B. Roebuck, "The Negro Numbers Man as a Criminal Type: The Construction and Application of a Typology," *Journal of Criminal Law, Criminology and Police Science* 54, no. 1 (March 1963): 48–60.

(any nonviolent means of making money, usually illegal) to live without working for wages and his *kick* (any act usually tabooed by the community). The most popular kick is drugs, in some progression from marihuana to hard drugs and hallucinogens (heroin, methedrine, cocaine and acid—LSD).[9]

Drug selling is a type of crime that is popular with hustlers or cats hurrying to achieve upward social mobility. It is a fast route out of the slums, and out of the fields of petty theft and living off the proceeds of prostitution. It is a get-rich-quick scheme compared to the orderly and earned advancement of the numbers man from runner, to pickup man, to an executive role in the bank or counting room of a major gambling oper-tion.

This is a rags-to-riches story of one hustler on the drug scene:

If he could last six months selling narcotics he was a rich man. He owned part of a bar on 138th Street. He had excellent credit with bookies and gamblers. All of this because of money. He had all the money he wanted and everything that money could buy, and it came in every day. He controlled the major cutting of the heroin from its high purity state to the retail product at street level, and he took greater risks than the others in the drug-selling mob, but it was the risk-taking which accounted for his huge profits. He was the distributor, the supplier of the pushers who sold to the junkies.[10]

Before, in the Roaring Twenties, a lucrative role in criminality had been held predominantly by the Irish, Italian, or German bootlegger, willing to risk arrest to bring his customers a supply of illegal whiskey and beer during America's Noble Experiment, the dry years. Of course, the harmful effects of drug selling is much greater than any harm from selling a fair quality of bootleg whiskey or beer, but the instant riches factor is quite similar.

The hustler in the ghetto of modern cities who specializes in the high-risk business of marketing illegal drugs will make money, but there is a lesser risk in the traditional hustler's role of pimp, thief, or numbers man. This is the new professional criminal in the ghetto: the drug boot-legger or the man with an angle.

Criminal Typologies

A recent system used to break up the universe of criminals combines the socio-psychological aspects of criminal behavior with the life-style of the criminal to create a typological classification system. The following

9. Harold Finestone, "Cats, Kicks and Color," *Social Problems* 5, no. 1 (July 1957): 3–13.
10. Alvin Moscow, *Merchants of Heroin—An In-Depth Portrayal of Business in the Underworld* (New York: Dial Press, 1968), p. 225.

factors are used to assign a criminal to one of the types of criminal behavior comprising this system:

1. Offense behavior (things done)
2. Interactional setting (crime scene; victim)
3. Role-career (life-style)
4. Offender's self-concept and attitudes
5. Family background, associates, and so forth.[11]

The descriptive titles given each distinguishable group of criminals in this array is more diversified than Byrnes' 1886 listing, ranging through the following role-careers in criminality:

1. Professional thief (confidence man, shoplifter, pickpocket)
2. Professional heavy (robber, burglar)
3. Professional fringe violator (doctors, attorneys, and other professional persons who violate laws)
4. Semiprofessional property criminal
5. White-collar criminal*
6. Fraud—check passing, non-professional (usually drawn against a personal account and returned because of insufficient funds)
7. Embezzler (dishonest employee)
8. Auto thief (joyrider)
9. Personal offender (assailant; one-time)
10. Property offender (one-time)
11. "Psycho" assailant
12. Sex offender —nonviolent
13. Sex offender—nonviolent (statutory rape)
14. Sex offender—violent
15. Addict—heroin.[12]

11. Don C. Gibbons, *Society, Crime and Criminal Careers—An Introduction to Criminality* (Englewood Cliffs, N.J.: Prentice-Hall, 1968), pp. 215–42.
*A broad definition of white-collar criminality is: "The violation of criminal law by a person of high socio-economic status in the course of occupational activity." See Earl R. Quinney, "The Study of White Collar Crime: Toward a Reorientation in Theory and Research," *Journal of Criminal Law, Criminology and Police Science* 55, no. 2 (June 1964): 208–14.
12. Don C. Gibbons, *Changing the Lawbreaker—The Treatment of Delinquents and Criminals* (Englewood Cliffs, N.J.: Prentice-Hall, 1965), pp. 96–128. (This typology of criminals was developed in association with Donald L. Garrity; see Don C. Gibbons and Donald L. Garrity, "Definition and Analysis of Certain Criminal Types," *Journal of Criminal Law, Criminology and Police Science* 53 (March 1962): 27–35.

While fashions in crime change over a half century, there is a re-markable similarity between this criminal typology and the prior class-ification of criminals by Tarde, the French criminologist, early in this century, and Byrnes, the New York chief of detectives, late in the nineteenth century. There is a differentiation between groups of crimi-nals where crime is a trade or major source of income (professional as op-posed to semiprofessional and one-time criminals). The semiprofessional and one-time subdivisions in this typology of Gibbons and Garrity allows for classification of both the situational and physical occasional offenders described by Dr. Foxe.

One of the more recent criminal typologies constructed by American criminologists is that of Marshall B. Clinard and Richard Quinney.[13] It is a behavioral-cultural typology that uses not only the offender's criminal behavior as a criteria of classification, but also considers the interrelation-ships of individual human behavior with the behavior of others, both in the offender's social group and in the community. This brings the crimi-nal deed and the offender into focus with the social context of the act and the perpetrator. This typology uses four major factors for analysis and classification:

1. Crime career
2. Support by offender's social group of the criminal behavior of offender
3. Relationship between the criminal behavior and noncriminal behavior in society generally
4. The reaction of the community (society) to the criminal behavior.

This innovative behavioral-cultural typology allows for eight types of offenders:

1. Violent criminals (murder, rape, aggravated assault)
2. Conventional criminals (robbery, burglary, theft)
3. Professional criminals (swindling, shoplifting, pickpocketing, counterfeiting, forgery)
4. Organized criminals (sale of narcotics and dangerous drugs, prostitution, gambling)
5. Occupational criminals (embezzlement, price fixing, fee split-ting, black marketeering)
6. Occasional property criminals (auto theft, shoplifting, forgery—checks, vandalism)

13. Marshall B. Clinard and Richard Quinney, *Criminal Behavior Systems—A Typology* (New York: Holt, Rinehart and Winston, 1967), 12–14.

7. Political criminals (treason, sedition, and protest defined as criminal)

8. Public order criminals (drunkenness, drug abuse or narcotic use, homosexuality, traffic violations).[14]

Criminal Careers

There is a cost to the entire community and its criminal justice system when a person becomes a criminal and begins a career in crime, which may be coterminous with his lifetime. There is a financial cost to victims of crime when money or property is stolen, an out-of-pocket cost when injuries or death are caused by crime, and the intangible social cost to the community of both criminal and victim. However, the most basic cost is the fiscal expenditure needed to process offenders in the criminal justice system from the beginning to the end of their criminal careers.

In a major study of offenders, it was reported that criminal career patterns of first arrests and subsequent rearrests revealed an average cost of $12,000 per individual. For instance, a sample of 1,000 offenders arrested initially for one of the FBI Index crimes (murder, nonnegligent manslaughter, forcible rape, robbery, aggravated assault, burglary, larceny of $50 or more, and auto theft) would build up to a total of 3,670 rearrests for Index crimes alone.[15]

In projecting crime-career costs, it was discovered that certain crimes could be identified with crime careers, which accounted for various segments of the community's crime-career cost:

1. Burglary (39 percent)
2. Theft—$50 and over (24 percent)
3. Automobiles (18 percent)
4. Aggravated assault (9 percent)
5. Robbery (7 percent)
6. Murder and nonnegligent manslaughter (2 percent)
7. Forcible rape (1 percent).[16]

In the rearrest crime-switch area of this study, it was reported that the professional or repetitive criminal was arrested three to four times in his life span of criminal behavior. For instance, a sample of 1,000 crimi-

14. Clinard and Quinney, *Criminal Behavior Systems—A Typology*, pp. 14–19.
15. U.S., The Institute of Defense Analyses, *Task Force Report: Science and Technology*, prepared for the President's Commission on Law Enforcement and Administration of Justice (Washington, D.C.: Government Printing Office, 1967), pp. 59–65.
16. Ibid., p. 64.

nals arrested initially for robbery, during their collective lifetime would total:

1. Fifty arrests for murder
2. Seventy arrests for rape (forcible)
3. Eight hundred more arrests (in addition to the first arrests) for robbery
4. Two hundred and fifty arrests for aggravated assault
5. Fourteen hundred arrests for burglary
6. Seven hundred and thirty arrests for larceny of $50 or over
7. Three hundred and seventy arrests for auto theft.[17]

While the FBI Index crimes are not representative of the universe of crimes committed, they are suggestive of crimes which can be classified as serious, and are commonly found in the American criminal justice process. Additionally, since the Index crimes do not include any offenses within the overreach of the criminal law, these patterns and their costs are for antisocial conduct justly termed criminal by law.

The existence of professional criminals whose recidivism develops into lifetime careers of repetitive criminal behavior indicates the importance of a classification system. This will aid and assist the judiciary in the sentencing dilemma, and aid and assist those responsible for custody and treatment in probation, institutional corrections, and parole. The continued development of offender typologies, both legal and behavioral, should have a much broader data base in the future. The information available from typical arrest reports (date, name, age, sex, offense, and physical characteristics) are insufficient for a basic typology of criminals that will meet the threefold needs of law enforcement and criminal justice (police, judiciary, corrections). The minimal data necessary for the construction of adequate typologies of criminals is: (1) educational achievement, (2) prior record (particularly while incarcerated or while on probation or parole), and (3) employment record and status.[18]

Data for Typologies

Ideally, a criminal typology should provide data about offenders in a fashion which would allow agents of criminal justice to better understand the offender as a person, and to better comprehend his criminal behavior.

17. Commission on Law Enforcement, *Science and Technology*, pp. 63–64.
18. Space-General Corporation, *A Study of the Prevention and Control of Crime and Delinquency* (El Monte, Calif.: Space-General Corporation, 1965), pp. 59–60.

Access to the following information would offer new horizons in this vital area:

1. Characteristics which are descriptive of criminals in each major category
2. Similarities and differences in the characteristics of criminals in the major groupings of the typology
3. The maturation factor, similarities and differences between early and later portions of criminal careers.[19]

Additionally, the organization of the collected data into offender classifications should be flexible enough to accept the threat to legal typologies inherent in the overreach of morality laws; the penalty inconsistencies of politics-as-usual in such laws as those relating to drug abuse; and the threat to criminal typologies by the cultural conflict which develops new types of professional criminals such as the cats and hustlers.

The data collected by police and stored in their records identifies criminals and offers a primary source of information about offenders and their crimes. The universe of known criminal offenses listed in police recording systems establishes the boundaries of any legal typology of criminals. The data as to the disposition of each event in the life record of a criminal identifies the offender as a repetitive or occasional criminal. Rearrests and the switch from one crime to another reveal development in a criminal career, or some progression. When an offender repeats his crimes, there is likely to be an occupational upward mobility. Beginners in crime are handicapped by a lack of confidence in their ability, and have yet to meet older career criminals whose help beginners need to reach the top rungs of the criminal ladder.[20]

The three most important data elements in police records concerning the offender are those facts which will identify the offender in case of rearrest, describe the crime committed, and state the disposition of the arrest.

Identification Data—To enable the search of police files for a prior record, the minimum data required is usually name; sex; race; date of birth; height; local, state and federal (FBI) identification number (local police assign a number to a person on his first arrest and this procedure is carried out at other levels of government); fingerprints; and physical description. Fingerprint data begins with the standard classification of pattern types and subgroups, and includes data on missing fingers. Because of their identification potential, visible scars, marks, tatoos, amputations, or deformities are recorded by police.

19. Space-General Corporation, *A Study*, p. 64.
20. Byrnes, *1886—Professional Criminals in America*, p. 1.

Standardized Offense Terms—A massive research project at all levels of government concerned with data about crime and criminals has developed a uniform and standard list of criminal offenses in the United States.[21] While the laws of the federal and state governments differ, this listing allows a grouping of similar crimes, nationally or locally. The universe of crimes for police records systems is as follows:

1. Sovereignty (treason, espionage, sabotage, sedition)
2. Military (desertion)
3. Immigration (illegal entry, smuggled aliens, false citizenship)
4. Homicide (murder, manslaughter, manslaughter by vehicle)
5. Kidnapping
6. Sexual assault (forcible and statutory rape, sodomy)
7. Robbery
8. Assault (aggravated, simple)
9. Abortion
10. Arson
11. Extortion
12. Burglary (including "Burglar's Tools")
13. Larceny (pocket picking, purse snatching, shoplifting, thefts from vehicles, buildings, yards, coin machines, U.S. mail)
14. Stolen vehicle (includes airplanes)
15. Forgery (forging and passing forged checks, counterfeiting)
16. Fraud (confidence game, swindle, mail fraud, fraudulent credit cards, "Not Sufficient Funds" checks—own name, and false statements)
17. Embezzlement
18. Stolen property (receive, possess, transport, sell)
19. Property damage (vandalism—private or public property)
20. Dangerous drugs (hallucinogens, heroin, opium, cocaine, synthetic narcotics, narcotic equipment, marihuana, amphetamines, barbiturates)
21. Sex offenses (child molesting, indecent exposure, peeping Tom, bestiality, incest, homosexuality)
22. Obscene material

21. Project SEARCH (*System for Electronic Analyses and Retrieval of Criminal Histories*) is a federal-grant project of the Law Enforcement Assistance Administration, the U.S. Department of Justice, and 10 participating states.

23. Family offenses (neglect, cruelty, nonsupport, bigamy, contributing to delinquency of minor)

24. Gambling (including possession and transportation of gambling devices, transmitting wagering information, tampering with sports events)

25. Commercial sex (brothel keeping, procuring, prostitution, homosexual prostitution)

26. Liquor (illegal manufacture, sale, possession; misrepresenting age)

27. Drunk

28. Obstruct police (resist officer, harbor fugitive, aid prisoner to escape, destroy evidence)

29. Flight—escape

30. Obstruct justice (perjury, contempt of court, obstructing court)

31. Bribery (give, offer, solicit, receive)

32. Weapons offense (includes "as" weapon, explosives, incendiary devices)

33. Public peace (anarchism, riot, unlawful assembly, false alarm, desecrate flag, disorderly conduct, loiter, disturb the peace, curfew)

34. Traffic offenses

35. Health and safety (adulterated or misbranded drugs, food and cosmetics)

36. Civil rights

37. Invade privacy (trespass, eavesdrop, wiretap)

38. Smuggle (contraband, to avoid duty, prison contraband)

39. Election laws

40. Antitrust

41. Tax—revenue (income, sales, liquor)

42. Conservation (animals, fish, birds)

43. Vagrancy.[22]

Disposition Data—In the beginning there is an arrest, and what follows through court proceedings and correctional custody and treatment is disposition. Studies of individuals as offenders against the law of crimes will be facilitated by this all-inclusive definition of disposition. There is need for more than the finding of guilt or innocence and the length of a

22. *Standardized Data Elements for Criminal History Files,* Project Search Staff, California Crime Technological Research Foundation (Sacramento: 1970), pp. E5–11.

sentence following conviction for a crime. The major court outcome is important to a criminal history, but of even greater importance is data about each institutionalization and each release on probation or parole.

When such data is part of the police records system, future criminal typologies will be able to trace the role-careers of offenders from arrest to rearrest. Adequate data on how the criminal offender left the court-and-corrections phase of the criminal justice system will allow the development of a matrix of "input" and "output" events in the life—and criminal history—of an offender.

Typologies of Delinquents

Classifications of juvenile and youthful offenders into criminal typologies include youngsters from 7 to 21 years of age. Children under seven are presumed incapable of committing crime, and the legal age of maturity is 21 years. To complicate the problem of constructing a typology of delinquency, the laws of many states have established the age of 18 as the age at which adolescence ceases and adulthood begins—and a few states have lowered this limit to the age of 16. At whatever age set within a state by statute law, a young person under 16, 18, or 21 is treated as a juvenile rather than as an adult and processed as a noncriminal by criminal justice agencies. Above the age established as the upper limit on juvenile delinquency, the young person is considered an adult with full criminal responsibility for his acts, and processed in an accusatory criminal proceeding.

To avoid a hasty conclusion that delinquency is only distantly related to criminality, it has been noted that there is an increased involvement of young people with violent and serious criminal behavior. The involvement of young people in real crimes is revealed in the official statistics of the FBI's uniform crime reports. These statistics reveal an increasing percentage of persons under the age of 18 arrested for the crimes of murder, aggravated assault, forcible rape, robbery, burglary, larceny-theft, and auto theft.[23]

A typology of delinquency based mainly on sociological theory, and which uses the same criteria for classifying offenders as in categorizing adult criminal behavior has been worked out by Don C. Gibbons.[24] He lists nine classes (types) of young persons in accordance with a four-dimensional criteria of: (1) offense behavior, (2) interactional setting, (3) self-concept, and (4) offender attitudes (to community agencies). These nine types are:

23. *Uniform Crime Reports* (Washington, D.C.: Federal Bureau of Investigation, U.S. Department of Justice, printed annually).
24. Don C. Gibbons, *Changing the Lawbreaker*, pp. 74–97.

1. Predatory (acquisitive or theft) gang delinquent
2. Conflict (fighting) gang delinquent
3. Occasional (casual) gang delinquent
4. Occasional (casual) non-gang delinquent
5. Auto thief—joy rider
6. Drug abuser
7. Overly aggressive delinquent
8. Female delinquent
9. Behavior-problem delinquent.

In this typology heavy emphasis is placed upon group behavior in delinquency: *the gang*. Three of the nine classifications are assigned to
gangs, either by the nature of the group or by the characteristics of the
young person's membership. Three of the classifications are concerned
with the occasional delinquent and the joy-riding auto thief who is not
considered a real thief—whose intent is to steal property (the auto) rather
than to temporarily use the property (for the ride). Another three classes
of young offenders who appear to have a natural grouping are drug abusers, overly aggressive delinquents, and behavior-problem delinquents.
Certainly, the drug abuser and the overly aggressive youngster can be
shown to have behavior problems. Lastly, the female offender group
needs several subdivisions for clarification. They are often gang members
in ghetto and barrio* areas. They are frequently drug abusers, and may
be classed as behavior-problem persons.

Another approach, based on psychology and psychiatry, views delinquency as a complex pattern arising from individual problems, intrafamily problems, and situations conducive to delinquency.[25] In it there
are four basic groups of identifiable delinquents. They are:

1. Organic damage delinquents—youths with brain damage,
   epilepsy, and genetic defects such as endocrine abnormality
2. Deprived or disadvantaged delinquents—early parental rejection and subsequent foster-parent or institutional care
3. Emotionally disturbed delinquents—mentally ill youngsters
4. Family situation delinquents—young people in reaction to
   stress of intrafamily tensions.[25]

*Ghettos dominated by Spanish-speaking residents: Mexican Americans (Chicanos) in the
Southwest and Pacific Coast areas, and persons of Puerto Rican or Cuban origins along the
East Coast.
25. K. R. H. Wardrop, "Delinquent Teenage Types," *British Journal of Criminology* 7, no.
4 (October 1967): 371–80.

K. R. H. Wardrop, the author of the foregoing typology of delinquency, presents four clear-cut types of adolescent delinquency. The first two groups of offenders (organic damage and deprived or disadvantaged delinquents) comprise a disabled population, while the remaining two groups are comprised of youngsters who are sick or verging on mental illness. This major division is evidenced by the concepts of sickness as opposed to disablement. Additionally, Wardrop constructs a fifth delinquent group to encompass youngsters who are nothing more than the products of their cultural background. These *situational delinquents* are generally described as young people with blocked goals who join aggressive or acquisitive gangs from the same cultural background. This subculture is marked by hostility to the rest of the community and its agencies, which often tolerate their violent behavior as the norm, and usually accept the acquisitive behavior of these neighborhood theft gangs as normal behavior.[26]

Both major typologies of delinquency, one with its origins in America and the other with its sources in Britain, reveal an ever-increasing stress on an *interactionist* theory of delinquency based on reaction to real-life situations. Both typologies strongly suggest that a heterogeneous mass of young persons interact with the circumstances of any given situation within a group of subcultural patterns of behavior determined by gang membership or ghetto residence.

Selected References

Books

Byrnes, Thomas. *1886—Professional Criminals in America.* New York: Chelsea House Publishers, 1969.

Clinard, Marshall B., and Quinney, Richard. *Criminal Behavior Systems—A Typology.* New York: Holt, Rinehart and Winston, 1967.

Foxe, Arthur, N. *Studies in Criminology.* New York: Nervous and Mental Disease Monographs, 1948.

Gibbons, Don C. *Changing the Lawbreaker—The Treatment of Delinquents and Criminals.* Englewood Cliffs, N.J.: Prentice-Hall, 1968.

Hall, Arthur Cleveland. *Crime in Its Relation to Social Progress.* New York: AMS Press, 1968.

Morris, Norval, and Hawkins, Gordon. *The Honest Politician's Guide to Crime Control.* Chicago and London: University of Chicago Press, 1969.

Polsky, Ned. *Hustlers, Beats and Others.* Chicago: Aldine Publishing Co., 1967.

Periodicals

Wardrop, K. R. H. "Delinquent Teenage Types," *British Journal of Criminology* 7, no. 4 (October 1967): 371–80.

26. Wardrop, "Delinquent Teenage Types," p. 376.

Chapter IV

Causative Factors in Criminal Behavior

As a human being grows, and wherever he goes, he is aware of being judged. The infant develops an awareness of whether a parent has a favorable or unfavorable reaction to some act. Young persons are particularly alert to social embarrassments and usually avoid actions likely to lead to humiliation. Older persons are very conscious of their social habits and tend to lessen any discomfort by adjusting habits to status in the social order. Judgment—approval or disapproval—turns upon interests shared by others, and the folkways and customs of the group. Social norms are established in the image of the group and its habits.

Social pressure to develop conformity among group members has two major forms: internal and external. Internal controls (conscience, superego, values, and beliefs) are the result of socialization by parents and other family members, school personnel, clergymen and church members, friends, and others in the community. They represent the first influence on the individual to adjust his behavior to conform to the behavior norms of the group, and to refrain from unacceptable behavior. External controls are devices such as sanction laws which control antisocial behavior after it breaks the bounds of internal controls. The death penalty, banishment and deportation, and imprisonment are external controls capable of removing the offender from the community which failed to socialize him. Ostracism is a lesser and informal external control. It is related to other social controls associated with the stigma of being a criminal offender (the "ex-con" image), and it ranges from loss of job, of spouse and of friends, to the denial of public office or public employment, and the loss of civil rights (voting, jury duty, etc.).

However, conscious and unconscious wishes, urges, motives, interests, desires, and passions are continually in operation in all persons, serving as cues for intentional actions of an individual. This often leads to a conflict situation in which the outcome wished for or desired is blocked by either internal or external controls. Unfortunately, the conflict situation is frequently resolved in favor of the wished-for outcome. Social pressure does not always lead to thoroughgoing conformity.

In the nineteenth century metaphysics and theology began to interface with the emerging scientific disciplines of biology, psychiatry, psychology, and sociology in seeking the reasons for criminal behavior. Defective social controls encompassed the first theory of criminal behavior. Inherited traits or predispositions to criminality followed quickly as a contemporary explanation of crime and criminals, and this concept was promptly shelved for a broader learning-theory concept: that criminal behavior was learned in the same manner as all behavior is learned.

In the following survey of the theories of crime causes, each theory of criminal behavior is identified with the scientist or scientists who contributed to its origin and development. Where possible, a relationship is shown between theories in the same major areas: (1) biological, (2) environmental, and (3) mental influences. Each theory is developed as if it were mutually exclusive and *could* be the single cause of criminal behavior. However, a multifactor theory of criminal behavior is discussed for the purpose of joining several theories, or all of them, as explanations of criminal behavior.

The traditional theories of the origin of criminal behavior can be grouped into three broad areas by the major thrust of the theory itself or by the professional area of the theorist. These are:

THEORY	PROFESSIONAL AREA
1. Criminal behavior is inherited.	Biology and Anthropology
2. Environment is the cause of criminal behavior.	Sociology
3. Mental factors or conditions are the cause of criminal behavior.	Psychiatry and Psychology

Researchers in the field of criminal behavior are motivated in the search for knowledge and insight about the origins of criminal behavior by the purpose of preventing it and making a significant reduction in the crime rate. The research goal is to determine *why* persons of this kind (individuals with similar characteristics) commit such crimes, and why some individuals with like characteristics do not commit criminal acts. These are sizable dimensions for any research as crime ranges from the emotional outbursts of assailants and killers to the planned activities of professional thieves.

The earliest theory of criminal behavior was that each person had free will to decide whether to commit a crime. The rules of law and their sanctions against disobedience largely assume this theory. Sanctions are those rules of the legal order that spell out the consequences of violating criminal law. Criminal punishment in sanction law is any disposition of an offender authorized by law for persons found guilty after a criminal trial.[1]

The next theory of criminal behavior developed out of the concept of determinism: a concept that is threaded through all subsequent theories of crime to date. This is that man is not a free agent, that various pressures and drives determine human behavior, and that the decision to commit a crime has little or no free will involved, but is determined by these forces acting upon a person at one place, and at one specific time.

The Classical and the Positive Schools*
of Criminology

In the beginning there were man-to-man disputes and acts considered as threats or hazards to personal safety. Causes were factual and functional; the thing done was self-explanatory to the victim and his kin. It was a time of direct action and private revenge. In the later half of the eighteenth century, there were some changes for the better. Courts abandoned any concept of vengeance: punishment became a deterrent to crime rather than pure revenge, although punishment ranged from the death penalty, through various forms of mutilation, to flogging and prison sentences for long periods of time.[2]

Eighteenth-century penologists believed in the pleasure vs. pain principle in motivating human behavior and rational decision making. Individuals avoided acts that caused pain, and repeated acts that gave pleasure. When faced with the unknown consequences of an act, most persons would test for the pain-pleasure outcome, and adjust their subsequent action to secure as much pleasure and as little pain as possible.

Cesare Bonesana, Marchese de Beccaria was the first of a group now known as the classical school of criminology to attempt modification of the overkill aspects of the severe sentences given criminals for minor crimes.

1. Herbert L. Packer, *The Limits of the Criminal Sanction* (Stanford, Calif.: Stanford University Press, 1968), pp. 33–37.
*Criminology is a field in which dissent is common; the term 'school' is used to indicate conceptual agreement among a group of criminologists.
2. Stephen Schafer. *Theories in Criminology—Past and Present Philosophies of the Crime Problem* (New York: Random House, 1969), pp. 97–109.

In full support of the freewill concept of decision making, and the pain-pleasure principle of motivation, Beccaria sought uniformity in sentencing offenders so that the punishment awarded for violation of a specific law would take cognizance of the seriousness of the offense and the proceeds or satisfaction gained by the offender. This theory would only make the punishment slightly more painful than the pleasure the offender could gain from the criminal act. Lengthy sentences—and the death penalty—would be cut back and tailored to the gain (pleasure) in crime as opposed to the loss when apprehended (pain), and not to the simplistic belief that the more severe the sentence, the greater the control of crime. The classical school of criminology based its scheme of criminality on the offense as the object of attention; the reaction to the offense as some punitive measure.[3]

In the late nineteenth century with the advance of scientific thought in other fields, a new school of criminology based on the doctrines of science set new directions for the study of criminal behavior. What is now known as the positive school of criminology suggested the scientific study of the origins of crime, and remedial action stressing rehabilitation, rather than punishment. The offender was the object of attention; the reaction to the offender was oriented to treatment.

The positivists originally viewed crime as a phenomenon in which the causative factors had roots in the anthropological criminal type. Later, the influence of environment was accepted by the positivists but always subordinated to the *born criminal* concept.[4] The positivists maintained that the offender was not the prime mover in criminality: the offender acted as a result of interaction between his personality and his environment. "In order to be a criminal it is rather necessary that the individual should find himself permanently or transitorily in such personal, physical and moral conditions, and live in such an environment, which become for him a chain of cause and effect, externally and internally, that disposes him to crime."[5]

The cofounders of the positive school of criminology were Cesare Lombroso and Enrico Ferri. Cesare Lombroso was educated in medicine and served as a physician in the Italian army. His first civilian practice was concerned with the mentally ill and he became interested in the problems of crime and insanity. This was a foreshadowing of his pioneer work in criminal anthropology. His most important book, *L'Uomo Delinquente*, was first published in 1876. In this text, Lombroso theorized that crime resulted from the anthropological characteristics of the criminal. In

3. Shafer, *Theories in Criminology*, pp. 105–37.
4. Thorsten Sellin, "Enrico Ferri, Pioneer in Criminology," in *The Positive School of Criminology: Three Lectures by Enrico Ferri*, ed. Stanley E. Grupp (Pittsburgh, Pa.: University of Pittsburgh Press, 1968), pp. 1–39.
5. Ferri, "Lecture I—Critique of the Classical School," in Sellin, *The Positive School of Criminology*, p. 54.

later writings, however, he gave an increasing weight to social forces in the determination of criminal behavior.[6]

Yet, in 1909, in responding to a letter of notification that the new American Institute of Criminal Law and Criminology had selected his latest text for translation into English, Lombroso writes of the born criminal and his discovery of numerous atavistic* characteristics among them and links these physical characteristics to savage races (low cranial capacity, skull thickness, blunted affections, etc.). He also noted a relationship between criminals and epileptics which manifests itself in deterioration of the moral and emotional sensibilities—among other things. He describes a *criminaloid* as differing from a born criminal in the physical marks of criminality, but having some connection with atavism and epilepsy.[7]

Enrico Ferri was a student of Lombroso, and a contemporary in his adult years. Ferri was educated for the legal profession, and became a professor of criminal law at several universities in Italy. Ferri supported Lombroso's concept of an anthropological criminal type, but his writings stress the application of the discipline of sociology to the problem of criminal behavior. Ferri's five types of criminal offenders include the born criminal.** He qualified his belief in this congenital predisposition to crime by pointing out that many born criminals were law abiding when their environment was favorable and did not offer a temptation to crime.[8]

Ferri's sociological orientation foreshadowed the present concepts of crime causation which cite environmental factors as the major force in determining criminal behavior. However, in maintaining some linkage with the Lombrosian doctrine of hereditary criminality, the positivist school is also in harmony with recent research on predispositions to criminal behavior which have sometimes been validated in studies of physique and temperament, chromosomal makeup, and pathological criminality.

The Theory of Differential Association

What will probably be known as the American school of criminology in future years has reached some agreement on the influence of environment on crime causation. The major theory accepted to date is the theory of differential association advanced in 1939 by Professor Edwin H.

6. Marvin E. Wolfgang, "Pioneers in Criminology: Cesare Lombroso (1835–1909)," *Journal of Criminal Law, Criminology and Police Science* 52, no. 4 (November–December 1961): 361–91.
*Lombroso's theory of atavism was based on personal confidence that he had discovered a marked resemblance between the typical criminal and the savage or prehistoric man.
7. Cesare Lombroso, *Crime—Its Causes and Remedies*, trans. Henry P. Horton (1911; reprint ed., Montclair, N.J.: Patterson Smith, 1968), pp. 363–76.
**Others were: the *insane criminal*, the *habitual criminal*, the *occasional criminal*, and the *passionate criminal*.
8. Enrico Ferri, *Criminal Sociology* (New York: Agathon Press, 1967), pp. 138–67.

Sutherland. Sutherland's theory is that persons become criminals because of exposure to an overabundance of associations with criminal behavior patterns, as opposed to associations with anticriminal behavior patterns.[9]

Differential association is essentially a process of learning. As a process, Sutherland's theory is:

1. Criminal behavior is learned.
2. Learning is in the interaction with others and the inherent two-way communication between self and others.
3. Person-to-person contacts and communications among friends, relatives, associates, neighbors, acquaintances are more significant to this learning process than mass communications and its media.
4. Learning criminal behavior involves tutoring in operating techniques of crime, and a reorientation of attitudes, rationalization drives, and motives. (Specific direction of attitudes, motives, and drives is learned in orientation to definitions of law. In some groups, majority opinion favors obedience to law; in other groups, the majority favors violation of law.)
5. An individual's behavior becomes criminal because he accepts definitions favoring criminal action rather than those which reject such acts.
6. Differential associations vary in priority, frequency, duration, and intensity (early influences may be as significant to learning as lengthy and repeated high intensity influences), and the process of learning criminal behavior involves all the mechanisms involved in other learning processes.
7. Criminal behavior is also an expression of general needs and values, but these general needs and values cannot be explained as a cause of crime (the same needs and values drive men to seek employment and to work hard).[10]

The Social Reality Theory

In a theory of crime related to Sutherland's differential association concept, criminal behavior is viewed as a product of the social process

9. Edwin H. Sutherland and Donald R. Cressey, *Criminology*, 8th ed. (1924; reprint ed., Philadelphia: J. B. Lippincott Co., 1970; originally published with Edwin H. Sutherland as sole author), pp. 78–79.
10. Ibid., pp. 75–77.

(continuing actions leading to a specific result), conflict between persons and groups, power (the ability of persons and groups to determine the conduct of others), and social action. This latter term, social action, is defined as implying that human behavior is goal oriented and crime occurs with an awareness of its consequences.

The core area of this theory of the social reality of crime is: 1. Criminal definitions describe (and limit) behavior in conflict with behavior approved by those groups in the community which have the power to control or shape public policy. 2. Criminal definitions (and sanctions) are applied by, or in response to pressure from these community groups. 3. Behavior patterns are structured within the various segments of society in relation to criminal definitions, and persons engage in actions that may be defined as criminal. 4. Conceptions of crime are constructed and diffused by many means of communication, usually in response to the power segments of a community's population.[11]

An initial basis for this theory of crime as a social reality is that legislatures *create* crime. There's no doubt that sin-as-crime, and the other areas of crime without victims covered in the overreach of the criminal law, has created criminals. Moreover, because Sutherland's theory of differential association is assumed or incorporated within this theory of the social reality of criminal behavior, it has support for one of its major propositions: that behavior patterns are behavior learned in the environmental setting of the individual.

Anomie: The Goals-and-Means Theory

Life chances in the opportunity structure differ with the race, residence, education, and socioeconomic background of a person. Normal behavior can be classed as behavior aligned with prescribed, permitted, or preferred behavior, or behavior that contributes to stability in the social system. Historically, *anomie* refers to the breakdown or absence of norms and values. More recently, it refers to the conflict between the community culture and that of a subgroup; and the growth of illegal or illicit success may enlarge the degree of anomie.[12]

There is always the possibility that one or more youngsters from a minority group, ghetto home, dropout-centered education, or family with little or no financial resources will move from the subculture of his

11. Richard Quinney, *The Social Reality of Crime* (Boston: Little, Brown and Co. 1970), pp. 8–24.
12. U.S., Department of Health, Education and Welfare, *New Perspectives for Research on Juvenile Delinquency*, Helen L. Witmer and Ruth Kotinsky, eds. (Washington, D.C.: Government Printing Office, 1955), pp. 24–49.

family and neighborhood to the subculture of the Ivy League college, the tennis club, and Wall Street. It doesn't happen often. Most people who die poor were born poor.[13]

Success is the broad goal of upward mobility. It means different things to persons from various socioeconomic and racial subgroups. In America, success is hinged to occupational status and money. There is a pressure to outdo competitors, despite the cliché that there is plenty of room at the top. There is also pressure from within a family group, usually because parents want a better life for their children, and this upgrading is generally equated with success.

The goals-and-means segments of a community's social structure is severely strained, however, when some individuals are socially disadvantaged in the competitive struggle to move upward occupationally and socioeconomically. Honesty and noncriminal employment are viewed by some of the disadvantaged as limitations on the opportunity and means to success. This strain exerts pressure on disadvantaged persons to achieve success by any means available.

Society, and its social structure for the control of behavior identified as criminal, forbids criminal activity regardless of goals. There is the pressure of law upon persons to conform, rather than to engage in nonconforming conduct. Living in accordance with the rules of the game or the norms of prescribed conduct blocks the goal of success to many minority group persons with little education and no resources. Deviating from this, an individual loses his cultural anchorage of winning under the rules of the game.

Anomie is the term used to describe this social phenomenon. It creates cultural chaos in the individual because of the pull-and-push of conflicting values. A climate of anomie exists when common values are violated or disregarded to serve private interests with the result that there is an end-means reversal of the cultural norm. The exaltation of the end justifies almost any means to achieve goals. Anomie arises from the contradiction of the American community's espousal of the good life and common success goals for the entire population while at the same time its social structure restricts or blocks the approved means of reaching such goals for considerable segments of the population. In turn, anomie is linked to criminal behavior by the fact that crime does pay under some circumstances and at some times. There is both a promise and a reward of high income from burglary, robbery, drug selling, and organized crime. Because of availability, the pressure for success leads to the use of illegitimate expedients to reach a life goal. This strain toward anomie and deviant behavior (often criminal) breaks down the normal regulatory

13. Alvin L. Schorr, *Poor Kids—A Report on Children in Poverty* (New York: Basic Books, 1966), pp. 23–48.

structure guiding human behavior as it develops a situation in which the approach-avoidance conflict is a simple weighing of two values: (1) calculation of personal advantage, and (2) fear of punishment.[14]

The utility of criminal behavior for breaking out of the ghetto has always been known to the immigrants and minority groups who reside in these low-rent and high-crime areas. To some youngsters the route of upward mobility is either theft, or the rackets of organized crime.[15]

A ghetto or slum area is a factory where society manufactures delinquents who evolve through a natural growth process into adult criminals and drug addicts. Pimping and prostitution are not characterized as crimes; the "hot goods" sales of thieves classify the selling of stolen property as a major ghetto industry; and crimes against police evoke no special consternation. Ghetto crime often consists of the side-actions made possible by the influx of visitors willing to pay for the services of prostitutes; but thieves steal from anybody, and drug addicts prey on the weakest of the ghetto's residents—women and the elderly.[16]

Anomie is a complex of poverty, limited opportunities, and a shared system of success symbols.[17]

The New School of Criminal Anthropology

The concept of grouping humanity in types by using anthropological methods of measurement emerged from investigations by medicine and psychiatry. Investigations into the build of the body by these experts were planned to probe the problem of the human constitution: the whole physical makeup of the individual, which comprises the individual's inherited qualities as modified by the environment. The landmark researcher in this field, Ernst Kretschmer, worked out a *constitution scheme* to record his investigations. Its major sections are:

1. *Measurement*—height, weight, length (legs, arms), breadth (shoulders, pelvis), circumference (chest, stomach, hips), and skull.

2. *Description of face and skull*—shape, profile, frontal outline, (various shapes), height proportions (middle face, chin), and nose.

14. Robert K. Merton, *Social Theory and Social Structure* (New York: Free Press, Macmillan Publishing Co., 1957), pp. 131–60.
15. Irving Speigel, *Racketville, Slumtown and Haulberg—An Exploratory Study of Delinquent Subcultures* (Chicago: University of Chicago Press, 1964), pp. 30–38, 47–53.
16. Clause Brown, "The Ghetto View of Crime," *Race Relations Reporter*, vol. 5, no. 21, November 1974, p. 16–18.
17. Robert K. Merton, "Social Structure and Anomie," *American Sociological Review* 3, no. 5 (October 1938): 672–82.

3. *Description of physique*—bones, musculature, fat; neck, shoulders, chest, stomach, pelvis, extremities (especially length), hands, and feet

4. *Hair*—color and where located on body, and skin condition

5. *Glands*—thyroid, mammary, testicles, genitalia, and sexual anomalies

6. *Temporal*—commencement of mental disease, puberty, fattening, emaciation and certain physical diseases.[18]

Kretschmer's position was that any constitutional types must include the whole of mankind, physically and psychically, and would have biological significance only when relations were discovered between types of physique and psychic types. To secure the necessary "typical" values in his investigation, Kretschmer presorted photographs of many subjects and then superimposed the photos of selected subjects so that the characteristics which fit over one another were sharply outlined, and thus became an average value or typical.

Three ever-recurring principal types of physique surfaced from these studies: (1) asthenic, (2) athletic, and (3) pyknic. Briefly, the descriptive data on each of these types and a fourth nontypical group is:

1. The male *asthenic* type is a lean man who appears taller because of a deficiency in the thickness development of his body. Asthenic women are not only thin, but also very short.

2. The male *athletic* type is medium to tall in height, has a well-developed physique, a superb chest, firm stomach, good legs and a v-shaped trunk, tapering from shoulders to pelvis. The female athletic type corresponds to her male counterpart, but she is fatter, although the fat is in good proportion and distributed in a feminine rounded figure.

3. The *pyknic* type male is a person of middle height with a rounded figure, a soft-looking broad face on a short and thick neck, a merging vaulted chest and potbelly stomach and a main covering of fat round the trunk area. Pyknic women are smaller than pyknic men, with the same general body build, except that the main covering of fat is concentrated around the breasts and hips.

4. *Dysplastic* types are representative of several small groups of in-

18. Ernst Kretschmer, *Physique and Character—An Investigation of the Nature of Constitution and of the Theory of Temperament,* 2d ed. (Atlantic Highlands, N.J.: Humanities Press, 1951), pp. 3–16.

dividuals who differ among themselves and from the three major types listed above. They are the rare type, and not the average specimen.[19]

Kretschmer reports the findings based on his research were "surprising and of great biological importance." He had uncovered a correlation between bodily makeup and the two major forms of mental illness or emotional instability. His reported results are:

1. There is a clear biological affinity between manic-depressive individuals and the pyknic body type; and only a weak affinity between schizophrenics and pyknics.
2. There is a clear biological affinity between the schizophrenic and the asthenic and athletic types; and only a weak affinity between manic-depressives and the two types of asthenic and athletic physique.[20]

In other words, the medium height, soft-looking pyknic was most often a manic-depressive person; and the thin, lean asthenic and the well-developed athletic was most likely to be schizophrenic.

This German scientist particularly disagreed with Lombroso's isolation of "petty peculiarities." In Kretschmer's physique and temperament study, a single characteristic was only significant for its contribution to the broad form of bodily makeup. Kretschmer rejected any "symptoms of degeneracy" such as the so-called "criminal ear," and credited such details as only one of the parts of a person's physique.[21]

Kretschmer's basic research was followed by the in-depth studies of William H. Sheldon, who developed an array of *somatotypes** and a theory of behavior based on physique. Apparently, Lombroso's theory of the biological factor in criminal behavior has a phoenix-like characteristic, rising again after being discredited by earlier researchers who had reviewed Lombroso's born-criminal concept of criminality.

The three somatotypes of Sheldon are: (1) *endomorphic* (round; soft); (2) *mesomorphic* (heavy; hard); and (3) *ectomorphic* (thin). In this scheme of behavior projection, each somatotype was identified with various temperaments.[22] In the three dimensions of physique and temperament, endomorphy is visceral development and is usually associated with vis-

19. Kretschmer, *Physique and Character*, pp. 17–35.
20. Ibid., pp. 36–37.
21. Ibid., pp. 39–40.
*A quantification of the three primary components determining the morphological structure of an individual, using a series of numerals. *See* William H. Sheldon, *Atlas of Men* (New York: Harper & Row, Publishers, 1954).
22. William H. Sheldon, *Varieties of Human Physique* (New York: Harper & Row, Publishers, 1949), pp. 234–39.

cerotonic temperament (comfort, sociability); mesomorphy is muscular development and frequently correlates with somatotonic temperament (assertiveness, competitiveness); and ectomorphy is related to the linear structure of a person's physique and is generally aligned with a restrained and sensitive temperament. Sheldon concluded that mesomorphy was the physique most favorable to criminal behavior. Mesomorphs were high on activity, and vigorous and bold action people without too many inhibitions as individuals.[23]

It is not easy to devise reliable experiments and plan valid research for the study of physique and temperament. The reported results of the studies of physique and behavior are likely to be contaminated by research procedures. In fact, some of Sheldon's reported correlations between physique and temperament are unbelievably large and suggest that some of the temperament variables are aspects of physique rather than independent of it.[24] Despite the longtime rejection of some correspondence between criminal behavior and inherited characteristics, there is some valid (uncontaminated) research to support a theory of relationship between body build and criminal behavior. Since many of the factors governing body build are inherited, any suggestion that one body build is predisposed to criminality is a throwback, more or less, to Lombroso and his born criminal concept of criminal behavior.

Support for the viewpoint of the "New School of Criminal Anthropology" was developed during independent research into the causative factors of delinquency. In a study of 500 delinquent children and 500 nondelinquent children, the delinquents as a group were found to be physically distinguishable from the nondelinquents as they were essentially mesomorphic in bodily makeup (solid, muscular). Among the delinquents, 60.1 percent were mesomorphs, and twice the proportion of mesomorphs were found in the delinquent group as compared to the nondelinquent group. In subsequent research review it was found that the reason for the excess of mesomorphs among the delinquent group was that this physique type is more highly characterized by the presence of traits suitable to the commission of aggressive acts, and the absence of many inhibitions.[25]

In summing up, Kretschmer's and Sheldon's research findings do not predict whether an individual will become a criminal on the basis of physique, but do hold that the forms of criminal behavior which might emerge will be related to an individual's physique. The research done by

23. William H. Sheldon, *Varieties of Delinquent Youth*, 2 vols. (1949; reprint ed., Darien Conn.: Hafner Publishing Co., Macmillan Publishing Co., 1970), vol. 1, pp. 14–30; vol. 2, p. 762.
24. Ephraim Rosen and Jan Gregory, *Abnormal Psychology* (Philadelphia: W. B. Saunders Co., 1965), pp. 113–21.
25. Sheldon Glueck and Elizabeth Glueck, *Physique and Delinquency* (New York: Commonwealth Fund, 1950), pp. 7–15, 217–27.

Sheldon and Elizabeth Glueck indicates that one type of physique (as isolated and identified by William Sheldon) was predominant among the juvenile delinquents of their research population.

A fast-breaking research finding related to the work of Lombroso, Kretschmer, and Sheldon surfaced during the investigation of a psychotic murderer. The breakthrough was the genetic finding that the presence of an extra Y chromosome makes boys and men unusually aggressive. It is a finding that appears to offer a genetic base for the Lombrosian concept that some men are born criminals.

Linkage between the chromosomal constitution of an individual and criminal behavior was discovered in 1965 in Scotland. A research team found seven out of 197 mentally abnormal male prison inmates were discovered to be XYY types; and this incidence of XYY males in a prison population far exceeded the percentage in the general population (approximately 1.3 in 1,000 live births). Therefore, it was a highly significant finding.

A human life begins as a single cell containing 46 chromosomes. Heritage has its beginning in a sperm cell (and there are millions in every drop of seminal fluid), and its union with an egg. At conception, the father's role in the child's heredity is encompassed in his sperm. Each single sperm carries 23 microscopic bodies called chromosomes (exactly half of the father's 46 chromosomes). The mother's role in her child's heredity is providing the egg into which the sperm enters. Each egg has a nucleus with 23 microscopic chromosomes, and a host arrangement for releasing the mother's 23 chromosomes (exactly half of her 46 chromosomes) when the father's sperm enters the egg and releases its chromosomes. These 46 chromosomes are the two sets of heredity factors that comprise the biological heritage of any child. By a process of division and redivision the chromosomes provide the new individual with genes. Genes contain the ultimate factors in heredity; each gene has a definite function in the creation and development of every person.

Genes are the prime units of life containing in their molecular structure a "blueprint" that controls the growth of the individual. There are both *dominant** and *recessive*** genes. In addition there are "freak" genes and supplementary genes. A confusing array, but the limitless combinations of genes are the origin of the varieties of human life. Genes set the color and shape of eyes, the color of hair, skin color, facial structure, overall size and shape, as well as the other less visible parts of the human organism.

The XYY individual is produced during formation of the sperm. Normal division of the sex chromosomes leads to sperm of two kinds: X

---

*Presence in father *or* mother establishes an equal (50–50) chance of appearance (of effect or defect) in the child.

**Presence in *both* parents is necessary to establish a chance of appearance (of effect or defect) in the child.

chromosome and Y chromosome. Female children are the result when an X chromosome fertilizes a normal ovum. (A normal female child is XX.) Male children are the result when a Y chromosome fertilizes a normal X ovum. (A normal male child is XY.) The ordinary aggressiveness of a normal XY male is apparently doubled in the XYY male. While this doesn't always imply criminal behavior, it does suggest that the inherited genes must be influenced by a favorable environment if the XYY person is not to become overly aggressive and possibly engage in criminal behavior.[26]

Chromosomal deviations offer some promise for effective research into the biological basis of criminal behavior. Such deviations have been found and identified in the areas of the mentally ill, mentally retarded, homosexuals, and criminals.

It is the extra male chromosome (Y) that is the primary factor in this theory of behavior. In reviewing several years of research, the following findings have been substantiated:

1. The physique of an XYY person is taller and thinner than persons in the control groups—the average XYY individual is over 6 feet tall.

2. The personality structure of XYY individuals was found to be defective (often verging on the psychopathic); and the XYY person was found to be more aggressive, and more often exhibited disturbed behavior.

3. The violent crime rate of XYY persons was high.

4. The XYY youngster began his criminal career at an early age (10–13 as opposed to 18).

5. The chance that a criminal is an XYY person is 60 times greater than that of the general population.[27]

Pathological Criminality

The advances made in psychiatry and psychology by mid-century have provided criminologists with many research findings about psychopathological criminals (persons whose behavior exhibits varying degrees of abnormality) and mental illness as it relates to criminal behavior.

In a 1931 report to the president of the United States, the National Commission on Law Observance and Enforcement (the "Wickersham Commission," named for its chairman, George W. Wickersham) reported that after extensive investigation into the causes of crime, it had been un-

26. M. F. Ashley Montagu, "Chromosomes and Crime," *Psychology Today* 2, no. 5 (October 1968): 42–49.
27. Menachem Amir and Yitzchak Berman, "Chromosomal Deviation and Crime," *Federal Probation* 34, no. 2 (June 1970): 55–62.

able to determine to what extent defective intelligence or any other mental abnormality was present in the nation's criminal population. Even when defective intelligence was disclosed among criminals, it could not be isolated and identified as a cause of crime.[28]

In 1952, however, it was reported that the normal criminal was a myth, and that refined methods of examining criminals (other than the occasional, accidental, or one-time offender) was likely to disclose that all delinquents and criminals suffer from some form of mental disorder: either a psychosis, neurosis, character disorder, or some other form of emotional disturbance.[29]

Some mental disorders may originate in the transmissibility of a predisposition to criminality. If one believes in psychological heredity and the inheritance of tendencies and attitudes, then there are grounds for belief in the possibility of transmitting tendencies predisposing or promoting criminal behavior. A predisposition to criminal behavior is a joinder of hereditary and acquired organic or psychological conditions which, by releasing aggressive forces and withholding inhibitory forces, lowers the threshold of resistance to engaging in criminal behavior. It also includes a heightened receptivity to criminality. The particular characteristics which make an individual receptive to external conditions leading to criminal behavior are an essential element of predisposition to criminal conduct.[30]

Psychological predispositions established early in childhood are based on experiences in the formative years (infancy, latency). An individual develops a pattern of expectancies and they become part of his self-concept. Untroubled or successful development leads to a healthy and mature self-concept. Early experience is of vital importance in the growth of a person and his personality. For normal personality growth, children require a close friendship with parents or parent substitutes. Any parental attitude that indicates rejection (overt rejection, perfectionism, inconsistency, overdominance) increases the likelihood of emotional disorders. Severe or lengthy episodes of stress outside of the parent-child relationship can also alter a personality at any time, but they are particularly destructive when they occur early in life. Serious illness or injury, shortage of food, ostracism by associates, war combat, threatened or actual economic loss, unemployment, divorce, rejection in love, death of a relative or close friend, and drastic loss of self-esteem are examples of nonfamilial stress situations.[31]

28. *Wickersham Commission Reports, No. 13, Report on the Causes of Crime*, vol. 1 (1931; reprint ed., Montclair, N.J.: Patterson Smith, 1968), pp. 60–61.
29. David Abrahamsen, *Who Are the Guilty? A Study of Education and Crime* (New York: Holt, Rinehart and Winston, 1952), p. 125.
30. Benigno DiTullio, *Horizons in Clinical Criminology* (New York: New York University Criminal Law Education and Research Center, 1969), pp. 59–60, 66–67.
31. Ephraim Rosen and Ian Gregory, *Abnormal Psychology* (Philadelphia: W. B. Saunders Co., 1965), pp. 64–65, 141–49.

Basic personality patterns and traits such as aggressiveness, mental alertness, and tendencies to smile, laugh, and make other interrelational responses, are governed by heredity, childhood experiences, and the environment of home, neighborhood and school. To date, there has been no proof of the existence of behavior or personality genes. However, the genes that determine size, shape, and general appearance have some influence on the life experiences of a person because other persons react to size, shape, and appearance.

The child's personality heritage from its parents is probably a wide ranging personality potential which is shaped into a narrower pattern by environmental influences during the child's growth. In regard to the various factors influencing personality, and—to some extent—behavior, hereditary factors may be classified as:

1. *Hereditary influence likely:* intelligence, reaction time, motor skills, sensory discrimination

2. *Hereditary influence possible:* Temperamental attributes— emotional balance, mood, activity, inactivity

3. *Hereditary influence unlikely:* attitudes, values, beliefs.[32]

The psychological processes that underlie human behavior motivate a person's attitude and reaction to a prevailing situation. A person's behavior corresponds to his whole personality. The personality of a person is the total individual expressing himself: integration of individual thinking, willing, and acting out. Personality consists of four layers or levels: (1) the *anatomical* level of skeleton, muscles, and organs; (2) the *physiological* level or normal functioning of the organs, their interrelationship, and capability to adjust to a person's needs; (3) the *psychological* level of a person's mind: the ability to recognize, integrate, remember, and discriminate; and (4) the *social* level or behavior output. Personality is a dynamic unit; behavior depends on how it functions in a particular person. The riddle of human conduct generally, and criminal conduct specifically, must be searched for in the personality.[33]

Multiple Causation of Crime

It is unwarranted to assume that the causation of crime can be attributed to any single-factor theory of criminal behavior. Many of the causative factors in the foregoing theories are too remote from the operational

32. Amram Scheinfeld, *Your Heredity and Environment* (Philadelphia: J. B. Lippincott Co., 1965), pp. 490–91.
33. David Abrahamsen, *Crime and the Human Mind* (New York: Columbia University Press, 1944), pp. 19–24.

mechanism of human behavior to be useful. The nexus between these causative factors of criminality and the physical and mental makeup of any particular individual must be determined. What distinguishes what kind of person (as one or more of these causative factors becomes more and more operational) will become a criminal? Why do some individuals *not* become criminals despite the influence of one or more of the causative factors listed in the theories of criminologists about criminality? A general theory of the causation of crime and delinquency should be composed of individual differences and social forces. The amount of crime at any time and in any society depends upon the extent of the social force pressure and the makeup of the persons subjected to it.[34]

A simple joining of the three major areas of the foregoing theories offers a multiple causation theory of some validity. This theory would develop along these lines: 1. There is a biological base for criminal behavior in some inherited predisposition. 2. There is an environmental force or influence on this predisposed individual. 3. There is a mental condition or illness which spurs on the actual commission of a crime or fails to block the operation of the first two causative factors. (See Figure 1.)

A multiple causation theory of criminal behavior is related to the direct causative factors, or indirect factors, with a cautious eye to the offender's most recent crime. Such a theory can be developed around the three following major factors:

1. The want or gain factor, the need for the act or the results of crime

2. The opportunity or event factor, the place and the time of the crime and the situation that tempts or makes possible the crime as an event

3. The restraint factor—or more properly, the lack of restraint— which inhibits the noncriminal population from committing the same act when confronted with an opportunity for crime and when there is a conscious or subliminal surfacing of the want or gain factor.

Additionally, a theory of delinquency has introduced another major factor suitable for inclusion in any multiple causation theory of criminal behavior: the mental attitude that criminal conduct is right and proper. This is supportive of the lack of restraint factor, or an extension of it in the form of justification for criminal behavior. These techniques of neutraliz-

34. Sheldon Glueck, *Crime and Correction: Selected Papers* (Reading, Mass.: Addison-Wesley Publishing Co., 1952), pp. 4–12.

ing a young person's internal inhibitions may take one or more of the following four forms:

1. The denial of responsibility
2. The denial of injury to the victim's person or property ("He asked for it." "He can afford the loss." "We only borrowed it.")
3. The denial that there is a victim (the victim is a vague abstraction in property crimes, attacks on premises in which the owner is absent, in crimes against the person, and against store employees who do not own the stolen money)
4. Condemnation—the denial of wrongdoing by accusing the accusers (store proprietors are dishonest, police are corrupt and brutal, and the judiciary is biased and prejudiced).[35]

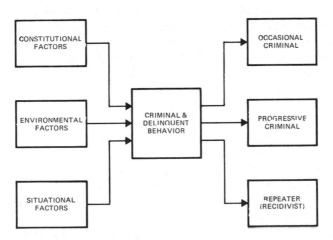

Figure 1. The Multiple-factor Theory of Crime   Criminal and delinquent behavior is caused by constitutional defects or deficiencies, environmental influences, and response to a situation—in some combination. The result may be occasional criminal behavior, progressive criminal behavior, or a confirmed repeating criminal—the recidivist. Occasional criminals may be one-time offenders; some will move to progressive criminality. From this plateau many become recidivists.

A number of persons may become criminals because of any single causative factor. Two or more factors may result in a like—or greater—number of individuals committing criminal acts. There is no possible rank order for the causative factors of criminal behavior. Each person, each social group, and each neighborhood acts as a different host for the actions of one or more of the factors. However, criminal behavior is in response to one or more of the causative factors discussed here.

35. Gresham M. Sykes and David Matza, "Techniques of Neutralization—A Theory of Delinquency," *American Sociological Review* 22, no. 6 (December 1957): 664–70.

Delinquency

The same multiple causation of crime accounts for the acts of juveniles which would have been criminal if committed by adults. Whether or not the youngster goes on to a career in adult crime has its origin in one or more of the areas described by the theories of criminality, coupled with the individual's own motivational makeup.

Strangely, the element of free will occurs again and again in contemporary theories of delinquency. The concepts of Beccaria are expressed almost in totality. According to one formulation, the will, desire, or intent to engage in delinquency develops under two kinds of circumstances: (1) when the young person is able to manage the technical skills needed to perform the crime and is capable of controlling the fear or apprehension associated with it; and (2) when a sense of unfairness and desperation (being pushed around) enhances the delinquent act itself by providing the youngster with a means of demonstrating his potency. The situation leading to an act of delinquency is simply a two-factor situation: the strength of the temptations vs. the strength of the controls.[36]

Some juveniles are easily discouraged from acts of delinquency because they feel inadequate about the technical skills of breaking-and-entering and the taking-and-selling of stolen property. Others find the unknown and unusual aspects of delinquency frightening and avoid it because of this apprehension component. Still others lack the self-doubt which fosters desperation as a causative factor in delinquency. The young persons who commit delinquent acts are victims of drift, a force midway between effective social control and freedom to act antisocially. They respond in turn to the temptations of delinquency and the demands of convention (a drifting between criminal and conventional behavior).[37]

Other studies of juveniles and crime have resulted in theories of delinquency closely associated with each of the major theories of criminality: from inherited traits or predispositions, through blocked goals and resultant anomie, to differential association and pathological criminality. Every typology of juvenile delinquents includes one or more categories labeled as maladjusted. This aligns with the theory of criminality that blames one cause of crime on personality disturbances. A major problem encountered by criminologists researching the etiology of delinquency is that while any one theory might quite satisfactorily explain the conduct of young persons in the lower socioeconomic brackets of the ghetto or barrio areas, the same theory falls short of the target in explaining the conduct

36. U.S., President's Commission on Law Enforcement and Administration of Justice Task Force on Juvenile Delinquency, *Task Force Report: Juvenile Delinquency and Youth Crime* (Washington, D.C.: Government Printing Office, 1967)
37. David Matza, *Delinquency and Drift* (New York: John Wiley & Sons, 1964), pp. 27–30, 184–91.

of youngsters in the middle-class socioeconomic brackets who reside in suburban areas or in the better neighborhoods. Conversely, a theory that is explanatory of middle-class delinquency does not account for the conduct of youthful hustlers and cats with their origins in lower-class neighborhoods.

No single cause has been identified and isolated as the prime mover in delinquency. However, based upon a developing consensus in this field, a scheme or pattern of delinquency has been developed for the average delinquent among lower-class young persons who are not maladjusted. This scheme or pattern of delinquency is:

1. The community has a limited ability to provide opportunities for young persons to achieve in accordance with middle-class values.

2. The young person's family has limited ability to maintain external controls.

3. The young person has developed in a family using only limited child rearing techniques which has led to ineffective internal controls.[38]

A similar theory of delinquency applicable to middle-class and upper-class young people can be dovetailed with the psychological and psychiatric theories which trace criminality to a breakdown in the identification process during preadult years. This would be applied to middle-class delinquent males as follows:

1. Middle-class boys who are less attracted to their community are more likely to engage in delinquency.

2. The less middle-class boys are attracted to their fathers, the more likely they are to engage in delinquency.

3. Middle-class boys who do less well in school are more likely to engage in delinquent behavior (apprehensive of failure when seeking employment in postschool years).[39]

From the above, it appears that delinquency among young persons from families in the lower socioeconomic levels has a subcultural origin, while the delinquency of young people from families in the middle and upper socioeconomic levels is a contracultural phenomenon.

38. Task Force on Juvenile Delinquency, *Juvenile Delinquency and Youth Crime*, pp. 210–11.
39. Jerome G. Miller, "Research and Theory in Middle-Class Delinquency," *British Journal of Criminology* 10, no. 1 (January 1970): 33–51.

The Criminality Idea

There is an instinctive reaction to crime and criminals in any community: the arrested and convicted person is regarded as among a class of persons separated from the remaining population (assumed to be law-abiding) by some strange or mystical difference. In tracing this general tendency to place criminals in a group apart from the law-abiding segment of society, its origin, most likely, is in the criminal law itself and the development of the concept of an abstract penalty, rather than the very personal revenge for a wrong or evil. Of course, early theological and ecclesiastical traditions established mental images of right as opposed to wrong, and revenge or vengeance was aligned with this ethical idea of right and wrong, or good vs. evil. However, the concept of penalty in sanction law went beyond personal retaliation for a wrong or evil, and possibly even beyond the concept of abstract justice. It verges on an extension of God's wrath. The relationship between the words of early criminal law and biblical terminology is supportive of this belief. The similarity between the penalties suggested by early religious writings and the penalties of sanction law are also noteworthy.

The setting of criminals, as a group, apart from the law-abiding, made the criminal an antagonist of the other noncriminal members of the community, an outcast. The early English concept of outlawry spelled this out, and it was carried to the new states in America. For over a century the westward thrust of the frontier stigmatized the criminal as an outlaw, a person to be hunted down. The *posse comitatus* of early England was also carried to America, and this "entire body of inhabitants liable to be summoned by the sheriff" became the sheriff's posse of the frontier and hunted down outlaws. The hue and cry of modern computer technology and microsecond communications across America in the searches for the FBI's "Ten Most Wanted Criminals" and lesser offenders, continues in modern form the concept of outlawry as describing a criminal group in American society.

On the other hand, there is good and sufficient evidence that the conduct of criminals has the same motivational thrust as the conduct of so-called normal human beings. Despite the fact that criminals are alleged to be born to criminality and to have a classic criminal ear and other anomalies not found in normal persons; alleged to be set apart from others by chromosomal differences, types of physiques, mental instability or emotional disturbance; or alleged to exist as the victims of an adversely conditioning environment, criminal acts are more properly viewed as common behavioral possibilities. The criminal should not be thought of as a special class of person, but as a person properly considered to be a normal human being.

In 1913, in a well-known text rebutting the Lombrosian concept of a born criminal, Dr. Charles Goring wrote:

Using the word "criminal" not necessarily in description of moral defectiveness, but merely to designate, in legal terminology, the fact that an individual has been imprisoned—using "criminal" in this sense implies a hypothetical character of some kind, a constitutional proclivity, either mental, moral or physical, present to a certain degree in all individuals, but so potent in some, as to determine for them, eventually, the fate of imprisonment.[40]

In this same text, Dr. Goring makes a strong case for a theory of "original equality." He asserts, "In view of the intricate nature of the mind of man, and of the mutability and complexity of environmental influences, it is impossible to state dogmatically, on *a priori* grounds, whether the criminal is born or made. . . . All we can assume, and what we must assume, is the *possibility* that constitutional as well as environmental factors, play a part in the production of criminality."[41]

The "Political" Criminal

A new and spreading rationale justifying the commission of crime is threatening the traditional approaches to crime, punishment, and rehabilitation. The basis for our system of punishment as deterrent to crime depends upon a fear of punishment, but an equally compelling basis for abiding by the law is a basic personal guilt in connection with the commission of crime; a sense of shame in facing family and friends when identified as a criminal. It may be connected with the religious ethic found in most prominent religions in America.

This increasing rationale or justification for crime in the political area is that the political system compels particular individuals, for a variety of reasons, to commit crime—that because of environment, race, or discrimination by employers, the political system has stacked the odds against an individual's chance to succeed. Accordingly, if one of these individuals steals, he takes only that which the political system has deprived him of—and thus belongs to him; or if he kills he is only a soldier in the revolution to correct the ills of the political system.

If an individual can thus rationalize his situation as an injustice inflicted upon him by the political system and convince his family of this fact, he can discuss theft and robbery with them and commit thefts and robberies without guilt feelings. If he is unemployed and a member of a minority group, he has ready-made reasons for feeling that the political system has deprived him of a livelihood, and he is ripe for a direct assault

40. Charles Goring, *The English Convict: A Statistical Study* (London: Darling and Son, for His Majesty's Stationery Office, 1913), pp. 26–27.
41. Ibid., p. 26.

on society in order to fight racism. If he is caught and sentenced to prison he becomes a "political" prisoner, no matter what crime he has committed.

To combat this justification for illegal behavior society generally must admit some validity to the complaint against the political system; that, at least to some degree, our American social system places certain segments of the general population in an undesirable position in the contest for employment (success). Minorities, parolees, and persons with an "arrest" record, have less chance for employment than Caucasians and persons who have no criminal history. As long as the system discriminates, this justification for crime will flourish among disadvantaged persons.

Prisons themselves, the institutions which society had hoped would rehabilitate convicted offenders, are becoming schools for political revolution and revolutionary indoctrination. The founding of radical "political" organizations whose whole existence is based upon the commission of the crimes of theft, robbery, kidnapping, and murder in order to destroy or reform the political system now takes place in prisons. (The revolutionary group calling itself the Symbionese Liberation Army is known to have been organized within the California state prison system.) Upon release, a member of one of these so-called political groups is a revolutionary in his own and the organization's eyes, and not a criminal rightfully subject to punishment for his acts.

In order to combat this growing menace it is not enough to increase penalties or to increase the sizes of police forces. Some change must be made in the social system's faults. As society is presently structured, some individuals are disadvantaged by poor education, inadequate family resources, minority group status, and a criminal history. The fact that a society does block the legitimate routes to the traditional success goal for some individuals lends a measure of credibility to the claims that certain thefts and crimes of violence are "political" acts rather than crimes. Perhaps the first place to start, or perhaps it is also the ultimate goal, is to give a total meaning in our society to the concept of equality of opportunity. The doctrine of equal justice before the law requires no less than equality of opportunity.

Selected References

Books

Abrahamsen, David. *Who are the Guilty? A Study of Education and Crime.* New York: Holt, Rinehart and Winston, 1952.
DiTullio, Benigno. *Horizons in Clinical Criminology.* New York: New York University Criminal Law Education and Research Center, 1969.
Ferri, Enrico. *Criminal Sociology.* New York: Agathon Press, 1967.

Glueck, Sheldon. *Crime and Correction: Selected Papers.* Reading, Mass.: Addison-Wesley Publishing Co., 1952.
—— and Glueck, Elizabeth. *Physique and Delinquency.* New York: Commonwealth Fund, 1950.
Kretschmer, Ernst. *Physique and Character—An Investigation of the Nature of Constitution and of the Theory of Temperament.* 2d ed. Atlantic Highlands, N.J.: Humanities Press, 1951.
Long, Elton; Long, James; Leon, Wilmer; and Weston, Paul B. *American Minorities and the Justice Issue.* Englewood Cliffs, N.J.: Prentice-Hall, 1974.
Matza, David. *Delinquency and Drift.* New York: John Wiley & Sons, 1964.
Merton, Robert K. *Social Theory and Social Structure.* New York: Free Press, Macmillan Publishing Co., 1957.
Packer, Herbert L. *The Limits of the Criminal Sanction.* Stanford, Calif.: Stanford University Press, 1968.
President's Commission on Law Enforcement and Administration of Justice. *Task Force Report: Juvenile Delinquency and Youth Crime.* Washington, D.C.: Government Printing Office, 1967.
Quinney, Richard. *The Social Reality of Crime.* Boston: Little, Brown and Co., 1970.
Schafer, Stephen. *Theories in Criminology—Past and Present Philosophies of the Crime Problem.* New York: Random House, 1969.
Sellin, Thorsten. "Enrico Ferri, Pioneer in Criminology." In *The Positive School of Criminology: Three Lectures by Enrico Ferri*, edited by Stanley E. Grupp. Pittsburgh, Pa.: University of Pittsburgh Press, 1968.
Sheldon, William H. *Varieties of Human Physique.* New York: Harper & Row, Publishers, 1949.
Spiegel, Irving. *Racketville, Slumtown and Haulberg—An Exploratory Study of Delinquent Subcultures.* Chicago: University of Chicago Press, 1964.
Sutherland, Edwin H., and Cressey, Donald R. *Criminology.* 8th ed. Phila., Penn.: J. B. Lippincott Co., 1970.

Periodicals
Amir, Menachem, and Berman, Yitzchak. "Chromosomal Deviation and Crime." *Federal Probation* 34, no. 2 (June 1970): 55–62.
Miller, Jerome G. "Research and Theory in Middle-Class Delinquency." *British Journal of Criminology* 10, no. 1 (January 1970): 33–51.
Montagu, M. F. Ashley, "Chromosomes and Crime." *Psychology Today* 2, no. 5 (October 1968): 42–49.
Sykes, Gresham M., and Matza, David. "Techniques of Neutralization—A Theory of Delinquency." *American Sociological Review* 22, no. 6 (December 1957): 664–70.
Wolfgang, Marvin E. "Pioneers in Criminology: Cesare Lombroso (1835–1909)." *Journal of Criminal Law, Criminology and Police Science* 52, no. 4 (November–December 1961): 361–91.

Part II
American Police

Chapter V

The American Police—
From Colonial Times
to 1900

The patterns of law enforcement in America have been closely aligned with municipal and county governments, rather than state and federal governments. For over two centuries, police services have provided for the control of criminal acts and the enforcement of local laws whenever a community and its local government believed police protection was necessary. In the settlements of colonial America, police services were viewed as necessary because "public watchmen" were essential to the protection of life and property. In rural areas and frontier communities, the employment of a sheriff, marshal or constable was viewed as essential because a willing and capable person was needed to confront armed criminals and bring them to justice.

The history of law enforcement in the United States reveals a steady growth in the number of police units but no trend toward consolidation into statewide police systems or one with national jurisdiction. Police units, because of their functional role in municipal and county governments, have similarities in the scope of their authority, prevailing practices, organization, and management, but there is no such thing as an American police system.[1]

The American police "system" has its roots in the Norman and Anglo-Saxon concept that groups of people have a basic responsibility to

1. Bruce Smith, *Police Systems in the United States* (New York: Harper & Row, Publishers, 1940), pp. 21–28.

guard against unlawful conduct in their community. In sixteenth-century England, the watch was a nighttime patrol which safeguarded the lives and property of the people of a community. Several of the residents of a town or village performed this duty each night. Assignments were rotated among the local citizens and service was compulsory—a civic responsibility. The *parish constable* system in England was also compulsory and without pay. The parish was a small community, and each resident parishioner was liable to one year's service as a constable. In addition, the parishioner performed his regular occupation. As communities increased in size, parishioners who did not wish to serve as constables were allowed to hire substitutes. In time, this led to the development of the role of constable as paid agent of the parish.[2] The London Metropolitan Police, organized in 1829 by Robert Peel, was a natural evolution of the watch and the constable systems into an agency which served to protect the local citizens and their property.

The office of constable predates the monarchy of England and its origin can be traced to the time of the Saxons. When the Statute of Winchester was enacted in 1285, during the reign of Edward I, one of its provisions was that two constables should be chosen from each *Hundred*. A Hundred contained ten *tithings*.* This unit had a corporate or community responsibility for the crimes of individual members of the Hundred. It was a control device initiated under the Saxon organization of England, but its roots go back to ancient German groups.

At that time, the law required that a constable should be *idoneus homo***: to have honesty to execute the office without malice, affection, or partiality; knowledge to understand what he ought to do; and ability as well as substance or estate, to enable him to conduct himself with utility to the public.[3] Early court decisions in both English and Scottish courts establish the fact that the constable was not an employee of a town or village, or a servant of the crown. He exercised his function and duties as an independent holder of a public office. He was a "professional citizen," paid to discharge the responsibilities of all citizens, but with an obligation only to the community as a whole. He was personally liable for false arrest, and he could not claim any of the immunities granted to servants of the crown. Additionally, a constable could not seek the refuge of the military services—the claim of acting upon orders of a superior.[4]

2. Patrick Pringle, *Hue and Cry—The Story of Henry and John Fielding and Their Bow Street Runners* (Great Britain: William Morrow and Co., 1964), pp. 12–16.
*Made up of ten *freeholders* (persons with title to realty), or *frank-pledges* (men who gave pledges, put up surety, or acknowledged the corporate responsibility) and their families.
**A responsible person; a good and lawful man.
3. Patrick Colquhoun, *A Treatise on the Police of the Metropolis* (1806; reprint ed., Montclair, N.J.: Patterson Smith, 1968), pp. 386–87.
4. Michael Banton, *The Policeman in the Community* (New York: Basic Books, 1964), pp. 5–6.

Unlike the British police system, the European police were nation-wide forces under the control of national governments. However, these systems had overtones of political control; of providing central governments with apparatuses for the control of citizens. Rather than being organized as watches to protect life and property in a community, these huge national police forces were organized primarily as political security police. In place of constables, these forces used military personnel.[5]

Fear of change may have been the major factor in developing what we now term the English model of policing. An attempt by Oliver Cromwell to establish central government control of localities may have contributed to this basic reluctance to change. In 1655, Cromwell divided England and Wales into 12 police districts, each under an army general and a force of from 100 to 1,500 armed men. Cromwell abandoned this project as a failure after 18 months because the people of England and Wales bitterly resented the system. He ordered the return to the constable system.[6]

Since the early settlers of our country had their roots in both the British Isles and Europe, there was a possibility that the natural growth of police services in the new land might have been patterned after the French or German models, instead of the British. The European police model, however, was in conflict with the new nation's rejection of tyranny. After the American Revolution, the new constitution provided for the preservation of order but not at any loss to individual liberty or fundamental freedoms. It is not surprising that the authors of a document stressing the citizen's right to personal freedom rejected a police model inherently oppressive because of central government control and potential unresponsiveness to the will of the people.

The framers of the United States Constitution adopted a federal system of government in which the powers are divided between the central government and the state governments. The Tenth Amendment reserves to the states respectively or to the people "all of the powers not delegated to the United States by the Constitution, nor prohibited by it to the states . . . ."[7]

The enumerated powers of the United States government are few, and a lesser number relate to the enforcement of laws related to crime and criminals. The federal government has the power to punish for counterfeiting; to define and punish crime on the high seas and against the law of nations; to declare the punishment for treason; to arrange the extradi-

5. Raymond B. Fosdick, *American Police Systems* (New York: Appleton-Century-Crofts, Meredith Corporation, 1921), pp. 76–81.
6. Pringle, *Hue and Cry*, pp. 12–16.
7. U.S., *Constitution*, Amend. 10. "The powers not delegated to the United States by the Constitution, nor prohibited by it to the States, are reserved to the States respectively, or to the people."

tion of fugitives; and to try criminal actions in federal courts. However, general law enforcement is reserved for the states. Within the states, the enforcement of law is generally delegated to the political subdivisions: cities, counties, towns, and villages. In many states, a state-wide police or highway patrol supplement local police agencies, particularly in rural areas and along major highways. [8]

Local Government and the Police

When the United States Constitution established a federal system of government it also established two power centers: (1) the national government, and (2) the state governments. Centralization is common in federal government. Decentralization is the pattern of operations within states, with the state being divided into counties for this purpose.

The county as a unit of local government is an Anglo-Saxon heritage. The basic territorial jurisdiction for local government in that period was the *shire*.* After the time of William the Conqueror, the shire became a county. In the colonies, in 1634, the populated area of Virginia was divided into eight shires or counties. In Massachusetts, colonists adapted a smaller unit of English local government to their needs; they formed towns, geographical areas roughly centered on one or more villages. In the Middle Atlantic colonies, both towns and counties were established. By the time of the Civil War, the county was established in its present and traditional form as the basic geographical subdivision of the state.

The county is the main political base for party organization. The political leader of the county is usually a key figure in local politics. Elective and appointive positions in the county government are a source of patronage for the political party in power. [9] Since the county is also the basic subdivision of the state court system, every county has a courthouse. This structure has traditionally served as the center for county government in its performance of the two types of functions characteristic of this unit of government: (1) duties required by the state, (2) activities not required by the state but permitted. [10]

The concept of home rule for city governments became firmly established in America as urban centers struggled with the problems of growth and the concept of self-government. In the middle of the twelfth century

8. Arthur C. Millspaugh, *Crime Control by the National Government* (Washington D.C.: Brookings Institution, 1937), pp. 43–48.
*One of the earliest territorial subdivisions of government in England.
9. Herbert S. Duncombe, *County Government in America* (Washington, D.C.: National Association of Counties Research Foundation, 1966), pp. 3–33.
10. Paul B. Wager, ed., *County Government Across the Nation* (Chapel Hill, N.C.: University of North Carolina Press, 1950), pp. 10–20.

the term _civitas_* began to have a precise meaning: a compact settlement having a special law with rights of self-government for its free men. It was normally walled, had a market, and some commerce and industry. The factor which encouraged the growth of a city was its focus as headquarters for trade and institutions which provided goods and services for the residents of the surrounding area. In ancient Greece and Rome _civitas_ embodied the concept of a city-state: a small unit with a central focus for its life and activities.[11]

While the specifics vary from state to state, the general idea is that when a community has reached the population levels normally earning classification as a city, control of local affairs is within the scope of a municipal government. Once incorporated as a local government unit, a municipality is self-governing within certain limits, and is not interfered with by the state government and its legislature. In California, the state's constitution was amended in 1879 to curtail the power of the state legislature in municipal affairs and to allow cities to run their own affairs.[12]

The primary business of local self-government is to provide public services. The cost of these services to the taxpayer depends upon the expertise and integrity of local public officials and employees. However, local government is often linked to local politics.

The "courthouse gang" refers to a group influential in decision making in county government and politics. The composition of this elite group in the local political scene varies from county to county, but there is little doubt that this group of local residents is the most powerful force in county politics.[13] Americans, from the time of the original settlements along the eastern seaboard, have believed that positions in a municipal government belong by right to the residents of the community, and that well-paying jobs in a municipality's government are a means of taking care of "worthy elements" among the city's residents—and voters.[14]

Before the turn of the century, urban police forces were tainted by the corruption in government. Political interference with day-to-day police operations was common. The residents of large cities identified police with corrupt city politics and the equally corrupt local government. Appointments to high police positions were made in accordance with the interests of the dominant political party. Municipal leaders were quick to respond to changes in public sentiment, and they used the de-

*The equivalent term in French was _ville;_ in German, _stadt;_ in Greek, _polis;_ and _town_ in English.
11. Robert E. Dickinson, _City and Region_ (London: Routledge and Kegan Paul, 1964), pp. 20, 49, 60.
12. Eugene P. Dvorin and Arthur J. Misner, _Introduction to California Government_ (Reading, Mass.: Addison-Wesley Publishing Co., 1966), pp. 97–99.
13. John C. Bollens, in association with John R. Bayes and Kathryn L. Utter, _American County Government_ (Beverly Hills, Cal.: Sage Publications, 1969), pp. 24–25.
14. Thomas R. Adam, _Elements of Government—An Introduction to Political Science_ (New York: Random House, 1960), pp. 265–67.

vice of short tenure to make certain that the police leader was equally responsive. It was a time of political partisanship and corruption.[15]

Municipal Police

The community of New Haven in the colony of Connecticut used special constables in place of a night watch as early as 1668. The law enforcement problem was centered at the iron works (the only industry in New Haven), and was primarily concerned with disorderly persons. In 1673, New Haven's selectmen (elected at a town meeting) appointed two constables for one-year terms to supplement the citizens who served as special constables. Apparently, this combination satisfied the town's residents, because the night watch was not reestablished until the hostilities of King Philip's War in 1675–76 threatened the safety of the community and its residents.[16]

In July 1772, the city fathers of Williamsburg, Virginia, roused to action by the activities of thieves (including the burglary of the local post office), created a town watch of four "sober and discreet people," whose duties were described as: "To patrol the streets of this city from ten o'clock every night until daylight the next morning, to cry the hours, and use their best endeavours to preserve peace and good order, by apprehending and bringing to justice all disorderly people."[17]

In 1801, the people of the community of Boston approved the establishment of a continuous night watch. Prior to this time, the people of Boston and its surrounding towns and villages would only be required to perform watch duty as required by local conditions. This continuous duty as public watchmen was incompatible with the earlier concept of watch service as a civic responsibility (refusal to serve required production of a substitute), and funds were voted to pay members of the watch. The watch patrolled the city of Boston from 10:00 P.M. or 10:30 P.M. to sunrise. The men on patrol were asked to cover their assigned section (or beat) once each hour and to prevent or suppress all disorders and disturbances. Members of the watch were authorized to stop and examine all persons reasonably suspected of unlawful designs and to question them as to their business and the purpose of being about the streets at night.[18]

New York City, at the beginning of the nineteenth century, had a history of both a citizen's watch and military patrols, and the city was pro-

15. Smith, *Police Systems in the United States*, pp. 4–10, 206–7.
16. Rollin G. Osterweis, *Three Centuries of New Haven, 1638–1938.* (New Haven: Yale University Press, 1953), pp. 70–73.
17. Arthur P. Scott, *Criminal Law in Colonial Virginia* (Chicago: University of Chicago Press, 1930), pp. 218–19.
18. Roger Lane, *Policing the City: Boston 1822–1885* (Cambridge, Mass.: Harvard University Press, 1967), pp. 7–10.

tected by a high constable, constables, marshals* and a night watch. In 1801, a local law made the high constable responsible for the peace of the city and the enforcement of all state laws and ordinances of the municipal corporation. This public officer was appointed by the mayor and supervised 16 constables. Constables were elected annually in each of the *wards*, political subdivisions of the municipality. City marshals were appointed by the mayor. In 1811, the state legislature limited the number of marshals in New York to no more than 60. Both constables and marshals served the various courts of the city and were essentially a day police force. The night watch served from sunset to sunrise. There were only 72 watchmen in 1800, but by 1826 the night watch consisted of 400 men. These men were divided among three watch districts in the city, each with a watch house. The entire watch was supervised by the Watch Committee of the city's Common Council. This council appointed all watchmen, captains, and assistant captains of the watch.[19]

In 1832, the state legislature—reacting to the pleas of the mayor— raised the allowable number of city marshals in the city of New York to 100. In 1845, the number of watchmen on nocturnal patrol in the growing city totaled 1,096. However, it was not until 1845 that New York City reformed their police structure along the lines of London's police.[20]

The civic responsibility of policing the city was established as the objective of a reorganized police force.** This objective was stated simply and became part of the city charter:

The Police Department and Police Force thereof has the power and it is their duty, at all times of the day and night to:

a. Protect life and property
b. Prevent crime
c. Detect and arrest offenders
d. Preserve the public peace
e. Enforce all laws, ordinances and provisions of the Administrative Code over which the Police Department has jurisdiction.[21]

*Termed "little sheriffs" because their work was also concerned with local courts as well as law enforcement. The provost marshal is a military officer responsible for military police and the administration of justice. Marshal is derived from an old German word *marah* (horse) and *scalh* (servant), a person who cared for horses.
19. James Richardson, *New York Police: Colonial Times to 1901* (New York: Oxford University Press, 1970), pp. 7–21, 32–33.
20. Ibid., pp. 29–49.
**The word *police* did not become common until late in the eighteenth century. F. W. Maitland in *Justice and Police* (London: Macmillan Co., 1885) suggests a definition: "Such part of social organization as is concerned immediately with the maintenance of good order, or the prevention or detection of offences."
21. *Rules and Regulations* (New York: New York City Police Department, 1956), p. 10.

In 1843, the legislators of the state of New York established a three-man Board of Police Commissioners for New York City and took the first step in the history of the country to eliminate the political control of urban police forces which had dominated this branch of government since colonial days. Prior to this time, arrangements for the control of police had been in the hands of common councils or mayors, public officials with broad executive power. The New York Board of Police Commissioners consisted of the mayor, the recorder, and the city judge. It was an administrative body that had full control of the good order and discipline of the police force. It was a model promptly adopted by other urban areas in the United States: New Orleans (1853); Cincinnati, San Francisco (1859); Detroit, St. Louis, Kansas City (1861); Buffalo, Cleveland (1866). From 1870 to 1880 most of the population centers of the country placed control of their police forces under a two- to twelve-man police board or commission.[22]

However, police boards in urban centers soon became political tools when state legislators enacted laws placing the appointing power in the hands of the governor. State control of such boards represented maneuvering by political parties at state levels to gain control over the police in a city usually dominated by the opposition party. When New York City's Board of Police Commissioners was placed under state control in 1857, the membership was increased to five, and the governor promptly appointed four members of his own political party and one man from the opposition. Maryland imposed a state-controlled plan in Baltimore in 1860: four commissioners of police to be chosen by the state legislature. Missouri, Illinois, Massachusetts, Michigan, Ohio, Louisiana, Indiana, and California also imposed state control over local municipal police in the years from 1857 to 1888.[23]

State political control of these police boards soon clashed with the home rule concept of municipal self-government. In 1870, New York City's local control of police was restored under a new city charter; in 1891, Michigan lawmakers eliminated state control in the city of Detroit as a contribution to effective local self-government; and, in 1902 the Ohio legislature rescinded any authority of the central government in cities. Under this law, the municipal authorities of Ohio cities have full control of police and their management.[24]

Critics said that bipartisan police boards or commissions never worked well and never would. These boards simply provided a means for the two leading political organizations to run the police force in a partnership under a gentleman's agreement. Municipal government requires a mayor with courage and conviction to place law enforcement and the ad-

22. Fosdick, *American Police Systems*, pp. 76–81.
23. Ibid., pp. 80–96.
24. Ibid., pp. 106–8.

ministration of justice above political ambition or advantage by appointing a competent person as the police executive and then supporting this public official as long as he is honest and faithful to his duties and responsibilities.[25]

The abandonment of the police board as an effective management technique led to a restoration of single-handed leadership in police forces in urban areas. The one-man system of executive control was substituted for the multiheaded control of police boards in city after city: New York and Detroit in 1901; Boston in 1906; Cleveland in 1908; Omaha in 1912; and Buffalo in 1916.

Detectives

Francis Tukey, a young attorney, was appointed as city marshal for Boston, Massachusetts, in 1846. His instructions from a reform mayor were to reorganize the night and day watch into a police force. Within a year, he installed a detective force. He transferred the most capable policemen to this new unit, several of whom were men who had served as constables before Tukey's appointment, and he specified that a detective's duties were to ferret out serious crimes and detect those who had committed them. Tukey was the first American police official to recognize the existence of certain police functions which a uniformed policeman cannot perform, because his uniform and badge publicly identify him as a police officer.[26]

It has long been recognized that criminal offenders who are not arrested at the crime scene or in flight from it, are likely to be professional criminals who have learned how to evade the uniformed police on patrol. While every crime scene can tell its story to modern evidence technicians and skilled investigators, the detectives in the early years of policing had to outwit the professional criminal by being knowledgeable about criminals and their *line*. They tended to specialize in the detection of pickpockets, hotel and boardinghouse thieves, confidence men, and bank burglars.[27]

At this time a precept of detectives was: "Criminals usually stick to their line." This belief led to the later development of *modus operandi* as a technique of criminal investigation—identifying a criminal from his method of operation recorded in reports of prior crimes.

---

25. William McAdoo, "Why the Police Are Not More Effective," in *The American City*, ed. Anselm L. Strauss (Chicago: Aldine Publishing Co., 1968), pp. 270–77.
26. Lane, *Policing the City*, pp. 44–66.
27. Duncan Matheson, "The Technique of the American Detective," *The Annals of the American Academy of Political and Social Science*, 116, November 1929: pp. 214–18.

George S. McWatters was the first American detective to write a nonfiction book on American detectives.[28] He was a New York detective who believed that without him and his fellow detectives the civilization of New York could not be maintained, and anarchy of a sort would prevail throughout the country. "Vigilance committees," McWatters wrote, "would be needed in all our cities, and be made up of inexperienced citizens, who—not knowing what to do—would make confusion more confounded, and run riot themselves."

McWatters was of the opinion that detectives were not fully understood by the majority of the people, who never knew how much of their peace and security depended upon the quiet, silent, effective operations of *master detectives*. This author describes the work of a master detective as follows:

> His field of labor is usually more thorny, and his work at times not only very perplexing, on account of the subtle characters he has to deal with, but very laborious in view of the much traveling, nights and days, which many jobs occasion. The tracking of bank robbers, searching for the hiding-places of their stolen treasures, and various like things, will suggest the great amount of real, hard, physical labor the detective sometimes has to perform. Only he can do it. He cannot delegate his powers to any great extent. If he employs others, it is only as aids, not as substitutes. He is expected to know everything in the ways of business, regular and irregular. If he would succeed as a detective of bank robbers, especially, he must not only know all the rogues in that class, but he must understand what class of "workmen" they are; for these industrious hardworking bank robbers all have different ways of doing their work; possess different degrees of skill; and when the robbery of a bank is reported to a detective, his first inquiry is directed to the manner in which the work was done. So the detective's calling is one which demands not only much cunning, but much general and accurate knowledge of human character, and not a little acquaintance with all sorts of business.[29]

Thomas Byrnes of the New York City police was considered the country's leading detective in post-Civil War years. Byrnes became chief of detectives in the New York City Police Department and he made his record in this position in a variety of ways. He trained his detectives in criminal techniques. When a theft occurred, his men were generally able to name the thief, making identification from their knowledge of the style of work of professional thieves: the signature aspect of a crime. Byrnes and his subordinates also built a network of informers in whose interest it was to report on other criminals. When these techniques proved inadequate for the solution of particular cases, Inspector Byrnes had no

28. George S. McWatters, *Knots Untied: or Ways and By-Ways in the Hidden Life of American Detectives* (Hartford, Conn.: J. B. Burr & Hyde, 1871), pp. 659–61.
29. Ibid., pp. 652–53.

hesitation about resorting to the third degree—or approving its use by his detectives. He personally solved the Manhattan Savings Institution robbery by patient inquiry in the underworld until he accumulated enough scraps of information to move in on the suspects and extract their confessions.[30]

Rural and Frontier Policing

While the first urban police forces in America had their origin in the watch and constabulary, the origin of policing in rural areas is the ancient English office of sheriff as representative of the crown.* The central government's control over the office of sheriff did not survive long in America. Control stabilized at county levels of government and the office became an elective one, with the county's electorate choosing a sheriff at two-, three-, or four-year intervals.

The sheriff of a rural area during the time of colonial and postcolonial government was probably a merchant or landowner of considerable wealth. But as the frontier moved southward and westward, the average incumbent sheriff was no more than a householder of the community. Additionally, the western sheriff never had much opportunity to perform the tasks of assisting local magistrates and tax collecting, which were characteristic of their early English counterparts. For the first time in the history of this office, the sheriff became personally active in the enforcement of law. This heroic figure of frontier history was no longer the "king's steward," but was an armed protector of life and property known for the frequency of his shoot-outs with gun-carrying cattle rustlers, horse thieves, and stagecoach and train robbers.[31]

The function and duties of the office of sheriff have been described as follows: "The sheriff is the conservator of peace in his county, and while serving in this capacity is the sovereign power of the state. He has a duty to commit all persons who break the peace, or attempt to do so, to jail, and to pursue and capture all felons and 'other misdoers' and he may command a *posse comitatus*—by a summons every person over 15 must obey."[32] The *posse comitatus* was the *levee en masse* of the adult male population of a county, which a sheriff might summon to his aid in preserving the peace, pursuing felons, etc.

30. Thomas Byrnes, *1886—Professional Criminals in America* (1886; reprint ed., New York: Chelsea House Publishers, 1969), pp. xii–xxvi.
*The *reeve* was a public official of a shire who had some law enforcement duties. He was called the shire-reeve, the origin of the word sheriff.
31. Smith, *Police Systems in the United States*, pp. 75–89.
32. August Vollmer and Alfred Parker, *Crime and the State Police* (Berkeley, Cal.: University of California Press, 1935), pp. 15–16.

Towns and villages within a county often hired constables or town marshals as their agents of law enforcement. Their territorial jurisdiction was limited to the boundaries of the village or township.

While the jurisdictional boundaries of sheriff, constable, and town marshal were usually respected in rural areas, the incumbents in these positions along the western frontier generally ignored them. The sheriff usually deputized his fellow lawmen and thus authorized countywide law enforcement jurisdiction, and sheriffs of adjoining counties were usually happy to have professional assistance in apprehending criminal offenders.[33]

At the request of a sheriff or other local public official, a governor of a state can summon the state militia (National Guard) for law enforcement duty. This system supports the office of sheriff as it allows the larger unit of government to step in and help when necessary. However, the reverse is not always true. Sheriffs may be unwilling to respond to the direction of a governor. After all, sheriffs are elected officials of a local government unit and are not in the employ of the state.[34]

State Police

In order to protect the lives and property of 30,000 American colonists during the Texas Revolution in 1835, a police force commonly known as the Texas Rangers was organized. The initial authorization was for a force of 60; two groups of 25, and one group of 10 rangers. A month later three companies of 56 men each were authorized; the men were enlisted for one year and placed under the command of a major and three captains. The rangers were neither state militia not a unit of the federal armed forces. They were armed men in a military-civilian organization. They were allowed $1.25 a day for "pay, food, clothing and horse service." On its frontier to the west, the residents of Texas justly feared the menace of roving bands of Indians intent on arson and murder. On the southern frontier of Texas, Mexican soldiers and citizens disputed the right of the Anglo-American residents to seize land they considered part of Mexico. The Republic of Texas was the governing unit of this territory from 1836 to 1845. In 1836 legislation provided for additional companies of mounted volunteers for the ranging service to protect three border counties. In 1884 and 1845, additional companies were formed for other counties along the western and southern frontiers of Texas. After Texas entered the Union in 1845 as a state, the rangers served as scouts for the U.S. Army in

33. Carl W. Breihan, *Great Lawmen of the West* (New York: Bonanza Books, Crown Publishers, 1963), pp. 10–12.
34. Bruce Smith, *The State Police—Organization and Administration* (1925; reprint ed., Montclair, N.J.: Patterson Smith, 1969), pp. 15–36.

its fight with the Mexican army to preserve the border of Texas as United States territory.[35]

The Arizona Rangers were organized in 1901 and the New Mexico Mounted Police in 1905. The assigned duty of both units was patrol, similar to the ranging of the Texas Rangers. In 1905, the Commonwealth of Pennsylvania established a state constabulary. In earlier years, Massachusetts and Connecticut appointed a few constables with authority to function within a statewide jurisdiction, but neither group was a police force managed by a commanding officer. Pennsylvania, in fact, was the first state to initiate a force similar to the Texas Rangers, but with general law-enforcement authority rather than specific border or frontier service.[36]

The concept of a state police did not spread rapidly. It was roadblocked by organized labor's resentment of the gathering of great numbers of state policemen in one place for strike duty. The Pennsylvania State Police were used for duty at many strikes as were other state police forces. The presence of a concentration of professional police attempting to preserve the peace and protect life and property may have frustrated some of the legitimate demands of organized labor. Legislators responsive to the voting power of an industrial area hesitated to be supportive of the state police concept. However, the rejection of the concept of a state police may not have originated in the use of such police in labor disputes, but rather from a local community's rejection of any armed force entering that community and taking over the privileges of the familiar local police.[37]

State police are an excellent solution for the problem of policing rural areas, substituting full-time, salaried, and trained police for part-time and often untrained sheriffs and constables. In New York, the state police have *troops* of police distributed at various zone headquarters and substations throughout the state, and they have the responsibility—along with the county sheriffs—for law enforcement outside of cities. The state police have the power to go into cities and make arrests whenever necessary. This police organization has proven itself for the past half-century to be a professional police force in the finest sense of the term. The troopers are known and respected by citizens throughout the state of New York.

Other states have units with similar powers, but many states have restricted the jurisdiction of their statewide police to traffic law enforcement. The California Highway Patrol is a nationally recognized professional police unit, but its jurisdiction is the highways of the state and its personnel, by legislative action, are termed state traffic officers, rather

35. Walter Prescott Webb, *The Texas Rangers* (Boston: Houghton Mifflin Co., 1935), pp. 21–34, 91–95.
36. Smith, *State Police*, pp. 36–42.
37. Ibid., pp. 53–65.

than state policemen. However, this specialization has been very effective as it concentrates a statewide police in a crisis area, the control of traffic, and at the same time provides local police and sheriff's deputies with a back-up force of highly trained police officers.

Federal Law Enforcement

The Judiciary Act of September 14, 1789 not only established a system of federal courts, but also established the Office of Attorney General and the position of federal marshal. U.S. marshals were appointed in each of 13 federal districts for four-year terms. Assigned duties were to serve the federal courts and execute all lawful orders directed to them under the authority of the United States. The U.S. marshal was empowered to appoint deputies and to command all necessary assistance in the performance of his assigned duties. In 1792, Congress granted U.S. marshals the same common-law powers in executing the laws of the United States as sheriffs possessed in their respective counties in the states.[38]

The U.S. marshal was the first agent of law enforcement in the federal government. He had the same powers under federal jurisdiction that sheriffs possessed at local levels, and his authority to command assistance equaled the ancient rights of sheriffs to call out the able-bodied men of a county as a posse comitatus.

In 1861, the attorney general was given control and responsibility for United States district attorneys and United States marshals. In 1870, Congress authorized a Department of Justice in the federal executive system and made the attorney general its chief executive.

In 1889, a U.S. marshal shot and killed a California citizen named Terry in the line of duty. The marshal acted in defense of the life of a judge he was protecting on orders from the U.S. attorney general. The U.S. marshal was jailed by California authorities. His defense was that he had acted pursuant to the law of the United States, and he sought review and release in an application for a writ of *habeas corpus*.* The case terminated in the U.S. Supreme Court.[39] In its opinion the court commented that there was a "peace of the United States," and that the U.S. marshal in this case was as much entitled to protect this peace as a California sheriff would have been in protecting the local peace under the same circumstances.[40]

The Secret Service had commenced operations against counterfeiters of the national currency in 1865 under legislation enacted by Congress to

38. Rita W. Cooley, "The Office of U.S. Marshal," *Western Political Quarterly* 12, no. 1, part 1 (March 1959): 123–40.
*Literally: produce the body; a legal remedy for persons unjustly imprisoned.
39. In re Nagle, 135 U.S. 1 (1890).
40. Ibid., p. 69.

restore public confidence in the country's money. Inherent in this legislation, which provided funds to detect and arrest persons violating the counterfeiting laws, was the authority to act against persons violating these laws and other federal laws regarding the U.S. Treasury. This new unit became a branch of the Treasury Department. The Secret Service was a small force in comparison to the awesome responsibilities of this new agency of law enforcement. Washington became the headquarters of the Secret Service, and its 30 investigators were distributed across the country in 11 field offices. In the announcement of the initiation of this group of federal agents and its single area of interest, U.S. marshals in each federal district were asked to cooperate.

The Secret Service operated under yearly grants of authority by Congress in annual appropriations acts providing various amounts of money for operating expenses. It was at the turn of the century that the protection of the president was assigned to the Secret Service (informally in 1901 after President William McKinley's assassination; formally in 1903 when Congress included this duty in its annual appropriations act funding the Secret Service).[41]

The Division of Inspectors of the Post Office Department existed as early as 1878. The U.S. Post Office Inspection Service is responsible for internal security (administrative inspection of post offices and postal accounts) and the detection of crime. In 1886 the office of chief inspector of this service was approved by a congressional appropriation of funds for this purpose. It quickly became a nationwide operation with postal inspection districts and a force of postal inspectors. Cases assigned to these men have included the rifling of mail, embezzlement, the transmission of forbidden matter, post office burglaries, and the robbery of postal employees and trains and other conveyances transporting mail.[42]

As late as 1906, Congress was authorizing the temporary assignment of Secret Service personnel to the Department of Justice; and it was not until 1909 that Congress appropriated sufficient funds for the attorney general to create and maintain a small detective force. These men were assigned to a new subdivision of the Department of Justice, the Bureau of Investigation—renamed the Federal Bureau of Investigation (FBI) in 1935.[43]

The Congress of the United States was apparently reluctant to take any action likely to contribute to the establishing of a national police. The intent of Congress was made clear by limiting the U.S. marshal's duties to crimes defined by federal statutes and to legal processes concerned with U.S. courts; by carefully delineating the restricted enforcement areas as-

41. Walter S. Bowen and Harry Edward Neal, *The United States Secret Service* (Philadelphia: Chilton Book Co., 1960), pp. 14–16, 126, 190–92.
42. Albert Langeluttig, "Federal Police," *Annals* 146, November 1929, pp. 41–54.
43. Harry Overstreet and Bonaro Overstreet, *The FBI in Our Open Society* (New York: W. W. Norton & Company, 1969), pp. 11–28.

signed to the Secret Service and the Postal Inspection Service; and by its delay until 1909 in providing investigators for the U.S. Department of Justice.

The post-Civil War years may have contributed to Congress' reluctance to install any federal police with general criminal jurisdiction. The states participating in the Civil War as part of the Confederacy were placed under the control of the United States Army. This was the only federal agency available to administer the national government's reconstruction policy. This policing under central government control was authorized by martial law. Military personnel serving as provost marshals were in charge of one or more districts. Military commissions and provost courts* functioned under federal control in place of the civil courts of many areas of the South.[44]

President Andrew Johnson's Proclamation of Peace on April 2, 1866, began the long process of changing over from military to civilian control in the South. The preamble of this proclamation is illustrative of the federal control over the region during this period.

> Whereas standing armies, military occupation, martial law, military tribunals, and the suspension of the privilege of the writ of *habeas corpus* are in time of peace dangerous to public liberty, incompatible with the individual rights of the citizen, contrary to the genius and spirit of our free institutions, and exhaustive of the national resources, and ought not, therefore, to be sanctioned or allowed except in cases of actual necessity for repelling invasion or suppressing insurrection or rebellion. . . .[45]

Police Status at the End of the Nineteenth Century

The history of the law enforcement officers who served their communities as constables, sheriffs, deputy sheriffs, or members of a city's police force from colonial times to 1900 has structured many of the stereotypes about police now held by the public. One that has apparently earned its right to a natural death and an R.I.P. burial is the stereotype of the "dumb cop." It is true that long ago, police applicants satisfying the rudimentary physical requirements of height and strength, were tested only as to their friendship with the political party in power at the time.[46]

*Derived from the use of provost marshal to designate the law enforcement official in the army.
44. John Richard Bennett, *The South As It Is: 1865–1866* (New York: Viking Press, 1965), pp. 220–23.
45. James E. Sefton, *The United States Army and Reconstruction: 1865–1877* (Baton Rouge, La.: Louisiana State University Press, 1967), pp. 5–33, 78.
46. Charles B. Saunders, Jr., *Upgrading the American Police—Education and Training for Better Law Enforcement* (Washington, D.C.: Brookings Institution, 1970), pp. 13–15.

A second stereotype slowly fading from the public mind is the image of the brutal policeman. Unfortunately, this was fostered in earlier years by press reports of police brutality when accused persons were interrogated. The *"third degree"* became the catchword for the employment of methods which inflict suffering, physical or mental, upon a person in order to obtain information about a crime.[47] Decisions of the U.S. Supreme Court in confession cases set new standards for police interrogations and police acceptance of these decisions erased this stereotype, or— at least—partially erased it from the public mind.[48]

However, there is a strong suspicion that another element in the public attitude about police brutality is an Anglo-American fear of a strong police force, first manifested in England in 1829, when Robert Peel proposed a municipal police. This fear is part of our national psychology, and is probably the major reason for our fragmented American police system.[49] Fear and distrust of government authority by a citizenry intent on preserving their fundamental freedoms, provided a receptive audience for every tale of police third degree methods.

The basic distrust of an armed, uniformed, and disciplined body of police is reflected in the failure to provide tenure for city police chiefs and the continuing popular election of sheriffs. Lack of tenure for an adequate number of years and popular elections are both devices used by communities for control of local police, and they are both aligned with the citizens' distrust of an armed, uniformed, and disciplined police.

Lastly, and probably another carry-over from the watchman's role of colonial days, is the American public's attitude that police are solely responsible for controlling crime.[50] This may also be a side effect of the American image of the western frontier and its lawman, sheriff, or marshal who took direct and personal action against criminals.

The outstanding features of the American police at the end of the nineteenth century were its local characteristics and its communal control.

The nature and growth of a great nation shaped the law enforcement area of government during these years, and fast-growing communities set the stage for the development of modern police organizations. Police in America, in their growth to professional organizations of full-time, salaried personnel, did provide the citizens of a growing nation with the protection necessary to "insure domestic tranquility," and they contributed in no small measure to establishing justice, and providing for the general welfare.

47. Zachariah Chafee, Jr., Walter H. Pollack, and Carl S. Stern, *Mass Violence in America: The Third Degree* (New York: Arno Press and the *New York Times*, 1969), p. 19.
48. The series of cases commonly known as the "confession cases" begin with Brown v. Mississippi, 297 U.S. 278 (1936), and climax in Miranda v. Arizona, 384 U.S. 436 (1966).
49. Saunders, *Upgrading the American Police*, pp. 13–15.
50. Ibid., p. 13.

Selected References

Books

Adam, Thomas R. *Elements of Government—An Introduction to Political Science* New York: Random House, 1960.

Bollens, John C., in association with Bayes, John R. and Utter, Kathryn L. *American County Government.* Beverly Hills, Calif.: Sage Publications, 1969.

Bowen, Walter S., and Neal, Harry E. *The United States Secret Service.* Philadelphia: Chilton Book Co., 1960.

Byrnes, Thomas. *1886—Professional Criminals in America.* 1886; reprint ed., New York: Chelsea House Publishers, 1969.

Duncombe, Herbert S. *County Government in America.* Washington, D.C.; National Association of Counties Research Foundation, 1966.

Fosdick, Raymond B. *American Police Systems.* New York: Appleton-Century-Crofts, Meredith Corporation, 1921.

Lane, Roger. *Policing the City: Boston 1822–1885.* Cambridge, Mass.: Harvard University Press, 1967.

McWatters, George S. *Knots Untied: or Ways and By-Ways in the Hidden Life of American Detectives.* Hartford, Conn.: J. B. Burr & Hyde, 1871.

Millspaugh, Arthur C. *Crime Control by the National Government.* Washington, D.C.: Brookings Institution, 1937.

Overstreet, Harry and Overstreet, Bonaro. *The FBI in Our Open Society.* New York: W. W. Norton & Co., 1969.

Pringle, Patrick. *Hue and Cry—The Story of Henry and John Fielding and Their Bow Street Runners.* Great Britain: William Morrow and Co., 1964.

Richardson, James. *New York Police: Colonial Times to 1901.* New York: Oxford University Press, 1970.

Ruchelman, Leonard. *Who Rules the Police?* New York: New York University Press, 1973.

Sefton, James E. *The United States Army and Reconstruction: 1865–1877.* Baton Rouge, La.: Louisiana State University Press, 1967.

Smith, Bruce. *Police Systems in the United States.* New York: Harper & Row, Publishers, 1940.

Webb, Walter P. *The Texas Rangers.* Boston: Houghton Mifflin Co., 1935.

Periodicals

Cooley, Rita W. "The Office of U.S. Marshal." *Western Political Quarterly* 12, no. 1, part 1 (March 1959): 123–140.

Matheson, Duncan. "The Technique of the American Detective," *The Annals of the American Academy of Political and Social Science*, 116, November 1929, pp. 214–18.

Cases

In re Nagle, 135 U.S. 1 (1890).

Chapter VI

The Police Mission and Role in a Democratic Society

The peace officer role in the history of Anglo-American government pre-dates the police role as law enforcer. The "king's peace" at one time sig-nified the absence of any disorder. Loyalty to the monarch entitled the king's subjects to a certain measure of peace and security. As the chief magistrate, the king appointed his stewards to extend the royal protection to loyal subjects. Later, the monarch delegated some of his magisterial authority to persons in his service and assigned them responsibility for a specified territorial area, a shire. These men had vice-regal powers in the beginning, convening their own courts in the king's name. They were also empowered to call upon any of the king's subjects to assist them in keeping the peace. One of the roles of the *posse comitatus* was to handle serious disturbances. Later, great landowners—the lords of the manors—became responsible for the peace and security of their dependents.[1]

The modern police officer responds to the needs of twentieth-century communities by assuming the role of an employee hired to keep the public order and to provide various related general services. It is a dual role inasmuch as police must always be on the alert for violations of law, and many times, when peace-keeping efforts fail, police must switch roles and invoke the formal arrest process.

The prototype of twentieth-century police organizations, London's Metropolitan Police, was organized to serve this dual function. It was an arm of the administration of justice, bringing persons accused of crime

1. Douglas G. Browne, *The Rise of Scotland Yard* (London: George G. Harrap & Co., 1956), pp. 13–14.

into court for trial, but it was also an agency for keeping the peace by official action less than the formal legal procedure of arrest and arraignment.[2] In October 1829, the membership of the Metropolitan Police were warned about rudeness "on the part of the police toward persons asking civil questions"; and a month later, in November, they were cautioned "to preserve peace and good order" by all possible means. One hundred and thirty-five years later, in 1964, an article in an authoritative police science and criminology journal concluded with these words:

> The real significance of the Metropolitan Police lay in its example to the nation as a model for subsequent national police reform legislation and organization. It proved that an efficient police could greatly decrease the use of troops against civilians; that it could protect life and property; and that it could be compatible with the English constitutional concepts of liberty.[3]

The Police Mission

The evolution of American policing over a century and a half has developed the mission of police as one element of the criminal justice system. It is supportive of the entire process of the administration of justice, and as the most visible of its agents and agencies its role in law enforcement and apprehension is critical.

The goals to be achieved by police are generally summed up as the prevention of crime and disorder; the preservation of the peace; the apprehension of offenders; the recovery of lost and stolen property; and the protection of life, property, and personal liberties.

The primary police techniques for achieving these measures are the crime-prevention-and-deterrence method, the apprehension process, the regulation of noncriminal conduct, the provision of public services, and the protection of personal liberties by appropriate control of police behavior and interaction with other units in the criminal justice system.[4]

Most police officers see their function and the police department's mission as primarily that of law enforcement. However, urban living in high-density population centers, the continuing industrial revolution and the increasing use of the automobile has realigned the police mission with the basic responsibility of keeping order. The twentieth century introduced a whole new set of interrelationships, and equally new

2. Egon Bittner, "The Police on Skid Row: A Study of Peace Keeping," *American Sociological Review* 32, no. 5 (October 1967): 699–715.
3. J. L. Lyman, "The Metropolitan Police Act of 1829," *Journal of Criminal Law, Criminology and Police Science* 55, no. 1 (March 1964): 141–54.
4. George D. Eastman, ed., *Municipal Police Administration* (Washington, D.C.: International City Management Association, 1969), pp. 3, 209, 322.

areas and avenues of conflict in these interactions. These order-keeping functions are more frequently aligned with the police officer as philosopher, guide, friend, or peace officer rather than the pursuer of criminals in the apprehension process.

The police mission in a democratic society is concerned with control, keeping the law from being violated, and apprehending law violators, but it is also concerned with the maintenance of order. Thousands of police officers in all sections of the country, day after day, function as keepers of the peace to preserve domestic tranquility.

A functional continuum has been suggested as illustrative of the basic police mission. This continuum would have the helping function at one end, and the punitive function at the other end;[5] or the supportive functions at one end and the control functions at the other end.[6]

That policemen are practicing social scientists is a reality long rejected by the academic world of social science and the professional arena of social work, but the facts of day-to-day performance of police as peace officers in many jurisdictions throughout the nation has established the police as de facto social scientists. The mission of police has not changed, but a basic part of that mission has developed as a function demanding new skills and more police manpower than the law enforcement segment of the police mission.

In a survey of the literature and commentaries on police management the following specific functions were outlined as goals for police:

1. Prevention and repression of crime
2. Maintenance of the peace (domestic tranquility)
3. Protection of persons and property (security)
4. Enforcement of laws
5. Detection of crime
6. Recovery of lost and stolen property
7. Apprehension of offenders
8. Regulation of noncriminal conduct
9. Protection of individual rights
10. Control of traffic
11. Miscellaneous public services
12. Preparation of cases for presentation in court.[7]

5. U.S., President's Commission on Law Enforcement and Administration of Justice, *The Police and the Community—The Dynamics of Their Relationship in a Changing Society*, prepared by Joseph D. Lohman and Gordon Misner (Washington, D.C.: Government Printing Office, 1966), p. 38

6. Elmer H. Johnson, "Police: An Analysis of Role Conflict," *Police*, January–February 1970, pp. 47–52.

7. Commission on Law Enforcement, *The Police and the Community*, p. 37.

The dominance of the order-keeping function has led to its classification as the *first* objective of a police department and the classification of the law enforcement function as the *second* objective.[8] A study of 652 calls to an upstate New York police department spanning an 82-hour period is illustrative of the merit of this reorientation of the police mission. Researchers found significant evidence of police acting out a peacekeeping role. A patrol car was dispatched in 75 percent of the 652 calls. In reports by these responding police, over 50 percent of the citizens wanted help or some form of support for personal or interpersonal problems. This research team found that responding police attempted to solve the problem, or guided the citizen to someone who might solve his problem. In on-the-scene problem-solving, police were found to provide support, either by offering friendly sympathy to the caller, by giving authoritative information to the citizen, or by helping two or more disputants agree on some plan for resolving the problem.[9]

Police as Law Enforcers: The Apprehension Process

The apprehension process is within the core area of the traditional role of police as law enforcers. In response to an event, the police invoke the formal process of arrest and arraignment in court.

The apprehension process was first formalized by the hue and cry, an arrest procedure in which an alarm was raised upon the commission of any felony. The practice dates back to Edward I (1285), when persons fleeing the scene of a crime were easily identified and pursued. When a hue and cry was raised, every person—on a constable's order—had to aid in the pursuit of the felon, or be liable to fine and imprisonment. During the time of George II (1735), a regulation was promulgated which provided for a forfeit of five pounds for any constable who "neglects making hue-and-cry."[10]

The apprehension process is a sequence of actions taken as a response to the event of a crime. The sequential action begins when a crime is detected by police, a victim or another citizen, or by an alarm device. The next step is a headquarters-to-patrol-unit broadcast over local police radio. Police on patrol respond and proceed to the crime scene. A search for the perpetrator of a crime has three phases: (1) *hot*, (2) *warm*, and (3) *cold*. The hot and warm searches are conducted at the crime scene and in the general area of the crime, respectively, and generally have a time

8. James Q. Wilson, "Dilemmas of Police Administration," *Public Administration Review* 28, no. 5 (September–October 1968): 407–17.

9. Elaine Cumming, I. Cumming, and Laura Edell, "Policeman as Philosopher, Guide and Friend," *Social Problems* 12, no. 3 (Winter 1965): 276–86.

10. Patrick Colquhoun, *A Treatise on the Police of the Metropolis* (1795, reprint ed., Montclair, N.J.: Patterson Smith, 1969), pp. 388–89.

limit associated with the time of the crime and the duration of the perpetrator's flight from the scene. The cold search may range far and wide, and its time span is limited only by the opportunities for getting results.[11]

Uniformed police, within the police function of patrol, usually conduct the hot and warm searches. Being on patrol nearby the scene of a crime, being available for instant receipt of the alarm broadcast, and having the mobility necessary to get to the crime scene without delay are the three factors which assign this portion of the apprehension process to police on patrol.

When the perpetrator is known to the victim, known to an eyewitness to the crime, or if there is an identification of a vehicle involved in the crime, the cold search is often initiated by the police radio dispatcher, and the patrol force often makes arrests on the basis of broadcasted data about the suspect, his vehicle, or both. When an arrest is not made in the first eight hours of the postcrime period, the case usually requires investigation.

When the victim can give no clue to the perpetrator's identity and there are no eyewitnesses (or such witnesses cannot provide any identification data), the search is investigative from its origin. The success of the apprehension process depends upon the ability of investigative personnel to identify the perpetrator from a study of the crime's circumstances and collected evidence: linkups to past crimes through comparison of modi operandi; the use of informants; or some combination of intuition and innovative handling of promising leads.[12]

Delegation of the continuing investigation—the cold search of the apprehension process—to the personnel of the investigative unit is necessary because the continuing investigation embraces all the work necessary for identifying the offender, apprehending him, and preparing the case for prosecution. The ready alert status of patrol officers and their assignment to the limited area of a post or sector interferes with this type of investigation. The cold search is more than surprising a perpetrator at a crime scene or skill in pursuing a criminal in flight from the scene. It is a search in which a patrol officer is likely to be handicapped by his uniform, frustrated by his patrol duties, and limited by his assignment to a territorial area (post or sector).

The Peace Officer Role of Police

In keeping the peace, police are confronted with three main types of public disorder: structural, collective, and individual. Structural disorder

11. U.S., The President's Commission on Law Enforcement and Administration of Justice, *Task Force Report: The Police* (Washington, D.C.: Government Printing Office, 1967), p. 58.
12. Paul B. Weston and Kenneth M. Wells, *Criminal Investigation*, 2d ed. (Englewood Cliffs, N.J.: Prentice-Hall, 1973), pp. 95–120.

results from noncriminal actions creating a collective disorder: the carelessly discarded match or cigarette can lead to huge conflagrations, and panic in a crowded restaurant or theater can result from an ill-chosen word such as "fire." The collective disorder results from the acts of several persons acting in concert. Riots, parades, demonstrations, meetings that become riotous, and mass picketing that gets out of hand are collective disorders. The common drunk or the "man down" are the classic illustrations of individual disorders—one is apparently an intoxicated person, the other is one lying in the street who may be drunk, sick, or injured.[13]

Peace keeping involves skill in the application of procedures to situations that do not involve the formal legal routine of arrest. Typical situations which are likely to result in action less than an arrest are:

1. *Supervision of licensed premises*—the inspectional role of police, from the scrutiny of licenses to the influencing of the licensee to cooperate with the police and other agencies of government—particularly in protecting the morals of young people

2. *The regulation of traffic*—the control of noncriminal conduct

3. *Minor criminal offenses*—the classic "low visibility" of American police when the law or the circumstances of the case are ambiguous and the police officer may act alternatively rather than make an arrest

4. *Crisis-intervention*—intervention in family and neighborhood matters that have no criminal aspects (and often no legal aspects) in order to aid people in trouble; to arbitrate family disputes; to care for the sick, injured or intoxicated person; and to pacify the rowdy and unruly

5. *Monitoring crowds and assemblies*—the police control role in an early stage of preventing disorder: monitoring is an informal control of groups in the incipient stages of disorder

6. *People with special problems*—police concern with the less-than-fully-competent persons: (a) children, (b) aged persons, and (c) the mentally ill; for people who are different—bohemians and vagabonds;[14] and the resident known criminal.

Keeping the peace requires officers on patrol to know a great deal about their posts or sectors. Officers assigned to a neighborhood should

13. Arthur L. Stinchcombe, "Institutions of Privacy in the Determination of Police Administrative Practice," *The American Journal of Sociology* 69, no. 2 (September 1963): 150–60.
14. Bittner, "The Police on Skid Row," pp. 701–15.

not be transferred without reason and certainly not until several years have been spent in the same neighborhood. The concept of police residing in their work areas would promote a firsthand knowledge of local conditions. The old-time foot patrolman had a rare knowledge of his post, and he usually did not live at any great distance from it.

Peace keeping has been described as a "craft," and skill at keeping the peace is developed as a result of an apprenticeship rather than any formal training or learning by the study of a written body of special knowledge. From the long-term acceptance of police intervention in disputes, differences, and difficulties of family and neighborhood, there is a recognition that when police inspect, direct, inform, warn, and take other action less than an arrest, they do this in some accord with the circumstances of the event threatening domestic tranquility.

This on-the-job training in the skills of peace keeping involves some trial and error actions and some ground rule coaching in what *not* to do. The grading process in these skills is job-related: winning or failing to win the approval of associates in the police patrol unit. Gains in the performance of police in their peace-keeping role are not likely to result from the formalization of procedures, nor in extensive training programs. The most significant action to improve police skills in peace keeping is to reorient the police administrators to emphasize and adequately reward the patrol officer and to develop assignment patterns which will increase the patrol officer's knowledge of a neighborhood and the problems of its people.[15]

The Police Mission—Organizing and Managing

Organizations are made up of people with a purpose, who work in groups, who use knowledge and method in their work, and who attempt to work together in interdependent relationships, but with some structuring and integrating of individual activities. The total task of achieving an organization's objectives is segmented so that particular persons or groups are responsible for the performance of specialized activities.

The executive is responsible for organizing and controlling all activity in achieving the ultimate objectives of an organization. He may establish program objectives for supervisors in charge of segments of the organization and delegate related duties to them. In turn, these officers in charge may set objectives for subordinates and delegate related duties. This is a pyramidal management structure. The various levels of management between the executive at the top and the operations personnel who turn out the product is primarily dependent upon the size of the organization.

Universally, police forces in America use location as a primary organizational base. The municipal, town or village police department, the

15. Wilson, "Dilemmas of Police Administration," pp. 413–15.

sheriff's office, and the state police are all responsible for certain geographical areas. This territorial jurisdiction is broken down into posts and sectors to secure a basic unit for the assignment of personnel. Concurrently, because police must provide services on a 24-hour and 7-day basis, there is also a universal division of work and responsibility by time: within the total territorial jurisdictional area of a police force there are one or more police officers on duty or available when required.

A police organization has a historical division of labor. The average organization of an American police department or sheriff's office is segmented by function into two major areas: the enforcement arms, and auxiliary or support services. In the evolution of American policing, preventing crime and responding to calls for services are the primary functions of the patrol division. Other more specialized functions are assigned to smaller units such as the detective or criminal investigation division, the traffic division, the juvenile or youth division, and the vice division. These enforcement-oriented units are supported in their field work by various auxiliary services from records management to vehicle maintenance.

The organizational structure of the police force of a major police department or sheriff's office depends a great deal upon its size. The division of work in a small police department may plan for one man to perform almost all of the police functions, or allow for some part-time specialization in the division of work. When a police force has a considerable number of men, the available personnel allows for more specialization.

Unit Beat Policing

There is a trend to combine the patrol and criminal investigation functions under a common supervisor. The traditional separation of these two functions has handicapped staff planning, both in the improvement of the apprehension process and in the solution of crimes which occur in a series pattern.[16]

Unit beat policing is an innovative British concept that recommends consolidation of these two functions into a new neighborhood police unit. Unit beat policing begins with a double assumption: (1) beat patrol is the basis of the British police service, and (2) police organizations have lost the struggle to provide adequate police patrol by conventional means. The concept of unit beat patrol is simple: a team of police will provide police service to a selected area. Each beat would be patrolled by a radio-equipped car manned by one or two officers and supplemented by two area constables and a detective constable.

16. Commission on Law Enforcement, *Task Force Report: The Police*, p. 53.

The essence of unit beat policing is teamwork. The detective constable is responsible for the incidence of crime on the beat, and for giving help and guidance to patrol officers and area constables in the solution of minor crimes. The area constables and the patrol officers are responsible for learning the crime patterns in their assigned area and getting to know the people in it, and helping the detective constable. The basic unit consists of: (1) the car and assigned personnel patrolling the beat 24 hours a day, (2) two area constables patrolling in a manner and time most beneficial to achieving the unit's objectives, and (3) the detective constable.[17]

American adaption of unit beat policing is termed "team" or geographic policing. Unfortunately, many of the team policing experiments in this country do not combine criminal investigation with the patrol function, and the major thrust of team policing is not crime control but the improvement of police relations with citizens in the team's assigned geographic area.

Styles of Policing

A new and interesting concept regarding police organizations is that each police department has a style of policing that can be determined by examining the policies and prevailing practices of a police force. The style of a police organization affords a convenient grouping of police organizations on the basis of the common characteristics of the role performance in these departments.

When police act as if keeping the peace rather than enforcing laws was their particular function, the department has a *watchman's* style. The law is used mainly as a means of maintaining order.

When police react to situations as law enforcers rather than peace officers, comparing observed behavior with the essential elements of a crime and making an arrest if all the essential elements are present, the police style of the organization is *legalistic*. A legalistic police style is usually the result of strenuous efforts by the management of a police organization to get the patrol officers to take the law enforcer's role and to measure community conduct against legal standards.

When the police of a community intervene frequently but not formally, and seriously review all called-for service requests, the police style is *service*. In these communities, the police protect a local definition of law and order against threats by unruly local residents or outsiders.[18]

17. Eric Gregory and Peter Turner, "Unit Beat Policing in England," *The Police Chief*, (July 1968), pp. 42–47.
18. James Q. Wilson,*Varieties of Police Behavior—The Management of Law and Order in Eight Communities* (Cambridge, Mass.: Harvard University Press, 1968), pp. 140–226.

Evaluation and Control of Role Performance

Since the concepts of crime and legal sanctions for violating laws belong to the legal system, police role performance as law enforcers is subject to review by the judiciary rather than by the managers of the police unit. Arrest, the first step in the formal legal prosecution of persons accused of crime, is rightfully subject to judicial review: (1) on the issue of probable cause justifying the police action, (2) on the lawfulness of the gathering of evidence, and (3) on the ultimate issue of guilt or innocence.

However, role performance in this law enforcer role is measurable by management. First, the offenses known to police tabulate the discernible universe of criminal operations. Second, the case clearance data reveals the cases cleared by arrest or other authorized administrative techniques for closing cases (unfounded; offender in prison; no further results possible; etc.). Lastly, the ratio of convictions to arrests indicates the successful prosecution of police cases.

The peace-keeping role of police is highlighted by police action less than an arrest. Therefore, there is no judicial review of police action. There is no criteria of probable cause, lawfulness of evidence gathering, or measure of guilt or innocence. There is no ratio of offenses known to the police and case clearances. Peace officers pretty much act without constraint or external direction. Control is exercised mainly through on-the-job consultation between supervisors and subordinates.[19]

There is a need to measure the peace-keeping role; to evaluate the ability of patrol officers to keep the peace on their post or in their sector. Supervisors and managers in the police organization will have to learn how to evaluate patrol officers on how they function as crisis interventionists in family fights, teenage rumbles, street-corner altercations, and during civil unrest and other disturbances.[20]

Since a significant percentage of the called-for services of any police unit involves family crisis situations, there is a potential for evaluation of role performance in this area. Homicides and serious assaults are more likely to occur in family quarrels than in disputes with strangers, and death and injury to patrol officers responding to family quarrels occur with disturbing frequency. Evaluation of a patrol officer's effectiveness when intervening in family disputes may be based on the total number of family disturbances on his post or in his sector (in some comparison with a control area); the recidivism rate; the recurrence of complaints by the same families; a reduction in the number of homicides and assaults involving family members; and an improved survival rate among police responding to complaints of family trouble.

19. Bittner, "Police on Skid Row," p. 704.
20. Wilson, "Dilemmas of Police Administration," pp. 412–13.

Evaluating the role performance of police officers may also be achieved by a costs-to-benefits analysis. The decision to arrest, or to intervene in any other fashion, is a decision which can be analyzed on the net loss or gain to the suspect, the neighborhood, and the officer himself. The dimensions of this analysis are twofold. Is the situation within the law enforcer or peace officer role? Is the response police-invoked or citizen-invoked?

In police-invoked law enforcement, the officer's action is measurable in the area of initiative and job interest as well as by justification of the action taken. In citizen-invoked law enforcement the officer's conduct is measurable primarily as a report taker.

In police-invoked order maintenance, the police officer's intervention is measurable by the justification for his action and the outcome of the event: was intervention justified, and was order maintained or disorder controlled? In citizen-invoked order maintenance, an assessment can be made of the officer's handling of the complaint and the outcome of his action.

Role conflict is a factor in police behavior that is not uncommon. Therefore, in examining role performance, there is a need to review the conduct of an officer in order to determine whether one or more of the common means of handling role conflict are operating to handicap any effective work performance. These techniques range from compartmentalization, through delegation and extension, to raising barriers against intrusions on the officer's time. An officer can "compartmentalize" his work and hew to his selected role as law enforcer or peace keeper, disregarding the circumstances of an event. In "delegation," a patrol officer rejects and refers to another agency any part of a situation not in harmony with his selected role as law enforcer or peace officer. In "extension," a patrol officer keeps himself busy in one role, law enforcer or peace keeper, and pleads lack of time to fulfill any other role. In discouraging people on his post or sector from inducing citizen-invoked police action, an officer erects "barriers against intrusion." Requests for some services, therefore, are rejected because the request relates to a nonpolice matter.[21]

In the control of police role performance the role of law enforcer lends itself to controls inherent in the legal system and judicial review of police action. In the control of police behavior in the peace officer's role, there is a pressing need for new management measures which will allow evaluation of role performance: is the police intervention warranted and in alignment with the police mission to preserve the public order and insure domestic tranquility?

21. Johnson, "Police: An Analysis of Role Conflict," pp. 51–52.

Selected References

Books

Banton, Michael. *The Policeman in the Community.* New York: Basic Books, 1964.

Browne, Douglas G. *The Rise of Scotland Yard.* London: George G. Harrap & Co., 1956.

Eastman, George D., ed. *Municipal Police Administration.* Washington, D.C.: International City Management Association, 1969.

Kast, Fremont E., and Rosenzweig, James E. *Organization and Management—A Systems Approach.* New York: McGraw-Hill Book Co., 1970.

O'Connor, George W., and Vanderbosch, Charles G. *The Patrol Operation.* Washington, D.C.: International Association of Chiefs of Police, 1965.

Sterling, James W., *Changes in Role Concepts of Police Officers.* Gaithersburg, Md.: International Association of Chiefs of Police, 1972.

U.S., The President's Commission on Law Enforcement and Administration of Justice, *The Police and the Community—The Dynamics of Their Relationship in a Changing Society.* Prepared by Lohman, Joseph D. and Misner, Gordon. Washington, D.C.: Government Printing Office, 1966.

U.S., The President's Commission on Law Enforcement and Administration of Justice, *Task Force Report: The Police.* Washington, D.C.: Government Printing Office, 1967.

Weston, Paul B., and Wells, Kenneth M. *Criminal Investigation: Basic Perspectives,* 2d ed. *Englewood Cliffs, N.J.: Prentice-Hall,* 1973.

Wilson, James Q. *Varieties of Police Behavior—The Management of Law and Order in Eight Communities.* Cambridge, Mass.: Harvard University Press, 1968.

Periodicals

Bard, Morton, and Berkowitz, Bernard. "Training Police as Specialists in Family Crisis Intervention: A Community Psychology Action Program." *Community Mental Health Journal* 3, no. 4 (Winter 1967): 315–17.

Bittner, Egon. "The Police on Skid Row: A Study of Peace Keeping." *American Sociological Review* 32, no 5 (October 1967): 699–715.

Cumming, Elaine; Cumming, I.; and Edell, Laura. "Policeman as Philosopher, Guide and Friend." *Social Problems* 12, no. 3 (Winter 1965): 276–86.

Gregory, Eric, and Turner, Peter. "Unit Beat Policing in England." *Police Chief,* July 1968, pp. 42–47.

Johnson, Elmer H. "Police: An Analysis of Role Conflict." *Police,* January–February 1970, pp. 47–52.

Lyman, J. L. "The Metropolitan Police Act of 1829." *Journal of Criminal Law, Criminology and Police Science* 55 (1964).

Wilson, James Q. "Dilemmas of Police Administration." *Public Administration Review* 28, no. 5 (September–October 1968): 407–17.

Chapter VII

The General Field Force

The general field force of a police department is comprised of a patrol division, a traffic unit, and a youth-services section. The major unit is the patrol division, with the traffic and youth-services units providing staff services and performing specialized work in their areas of traffic and the control of juvenile delinquency and youth crime. The members of a general field force now perform the traditional tasks of a patrol division as well as most of the work performed in the past by specialized traffic and youth-services units.

The problems of traffic congestion and reducing traffic accidents placed increasing demands upon police departments. Patrol divisions were hampered in their primary work because of the transfer of personnel to traffic units. The assignment of greater responsibility for traffic control to the patrol division has been evolutionary and defensive.

The increase in youth crime and juvenile delinquency in the early years of drug abuse by young people led to greater burdens on patrol division officers, and a realization has developed that *all* officers should be trained in the special techniques of police-juvenile contacts and service referrals. In this instance, change was brought about not by the drain of manpower from the patrol division to handle the problem, but rather by the growth of the problem of juvenile delinquency and its on-the-street confrontation by members of the patrol division.

The general field force concept in which all officers are assigned to a patrol division but perform traffic and youth-service duties, as well as general patrol duties, does not include the follow-up work of criminal investigators who handle a case after the patrol force has completed its on-the-scene investigations. This is still the work of the detective division.

The Patrol Division

The police patrol force, always visible in distinctive police uniforms and marked cars and always at or near the area of conflict or where police services are called for, most directly represents to the public the total police performance in crime control and maintaining public order. It is the major unit of police which is on duty 24 hours a day every day.

Activities of a police patrol force are centered on crime-prevention, protection of life and property, and response to calls for police services. Generally, police patrol activity includes:

1. Patrol and observation
2. Duty at public meetings
3. Miscellaneous services
4. Response to calls
5. Investigation
6. Collection and preservation of evidence
7. Apprehending offenders
8. Report preparation
9. Testimony in court.[1]

The prevention aspect of police patrol is based on planned random patrol by uniformed officers on foot, or in plainly-marked automobiles or other vehicles. Police observation while patrolling is enhanced by training and experience. This police expertise has been recognized by the U.S. Supreme Court as a special talent possessed by police allowing them to objectively identify behavior as suspicious and therefore being possible preparation for criminal activity.[2] Inspection by roving police patrols of licensed premises such as bars and pool halls, places where juveniles congregate, and the known resorts of hoodlums and thieves are common to aggressive patrol, as is the field interrogation* of suspicious persons. Inspectional tasks also include visits to places likely to be the targets of criminals.

1. George D. Eastman and Esther M. Eastman, eds., *Municipal Police Administration*, 6th ed. (Washington, D.C.: International City *Management Association*, 1969), p. 78.
2. Terry v. Ohio, 392 U.S. 1 (1968).
* Suspicious persons are stopped and questioned; a police report of a field interrogation stop can be useful to police investigating crimes possibly connected to the presence of the person or persons stopped and questioned, particularly crimes in the area in which the field interrogation was made.

Preventive Police Patrol

Preventive police patrol is a projection of the threat of apprehension inherent in the police *presence*. It is the threat that a policeman or a police vehicle will suddenly appear and inquire into any suspicious activity that justifies the classification of police patrol as a crime-prevention activity. Such preventive patrol by police is unlikely to change the desire, wish, or drive for criminal activity, but it often causes a potential criminal to postpone the actual commission of a crime or displaces the criminal action to another locale. Delay or displacement may lead to total discouragement.

When a potential criminal does not postpone or "move" his criminal activity, the theory and practice of preventive police patrol requires police assigned to this activity to prevent the actual criminal event by detecting the crime or its attempt and arresting the offender.

Of course, many crimes are not postponed or displaced, some criminals are not discouraged by police patrol, and many criminals are not apprehended while their crime is in progress or during flight. However, police vigilance as represented by an "ever-present patrol" has a considerable potential for crime control.[3]

Crime prevention by police patrol is directed at avoidable and observable crimes such as armed robbery, purse-snatch robbery, assaults, auto theft, thievery from parked vehicles, and burglaries detectable because of forced doors, broken glass, or stolen property.

The protection of life and property is a generalized police responsibility. Crime prevention, supplying help to injured crime victims, recovering stolen property, and emphasis on the apprehension and prosecution of violent and dangerous criminals are all police activities which safeguard life and property.

The response aspect of police patrol is concerned with called-for police services: crimes, suspicious events (possible crimes-in-progress), and general police services. Primarily, the crime-control factor of police responding to a crime scene rests in the ability of such police to apprehend the crime's perpetrator while at the scene or in immediate flight from it. For this reason, the likelihood of police apprehending an offender under these circumstances is directly related to the time elapsed since the crime was committed. This elapsed-time element consists of:

1. Time between detection of criminal event and the call to the police

3. Eastman and Eastman, *Municipal Police Administration*, p. 78.

2. Time necessary to process the call in the police communications center

3. Travel time for the responding police officer or officers.[4]

While officers on patrol discover crimes by their observations and inspection, it is the public who usually reports crimes and other events requiring police response to the scene.

In recent years police management has made remarkable progress in reducing the time lag common to processing calls. A common or easily remembered number such as 911, the common emergency number nationally, or 1234, a frequently used local police emergency number, speeds the call initially. A considerable number of police departments have automated their communications complex to lessen the time between receipt of such calls and actual dispatch by radio of police. It is a practice nationally to set up priorities so that some police units are always available for response to emergencies and serious crimes.

Patrol Availability and Mobility

For years the key to police patrol has been *availability* and *mobility*. At one time, the availability of police was limited by the slowness of communications, but two-way radio solved that problem at just about the time that the amount of work to be performed in response to called-for services increased so markedly that many patrol units were unavailable for immediate response. At one time mobility was limited to an officer's foot power or available public transportation or private (commandeered) vehicles; police automobiles and other vehicles now provide patrolling officers with more than adequate mobility. In addition, the assignment of patrol units to segments of the total area of a jurisdiction placed one or more such units in close proximity to crime scenes, measurably reducing travel time when cars on preventive patrol nearby are available to respond to a service call. When the car assigned to the sector in which the called-for service is required is not available, then the call is given to one or more available patrol units in an adjoining sector.

Forecasting the need for called-for services requiring police response is a problem of space and time. The demand fluctuates by areas, time of day, day of week, and season. However, the need for roving patrol units for crime prevention allows police managers to put personnel and vehicles on patrol to make an adequate number of patrol units available

4. U.S., Department of Justice, Law Enforcement Assistance Administration, National Institute of Law Enforcement and Criminal Justice, *Allocation of Resources in the Chicago Police Department*, prepared by the Operations Research Task Force of the Chicago Police Department, (Washington, D.C.: Government Printing Office, 1972), pp. 7–9.

for response duty. In no other way could the availability factor vital to this response duty be held at a reasonable level. Patrol officers and ve- hicles performing preventive patrol are in readiness to respond, and when they have serviced the event they return to their planned random patrol and inspectional work.

Forecasting demands on the patrol force also requires a decision about what blocks of eight hours (there is some experimentation with 10-hour days, but 8 hours is still the basic tour of duty) will comprise the three basic tours of duty, and whether one or more additional shifts are necessary to handle the expected work load. Present practice among police managers is to schedule three shifts along with one peak-load over- lapping shift:

Shift	Tour of Duty
#1—Morning	12:01 A.M. (0001) to 8:00 A.M. (0800)
#2—Day	8:01 A.M. (0801) to 4:00 P.M. (1600)
#3—Evening	4:01 P.M. (1601) to 12 Midnight (2400)
#4—Special	As required

The actual area of each sector on any one shift depends upon the forecast of the need for police services, and this usually varies from shift to shift. It is common knowledge among police managers that at certain times of the day relatively few patrol units are required. Traditionally, the area of each sector on any shift has been expected to reflect relative need. However, more and more police managers are noting the impor- tance of the travel time of police patrol units responding to calls. This has led to a new concept, the "five minute basic sector," in which the area of the sector is set by the travel time of patrol units in responding to calls. As the phrase implies the maximum travel time to any location in the sector under non-rush hour traffic conditions is five minutes.[5] This new concept increases the police effort that can be devoted to preventive patrol, and lessens the strain on patrol units responding to calls, enabling them to ar- rive more promptly.

Kinds of Patrol

At one time officers were stationed in sentrybox booths, or at fixed posts located at important street intersections. These booths and posts manned by uniformed police had a high visibility and the local citizenry knew where policemen could be easily found in case of emergency. The booth was equipped with a telephone to police headquarters. The fixed

5. *Resources in the Chicago Police Department*, pp. 41–43.

post locations usually had a recall signal (light) and a "call-box" telephone to headquarters on a nearby street-light post.

Roving police patrol grew from a belief that police should discover or detect crime rather than wait until a citizen alerted a policeman in a booth or at a fixed post, or headquarters notified the officer of a citizen's need. At first it was patrol at night and by squads of police; then a day patrol was initiated and squad patrol reduced to patrol by a single officer. Early patrol officers were expected to patrol "continuously," covering their entire post each day when they first came on duty and again just before their duty tour was completed.[6]

The objectives of such regulations were to develop careful attention to duty on the part of the patrolman and thus to give the citizens fuller police protection. Traces of these early regulations still exist. A contemporary measure of patrol effectiveness is the theoretical repetition rate at which a police patrol vehicle would, on the average, pass a randomly selected point in the assigned area being patrolled. This patrol cycle time gives the average time span between successive passages of a patrol unit past the randomly chosen location. An observant citizen at such location would see a patrol car, on the average, every "x" number of hours and minutes, with "x" being a factor of average patrol speed, street mileage in the assigned sector, and time the car was "out of service" responding to calls or for other reasons.[7]

Police booths and "booth posts" are still used in American policing. The New York City Police Department's Rules and Regulations contain the following provisions regarding police booths:

Rule and Regulation 1.19. A booth post is a booth to which a member of the force is assigned to observe, receive and answer calls for police duty.

Rule and Regulation 100.0. A patrolman assigned to a booth shall not go more than 20 feet from it except on police duty. At night he shall keep all inside and outside lights properly lighted. Except during inclement weather or as specially directed, he shall remain outside and in such a position that he can observe everything in the vicinity of the booth. He shall not read or write except in the performance of official business and shall send or receive police messages.

The high visibility of uniformed police stationed at a police booth has been used in recent years by builders of single- and multiple-family resi-

6. Leonard Felix Fuld, *Police Administration* (New York: G. P. Putnam's Sons, 1910), p. 116.
7. U.S., Department of Justice, Office of Law Enforcement Assistance, *Reports, Records and Communications in the Boston Police Department: A System Improvement Study,* prepared by the Boston Police Department and Arthur D. Little, Inc., (Washington, D.C.: Government Printing Office, 1968), p. 82.

dences to enhance the security of the residents. This use is associated with walled enclaves, and a police booth and its uniformed private police officer serves as a sort of medieval gatehouse and guard at the only pedestrian or vehicle access road. The fact that residents of these housing developments are willing to assume the costs of such private police protection indicates an awareness of the need for the presence of police.

A foot post was the original patrol post. Its boundaries necessarily delimited a small territory to be patrolled, and the assigned officer was not expected to patrol the interior of buildings. Foot patrol provides the best opportunity for observation within the range of the senses and for a close contact with people and things within an assigned geographical area, enabling the foot patrolman to be of maximum service as an information source and a counselor to the persons residing in the area, with business interests or employed there, or visiting for one reason or another. Because of this interaction between the foot patrolmen and the public served on their posts, these officers have been described as the "eyes and ears of the police department."[8]

Foot patrol was abandoned in post World War I years when criminals became motorized. Flight from a crime scene at 60–70 m.p.h. literally left the foot patrolman flat-footed. Police managers secured funds for automobiles, and police patrol became motorized with a pursuit capability to match the equipment of most criminals. The old police "signal" light and the police "call box" were replaced by radios in the police cars. At first it was a one-way (headquarters to car) system, then it became two-way, and now it is multi-channel three-way communications.

This combination of increased availability and extended mobility of radio-equipped automobiles allowed for a new dimension of police patrol: the sector. Sectors were developed which were five to ten times as large geographically as one average foot post.

The transition from foot to motor patrol was a professional evolution. Motorized patrol was less monotonous and presented greater opportunities for job enlargement and enrichment. The extensive territory assigned to each patrol vehicle and its officer or officers, and the multiplicity of crime-control problems over those common to any one foot post, meant more work for personnel, but it also meant greater job satisfaction. The radio contacts between headquarters and the crew of a patrol vehicle, and with associates in other cars, contributed to this job satisfaction by joining the work of the individual officer or officers in a patrol car with associates in the field and at headquarters. Group effort on a common problem tends to raise the level of employee motivation to work as it develops the belief that above-average job performance will be discovered and recognized.

8. O. W. Wilson and Roy Clinton McLaren, *Police Administration*, 3d ed. (New York: McGraw-Hill Book Co., 1972) p. 334.

To a limited extent foot patrol has made a comeback. It is particularly useful in areas offering many opportunities for criminal operations or in which personal contacts between police and members of the community are important. Foot patrol officers have a greater opportunity to inspect occupancies (properties and places and their use), and to meet and learn the identity of owners and employees and their business routines. Suspicious persons and vehicles are easier to identify when officers are well informed of the usual activity in a neighborhood. The personal contacts common to officers on foot patrol also have an excellent police-community relations value. The mutual understanding that can be developed in these personal interactions give police feedback on the attitudes of local people to the work and problems of police, and afford the members of the community an opportunity to get better acquainted with a police officer, and through him with the goals and problems of law enforcement generally.

In some police agencies there is a joining of foot and motor patrol. In a one-man car assignment, the officer spends part of his tour of duty on foot patrol in a high-risk or high-crime area. In a two-man car assignment, one officer patrols a designated area on foot at specified times. Portable radios or paging devices are used to keep communications open with such officers, and assigned or nearby police vehicles offer them assistance and mobility when necessary.

The Patrolman as Investigator

Another professional change which has also led to new horizons of job satisfaction among police on patrol is the projection of the duties and responsibilities of the first police officer at the scene of a crime to include the preliminary investigation of crimes.

In earlier years the patrol officer or officers responding to the scene of a serious crime were expected to arrest the guilty person or persons if still on the scene at the time of arrival, to "freeze" the scene to protect evidence, to hold all witnesses, and to get and transmit to headquarters sufficient descriptive data about the perpetrator and crime partners, if any, for a radio broadcast alerting other police to the fact of the crime and describing the wanted person or persons and their vehicle, if any. When one or more detectives arrived, the scene would be searched and the witnesses questioned, and the assigned detective would assume responsibility for the remainder of the investigation.

The present-day American practice is to assign the entire preliminary investigation to one or more of the responding patrol officers, with one officer designated as the reporting officer. The work of preliminary investigation concentrates on three of the basic elements of criminal investigation: searching the scene of the crime; collecting, preserving, and transporting physical evidence found at the scene; and locating and interviewing witnesses available at or about the scene. Illustrative of the enlargement of the work of patrol officers are the following duties of an officer conducting a preliminary investigation:

1. Establish whether a crime has been committed; arrest the perpetrator, and determine the type of crime by category, and if possible, by specific classification.

2. In eyewitness cases, secure a description of the perpetrator, his vehicle (if any), and direction of flight; transmit data to the dispatcher for radio broadcasting to other police as an alarm or "want."

3. Locate and interview the victim and witnesses; record stories and take statements, when warranted; secure and accurately record identity, addresses, and other necessary data for future contacts.

4. Protect the crime scene; search for and collect objects and traces that are obviously evidence or likely to be evidence; mark evidence for identification and protect it from change, loss, damage, or contamination; safeguard it to protect its integrity by maintaining control from the time the evidence is found to the moment it becomes an exhibit in the prosecutor's case.

5. Determine how the crime was committed, the extent of personal injuries, and the nature and value of property taken.

6. Record in field notes and sketches all data about the crime, the stories of the various participants and witnesses, the crime-scene search and evidence collected and its disposition, measurements taken at the scene, and other pertinent information; arrange for a photographic summary of the crime scene and major items of evidence, make required reports.[9]

Vehicular Patrol

The automobile is now the standard police patrol vehicle in America. The auto aids in reducing fatigue common to police work; protects the crew from rain, snow, and cold; transports a miscellany of equipment and supplies, as well as prisoners or other persons; provides cover and some protection in armed combat; and provides a pursuit capability for overtaking offenders fleeing in automobiles. The automobile is an indispensable police patrol vehicle.[10]

9. Paul B. Weston and Kenneth M. Wells, *Criminal Investigation: Basic Perspectives*, ed ed. (Englewood Cliffs, N.J.: Prentice-Hall, 1974), pp. 28–29.
10. Eastman and Eastman, *Municipal Police Administration*, pp. 84–85.

Posts can also be patrolled by officers using bicycles; motorcycles (including scooter bikes); horses; boats; helicopters, aircraft designed for short takeoffs and landings; 4-wheel drive vehicles; and snowmobiles.

Using a bicycle has many of the disadvantages of being on foot, but because of its silence and its speed in comparison with a person fleeing on foot there has been some contemporary use of this type of patrol. Also, bicycles are inexpensive.

Motorcycles and scooter bikes have recently been adapted to police patrol purposes. Motorcycles used by traffic personnel have a great capacity to get to accident scenes without loss of time despite traffic congestion. So-called "trail" motorcycles have enhanced this capability to go where automobiles cannot travel and continued research may develop this vehicle as a supplement to police patrol in automobiles. It conserves gasoline, and initial costs and the cost of upkeep is reasonable.

Horses, boats, and helicopters have a high ratio of expense to utility, and for this reason their use is limited. However, special conditions in parks can justify horse patrol; the enforcement of laws regulating the use of boats justifies marine patrol in the general interest of the safety of the many people now engaging in boating and water skiing; and the "eye in the sky" of the helicopter has been proven in recent years to be effective and unique with capabilities unmatched by other patrol vehicles. Short take-off and landing aircraft may prove to have similar advantages and be less costly to operate.

Four-wheel drive vehicles are not much more expensive to purchase and maintain than the basic police car. They can travel across open areas and up crude roads in forests and mountains. Snowmobiles are not expensive items of equipment and earn their cost when police must perform in heavy snow.

Patrol and Public Awareness

Public awareness of police on patrol and the resulting reassurance among members of a community that they are being protected from criminal depredations when the police are seen overtly at work may justify police patrol activity despite the difficulty of measuring the success-failure ratio of crime prevention by patrol units, and the minimal number of apprehensions usually made by police responding to crime scenes. Police patrol as a technique that develops this awareness is a means of enhancing public confidence in police services and securing enriched cooperation from members of the community.

Public awareness of the police presence is difficult to measure as a gain or loss in assessing a police department's drive toward its major objectives. For over ten years the New York City Police Department fielded an elite corps of vigorous and active men called the Midtown

Squad. Their area was in the middle of New York's skyscrapers, centering on Park, Madison, and Fifth Avenues. They worked 9 A.M. to 6 P.M. on weekdays, with an hour for lunch, thus matching the normal working hours of the million or more clerks, stenographers, and other office workers in this area. Members of the squad were identifiable by their MTS insignia, and spit-and-polish appearance. They were assigned to short, straightaway foot posts, and were supervised by "walking" and uniformed sergeants and lieutenants. Squad members spent all of their time on active patrol. They daily aided many persons, such as the ill or those seeking information; arrested robbers, sneak thieves, and purse-snatchers; settled many disputes common in any high-density use area. By their presence they prevented an unmeasurable number of crimes and at the same time reassured the mass of workers that the police were about and working. The squad was abandoned in 1952 because survey analysts could not measure the squad members' activities in units common to police management at that time: arrests and summonses.[11]

The fresh and untrammeled approach of the Midtown Squad to a return to foot patrol warrants careful review, not only for the factor of preventive patrol, but also because the squad members' high visibility and superior appearance added positively to the public awareness of the police and reflected credit upon the police force as a whole.

Continued job enlargement and the innovative use of every form of patrol, supplemented by new scientific devices, can develop well-motivated personnel sincerely discharging their responsibility for preventive patrol as well as their duty to respond to called-for services, and doing so with an increasing visibility is likely to interact beneficially with the public.

The Traffic Control Function

Public clamor over the increasing number of traffic accidents and delays due to traffic congestion caused police officials to field special units to study and reduce accidents, and to control traffic and relieve congestion. While specialized traffic forces did bring the problem under control, the general patrol force divorced itself from traffic law enforcement. As early as 1954 the need to reorient the patrol force to aid in the work of a specialized traffic division was recognized and plans were made to train the general patrol force to assume an increasing share of the burden of traffic control and enforcement.[12]

11. Bruce Smith, *The New York Police Survey* (New York: Institute of Public Administration, 1952), pp. 19–20.
12. Franklin M. Kreml, "The Specialized Traffic Division," *The Annals of the American Academy of Political and Social Science.* (New Goals in Police Management), Volume 291 (January 1954): 63–77.

The basic function of traffic law enforcement—the police activity specifically directed toward controlling traffic violations and accidents through preventive patrol and enforcement, case preparation, and court testimony—includes line patrol (major highways), area patrol, and selective location patrol. The primary purpose of traffic law enforcement is to induce voluntary compliance with reasonable traffic regulations. Warnings, citations, and arrests are the means used to obtain voluntary compliance.[13]

The basic function of traffic accident investigation includes: traffic control at the scene, aid to injured, initial investigation, followup investigation, enforcement action, records, reports, and notifications.

In addition to responsibility for traffic law enforcement and accident investigation, the general field force is partially responsible for the problem of traffic congestion. Traffic engineers and departments of traffic have as their major responsibility the safe and economical movement of pedestrian and vehicular traffic. They erect and maintain traffic signal systems, monitor public parking, and supervise physical changes in the local street and highway system. However, when accidents, weather, or other factors cause traffic congestion, despite the work of the local traffic engineering agency, police are expected to take appropriate action to relieve the congestion.

Traffic law enforcement is meaningful work for all officers on patrol. Every police officer has witnessed the pain and suffering of traffic accident victims, and knows that illegal behavior behind the wheel of a vehicle is often the cause of vehicle accidents.

Accident investigation has the on-the-job satisfaction of successfully reconstructing an accident and preparing a report which is of use to participants in the accident and to analysts seeking from each such report cumulative data as to accident causation. The challenge of traffic accident investigation is in piecing together the available evidence to produce a story of how the accident happened and to identify the participant or participants who caused it.

The emergency aspect of backed-up vehicles and impatient drivers offer police a continuing challenge to move traffic without contributing to delays or secondary accidents. This is a helping function of police traffic control.

Juvenile and Youth Services

The prevention and control of juvenile delinquency is the joint responsibility of youth-services units and the patrol division, with some di-

13. Paul B. Weston, *The Police Traffic Control Function*, 2d ed. (Springfield, Ill.: Charles C. Thomas, Publisher, 1968), p. 57.

vision of duties and responsibilities. Police officials have agreed to all kinds of help programs, even to those concerned with guidance and recreation, but cost-conscious police managers now attempt a dual handling of the problem of juvenile delinquency, charging the patrol force with general responsibility for preventing delinquent behavior and taking appropriate action when delinquency occurs, while assigning to juvenile specialists the specific responsibilities for appropriate action once juveniles have been identified as delinquents.

Police on patrol have the duty to be alert for juvenile misbehavior before it becomes delinquent behavior. For this purpose, they have authority to stop children and warn and admonish them or, if warranted, to take them into custody for non-criminal acts. They also have the authority to take action less than actual physical restraint and custody when a juvenile commits an act which would be criminal if committed by an adult, unless the act done is a serious crime.

Juvenile specialists in police youth divisions are assigned responsibility for developing data on identified predelinquent, delinquent, or neglected children which would be useful in evaluating the youth's problems, life situation, and family resources. They make recommendations to the juvenile's parents or, in serious crime cases or if there is a pattern of continuing delinquency or neglect, to the probation department or juvenile court. The role of the police juvenile specialist is to learn and understand the problems of juveniles and seek out the disposition in each case most likely to be of benefit to the juvenile and the community.

Patrol officers and police juvenile specialists share responsibility for pre-judicial dispositions. The patrol officer's close relations with the neighborhood and associates of a juvenile is qualification for this type of screening, as is the police juvenile specialist's training and knowledge of the capabilities of local agencies working with predelinquent and delinquent youths. While pre-judicial screening by police is an informal dispositional process, it should be based on stated criteria in order that the process can be reviewed by police supervisors.[14]

Auxiliary Services

Communications, records, and transportation are support services vital to the work of the general field force. Identification personnel and techniques generally service and aid in the apprehension of offenders. Management planning, particularly in the area of crime analysis and the forecasting of the time and place of future crimes, aid officers charged

14. U.S., The President's Commission on Law Enforcement and Administration of Justice, Task Force on Juvenile Delinquency, *Task Force Report: Juvenile Delinquency and Youth Crime* (Washington, D.C.: Government Printing Office, 1967), pp. 18–19.

with deploying the patrol force. Lastly, personnel management techniques contribute to the professionalization of the police hierarchy, from operations personnel to executives, by providing the field force with trained and motivated personnel. The job enlargement and enrichment inherent in the field force concept are establishing all these practices among police in America. More and more, police duty in uniform is becoming interesting, meaningful, and significant to its practitioners and the public.

Selected References

Books

Chapman, Samuel G., *Police Patrol Readings*, 2d ed. Springfield, Ill.: Charles C. Thomas, publisher, 1970.

O'Connor, George W., and Vanderbosch, Charles V. *The Patrol Operation*. Washington, D.C.: International Association of Chiefs of Police, 1967.

U.S., National Advisory Commission on Criminal Justice Standards and Goals. *Report on Police*. Washington, D.C.: Government Printing Office, 1973.

U.S., The President's Commission on Law Enforcement and Administration of Justice, Task Force on Juvenile Delinquency. *Task Force Report: Juvenile Delinquency and Youth Crime*. Washington, D.C.: Government Printing Office, 1967.

Weston, Paul B. *The Police Traffic Control Function*, 2d ed. Springfield, Ill.: Charles C. Thomas, Publisher, 1968.

Chapter VIII

Criminal Investigation

Criminal investigation is a major function of police. Uniformed police assigned to limited geographic areas and busy therein with crime prevention and response to called-for services are handicapped in conducting follow-up investigations. Unlike preliminary investigations, whose locale is the crime scene to which uniformed police respond in fulfillment of the patrol function, the area of a continuing investigation can be very extensive. Continuing investigations often extend beyond one tour of duty, and may be kept in an active status for long periods of time.

Personnel assigned to the detective division perform the usual follow-up investigation. Special squads, in coordination with detectives and the general field force, are usually assigned the additional responsibility for the investigation of vice, drugs and narcotics control, and the new role of collecting and using intelligence.

The Detective Division

A few years prior to 1900, Dr. Hans Gross, European magistrate and investigator, and professor of criminology at the University of Prague, declared in his authoritative text, *System Der Kriminalistik*, that the detective should:

1. Be possessed of abundant energy, initiative, ingenuity, vigilance, tact, courage, and have an acquaintance with languages.
2. Be mentally and bodily fit, and possess an encyclopaedic culture: have observed life and undergone many experiences

121

3. Have a devotion to his profession so that he will always be seeking to learn something calculated to extend his knowledge ("Every day he must be picking up something which may be helpful to him in his work.")

4. Be willing to devote himself completely and continually to his work, and where the investigation demands it never pause for rest

5. Have a capacity for recognizing the exact moment in a criminal investigation when a definite opinion can be formed as to how the crime was committed, the motive, and who did it (". . . a definite opinion on an affair as a whole will not come to him all of a sudden; to arrive at it he must advance step by step.").[1]

In 1910 the two fundamental principles for successfully administering the criminal investigation function were (1) a permanent chief of detectives, and (2) tenure for the individual detective contingent on his giving good service.[2] Leadership of the detective division was not viewed as an assignment to be filled by any superior officer with adequate rank, but rather as the job of a superior officer who had made criminal investigation his life work. Conditional tenure allowed officers the time to become acquainted with criminal investigation, but gave superiors in the division the power to send back to patrol duty those individuals unable to meet the standards of satisfactory job performance. Coupled with careful selection of patrol officers, this conditional tenure assured the chief of detectives a reasonable chance at gaining efficient and competent criminal investigators.

These fundamentals of Gross and Fuld have not only survived the intervening years, but have also become the foundation of a professionalized concept of criminal investigation in the United States. Detectives must have the characteristics and perfectionist drive toward problem solving specified by Gross, even though criminal investigation is a highly personal art that varies with the personal makeup of each of its practitioners. A detective division must be organized for leadership and staffing as outlined by Fuld; without such safeguards there is a structural deficiency likely to subvert attempts at excellence. These are the principles, tested by time, which have resulted in the high level of professionalism among police detectives in the United States.

Over the years, the decisions of the United States Supreme Court have also tended to upgrade and professionalize criminal investigation. A

1. John Adam and J. Collyer Adam, *Criminal Investigation*, adapted from the *System Der Kriminalistik* of Dr. Hans Gross, 5th ed., ed. Richard Leofric Jackson (London: Sweet and Maxwell, 1962), pp. 1–5.
2. Leonhard Felix Fuld, *Police Administration* (New York: G. P. Putnam's Sons, 1910), pp. 180–181.

long series of "confession" cases developed court-acceptable rules for custodial interrogation.[3] Supreme Court opinions have specified approved
pretrial investigative conduct in other major areas: in the use of eyewitnesses to identify offenders,[4] in search and seizure,[5] in electronic eavesdropping,[6] and in the employment of informers.[7]

The step from patrolman or patrolwoman to detective is handled
administratively in most police departments, with the officer's qualifications for the work being the controlling factor. Oftentimes, such assignments are alleged to originate in local governmental politics or the internal politics of the police department. The factual reality is that the
superior officers of a detective division responsible for the initial selection
of promising personnel are so conscious of the demands of criminal investigation that applicants whose sole claim to this assignment are based on
political connections are usually rejected quickly but gracefully. This
does not mean that some applicants who have political friendships do not
become detectives, but it is usually because they possess the basic skills
and motivations likely to make them good investigators—and their political affiliations are not of a depth or nature to invalidate such skills and
motivations.

Continuing Investigation

Investigative efforts to arrest perpetrators of crimes are the concern
of the detective division; detectives are specifically responsible for work
on assigned investigations of crimes which have not resulted in the arrest
of the person or persons responsible by the patrol force during or shortly
after the preliminary investigation. They are a follow-up force to the preventive patrol and response-to-calls work of the patrol division. Unless a
crime has dimensions of enough seriousness to warrant detectives participating in the preliminary investigation, the men and women of this division are mainly assigned to continuing investigations.

A continuing investigation picks up a case after the preliminary investigation has been terminated without an arrest; or when an arrest has
been made by members of the patrol division, but there is a need to apprehend crime partners, locate witnesses, or follow other leads to close
out the case. Included in a continuing investigation are:

3. From Brown v. Mississippi, 297 U.S. 278 (1936) to Miranda v. Arizona, 384 U.S. 436
(1966).
4. United States v. Wade, 388 U.S. 218 (1967); Kirby v. Illinois, 406 U.S. 682 (1972);
United States v. Ash, 37 L. Ed. 2d 619 (1973).
5. Mapp v. Ohio, 367 U.S. 643 (1961); Chimel v. California, 395 U.S. 752 (1969); United
States v. Robinson, 38 L. Ed. 2d 427 (1974); Gustafson v. Florida, 38 L. Ed. 2d 456 (1974).
6. Katz v. United States, 389 U.S. 347 (1967).
7. McCray v. Illinois, 386 U.S. 300 (1967).

1. Follow up of the preliminary investigation and the initiation of or the continuation of inquiries

2. Development and revision of a scheme of the crime

3. Analysis of the legal significance of information and evidence

4. Continued search for witnesses, liaison with witnesses interviewed during the preliminary investigation, interviews with new witnesses, and the necessary re-interviews with original witnesses

5. Establishment of liaison with laboratory technicians and access to the reports of their analyses of physical evidence

6. Identification of the perpetrator and accomplices, if any

7. Preparation of wanted notices for the perpetrator and associates, if any

8. Conducting appropriate surveillance, interrogation, and lie detector testing

9. Recommending suspension of the case if an arrest is not made in a reasonable time

10. Preparation of the case and conferences with the prosecutor. [8]

Detectives investigate crime along general lines of inquiry concerned with motive and opportunity: (1) Who "wanted" the crime? (2) Who had the opportunity to commit it? In some cases, *prime suspects* with motive or opportunity, or both, are identified by victims or witnesses; in others, identity must be developed by the result of this two-pronged investigation. [9]

Clues and traces found at a crime scene, modus operandi of the crime, the victim, and other evidence provide detectives with *basic leads* which contributes to the establishing of a group of suspects, and/or the identification of the guilty person once a group of suspects has been developed. Standard basic investigative leads are:

1. Victim (background)

2. Informants

3. Benefit (motive)

4. Knowledge (persons with access to crime scene; knew value of stored property or routine of employees, etc.)

5. Field interrogation reports (stop-and-frisks by patrol officers)

8. Paul B. Weston and Kenneth M. Wells, *Criminal Investigation: Basic Perspectives,* 2d ed. (Englewood Cliffs, N.J.: Prentice-Hall, 1974), p. 31.
9. Brendan P. Battle and Paul B. Weston, *Arson: A Handbook of Detection and Investigation* (New York: Arco Publishing Co. 1960), pp. 137–139.

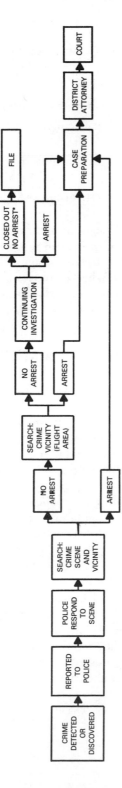

*Under exceptional circumstances: suicide of offender, offender in custody elsewhere, extradition refused, etc.

Figure 2. Place of the Continuing Investigation in the Police Apprehension Process.

6. Motor vehicles

7. Weapons, wounds (in firearm cases, bullets, cartridge cases, etc.)

8. Fingerprints

9. Stolen property (tracing recovered stolen property to thief)

10. Modus operandi (choice of particular crime and *method* of committing it)

11. Photographs of known criminals (shown to eyewitnesses for possible identification)

12. Injured suspects (injury related to crime or flight from scene).[10]

Detectives are given a reasonable amount of time to complete an assignment, but reports of work done must explain temporary setbacks. It is the progress reports of assigned investigators upon which detective division superiors depend for data as to whether to continue an investigation because results are possible, or to suspend it because all possible leads have been investigated without results.

The Control of Vice: Prostitution and Gambling

Crimes connected with prostitution and gambling are different from crimes against persons and property such as homicide and robbery, and burglary and theft; and as a result, the techniques of investigation also differ. Prostitution and gambling are crimes without victims: the willing exchange, among adults, of strongly demanded but legally proscribed goods and services. In crimes with victims police rely on the victim for the discovery of the crime, or someone observing or discovering the crime to report it. In prostitution and gambling the police must investigate in order to discover and expose criminal operations. It is *not* a continuing investigation as it is *not* a follow-up to the offense report (preliminary investigation by patrol division personnel), but an investigation which must discover criminal operations and then secure evidence warranting prosecution.

Public apathy, police attitudes, and the control of prostitution and gambling by organized crime* work against police efforts to enforce laws forbidding prostitution and gambling. While various reform groups surface now and then in a community, they represent an outcry against conditions which should have been suppressed by police long before they peaked and came to public notice, and their effectiveness is usually

10. Weston and Wells, *Criminal Investigation*, pp. 95–120.
* See Chapter XX, Organized Crime.

short-lived. Police attitudes may also account for the short life of reform in the control of prostitution and gambling. Since the people they serve in a community only develop sporadic expressions of morality, it is difficult for many police to view prostitution and gambling as criminal. Knowledge by police that some of the clients of both of these illicit services are substantial citizens locally also fosters this attitude. The local entrepreneurs managing these operations for the national crime syndicate use both the public attitude and the viewpoint of police to overcome police reluctance to accept bribes for allowing prostitution and gambling to exist at levels of business that insure a substantial income for all concerned.

In Chicago, in 1911, the only public pressure on police in regard to prostitution was to prohibit soliciting from doors and windows of houses of prostitution, and to prohibit such houses along street car lines. An early crime commission report noted: "The vice itself is bad enough without being flaunted in the faces of thousands of decent and law-abiding men and women who are compelled to daily patronize the car lines on the streets where these places have existed."[11]

In 1973, a report of a crime commission in New York stated that police activity against prostitution was responsive to public pressure but that it only resulted in periodic "clean-ups" of one area or another; that neither public pressure nor police response had the objective of arresting and prosecuting those who ran such operations. Visible objectives were only to move the more obvious brothels, "massage" parlors, prostitute bars and the highly-visible street-walkers to other areas until the public hue and cry diminished. "It is clear," this report states, "that current police practices have had little effect on curtailing illegal prostitution. Prostitutes operate openly and are likely to continue to do so."[12]

The survival of gambling as a profitable underworld source of income no doubt spans the same number of years as the survival of prostitution, and for similar reasons. Public and police officers view such illegal operations as unlawful but socially acceptable.

As in prostitution, conspicuousness is a major element in whether laws forbidding commercialized gambling are enforced. Gambling operations extend from illegal casinos offering several games of chance, to "floating" dice and card games operating "sub-rosa" and moving to different places every few days or weeks, and to book-making—accepting bets on horses and sports events.

11. Chicago Civil Service Commission, *Final Report: Police Investigation—1910 to 1912* (1912; reprinted in *Police in America* New York: Arno Press and the *New York Times*, 1971) pp. 16–17.
12. The Committee to Investigate Alleged Police Corruption (Knapp Commission after its chairman Whitman Knapp), *The Knapp Commission Report on Police Corruption* (New York: George Braziller, 1973), pp. 116–122.

The foregoing crime commission reports note the following about gambling and bribery of members of the local police:

1. *Chicago.* The commission feels that it has fully proved that a criminal conspiracy existed between certain commanding officers of the police department and certain gamblers operating and attempting to operate within the city limits, and is satisfied that money has been paid by these gamblers to secure protection for illegal games of chance.[13]

2. *New York.* The collection of tribute by police from gamblers has traditionally been well organized and has persisted unchanged for years despite periodic scandals, departmental reorganizations, massive transfers in and out of the units involved, and the folding of some gambling operations and the establishment of new ones.[14]

In addition to prostitution and gambling, vice operations include:

1. Manufacture and sale of untaxed alcohol (bootlegging)
2. Pornography and obscenity.

Unlike prostitution and gambling, these related activities have been viewed with some hostility by public and police. Untaxed alcohol has killed and blinded many people; the explicitness of contemporary pornography and obscene plays and motion pictures has been resented by many members of the community. However, underworld operators attempt to diminish police activity in these areas with the same offers of bribery as are made on behalf of prostitution and gambling. The rationale of the bribe solicitor is that the only victim of bootlegging is the government (taxes), and that sex crimes are reduced by "porno" and x-rated movies.

Local police executives are knowledgeable about public apathy toward vice conditions. There is even pressure from some members of the business community to "open up" and attract visitors to the community. The police executives are cognizant of the existence of certain tolerant attitudes toward vice among police generally, and the means used to exploit these attitudes by the bribe-offering minions of organized crime; but they are usually keenly aware that vice operations are devoid of social utility, exploit human weaknesses, and can be directly linked to more serious crimes:

1. Robberies and related assaults and felony murders by vice customers, prostitutes, and participants in card, dice, and other gambling games

13. *Chicago Police Investigation*, p. 9.
14. *Knapp Commission Report*, p. 71.

2. Assaults and murders to enforce the underworld's code of silence (police informers), and to discipline criminal syndicate members

3. "Rip-offs": victimization of customers by theft, blackmail, extortion, cheating and what may be described as consumer fraud

4. Corruption of public officials

5. Violations of state regulations controlling the operations of premises licensed for on-premises sale of alcoholic beverages.

Police officials are also aware that public opinion has not turned away from the belief that vice is fundamentally evil. The failure of other states to follow Nevada's example in legalizing gambling is illustrative, as is the slow progress of legalizing off-track betting systems.[15]

For these reasons enforcement policy must articulate the objectives and responsibility of police in controlling local vice operations, and establish a framework for enforcement activities along dual lines:

1. Enforcement by patrol division

2. Comprehensive investigation and enforcement by full-time specialists in this area of investigation.

Uniformed patrol officers can deter open and notorious vice operations, and can suppress such activity when it surfaces in their presence through a report of their observations or a summary arrest, if warranted. Full-time investigators can follow up on reports of the patrol force, complaints from citizens, or undercover investigations. The aim of patrol force action is to harass; the goal of investigators is to develop cases against the leadership of vice operations locally, those who profit the most from these illegal operations, rather than the prostitutes and other operational personnel

While the control of vice can be the responsibility of the detective division, its crime-without-a-victim classification, the close connection of this illicit traffic with organized crime, and the need for special investigative techniques other than those of the standard continuing investigation suggest the assignment of this responsibility to a special squad or division. This is in addition to allocating to the patrol force a partial share of the responsibility for enforcing the laws regarding prostitution and gambling, bootlegging, pornography, and obscenity.

Recurring scandals have been common among so-called vice squads. Chiefs of police have been terminated—sometimes with prejudice—because of the corrupt practices of these squads. It is still a prevailing practice to group this work of vice control and assign it to a special squad,

---

15. Rufus King, *Gambling and Organized Crime* (Washington, D.C.: Public Affairs Press, 1969), pp. 11–12.

but police executives have established various measures of control in an attempt to insure the integrity of the work performed. First, the term "vice squad" has gone into disuse, primarily because it seemed to forecast the corrupt behavior of squad personnel. Secondly, assignments to this work are carefully considered: background and continuing net worth investigations are common; control by reporting procedures have been standardized to account for all of the activity and on-the-job time of personnel; short assignments to this work rather than lengthy periods of duty reduce the environmental hazards of working with whores, pimps, and the gambling fraternity; and personnel on the career ladder have been utilized rather than rank and file officers in the belief that pending promotion to supervisor or assignment to the detective division may lessen an officer's susceptibility to being corrupted. Lastly, police executives place the squad responsible for vice control under their personal command or directly responsible to the chief of detectives, to avoid any insulation which would result in a loss of executive control.

The Control of the Illegal Traffic in Drugs and Narcotics

Every police department is confronted with violations of law regarding the possession and sale of dangerous drugs and narcotics. It is no longer a problem of control by detectives or special squads. Officers on patrol are daily taking action on the drug "scene," enforcing laws, reporting suspicious activity, or helping drug abusers who are victims of drug withdrawal or overdose.

Narcotic and drug investigations also encounter problems common to vice control. Drug abuse is classed as a crime without a victim (not that drug abusers are not victims of their own addiction, but because drug abusers do not report the event of a crime as do other victims of crime), and it is an area of investigation requiring techniques different from the follow-up techniques of detectives investigating property crimes and crimes against the person. Undercover agents, purchases of drugs and narcotics, and the utilization of search warrants as a primary investigative tool are common to drug and narcotic investigations. In addition, the clear indication that organized crime is heavily involved in drug-selling aligns enforcement with vice control rather than with the detective's investigation of crimes by individuals or small local groups.

Intelligence Operations

For many years police officials were satisfied with the patrol force as a source of information about crime and criminals. Posts and sectors are sources of reportable information. In criminal investigation, detectives have long cultivated bartenders, waitresses, cab drivers, and other "night people" as sources, and have labored hard to "turn" some criminals into informants reporting on the activity of friends and associates.

Originally what is now termed intelligence collection began with frustrations attendant on homicide investigations of gangland killings. Police followed out the standard basic leads but ended up against a blank wall. No one cooperated in revealing data, and the actual killers could not be linked to the murder by standard inquiries as to who had a motive for the murder or who had been present at the crime scene.

Covert physical surveillance of the movements of suspected persons was one of the initial means used to discover associates of suspects, places they visited, and their general patterns of association and activity. Because of the limitations of visual surveillance, wire-tapping and other forms of electronic surveillance such as hidden microphones and recording devices were used to gather information. Legal restrictions on electronic surveillance led to attempts to develop informants, but the difficulty of turning a trusted member of the underworld into an informant led to the use of undercover agents. However, infiltration of any criminal operation or syndicate normally requires newcomers to exhibit their criminality by participating in a serious felony such as armed robbery or murder. It is almost impossible to get an undercover police agent into the hierarchy of a major criminal group.[16]

Despite these handicaps many gangland homicides were solved by "intelligence" leading to conclusive evidence of guilt on the part of one or more of the killer team, and prosecutors developed these lower-level thugs into accomplice-witnesses against the gangland bosses who ordered the killings.[17] However, thoughtful police officials realized that the collection of data should be on a continuing basis, rather than being a post-murder activity. When a gangland killing did occur, police could then promptly trace back through the victim's associational and activity patterns the persons likely to have both motive and opportunity to commit the murder.

Intelligence should be organized as a staff unit separate from actual police enforcement. In smaller agencies the intelligence specialist should be required to take direct enforcement action only where limited agency resources make it absolutely necessary. In larger agencies such action should be taken only where a serious threat to life or property makes it absolutely necessary.

16. Technical Assistance Division, Office of Criminal Justice Assistance, Law Enforcement Assistance Administration, *Basic Elements of Intelligence*, prepared by E. Drexel Godfrey and Don R. Harris (Washington, D.C.: Government Printing Office, 1971), p. 21.
17. Burton B. Turkus and Sid Feder, *Murder, Inc.*, (New York: Farrar, Straus & Giroux, 1951), pp. 61–73.

Selected References

Books

Fitzgerald, Maurice J. *Handbook of Criminal Investigation.* New York: Arco Publishing Co., 1956.

Weston, Paul B. and Wells, Kenneth M. *Criminal Investigation: Basic Perspectives*, 2d ed. Englewood Cliffs, N.J.: Prentice-Hall, 1973.

Cases

Katz v. United States, 389 U.S. 347 (1967).

McCray v. Illinois, 386 U.S. 300 (1967).

Chapter IX

Crime Prevention

The public's fear of crime is by far the greatest single problem confronting American police systems. Police efforts to convince people that fear of crime is more harmful than crime itself has had little impact. One can see why people feel this way even if sometimes it is exaggerated. The actual incidence of crime across the nation has reached levels where a substantial percentage of the population have either been victims of crime or have personally known persons who have been crime victims.

The frequent generalization that crime in the streets is prevalent and violent leads to demands that police should work to make the public streets safe corridors to and from residences. This concept of the home as a haven, one of the few places secure from crime, lowers the barriers to criminal activity. As people withdraw, neighbors are isolated from neighbors leaving the criminal freer to act. The social mechanisms and interdependencies which reduce the danger and incidence of crime are falling into disuse.

A frightening aspect of this fear of crime, insofar as it affects achieving the mission and goals of police generally, is the abandonment of the responsibility of being a resident of a community, a householder, a parent, or a spouse, and as such, actively participating in the battle against crime. There is not only a general mistrust of strangers, but there is a fear of retaliation from criminals that is apparent in the public failure to intercede while a crime is in progress or even to inform the police. As the possibility of mutual help among the law-abiding diminishes, the opportunity for criminals to operate without interference increases.

Police administrators are responsible for providing police services that prevent crime and control crime that has not been prevented. Effective police management must seek ways to lessen the insulation between

133

the police and the community, and to involve both in the planning and implementing of new policies and procedures.

✗ Team or Geographic Policing

Team or *geographic policing* is innovative in that it is likely to develop among working patrol officers and investigators a consumer-oriented philosophy of police services. Among involved citizens, it leads to a greater recognition and understanding of the police posture in regard to community pressures and professional law enforcement.

Police must also participate in "corrective" and "mechanical" crime prevention as well as the traditional use of "punitive" prevention. These processes range from eliminating the causes of criminal behavior to "hardening the target," making crime more difficult or less profitable. In addition, police must cooperate with the private police forces that guard against crime at no out-of-pocket cost to taxpayers.

Team or geographic policing can be defined as: (1) combining all line operations of patrol and investigation into a single group under common supervision; (2) forming teams with a mixture of generalists and specialists; (3) permantly assigning the teams to geographic areas; and (4) charging the teams with responsibility for all police services within their respective areas.

This type of policing builds on the unit beat policing approach to lessen the growing isolation of police from the community which has risen from the difference in attitudes between police and public over the dimensions of the local crime problem and the best techniques of crime control.

The working police officer is placed in an environment that encourages cooperation with the public and thus reduces isolation. Team or geographic policing enables individual officers to cultivate community support and build personal relationships. A key premise of this innovative policing is that the public, when informed of the team policing objectives and goals, will respond to and assist police, particularly if solicited actively. When local residents participate in the planning stages, commitment can be encouraged by seeking the opinions, ideas, and assistance of citizens in resolving problems of mutual concern.

Officers assigned to geographic policing programs are responsible for the control of crime within their area. The resulting feeling of accountability for the crime rate makes officers more concerned with crimes happening in their assigned area, and it should develop men and women who will initiate effective action to cope with the neighborhood's police problems.[1]

1. U.S. National Advisory Commission on Criminal Justice Standards and Goals, *Report on Police* (Washington, D.C.: Government Printing Office, 1973), p. 63.

When police within an assigned area necessarily join with local residents in a common cause of crime and delinquency prevention and reduction there are bound to be improved interrelationships. When team members meet and discuss crime problems of the area with its residents and merchants, there develops an understanding of each other's problems. Crime and delinquency is a social problem. Any prevention or reduction program by police must be supported by the people of a community.

Team policing has been viewed by some as a return to a bygone age of police work typified by the foot patrolman. A better viewpoint is that this is a police style devoted to major police objectives, which also services public complaints, helps citizens, establishes good public relations locally, and builds new horizons of crime prevention into policing.

Punitive Crime Prevention

Preventive patrol by the police general field force, prompt response by police on patrol to crime scenes, and the followup investigation of those cases in which responding police do not arrest offenders at, or in flight from, crime scenes may forestall crime by highlighting the omnipresence of police and thus a probability of apprehension. *Punitive* prevention is the threat of punishment accompanying police apprehension of offenders, the trial and conviction of offenders which leads to the stigma of criminality, and the threat of actual imprisonment.

Mandatory prison sentences, rather than release on probation at judicial discretion, and a specified minimum period in prison before parole eligibility can be established, are two techniques of law-makers to increase fear in potential offenders. "Tough" laws which specify lengthy terms of imprisonment are an attempt to guard against so-called "soft" treatment by the judiciary or parole personnel. Lengthy periods of parole supervision for recidivists, even lifetime parole, has also surfaced as an attempt to control repeating criminals by toughening the penalties associated with arrest and conviction.

There is some doubt about the effectiveness of this attempt to induce fear since all criminals are not rational analysts who evaluate their risk-taking behavior. If the fear of apprehension-punishment is to have much crime prevention value the police must increase the certainty of arrest. But certainty of arrest is not enough.

Police must also make every effort to increase the certainty of conviction upon trial by use of contemporary methods of collecting and examining physical evidence. To these must be added the professional techniques of interrogating suspects and interviewing witnesses. While police have traditionally refrained from any action to influence judicial discretion in imposing sentences on a convicted defendant, police attitudes regarding certain classes of offenders have been made known to legislators. These attitudes have been influential in the legislative limiting of judicial discretion by such means as setting mandatory terms of imprisonment and restricting the early release options available to parole personnel. The fear of arrest alone is meaningless to most offenders, unless it is supported by the real likelihood of conviction upon trial and the probability of imprisonment after sentencing. Police action as crime prevention must have a punitive capability if it is to deter or prevent crime.

Corrective Crime and Delinquency Prevention

The basic responsibility for developing good habits, character, and social responsibility among members of a community rest on the cultural institutions of church, family, and schools. The purpose of social control is to develop a commonality of behavior that is acceptable to the community generally. Social control by the institutions of a community fails when an unusual percentage of local citizens engage in anti-social behavior.

There is no doubt that blocked success goals among ghetto youths have led to drug abuse, and the need for money to buy drugs leads to crime.[2] The concept is not the simple one that poverty leads to crime; it is that drug abuse may result from the fact that legitimate routes to success (quality education, supportive family resources, social acceptance) are blocked to youths whose family roots are in poverty-stricken areas such as the low-rent slum ghettos where black or Spanish-speaking residents predominate.

An innovative extension of police action to the field of "corrective" prevention of crime and delinquency is the program known as Treatment Alternative to Street Crime (TASC). This is a program for the diversion of drug-using offenders, juvenile or adult, from the criminal justice process. It is aimed at the link between drug addiction and criminal behavior. It is a program which involves the addict-arrestee's referral to a community treatment center in lieu of further processing by criminal justice agencies.

Although it is difficult to prove, there is a general consensus among police officials that 50 to 60 percent of so-called street crimes and burglaries are caused by drug dependence and the need for funds to buy drugs. While many police are cynical about the long-term effectiveness of any drug treatment program, they are aware that prison-as-treatment is ineffective. The traditional process of imprisoning drug-dependent criminals does little more than postpone further criminal activities until the of-

2. Paul B. Weston and Hon. Robert W. Cole, *Case Studies of Drug Abuse and Criminal Behavior* (Pacific Palisades, Calif.: Goodyear Publishing Company, 1973),pp. 1–28.

fender is released, when he must cope with the same problems that originally led to his drug abuse and criminal behavior.

Police participation consists in identifying those arrestees who are dependent on the "hard" drugs and offering them the opportunity of treatment after such identification. This implies more than the identification by defense counsel of a client against whom a criminal case is pending (or has been successfully prosecuted). It is a probing by police into the circumstances of many arrests, particularly arrests for the violent crimes of murder and nonnegligent manslaughter, aggravated assault, rape, and robbery; and the property crimes of burglary and theft. It is a search, within constitutional limitations, for persons who are dependent on narcotics and dangerous drugs. Its potential crime prevention value also suggests that police should encourage the cooperation of persons found to be drug-dependent at the time of arrest.

TASC involves police in arranging for urinalysis and physical examination, and in interviews with persons arrested, for the positive identification of drug dependent persons. During these interviews the advantages of diversion to a treatment program are likely to be discussed, and there is a possibility the arrested person will admit to extensive drug abuse. As a result, there is a need to insure that these interviews will not be used to gain evidence of any crime against the defendant for use in any prosecution for crime. Ethical and constitutional requirements demand no less.

The same concept of blocked success goals relates to crimes originating in the circumstances of a person's life style. Persons confronted with the reality that legitimate routes to success are closed to them will engage in criminal behavior to achieve financial success, or to act out emotional needs for excitement, danger, or self-destruction. The assumption made is that crime is the result of causative factors arising from low income, restricted social mobility, and adverse psychological influences.

Police organizations under the contemporary thrust of management by objectives, and funded under budgets limiting the expenditure of funds to programs aligned closely with stated police objectives, cannot become a social welfare or treatment-centered agency. On the other hand, police have traditionally exhibited a kinship for the poor and others needing help in a community. At the turn of the century, New York City's police stations were the only haven for a night's rest available to the city's indigent population.

For many years, police officials have stimulated community service agencies to extend their corrective crime and delinquency prevention activities to reach the disadvantaged segments of the local population who are the victims of poverty, substandard education, and lack of employment opportunities. Illustrative of this extension of the police role has been the police management of many programs to help young people, particularly in finding juveniles summer jobs, and in providing recreational activities. Some years ago, the police management of recreational programs for disadvantaged young people was severely criticized by management experts and civic leaders, yet the police were only performing a service which they believed should have been provided—as corrective delinquency and crime prevention—by other community agencies, but which had been ignored or neglected by such agencies.

Mechanical Crime Prevention

Often termed hardening the target*, mechanical crime and delinquency prevention is the process of reducing the potential gain or profit from a crime, or placing obstacles in the path of criminals intent on crime. It may only displace crimes, causing criminals to seek out more profitable or less risky victims in other areas, but it has excellent potential to prevent and reduce crime.

Mechanical prevention is the most immediate and positive method of prevention available to police. Typical means include:

1. Security guards, doormen, and tenant or citizen patrol
2. "No cash," "exact change" routines; intrusion-resistant safes with keys restricted to armored-car personnel
3. Mechanical and electronic devices: locks, fences, window guards; and alarms, and electronic sensors to detect intruders
4. Surveillance cameras to monitor target areas and record crimes in progress or suspicious persons
5. Dyes, chemicals, and visual markings to identify cash and other property which may be taken in the course of a robbery or theft.

Police accept security guards and doormen as semi-professionals in the business of guarding against intruders, but patrols by citizens, whether tenants of a building or residents of a neighborhood, have not received full police approval. The presence of these citizen patrols in and about buildings or patrolling the streets of a neighborhood tends, at the least, to displace crime, and may even discourage some offenders. In time, it may be accepted by police as a valid means of preventing and reducing crime and delinquency.

There are money-handling techniques that are aimed at establishing

*See "Victim Distribution: Hardening the Target," in Chapter II, Crime: The Offender-Victim Relationship.

conditions which discourage the commission of a crime by lessening the potential gain of a criminal act. Gas stations open at night may only accept credit cards or the correct amount in cash, and such cash receipts are likely to be deposited in an intrusion-resistant safe complete with signs that the service station attendant does not have the key, only armored-car register device can also be intrusion-proof. Cab drivers no longer carry change for large bills, and they may be protected from robbery attempts by intrusion-proof barriers between the driver's compartment and the passenger area.

There are other devices which increase the risks of apprehension at the crime scene. There are silent alarms, triggered by either burglars or robbery victims, which speed police to the scene while the crime is in progress. Television cameras monitor a segment of a public thoroughfare or the interior of a building and discover intruders and prowlers, thus allowing the response of private police, security guards, or the local patrol force of police.

Cameras in banks, liquor stores, and other targets of robbers not only aid in the apprehension of offenders, but also offer the police and prosecutor excellent evidence of the identity of the criminal. So-called "bait money" also has this potential: it is easily identifiable currency (serial numbers or markings) which is given to robbers upon demand, and which—if recovered by police in the possession of suspects—can be used to connect up the suspect or suspects with the commission of the crime. Dyes and fluorescent powders also identify suspects who have been in contact with stolen property or the place from which the property was taken.

In mechanical crime and delinquency prevention there is the potential for police to study persons and places that are victims of criminals so as to determine what obstacles are most likely to be effective in preventing such crimes.

The extension of defended space[3] can lead to the denial of the opportunity to commit a crime. A number of cities have passed local laws that require minimum security devices to prevent burglaries in commercial and business premises. These local laws, which are generally made a part of the local building code, authorize the police to enforce their provisions through timely inspections. Officers investigating a commercial or business burglary are required to file a report as to the method of attack upon the victim's premises, and in most of these cities the victim is required to add whatever physical security measures are necessary to prevent a recurrence of the same type of criminal intrusion.

3. *See* Oscar Newman, *Architectural Design for Crime Prevention* (Washington, D.C.: Government Printing Office, 1973), Chapter 3, "Defensible Space Hypotheses."

Private Police

Private security services provided by adequately equipped high quality personnel complement the public police by providing services where public police are not given adequate resources or where they are legally restrained. The term private police is generally applied to agents and agencies with a responsibility to protect life and property and prevent crime in a designated area.

Contract security agencies operate on a fee basis; in-house forces are not for outside hire as they provide services exclusively for their employer. A wide variety of consumers use such services: retail establishments, banks, insurance companies, hospitals, industrial firms, educational institutions (school and campus police), apartment houses, residential housing developments, and individuals.

Contract or in-house security agencies may provide one or more of the following services:

1. Guard
2. Patrol (foot and motor)
3. Armored-car escort
4. Central station alarm (wired premises)
5. Investigation (credit, insurance, preemployment background, pretrial for civil or criminal cases).[4]

The rising crime rate, property losses, and fear of crime have all contributed to the growth of the private police security industry. Security measures are also related to insurance. Increased rates or the threat of refusing coverage encourages business and commercial organizations to use private police as well as strengthening physical security of occupancies.

There is a great crime and delinquency prevention potential in the acts of private police. They can and do prevent, detect, and report criminal acts on private property; they provide security against loss from shoplifting, pilferage, dishonest employees and theft.

Selected References

Books

Kakalik, James S. and Wildhorn, Sorrel. *Private Police in the United States: Findings and Recommendations.* vol. 1: R-869/DOJ Santa Monica, Calif.: The Rand Corporation, 1971.

---

4. James S. Kakalik and Sorrel Wildhorn, *Private Police in the United States: Findings and Recommendations*, vol. 1: R-869/DOJ (Santa Monica, Calif.: The Rand Corporation, 1971),

Newman, Oscar. *Architectural Design for Crime Prevention*. Washington, D.C.: Government Printing Office, 1973.

U.S., National Advisory Commission on Criminal Justice Standards and Goals. *A National Strategy to Reduce Crime*. Washington, D.C.: Government Printing Office, 1973.

―――. *Community Crime Prevention*. Washington, D.C.: Government Printing Office, 1973.

Part III
Individual Rights

Chapter X

Individual Rights vs. State Power

The Constitution of the United States and its amendments serve as a buffer in the conflict between the political sovereign and the individual citizen: the conflict between order and liberty. The Constitution is the basic law of our country, and it contains guidelines delineating the rights of citizens and the limits of state power.

The Constitution should be judged by its survival as the supreme law of the land.[1] It foreshadowed a progressive form of government at a time when the democratic ideal was as yet little developed, and it has served as a framework for a democratic national government in the twentieth century. This document of 1787 now functions in a populous nation, with an urban-industrial environment and economy. The value of this written Constitution lies in the way it stabilizes a government in which frequent popular elections peacefully oust one set of officials and select their successors.

In its provision for judicial review, the Constitution places limitations on both legislative and executive action. A document such as the Constitution is nothing but empty words if it cannot be enforced by court action. The people of the United States enacted a written Constitution in which the theme is limitations on government power. Determination of the constitutionality of laws and government action is the essential ele-

---

1. U.S., *Constitution*, Art VI, Clause 2. This Constitution, and the Laws of the United States which shall be made in Pursuance thereof; and all Treaties made, or which shall be made, under the Authority of the United States, shall be the supreme Law of the Land; and the Judges in every State shall be bound thereby; any Thing in the Constitution or Laws of any State to the Contrary notwithstanding.

145

ment of judicial power under our Constitution. The doctrine of the supremacy of law dominated the thinking of the founders of the new nation, and this dominance probably accounts for the failure to specifically spell out the concept of judicial review in the Constitution. At that time, judicial review was the essence of government of laws and not of men, and was part of the legal tradition.[2] Judicial power, vested in a Supreme Court with tenure and salary protection which would insure an independent judiciary, was spelled out in Article II, Section 1, of the Constitution:

> The judicial Power of the United States, shall be vested in one supreme Court, and in such inferior Courts as the Congress may from time to time ordain and establish. The Judges, both of the supreme and inferior Courts, shall hold their Offices during good Behaviour, and shall, at stated Times, receive for their Services, a Compensation, which shall not be diminished during their Continuance in Office.

The unamended Constitution provided for judicial review, and an adequate and speedy legal remedy in cases of illegal imprisonment by providing that the writ of habeas corpus should not be suspended except for public safety in time of war or rebellion.[3]

However, the document lacked a "bill of rights" for its citizens. This listing of the rights of an individual was delayed by the amending procedure[4] until 1791.

The absence of a bill of rights was justified initially because: (1) the new government was one of specific and enumerated powers and possessed no authority except in those spheres where it had received a grant of power; (2) an enumeration of the rights of the people as against the new government was by implication restrictive; and (3) in any attempt to enumerate the rights of the people, the enumeration must be complete, because everything not expressly mentioned will be presumed to be purposely omitted.[5] Criticism of the absence of a bill of rights led to

2. Bernard Schwartz, *A Commentary on the Constitution of the United States, Part I: The Powers of Government* (New York: Macmillan Publishing Co., 1963), pp. 17–23.
3. U.S., *Constitution*, Art. I, sec. 9, Clause 2: The Privilege of the Writ of Habeas Corpus shall not be suspended, unless when in Cases of Rebellion or Invasion the public Safety may require it.
4. U.S., *Constitution*, Art. V: The Congress, whenever two thirds of both Houses shall deem it necessary, shall propose Amendments to this Constitution, or, on the Application of the Legislatures of two thirds of the several States, shall call a Convention for proposing Amendments, which, in either Case, shall be valid to all Intents and Purposes, as Part of this Constitution, when ratified by the Legislatures of three fourths of the several States, or by Conventions in three fourths thereof, as the one or the other Mode of Ratification may be proposed by the Congress; Provided that no Amendment which may be made prior to the Year One thousand eight hundred and eight shall in any Manner affect the first and fourth Clauses in the Ninth Section of the first Article; and that no State, without its Consent, shall be deprived of its equal Suffrage in the Senate.
5. Alfred H. Kelly and Winfred A. Harbison, *The American Constitution*, 3d ed. (New York: W. W. Norton & Company, 1963), pp. 152–53.

a drive for the adoption of such legislation by amendment once the new government set up business.

The Bill of Rights

The first ten amendments to the Constitution are known as *The Bill of Rights*. They were proposed by Congress and ratified by the legislatures of the states in accordance with Article V of the original Constitution. The provisions of these ten amendments went into effect on December 15, 1791. They are as follows:

I. Congress shall make no law respecting an establishment of religion, or prohibiting the free exercise thereof; or abridging the freedom of speech, or of the press; or the right of the people peaceably to assemble, and to petition the Government for a redress of grievances.

II. A well regulated Militia, being necessary to the security of a free State, the right of the people to keep and bear Arms, shall not be infringed.

III. No Soldier shall, in time of peace be quartered in any house, without the consent of the Owner, nor in time of war, but in a manner to be prescribed by law.

IV. The right of the people to be secure in their persons, houses, papers, and effects, against unreasonable searches and seizures, shall not be violated, and no Warrants shall issue, but upon probably cause, supported by Oath or affirmation, and particularly describing the place to be searched, and the persons or things to be seized.

V. No person shall be held to answer for a capital, or otherwise infamous crime, unless on a presentment or indictment of a Grand Jury, except in cases arising in the land or naval forces, or in the Militia, when in actual service in time of War or public danger; nor shall any person be subject for the same offence to be twice put in jeopardy of life or limb; nor shall be compelled in any criminal case to be a witness against himself, nor be deprived of life, liberty, or property, without due process of law; nor shall private property be taken for public use, without just compensation.

VI. In all criminal prosecutions, the accused shall enjoy the right to a speedy and public trial, by an impartial jury of the State and district wherein the crime shall have been committed, which district shall have been previously ascertained by law, and to be informed of the nature and cause of the accusation; to be confronted with the witnesses against him; to have compulsory process for obtaining witnesses in his favor, and to have the Assistance of Counsel for his defense.

VII. In Suits at common law, where the value in controversy shall exceed twenty dollars, the right of trial by jury shall be preserved, and no fact tried by a jury, shall be otherwise re-examined in any Court of the United States, than according to the rules of the common law.

VIII. Excessive bail shall not be required, nor excessive fines imposed, nor cruel and unusual punishments inflicted.

IX. The enumeration in the Constitution of certain rights, shall not be construed to deny or disparage others retained by the people.

X. The powers not delegated to the United States by the Constitution, nor prohibited by it to the States, are reserved to the States respectively, or to the people.

In tracing the history of these amendments to our Constitution there is a direct relationship to the English "Bill of Rights." In 1215, the Magna Charta was signed by King John of England. This document was a written agreement in which the sovereign granted to the people certain rights. Later, after James II fled England in early 1689, the English Parliament offered the crown conditionally to William and Mary. The condition was that the new rulers accept a declaration of the rights of the people. It was so agreed and the English Bill of Rights of 1689 became a written compact between rulers and subjects.

This compact is reported in full to permit comparison with the content of the first ten amendments to the U.S. Constitution. It reads:

1. That the pretended Power of Suspending of Laws, or the Execution of Laws, by Regall Authority, without Consent of Parlyament is illegall.

2. That the pretended Power of Dispensing with Laws, or the Execution of Laws, by Regall Authoritie, as it hath beene assumed and exercised of late, is illegall.

3. That the Commission for erecting the late Court of Commissioners for Ecclesiasticall Causes, and all other Commissions and Courts of like nature, are illegall and pernicious.

4. That levying Money for or to the Use of the Crowne by pretence of Prerogative, without Grant of Parlyament for longer time or in other manner than the same is or shall be granted, is illegall.

5. That it is the Right of the Subjects to petition the King, and all Commitments and Prosecutions for such Petitioning are Illegall.

6. That the raising or keeping a standing Army within the Kingdom in time of Peace, unlesse it be with Consent of Parlyament, is against Law.

7. That the subjects which are Protestants may have Arms for their Defence suitable to their Conditions, and as allowed by Law.

8. That Election of Members of Parlyament ought to be free.

9. That the Freedome of Speech, and Debates or Proceedings in Parlyament, ought not to be impeached or questioned in any Court or Place out of Parlyament.

10. That excessive Baile ought not to be required nor excessive Fines imposed; nor cruell and unusuall Punishments inflicted.

11. That Jurors ought to be duely impannelled and returned, and Jurors which passe upon Men in Trialls for High Treason ought to be Free-holders.

12. That all Grants and Promises of Fines and Forfeitures of particular persons before Conviction, are illegal and void.

13. And that for Redresse of all Grievances, and for the amending, strengthening, and preserveing of the Lawes Parlyament ought to be held frequently.[6]

A comparison of the foregoing text indicates that the English Bill of Rights and the first ten amendments of our Constitution are remarkably similar and point to the former as the major source of the latter.

In 1833, the Supreme Court's decision in *Barron* v. *Baltimore*[7] rejected a claim that the Fifth Amendment guarantee of due process was applicable to the actions of state governments. Chief Justice John Marshall wrote the opinion in which the Bill of Rights was interpreted as placing limitations on the federal government only, and not upon the state governments.

The reasoning expressed in the opinion of the Court was based on its recollection of the Constitutional Conventions:

It is a part of the history of the day that the great revolution which established the Constitution of the United States was not effected without immense opposition. Serious fears were extensively entertained that those powers which the Patriot Statesmen who then watched over the interests of our country, deemed essential to union and to the attainment of those invaluable objects for which union was sought, might be exercised in a manner dangerous to liberty. In almost every convention by which the Constitution was adopted, amendments to guard against the abuse of power were recommended. These amendments demanded security against the apprehended encroachments of the general government—not against those of the local government. In compliance with a sentiment thus generally expressed, to quiet fears thus extensively entertained, amendments were proposed by the required majority in Congress, and adopted by the states. These amendments contain no expression indicating an intention to apply them to the state governments. This court cannot so apply them.[8]

The Fourteenth Amendment and the Bill of Rights

It is sometimes difficult to understand how a constitutional amendment, conceived as a device to make citizens of the nation's black popula-

6. Theodore F. T. Plucknett, *A Concise History of the Common Law*, 5th ed. (Boston: Little, Brown and Co., 1956), pp. 59–60.
7. Barron v. Baltimore, 7 Peters 243 (1833).
8. Ibid.

tion, has served to guarantee to all citizens, black or white, that state governments would not take away the rights to life, liberty, or property guaranteed by the Bill of Rights without due process of law.

The original Constitution protected slavery in states in which it had taken root, set up a formula for counting slaves in apportioning congressional representation, and prohibited Congress from interfering with the importation of slaves before 1808. In 1857, the Supreme Court's opinion in the _Dred Scott_ case[9] stated that Negroes were not included under the word citizen in the Constitution and, therefore, could not claim any of the rights and privileges of the Constitution provided for and secured to citizens of the United States.

In 1865, after a divisive war on the issue of slavery between the North and the South, slavery was abolished. A year later, Congress drafted the Fourteenth Amendment, and by 1868 the necessary three-fourths of the states had ratified it. The Fourteenth Amendment, in effect, reversed the Supreme Court's opinion in the _Dred Scott_ case by amending the Constitution, and returned to the central government the powers that the _Dred Scott_ decision had given to the states.[10]

The framers of the Fourteenth Amendment intended to remedy the absence of a citizenship clause in the Constitution; to confer citizenship upon Negroes; to guarantee individual rights against interference through the power of state governments; and to warn the states (the equal protection clause) not to discriminate against Negroes.[11]

While the Fourteenth Amendment was only one part of a comprehensive action plan of reconstruction, the main purpose of the 1866 Radical Republican majority in Congress was to establish the citizenship of free Negroes and to certify beyond doubt that all persons, black as well as white, who were born or naturalized in the United States, are U.S. citizens.

The Fourteenth Amendment reads as follows:

Section 1. All persons born or naturalized in the United States, and subject to the jurisdiction thereof, are citizens of the United States and of the State wherein they reside. No State shall make or enforce any law which shall abridge the privileges or immunities of citizens of the United States; nor shall any State deprive any person of life, liberty, or property, without due process of law; nor deny to any person within its jurisdiction the equal protection of the laws.

Section 2. Representatives shall be apportioned among the several States according to their respective numbers, counting the whole number of per-

9. Dred Scott v. Sanford, 19 Howard 393 (1857).
10. Michael J. Hindelang, "Equality Under the Law," _Journal of Criminal Law, Criminology and Police Science_ 60, no. 3 (September 1969): 306–13.
11. Kelly and Harbison, _The American Constitution_, pp. 460–61.

sons in each State, excluding Indians not taxed. But when the right to vote at any election for the choice of electors for President and Vice President of the United States, Representatives in Congress, the Executive and Judicial officers of a State, or the members of the Legislature thereof, is denied to any of the male inhabitants of such State, being twenty-one years of age, and citizens of the United States, or in any way abridged, except for participation in rebellion, or other crime, the basis of representation therein shall be reduced in the proportion which the number of such male citizens shall bear to the whole number of male citizens twenty-one years of age in such State.

Section 3. No person shall be a Senator or Representative in Congress, or elector of President and Vice President, or hold any office, civil or military, under the United States, or under any State, who, having previously taken an oath, as a member of Congress, or as an officer of the United States, or as a member of any State legislature, or as an executive or judicial officer of any State, to support the Constitution of the United States, shall have engaged in insurrection or rebellion against the same, or given aid or comfort to the enemies thereof. But Congress may by a vote of two-thirds of each House, remove such disability.

Section 4. The validity of the public debt of the United States, authorized by law, including debts incurred for payment of pensions and bounties for services in suppressing insurrection or rebellion, shall not be questioned. But neither the United States nor any State shall assume or pay any debt or obligation incurred in aid of insurrection or rebellion against the United States, or any claim for the loss or emancipation of any slave; but all such debts, obligations and claims shall be held illegal and void.

Section 5. The Congress shall have power to enforce, by appropriate legislation, the provisions of this article.

In this amendment, the rule of citizenship is delineated in section 1; the loss of political representation is itemized in section 2 as a means of gaining voluntary compliance by the states; and the fact of only one victor is suggested strongly in section 3. There is also a reassurance that the federal government would pay its just debts which had been incurred during the war, but there would be no reimbursement in any fashion of debts incurred by the Confederacy or to any persons for losses caused by the freeing of their slaves. Lastly, section 5 specifies that the federal government intends to enforce the amendment and delegates this power to Congress.

In the half century following the passage of the Fourteenth Amendment there was only limited judicial recognition of the rights of citizens as opposed to the power of government:

1. In an 1886 case the Supreme Court criticized a federal court and its agents for its methods of collecting evidence, stating in its opinion: "It is the duty of courts to be watchful for the Constitu-

tional rights of the citizen, and against any stealthy encroachments thereon."[12]

2. In a 1914 case, the decision of the Courts forbade any illegal search and seizure by federal government agents and warned that such evidence could not be used against the person whose privacy had been unlawfully invaded. In its opinion the court stated: "The Fourth Amendment was a limitation and restraint upon the actions of the Federal courts and officials, and the use of evidence seized by Federal authorities in violation of the Fourth Amendment was a denial of the Constitutional rights of the accused."[13]

Applicable to the States By Reason of the Due Process Clause of the Fourteenth Amendment

Fifty-six years after the ratification of the Fourteenth Amendment, the Supreme Court merged the rights of a citizen under the Fourteenth Amendment with those of the Bill of Rights. This was accomplished by the decision in the case of *Gitlow* v. *New York*.[14] Gitlow was indicted and convicted under New York law on a charge of advocating the overthrow of government by unlawful acts. The main evidence at the trial was a series of writings published by Gitlow. The major argument presented by counsel for Gitlow was on the constitutional question that the liberty protected by the Fourteenth Amendment included the liberties of speech and of the press, and that deprivation of such liberty of expression by state courts was a violation of the due process clause of the Fourteenth Amendment. In its opinion in this case, the Court affirmed Gitlow's conviction on the grounds that it was a fundamental and long-established principle that the freedom of speech and of the press which is secured by the Constitution does not confer an absolute right to speak or publish without responsibility, and does not prevent the punishment of those who abuse this freedom. However, in a landmark "assumption," the Court stated:

> For present purposes we may and do assume that freedom of speech and of the press—which are protected by the First Amendment from abridgment by Congress—are among the fundamental personal rights and "liberties" protected by the due process clause of the Fourteenth Amendment from impairment by the States.

12. Boyd v. United States, 116 U.S. 616 (1886).
13. Weeks v. United States, 232 U.S. 383 (1914).
14. Gitlow v. New York, 268 U.S. 652 (1925).

The *Gitlow* doctrine was affirmed six years later in the 1930 case of *Stromberg* v. *California*.[15] It was another First Amendment "freedoms" case, and concerned a conviction under a California law against advocating revolution. Counsel for Stromberg claimed the law was vague and indefinite. The Court's opinion noted that it had been previously determined in the *Gitlow* case that the concept of liberty under the due process clause of the Fourteenth Amendment embraced the right of free speech, but that this right was not absolute and a state could punish those who incited to violence and crime and threatened the overthrow of organized government by unlawful means. However, the court reversed Stronberg's conviction because the California law was found to be so vague and indefinite as to threaten the right of free speech and was, therefore, repugnant to the guarantee of liberty contained in the Fourteenth Amendment.

It was not until 1937 that the United States Supreme Court clarified the issue of just how many of the rights guaranteed by the Bill of Rights were protected against state action by the due process clause of the Fourteenth Amendment. This was the case of *Palko* v. *Connecticut*.[16] Palko applied to the high court for a legal remedy as the result of an unusual Connecticut law which permitted appeals by the prosecutor from the verdict of a trial jury. Palko had been found guilty of murder in a jury trial and sentenced to life imprisonment, but the indictment had specified murder in the first degree and the jury had reduced this charge in their verdict to second degree murder. The prosecutor appealed, the Connecticut Supreme Court of Errors reviewed the case, and ordered Palko retried on the first degree murder charge. He was tried again, and his counsel made timely objections that the new trial placed Palko twice in jeopardy for the same offense and, in so doing, violated his constitutional rights under the Fourteenth Amendment. The objections were overruled, and Palko was convicted of murder in the first degree.

The following extracts from the Court's opinion in the Palko case develop the concept of "ordered liberty" and "fundamental freedoms and rights":

The due process clause of the Fourteenth Amendment may make it unlawful for a state to abridge by its statutes the freedom of speech which the First Amendment safeguards against encroachment by the Congress; or the like freedom of the press; or the free exercise of religion; or the right of peaceable assembly, without which speech would be unduly trammeled; or the right of one accused of crime to the benefit of counsel. In these and other situations, immunities that are valid as against the federal government by force of the specific pledges of particular amendments (Amendment I and VI) have been

15. Stromberg v. California, 283 U.S. 359 (1931) pp. 368–69.
16. Palko v. Connecticut, 302 U.S. 319 (1937).

found to be implicit in the concept of ordered liberty, and thus, through the Fourteenth Amendment, become valid as against the states.

Our survey of the cases serves, we think, to justify the statement that the dividing line between them, if not unfaltering throughout its course, has been true for the most part to a unifying principle.

The line of division may seem to be wavering and broken if there is a hasty catalogue of the cases on the one side and the other. Reflection and analysis will induce a different view. There emerges the perception of a rationalizing principle which gives to discrete instances a proper order and coherence.

The right to trial by jury and the immunity from prosecution except as the result of an indictment may have value and importance (Amendment VI and V). Even so, they are not of the very essence of a scheme of ordered liberty. To abolish them is not to violate a principle of justice so rooted in the traditions and conscience of our people as to be ranked as fundamental. Few would be so narrow or provincial as to maintain that a fair and enlightened system of justice would be impossible without them. What is true of jury trials and indictments is true also, as the cases show, of the immunity from compulsory self-incrimination (Amendment V).

On which side of the line the case made out by the appellant has appropriate location must be the next inquiry and the final one. Is that kind of double jeopardy to which the statute has subjected him a hardship so acute and shocking that our polity will not endure it? Does it violate those fundamental principles of liberty and justice which lie at the base of all our civil and political institutions?

The conviction of appellant is not in derogation of any privileges or immunities that belong to him as a citizen of the United States.[17]

The unifying principle that comes through strong and clear in the *Palko* opinion is that freedom of speech, press, religion, and assembly, and the right to counsel are fundamental principles of liberty and justice implicit in the concept of ordered liberty. Additionally, to abolish them is to violate a principle of justice so rooted in the traditions and conscience of our people as to be ranked as fundamental. On the other side of the dividing line are the rights to jury trial, prosecution by indictment, and immunity from compulsory self-incrimination. These rights were classed by the Court as of value and importance, but not of the very essence of a scheme of ordered liberty.

The legislation that had been enacted primarily to make citizens of ex-slaves and guarantee them the rights of citizens against any state denial, was now being utilized for the protection of all citizens against state government power. However, the words "nor shall any state deprive any

17. Palko v. Connecticut, 302 U.S. 319 (1937) pp. 324–28. In 1969, in Benton v. Maryland (395 U.S. 784), the double jeopardy clause of the Fifth Amendment was made applicable to the states through the Fourteenth Amendment. The guarantee against double jeopardy is fundamental to the American scheme of justice.

person of life, liberty or property, without due process of law" were being
limited in their application by the concept of ordered liberty and the
fundamental freedoms and rights doctrine.

It was not until 1949 that the Court decided that the right to privacy
(to be safe from unreasonable searches and seizures) was a citizen's right
guaranteed against state infringment by the due process clause of the
Fourteenth Amendment. This was the case of _Wolf v. Colorado,_[18] and
while the Court's decision was noted for its reluctance to use any form of
federal intervention upon state governments, the opinion of the Court
did incorporate the Fourth Amendment right of privacy into the scope of
the Fourteenth Amendment. The Court stated:

> We have no hesitation in saying that were a state affirmatively to sanction
> such police invasion into privacy it would run counter to the guaranty of the
> Fourteenth Amendment. Security of our privacy against arbitrary intrusion
> by the police is implicit in the concept of ordered liberty and as such en-
> forceable against the states through the Due Process Clause.

A dozen years later, in 1961, in the landmark case of _Mapp v. Ohio,_[19]
the Fourteenth Amendment was used to safeguard citizens against unreasonable searches and seizures. The Court ruled that all evidence obtained by searches and seizures in violation of the Constitution (Fourth
Amendment) is inadmissible in a criminal trial in a state court.

The facts of this case are: Dolly Mapp was convicted of knowingly
having had in her possession and under her control certain lewd and lascivious books, pictures, and photographs in violation of the laws of Ohio.
The Supreme Court of Ohio found that her conviction was valid though
based primarily upon the introduction in evidence of lewd and lascivious
books and pictures unlawfully seized during an unlawful search of the defendant's home.

The Supreme Court reversed the Ohio courts, and the following extracts from the _Mapp_ case clearly indicate the Court was no longer reluctant to use the inherent power of the Fourteenth Amendment to protect a
citizen from the illegal use of state power:

> Since the Fourth Amendment's right of privacy has been declared enforce-
> able against the States through the Due Process Clause of the Fourteenth, it
> is enforceable against them by the same sanction of exclusion as is used
> against the Federal Government. Were it otherwise, then just as without the
> _Weeks_ rule* the assurance against unreasonable federal searches and sei-

18. Wolf v. Colorado, 338 U.S. 25 (1949).
19. Mapp v. Ohio, 367 U.S. 643 (1961).
*The Court ruled in Weeks v. United States, 232 U.S. 383 (1914), that "in a federal prosecu-
tion the Fourth Amendment barred the use of evidence secured through an illegal search
and seizure." (In _Weeks,_ the Court used its supervisory authority over the federal courts to
enforce its ruling, and not the Fourteenth Amendment.)

zures would be "a form of words," valueless and undeserving of mention in a perpetual charter of inestimable human liberties, so too, without that rule the freedom from state invasions of privacy would be so ephemeral and so neatly severed from its conceptual nexus with the freedom from all brutish means of coercing evidence as not to merit this Court's high regard as a freedom "implicit in the concept of ordered liberty."

Moreover, our holding that the exclusionary rule is an essential part of both the Fourth and Fourteenth Amendments is not only the logical dictate of prior cases, but it also makes very good sense. There is no war between the Constitution and common sense. Presently, a federal prosecutor may make no use of evidence illegally seized, but a State's attorney across the street may, although he supposedly is operating under the enforceable prohibitions of the same Amendment. Thus the State, by admitting evidence unlawfully seized, serves to encourage disobedience to the Federal Constitution which it is bound to uphold.

Having once recognized that the right to privacy embodied in the Fourth Amendment is enforceable against the States, and that the right to be secure against rude invasions of privacy by state officers is, therefore, constitutional in origin, we can no longer permit that right to remain an empty promise. Because it is enforceable in the same manner and to like effect as other basic rights secured by the Due Process Clause, we can no longer permit it to be revocable at the whim of any police officer who, in the name of law enforcement itself, chooses to suspend its enjoyment. Our decision, founded on reason and truth, gives to the individual no more than that which the Constitution guarantees him, to the police officer no less than that to which honest law enforcement is entitled, and to the courts that judicial integrity so necessary in the true administration of justice.[20]

The Fourteenth Amendment and Criminal Prosecutions

In the decade that followed, most of the rights guaranteed in the Bill of Rights relating to criminal prosecutions were made applicable to the states by the Fourteenth Amendment. This was a selective incorporation of individual rights within the scope of the due process clause of the Fourteenth Amendment. A selected chronological review of landmark cases concerned with the rights of persons accused of crime indicates the balancing of community interest in law enforcement with the Constitutional rights of the accused persons. Additionally, extracts from these court decisions are illustrative of the mechanics of selected incorporation of a Constitutional Amendment within the due process clause of the Fourteenth Amendment.

In 1962, the Eighth Amendment protection against cruel and unusual punishment was made applicable to the states by the Fourteenth

20. Mapp v. Ohio, 367 U.S. 643 (1961) pp. 655–657.

Amendment. In this case, *Robinson* v. *California*,[21] the defendant Robinson had been prosecuted and convicted and sentenced to prison under a California law which made it a misdemeanor for any person to be addicted to narcotics. The California Supreme Court, on Robinson's appeal, affirmed the conviction on the grounds that this law made the "status" of narcotic addict a criminal offense for which the offender could be prosecuted at any time before he reformed, even though he had never used or possessed narcotics, or been guilty of any criminal behavior in the state.

In its decision involving this Eighth Amendment area, the Court indicated that the California law as used in this case was cruel and unusual punishment and violated Robinson's rights; and that the due process clause of the Fourteenth Amendment forbade this type of state action. Therefore, the law was unconstitutional.

The following extracts from the opinion of the Court, delivered by Justice Potter Stewart, explain this decision:

> It is unlikely that any State at this moment in history would attempt to make it a criminal offense for a person to be mentally ill, or a leper, or to be afflicted with a venereal disease. A State might determine that the general health and welfare require that the victims of these and other human afflictions be dealt with by compulsory treatment, involving quarantine, confinement, or sequestration. But, in the light of contemporary human knowledge, a law which made a criminal offense of such a disease would doubtless be universally thought to be an infliction of cruel and unusual punishment in violation of the Eighth and Fourteenth Amendments.
>
> We cannot but consider the statute before us as of the same category. In this Court counsel for the State recognized that narcotic addiction is an illness. Indeed, it is apparently an illness which may be contracted innocently or involuntarily. We hold that a state law which imprisons a person thus afflicted as a criminal, even though he has never touched any narcotic drug within the State or been guilty of any irregular behavior there, inflicts a cruel and unusual punishment in violation of the Fourteenth Amendment.[22]

Justice William Douglas, in a concurring opinion,* sums up the selective incorporation of the Eighth Amendment within the Fourteenth Amendment in these words:

> The command of the Eighth Amendment, banning "cruel and unusual punishments," stems from the Bill of Rights of 1689. And it is applicable to the States by reason of the Due Process Clause of the Fourteenth Amendment.[23]

21. Robinson v. California, 370 U.S. 660 (1962).
22. Ibid. pp. 666–67.
*Filed when a justice votes with the majority, but differs with the opinion of the court, and wishes to place his views in the record of the case.
23. Robinson v. California, p. 675.

Despite the U.S. Supreme Court's decisions in *Palko* v. *Connecticut* and *Powell* v. *Alabama*,[24] which classified the Sixth Amendment right to legal counsel within "the concept of ordered liberty" and as a necessity when a defendant faces "the danger of conviction because he does not know how to establish his innocence," the 1942 case of *Betts* v. *Brady*[25] refused similar classification to the appointment of legal counsel for an impoverished state court defendant who wished to hire an attorney of his own selection. The Sixth Amendment right of a person accused of crime to have legal assistance had been recognized in the federal court system and the practice of appointing counsel for indigent defendants was standard in federal courts since 1938. The implementation of this Sixth Amendment right was formalized in 1946 by Rule 44 of the Federal Rules of Criminal Procedure.

Gideon v. *Wainwright*[26] is the case that extended the Sixth Amendment right to legal assistance to any person accused of crime. The holding of the Court in *Gideon* was: "The right of an indigent defendant in a criminal trial to have the assistance of counsel is a fundamental right essential to a fair trial, and petitioner's trial and conviction without the assistance of counsel violated the Fourteenth Amendment."

Gideon brought his case before the Supreme Court in a handwritten petition for habeas corpus which began with the words: "I, Clarence Earl Gideon, claim that I was denied the rights of the 4th, 5th and 14th amendments of the Bill of Rights."* Gideon then went on to reveal the facts of his case. He had been charged in a Florida court with a noncapital felony, and had appeared without counsel. At this time, he informed the court that he was without funds and asked for appointed counsel. His request was denied by the court on the grounds that Florida law only permitted the appointment of counsel for defendants without funds to hire counsel in capital cases. Gideon conducted his own defense, and he was convicted and sentenced to imprisonment. The Florida Supreme Court denied Gideon's applications for relief.

The *Gideon* case is unique in that it was a rerun of the question of appointing legal counsel for defendants who could not afford to hire such counsel. Back in 1942, in the case of *Betts* v. *Brady*,[27] the Supreme Court had ruled that the appointment of legal counsel for indigent defendants, in accord with the Sixth Amendment guarantee of legal assistance, was not a fundamental right essential to a fair trial, and was not "made obligatory upon the states by the Fourteenth Amendment."

24. Palko v. Connecticut, 302 U.S. 319 (1937); Powell v. Alabama, 287 U.S. 45 (1932).
25. Betts v. Brady, 316 U.S. 455 (1942).
26. Gideon v. Wainwright, 372 U.S. 335 (1963).
*Normally the Supreme Court requires 40 printed copies of a petition, an expensive process. However, under a 1915 law, if a petitioner states he is too poor to do this (*in forma pauperis*) he need send in only one handwritten copy.
27. Betts v. Brady, 316 U.S. 455 (1942).

The following extracts from the Court's opinion in *Gideon* reveal the overruling of *Betts* v. *Brady* and the new doctrine of *Gideon:*

The fact is that in deciding as it did—that "appointment of counsel is not a fundamental right, essential to a fair trial"—the Court in *Betts* v. *Brady* made an abrupt break with its own well-considered precedents. In returning to these old precedents, sounder we believe than the new, we but restore constitutional principles established to achieve a fair system of justice. Not only these precedents but also reason and reflection require us to recognize that in our adversary system of criminal justice, any person haled into court, who is too poor to hire a lawyer, cannot be assured a fair trial unless counsel is provided for him.

The Court in *Betts* v. *Brady* departed from the sound wisdom upon which the Court's holding in *Powell* v. *Alabama* rested. Florida, supported by two other States, has asked that *Betts* v. *Brady* be left intact. Twenty-two States, as friends of the Court, argue that *Betts* was "an anachronism when handed down" and that it should now be overruled. We agree.

The judgment is reversed and the cause is remanded to the Supreme Court of Florida for further action not inconsistent with this opinion.[28]

In 1963, in *Ker* v. *California,*[29] the Supreme Court supplemented the *Mapp* decision by spelling out the standards of reasonableness in searches and seizures.

Having reason to believe that Ker or one of his associates was selling marihuana and had just purchased some from a person who was known to be a dealer, California police officers, without a search warrant, used a passkey to enter an apartment and arrested George and Diane Ker. It was argued at the trial that the arrest was made without probable cause and entry was made without notice, in violation of the defendants' constitutional rights under the Fourth Amendment. Both Kers were convicted and the California District Court of Appeal affirmed the convictions. The U.S. Supreme Court upheld the action of the California courts.

The following extracts from the Court's opinion in this case not only establish Fourth Amendment guidelines, but also highlight the incorporation of the Fourth Amendment within the Fourteenth Amendment's due process clause:

In *Mapp* v. *Ohio,*[30] we followed *Boyd* v. *United States,*[31] which held that the Fourth Amendment, implemented by the self-incrimination clause of the

28. Gideon v. Wainwright, 372 U.S. 335 (1963) pp. 343–45.
29. Ker v. California, 374 U.S. 23 (1963). For an application of reasonable standards where a search was conducted incident to a lawful arrest yet limited to the "within reach" area of the arrestee (when there is no search warrant), *see:* Chimel v. California, 395 U.S. 752 (1969).
30. Mapp v. Ohio, 367 U.S. 643 (1961).
31. Boyd v. United States, 116 U.S. 616 (1886).

Fifth, forbids the Federal Government to convict a man of crime by using testimony or papers obtained from him by unreasonable searches and seizures as defined in the Fourth Amendment. We specifically held in *Mapp* that this constitutional prohibition is enforceable against the States through the Fourteenth Amendment. This means, as we said in *Mapp*, that the Fourth Amendment "is enforceable against them (the states) by the same sanction of exclusion as is used against the Federal Government," by the application of the same constitutional standard prohibiting "unreasonable searches and seizures." We now face the specific question as to whether *Mapp* requires the exclusion of evidence in this case.

Preliminary to our examination of the search and seizures involved here, it might be helpful for us to indicate what was not decided in *Mapp*.

First, it must be recognized that the "principles governing the admissibility of evidence in federal criminal trials have not been restricted . . . to those derived solely from the Constitution. In the exercise of its supervisory authority over the administration of criminal justice in the federal courts . . . this Court has . . . formulated rules of evidence to be applied in federal criminal prosecutions."[32] *Mapp*, however, established no assumption by this Court of supervisory authority over state courts, and, consequently, it implied no total obliteration of state laws relating to arrests and searches in favor of federal law. *Mapp* sounded no death knell for our federalism; rather, it echoed the sentiment of *Elkins* v. *United States*,[33] that "a healthy federalism depends upon the avoidance of needless conflict between state and federal courts" by itself urging that "federal-state cooperation in the solution of crime under constitutional standards will be promoted, if only by recognition of their now mutual obligation to respect the same fundamental criteria in their approaches."

Second, *Mapp* did not attempt the impossible task of laying down a fixed formula for the application in specific cases of the constitutional prohibition against unreasonable searches and seizures; it recognized that we would be met with recurring questions of the reasonableness of searches and that, at any rate, "reasonableness is in the first instance for the (trial court) . . . to determine," thus indicating that the usual weight be given to findings of trial courts.

Mapp, of course, did not lend itself to a detailed explication of standards, since the search involved there was clearly unreasonable and bore no stamp of legality even from the Ohio Supreme Court. This is true also of *Elkins* v. *United States*,[34] where all of the courts assumed the unreasonableness of the search in question and this Court "invoked" its "supervisory power over the administration of criminal justice in the federal courts," in declaring that the evidence so seized by state officers was inadmissible in a federal prosecution.

32. McNabb v. United States, 318 U.S. 332 (1943).
33. Elkins v. United States, 364 U.S. 206 (1960).
34. Ibid.

Implicit in the Fourth Amendment's protection from unreasonable searches and seizures is its recognition of individual freedom. That safeguard has been declared to be as of the very essence of constitutional liberty the guaranty of which is as important and as imperative as are the guaranties of the other fundamental rights of the individual citizen. While the language of the Amendment is "general," it forbids every search that is unreasonable; it protects all, those suspected or known to be offenders as well as the innocent, and unquestionably extends to the premises where the search was made.

This Court's long-established recognition that standards of reasonableness under the Fourth Amendment are not susceptible of Procrustean application is carried forward when that Amendment's proscriptions are enforced against the states through the Fourteenth Amendment. And, although the standard of reasonableness is the same under the Fourth and Fourteenth Amendments, the demands of our federal system compel us to distinguish between evidence held inadmissible because of our supervisory powers over federal courts and that held inadmissible because prohibited by the United States Constitution. We reiterate that the reasonableness of a search is in the first instance a substantive determination to be made by the trial court from the facts and circumstances of the case and in the light of the "fundamental criteria" laid down by the Fourth Amendment and in opinions of this Court applying that Amendment. Findings of reasonableness, of course, are respected only insofar as consistent with federal constitutional guaranties. As we have stated above and in other cases involving federal constitutional rights, findings of state courts are by no means insulated against examination here. While this Court does not sit as in *nisi prius** to appraise contradictory factual questions, it will, where necessary to the determination of constitutional rights, make an independent examination of the facts, the findings, and the record so that it can determine for itself whether in the decision as to reasonableness the fundamental—i.e., constitutional—criteria established by this Court have been respected.

The states are not thereby precluded from developing workable rules governing arrests, searches and seizures to meet the practical demands of effective criminal investigation and law enforcement in the states, provided that those rules do not violate the constitutional proscription of unreasonable searches and seizures and the concomitant command that evidence so seized is inadmissible against one who has standing to complain. Such a standard implies no derogation of uniformity in applying federal constitutional guaranties but is only a recognition that conditions and circumstances vary just as do investigative and enforcement techniques.

In 1968, the U.S. Supreme Court in *Terry* v. *Ohio*[35] approved the kind of search termed by police the "protective frisk"—an investigative stop based on less than probable cause to arrest but upon objective obser-

---

*Examination of issues of fact; trial courts, rather than appellate courts.
35. Terry v. Ohio, 392 U.S. 1 (1968).

vation and police expertise. The Court approved a limited search or "pat-down" of outer clothing whenever the officer had reasonable belief that the suspect was armed, and stated that the officer was justified in removing any weapons found. In this decision the Court acknowledged the necessity for an investigating police officer to be protected from assault by a concealed weapon. However, the decision in *Terry* did not justify a full search, only one limited to that necessary for the discovery of weapons.

In 1969, in *Chimel* v. *California*,[36] the U.S. Supreme Court limited the police search of the *place* of arrest without a search warrant. The Court noted that it was reasonable to search the person arrested in order to remove any weapons, and to search for and seize any evidence on the arrestee's person in order to prevent its concealment or destruction. But it determined that this did not mean that in a *place* of arrest made without a warrant a search could include the entire area but rather *only* that part within that space that the arrestee could reasonably be expected to reach to hide weapons or destroy evidence.

The 1964 decision in *Malloy* v. *Hogan*,[37] protects the right to silence. Petitioner Malloy was arrested during a gambling raid in 1959 by the police of Hartford, Connecticut. He pleaded guilty to the crime of pool selling, a misdemeanor, and was sentenced to one year in jail and fined $500. The sentence was ordered to be suspended after 90 days, at which time he was to be placed on probation for two years. About 16 months after his guilty plea, petitioner was ordered to testify before a referee appointed by the Superior Court of Hartford County to conduct an inquiry into alleged gambling and other criminal activities in the county. The petitioner was asked a number of questions related to events surrounding his arrest and conviction. He refused to answer any question "on the grounds it may tend to incriminate me." The superior court adjudged him in contempt, and committed him to prison until he was willing to answer the questions. Petitioner's application for a writ of habeas corpus was denied by the superior court, and the Connecticut Supreme Court of Errors affirmed. The U.S. Supreme Court granted *certiorari*.*

In this case the U.S. Supreme Court was asked to reconsider prior decisions holding that the privilege against self-incrimination is not safeguarded against state action by the Fourteenth Amendment: *Twining* v. *New Jersey*, 211 U.S. 78; *Adamson* v. *California*, 332 U.S. 46. (In both cases the question was whether comment upon the failure of an accused to take the stand in his own defense in a state prosecution violated the privilege. It was assumed, but not decided, in both cases that such comment in a federal prosecution for a federal offense would infringe the provision of the Fifth Amendment that "no person . . . shall be compelled

36. Chimel v. California, 395 U.S. 752 (1969).
37. Malloy v. Hogan, 378 U.S. 1 (1964).
*A judicial process calling upon an inferior court to send up a case or proceeding for review.

in any criminal case to be a witness aggainst himself.") The Court held that the Fourteenth Amendment guaranteed the petitioner the protection of the Fifth Amendment's privilege against self-incrimination, and that under the applicable federal standard, the Connecticut Supreme Court of Errors erred in holding that the privilege was not properly invoked, and reversed the lower court's action.

The court's opinion in *Malloy* is a fine review of the Fourteenth Amendment and the Bill of Rights. It indicates that some, but not all, of the amendments are made applicable to the states and their agents and courts. These extracts from the Court's opinion in *Malloy* are a running commentary that solidifies the Court's action in case after case:

> The extent to which the Fourteenth Amendment prevents state invasion of rights enumerated in the first eight Amendments has been considered in numerous cases in this Court since the Amendments' adoption in 1868. Although many Justices have deemed the Amendment to incorporate all eight of the Amendments, the view which has thus far prevailed dates from the decision in 1897 in *Chicago, B. & Q. R. Co.* v. *Chicago*, 166 U.S. 226, which held that the Due Process Clause requires the States to pay just compensation for private property taken for public use.[38] It was on the authority of that decision that the Court said in 1908 in *Twining* v. *New Jersey*,[39] that "it is possible that some of the personal rights safeguarded by the first eight Amendments against National action may also be safeguarded against state action, because a denial of them would be a denial of due process of law."

> The Court has not hesitated to reexamine past decisions according the Fourteenth Amendment a less central role in the preservation of basic liberties than that which was contemplated by its Framers when they added the Amendment to our constitutional scheme. Thus although the Court as late as 1922 said that neither the Fourteenth Amendment nor any other provision of the Constitution of the United States imposes upon the States any restrictions about "freedom of speech," three years later, *Gitlow* v. *New York*, 268 U.S. 652 (1925), initiated a series of decisions which today hold immune from state invasion every First Amendment protection for the cherished rights of mind and spirit—the freedoms of speech, press, religion, assembly, association, and petition for redress of grievances.

> Similarly, *Palko* v. *Connecticut*, 302 U.S. 383 decided in 1937, suggested that the rights secured by the Fourth Amendment were not protected against state action, citing the statement of the Court in *Weeks* v. *United States*, 232 U.S. 383 that "the Fourth Amendment is not directed to individual misconduct of (state) officials." In 1961, however, the Court held that in the light of later decisions,[40] it was taken as settled that "the Fourth

---

38. In Barron v. Baltimore, 7 Peters 243 (1833), decided before the adoption of the Fourteenth Amendment, Chief Justice Marshall, speaking for the Court, held that this right was not secured against state action by the Fifth Amendment provision: "Nor shall private property be taken for public use, without just compensation."
39. Twining v. New Jersey, 211 U.S. 78 (1908).
40. Wolf v. Colorado, 338 U.S. 25 (1949); Elkins v. United States, 364 U.S. 206 (1960).

Amendment's right of privacy has been declared enforceable against the States through the Due Process Clause of the Fourteenth.[41]

Again, although the Court held in 1942 that in a state prosecution for a non-capital offense, "appointment of counsel is not a fundamental right,"[42] only last Term this decision was re-examined and it was held that provision of counsel in all criminal cases was "a fundamental right, essential to a fair trial," and thus was made obligatory on the States by the Fourteenth Amendment.[43]

We hold today that the Fifth Amendment's exception from compulsory self-incrimination is also protected by the Fourteenth Amendment against abridgment by the States.

The Fourteenth Amendment secures against state invasion the same privilege that the Fifth Amendment guarantees against federal infringement—the right of a person to remain silent unless he chooses to speak in the unfettered exercise of his own will, and to suffer no penalty, as held in *Twining*, for such silence.

This conclusion is fortified by our recent decision in *Mapp* v. *Ohio*,[44] overruling *Wolf* v. *Colorado*,[45] which had held "that in a prosecution in a State court for a State crime the Fourteenth Amendment does not forbid the admission of evidence obtained by an unreasonable search and seizure." *Mapp* held that the Fifth Amendment privilege aginst self-incrimination implemented the Fourth Amendment to make the exclusionary rule obligatory upon the States.

In a 1965 case, *Pointer* v. *Texas*,[46] the Sixth Amendment right of an accused to confront witnesses against him was upheld. The Court in this case stated that: "The right granted to an accused by the Sixth Amendment to confront the witnesses against him, which includes the right of cross-examination, is a fundamental right essential to a fair trial and is made obligatory on the States by the Fourteenth Amendment."

Pointer and his crime partner were arrested in Texas and taken before a state judge for a preliminary hearing (in Texas called the examining trial) on a charge of " . . . robbery by assault, or violence, or by putting in fear of life or bodily injury, in violation of the Texas penal code." At this hearing an assistant district attorney examined witnesses, but neither of the defendants, both of whom were laymen, had a lawyer. The robbery victim, a man named Phillips, gave his version of the robbery in detail, identifying Pointer as the man who had robbed him at gunpoint. Pointer

41. Mapp v. Ohio, 367 U.S. 643 (1961).
42. Betts v. Brady, 316 U.S. 455 (1942).
43. Gideon v. Wainwright, 372 U.S. 335 (1963). *See also* Robinson v. California, 370 U.S. 660 (1962) which, despite prior decisions, made applicable to the States the Eighth Amendment ban on cruel and unusual punishments.
44. Mapp v. Ohio, 367 U.S. 643 (1961).
45. Wolf v. Colorado, 338 U.S. 25 (1949).
46. Pointer v. Texas, 380 U.S. 400 (1965).

did not cross-examine the victim, although it was said he tried to cross-examine some other witnesses at the hearing. Pointer was subsequently indicted on a charge of robbery. Some time before the trial was held the victim moved to California, and the State at the trial offered the transcript of the victim's testimony given at the preliminary hearing as evidence against petitioner. Petitioner's counsel immediately objected to introduction of the transcript, stating, "Your Honor, we will object to that, as it is a denial of the confrontment of the witnesses against the Defendant." Similar objections were repeatedly made by petitioner's counsel but were overruled by the trial judge. The Texas Court of Criminal Appeals, the highest state court to which the case could be taken, affirmed the petitioner's conviction, rejecting his contention that use of the transcript to convict him denied him rights guaranteed by the Sixth and Fourteenth Amendments. The U.S. Supreme Court granted certiorari to consider the important constitutional question involved in the case.

The extracts below from the Court's opinion in *Pointer* v. *Texas* reveals the basis for the incorporation of this Sixth Amendment right within the scope of the Fourteenth Amendment:

> The Sixth Amendment is a part of what is called our Bill of Rights. In *Gideon* v. *Wainwright*,[47] in which this Court held that the Sixth Amendment's right to the assistance of counsel is obligatory upon the States, we did so on the ground that a provision of the Bill of Rights which is "fundamental and essential to a fair trial" is made obligatory upon the States by the Fourteenth Amendment.

> We hold today that the Sixth Amendment's right of an accused to confront the witnesses against him is likewise a fundamental right and is made obligatory on the States by the Fourteenth Amendment.

> We are aware that some cases, particularly *West* v. *Louisiana*,[48] have stated that the Sixth Amendment's right of confrontation does not apply to trials in state courts, on the ground that the entire Sixth Amendment does not so apply. But of course since *Gideon* v. *Wainwright*, it no longer can broadly be said that the Sixth Amendment does not apply to state courts. And as this Court said in *Malloy* v. *Hogan:* "The Court has not hesitated to re-examine past decisions according the Fourteenth Amendment a less central role in the preservation of basic liberties than that which was contemplated by its framers when they added the Amendment to our constitutional scheme."[49] In the light of *Gideon*, *Malloy*, and other cases cited in those opinions holding various provisions of the Bill of Rights applicable to the States by virtue of the Fourteenth Amendment, the statements made in *West* and similar cases generally declaring that the Sixth Amendment does not apply to the States can no longer be regarded as the law.

47. Gideon v. Wainwright, 372 U.S. 335 (1963).
48. West v. Louisiana, 194 U.S. 258 (1903).
49. Malloy v. Hogan, 378 U.S. 1 (1964), p. 5.

We hold that petitioner was entitled to be tried in accordance with the protection of the confrontation guarantee of the Sixth Amendment, and that that guarantee, like the right against compelled self-incrimination, is "to be enforced against the States under the Fourteenth Amendment according to the same standards that protect those personal rights against federal encroachment."

Because the transcript of Phillips'* statement offered against petitioner at his trial had not been taken at a time and under circumstances affording petitioner through counsel an adequate opportunity to cross-examine Phillips, its introduction in a federal court in a criminal case against Pointer would have amounted to denial of the privilege of confrontation guaranteed by the Sixth Amendment. Since we hold that the right of an accused to be confronted with the witnesses against him must be determined by the same standards whether the right is denied in a federal or state proceeding, it follows that use of the transcript to convict petitioner denied him a constitutional right, and that his conviction must be reversed.[50]

Selected References

Books

Kelly, Alfred H., and Harbison, Winfred A. *The American Constitution*, 3d ed. New York: W. W. Norton & Company, 1963.
Schwartz, Bernard. *A Commentary on the Constitution of the United States, Part I: The Powers of Government.* New York: Macmillan Publishing Co., 1963.

Periodicals

Hindelang, Michael J. "Equality Under the Law." *Journal of Criminal Law, Criminology and Police Science* 60, no. 3 (September 1969): 306–13.

Cases

Barron v. Baltimore, 7 Peters 243 (1833).
Benton v. Maryland, 395 U.S. 784 (1969).
Betts v. Brady, 316 U.S. 455 (1942).
Boyd v. United States, 116 U.S. 616 (1886).
Chimel v. California, 395 U.S. 752 (1969).
Dred Scott v. Sanford, 19 Howard 395 (1857)
Gideon v. Wainwright, 372 U.S. 335 (1963).
Gitlow v. New York, 268 U.S. 652 (1925).
Ker v. California, 374 U.S. 23 (1963).
Malloy v. Hogan, 378 U.S. 1 (1964).
Mapp v. Ohio, 367 U.S. 643 (1961).
Palko v. Connecticut, 302 U.S. 319 (1937).

---

*The victim in the robbery for which Pointer was indicted, tried, convicted, and sentenced.
50. Pointer v. Texas, 380 U.S. 400 (1965) pp. 403, 406–7. *See also* California v. Green, 399 U.S. 149 (1970).

Pointer v. Texas, 380 U.S. 400 (1965).
Powell v. Alabama, 287 U.S. 45 (1932).
Robinson v. California, 370 U.S. 660 (1962).
Stromberg v. California, 283 U.S. 359 (1931).
Terry v. Ohio, 392 U.S. 1(1968).
Weeks v. United States, 232 U.S. 383 (1914).
Wolf v. Colorado, 338 U.S. 25 (1949).

Chapter XI

The Right to Counsel

In England, prior to 1836, the accused was not allowed legal counsel in felony cases unless the charge was associated with treason, but defendants in minor cases had legal right to appear with counsel. It was an incongruous practice as the accused was denied the assistance of counsel in cases where death was likely to be the most common penalty, yet was allowed counsel in cases involving a fine or, at most, short imprisonment. Judges, aware of the ironic circumstances, usually permitted counsel. Between 1836 and 1850, there was some legislative action for reform and, in 1850, Parliament specifically provided that all persons tried for felonies should be allowed, after the close of the case for the prosecution, to make full answer and defense to the prosecution's case, by counsel "learned in the law."[1]

In America, the colonists were aware that an accused, undefended by counsel, was at a serious disadvantage. After the Revolution, most states included a clause respecting the right to counsel in their state constitutions; and, in 1791, the right to the assistance of counsel became part of the Constitution as a clause in the Sixth Amendment's specification of the mode of criminal proceedings: ". . . and to have the Assistance of Counsel for his defense."

A defendant's need for a lawyer is nowhere better stated than in the moving words of Mr. Justice George Sutherland in *Powell* v. *Alabama:*

> The right to be heard would be, in many cases, of little avail if it did not comprehend the right to be heard by counsel. Even the intelligent and educated layman has small and sometimes no skill in the science of law. If charged with crime, he is incapable, generally, of determining for himself whether the in-

1. William M. Beaney, *The Right to Counsel in American Courts* (Ann Arbor: University of Michigan Press, 1955), pp. 8–24.

dictment is good or bad. He is unfamiliar with the rules of evidence. Left without the aid of counsel he may be put on trial without a proper charge, and convicted upon incompetent evidence, or evidence irrelevant to the issue or otherwise inadmissible. He lacks both the skill and knowledge adequately to prepare his defense, even though he has a perfect one. He requires the guiding hand of counsel at every step in the proceedings against him. Without it, though he be not guilty, he faces the danger of conviction because he does not know how to establish his innocence.[2]

While a defendant in a criminal proceeding also has a constitutionally guaranteed right to represent himself (to appear *pro se*) at trial, this right has long been aligned with the common saying that "a man who represents himself in the legal arena has a fool for a client." In fact, courts not only recognize the need for counsel by defendants without funds to employ their own lawyers, but also acknowledge the fact that many illiterate or uneducated inmates of correctional institutions do not have access to qualified attorneys. They may use their right to counsel to seek help from a knowledgeable fellow inmate who can prepare applications for habeas corpus and other legal remedies.

The right of an accused to legal assistance at trial has always been linked with the right to effective counsel, and courts have uniformly allowed time for retained or appointed counsel to prepare their cases prior to trial. Traditionally, appointed or assigned counsel are appointed early in the proceedings. This has always meant not later than the first judicial appearance. Appointment of counsel subsequent to this stage of criminal proceedings is considered an untimely appointment and creates a presumption that the defendant's rights were prejudiced, and this shifts the burden of showing the contrary to the state. Aligned with this time needed for preparation and the concept of effective counsel, recent decisions of the Supreme Court have extended the right of legal counsel to the pretrial period.

Three important cases[3] in the area of criminal procedure established new horizons in the "time clock" of criminal justice. The Court's decisions in these cases advanced the right to counsel to the time at which: (1) an investigation focuses upon one suspect; (2) a suspect is subjected to custodial interrogation; and (3) a suspect is made part of a post-indictment lineup for identification by eyewitnesses. In addition to having advanced the time at which a person suspected or accused of a crime is entitled to legal counsel to the pretrial period necessary for preparation of the case for the defense, the Court has established an additional procedural safeguard in requiring the police to warn a suspect or accused person of his constitutional rights to silence *and* legal counsel.[4]

2. Powell v. Alabama, 287 U.S. 45 (1932) pp. 68–69.
3. Escobedo v. Illinois, 378 U.S. 478 (1964); Miranda v. Arizona, 387 U.S. 436 (1966); United States v. Wade 338 U.S. 218 (1967).
4. Miranda v. Arizona, 387 U.S. 436 (1966), and Escobedo v. Illinois, 378 U.S. 478 (1964).

The Indigent Accused

The right to counsel is never a problem when the accused has sufficient funds to retain a lawyer of his own choosing. Even prior to the ratification of the Sixth Amendment, legislation was enacted stating that every person indicted for treason or other capital crime would be allowed to make a full defense by counsel. In felony cases less serious than capital crimes, some members of the judiciary made a practice of appointing lawyers to defend accused persons without funds, but it was not a common practice.

Over many, many years, however, an emerging belief developed for the right to counsel by indigent defendants in all criminal proceedings. In 1963, a convict in Florida finally achieved this goal. Clarence Earl Gideon sent a handwritten appeal to the U.S. Supreme Court, along with a written motion to proceed in *forma pauperis* (as a person without funds for an attorney or formal documents), and papers showing that the Florida Supreme Court had denied his application for a writ of habeas corpus (an order to free him because he was unjustly imprisoned). Gideon claimed his trial for a felony without an attorney deprived him of the due process of law.[5]

The high court responded to Gideon's appeal for a legal remedy and in the landmark case of *Gideon* v. *Wainwright*[6] they reversed his conviction and ordered a new trial. The essence of the U.S. Supreme Court's decision in this case was that America was a country in which a person accused of crime would be capably defended no matter what his financial circumstances, and that the lawyer representing an indigent defendant would do so with pride and a knowledge that all of the support necessary to prepare an adequate defense would also be available. The Court held that every defendant in a criminal proceeding who desires a lawyer should have one (even if legal counsel had to be appointed at state expense for indigent defendants). This was guaranteed by the Sixth Amendment right to counsel.

Some of the key language of the *Gideon* majority opinion indicates the court's viewpoint about the right to counsel for indigent persons accused of crime. For instance:

1. Reason and reflection require us to recognize that any person haled into court, who is too poor to hire a lawyer, cannot be assured a fair trial unless counsel is provided for him.

2. Lawyers in criminal courts are necessities, not luxuries.

3. This noble ideal (fair trial) cannot be realized if the poor man charged with crime has to face his accusers without a lawyer to assist him.

5. Anthony Lewis, *Gideon's Trumpet* (New York: Random House, 1964), pp. 3–10, 205–10.
6. Gideon v. Wainwright, 372 U.S. 355 (1963).

The right to appointed counsel cannot logically be based on the name given a crime. It is simply impossible to draw a distinction between the right to counsel in misdemeanor, high misdemeanors, and felony cases merely because of terminology. The possible loss of liberty to an innocent person charged with a misdemeanor, who does not know how to defend himself, is too important a right to be sacrificed on the altar of expedience. A community that can afford a professional prosecuting attorney to prosecute these lesser crimes can also assume the burden of providing adequate defense counsel for accused persons financially unable to employ counsel, so that the innocent accused will not be convicted because of an inadequate defense.

The President's Commission on Law Enforcement and Administration of Justice made the following recommendation:

> The objective to be met as quickly as possible is to provide counsel to every criminal defendant who faces a significant penalty, if he cannot afford to provide counsel himself. This should apply to cases classified as misdemeanors as well as those classified as felonies.[7]

It is the duty of counsel appointed to represent an indigent defendant to respond to the needs of this client as he responds to the needs of other clients who retain him, and to remain in the case until prosecution is terminated or until other counsel is assigned in the trial court. His duties include informing any succeeding counsel, by way of a brief report, of all action previously taken and of any information relevant to the defendant's case.

The Public Defender

Los Angeles County, California, began its public defender system in 1913, the first in the United States. It is now a complex organization with a central office and branch offices. From that early beginning, the public defender concept has spread throughout California and, in other forms, throughout the nation. This system for providing legal counsel for indigent defendants is now providing qualified lawyers for accused persons in both felony and misdemeanor cases, and for juveniles appearing in juvenile court on petitions of delinquency. In addition, counsel is provided for hearings in relation to insanity, such as sexual psychopath proceedings and mental illness hearings. Its services range from implementation of the *Miranda* rule (police interrogations) and release on personal

---

7. U.S., The President's Commission on Law Enforcement and Administration of Justice, *The Challenge of Crime in a Free Society* (Washington, D.C.: Government Printing Office, 1967), p. 150.

recognizance in lieu of bail, through the preliminary hearings and trial on the issue of guilt or innocence, to appeals. For an accused person to be eligible for the services of a defender he must be financially unable to employ legal counsel. Courts can appoint counsel for indigent defendants, but such appointments are coordinated with the public defender's office to make certain the additional cost is justified. To insure full use of the public defender system, county officials or local agencies only approve payment to appointed counsel when the public defender cannot supply an attorney, or there is a conflict of interest.

In 1960, a state agency was established to perform similar services throughout Massachusetts: The Massachusetts Defenders Committee. In 1967, a new statewide public defender system was established in New Jersey. In various forms, this concept of a public or voluntary agency that serves as a central supply of attorneys to represent indigent defendants is spreading at either county or state levels.

The public defender system is more economically valuable to the community than the old system of appointing lawyers from a pool of attorneys willing to accept such work, and paying appropriate fees for each case. It is claimed that it is better than a system based on a pool of lawyers who volunteered in the public interest (or were coerced into volunteering by a local court) and who were paid no more than token fees, if anything. Public defenders offer every indigent defendant an established competency and experience in legal services, and the support of an office well-staffed with clerical and stenographic help and competent investigators. In the past, some appointed attorneys could ill afford the necessary time to defend an indigent client. In the public defender system, all of the time of a public defender is spent on behalf of indigent clients, just as all of the time of a prosecuting attorney is spent on prosecuting accused persons.

Success in the defense of any client accused of crime depends upon many things and various circumstances—as well as the competency of defense counsel. There is a belief throughout the country that the public defender system is less costly to government and better serves the interests of indigent defendants than past systems which appointed legal counsel for indigent defendants.

Counsel Pro se

When a person accused of crime intelligently waives his right to legal counsel and asks that the court permit him to represent himself, he appears *pro se:* in his own behalf. In some county jails in California, *pro se* defendants who have been unable to arrange release on bail or personal recognizance, are given cells in which telephones are installed. They can then conduct their defense more adequately despite confinement prior to trial.

While a defendant has the right to defend himself without the assistance of counsel, and an equal right to discharge his attorney and defend *pro se,* a trial court should have a basis for allowing the defendant to represent himself. To allow such action, a trial court should be convinced that to do otherwise would be to prejudice the rights of the defendant. However, the court cannot compel a defendant to accept a lawyer he does not want; a competent person accused of crime can refuse professional legal assistance and conduct his own defense.

The defendant must fully understand his right to retained or assigned counsel, and the court must ascertain whether the waiver of counsel is made intelligently and with full knowledge of the duties of legal counsel. The court must also be assured by the defendant's background (education or experience) that he has the capability of representing himself adequately, and be assured by the defendant's actions and attitudes that there will be no undue interference with the orderly procedure of the trial.

Counsel—When a Case Focuses

The 1964 case of *Escobedo* v. *Illinois*[8] initially established the right of counsel when a police investigation is no longer a general inquiry into an unsolved crime, but has begun to focus on a particular suspect already in police custody.

Police arrested Escobedo for the homicide of his brother-in-law, but he made no statement, and secured an attorney. His counsel filed for habeas corpus in a state court and Escobedo was ordered released. About ten days later, police again arrested Escobedo and took him to police headquarters for interrogation. Escobedo now made several requests to see his lawyer, who, though present in the building, and despite persistent efforts, was refused access to his client. Petitioner was not advised by the police of his right to remain silent and, after persistent questioning by the police, made a damaging statement which was admitted at the trial. Convicted of murder, he appealed to the state supreme court, which affirmed the conviction.

When a police investigation ceases to be a general inquiry into an unsolved crime and begins to focus on a particular suspect in police custody, if that suspect has been refused an opportunity to consult with his counsel and has not been warned of his constitutional right to keep silent, then the procedures have been in violation of the Sixth and Fourteenth Amendments. No statement extracted by the police during the interrogation may be used against him at a trial.

8. Escobedo v. Illinois, 378 U.S. 478 (1964).

The critical question in this case is whether, under the circumstances, the police refusal to honor the petitioner's request to consult with his lawyer during the course of an interrogation constitutes a denial of the assistance of counsel. This is in violation of the Sixth Amendment to the Constitution as made obligatory upon the states by the Fourteenth Amendment; and thereby renders inadmissible in a state criminal trial any incriminating statement elicited by the police during the interrogation.

The following are selected extracts from the Court's majority opinion in *Escobedo:*

The interrogation here was conducted before petitioner was formally indicted. But in the context of this case, that fact should make no difference. When petitioner requested, and was denied, an opportunity to consult with his lawyer, the investigation had ceased to be a general investigation of an unsolved crime. Petitioner had become the accused, and the purpose of the interrogation was to get him to confess his guilt despite his constitutional right not to do so. At the time of his arrest and throughout the course of the interrogation, the police told petitioner that they had convincing evidence that he had fired the fatal shots. Without informing him of his absolute right to remain silent in the face of this accusation, the police urged him to make a statement.

It is argued that if the right to counsel is afforded prior to indictment, the number of confessions obtained by the police will diminish significantly, because most confessions are obtained during the period between arrest and indictment, and any lawyer worth his salt will tell the suspect in no uncertain terms to make no statement to police under any circumstances. This argument, of course, cuts two ways. The fact that many confessions are obtained during this period points up its critical nature as a stage when legal aid and advice are surely needed. The right to counsel would indeed be hollow if it began at a period when few confessions were obtained. There is necessarily a direct relationship between the importance of a stage to the police in their quest for a confession and the criticalness of that stage to the accused in his need for legal advice. Our Constitution, unlike some others, strikes the balance in favor of the right of the accused to be advised by his lawyer of his privilege against self-incrimination.

We have learned the lesson of history, ancient and modern, that a system of criminal law enforcement which comes to depend on the "confession" will, in the long run, be less reliable and more subject to abuses than a system which depends on extrinsic evidence independently secured through skillful investigation.

We have also learned the companion lesson of history that no system of criminal justice can, or should survive if it comes to depend for its continued effectiveness on the citizens' abdication through unawareness of their constitutional rights. No system worth preserving should have to fear that if an accused is permitted to consult with a lawyer, he will become aware of, and exercise, these rights. If the exercise of constitutional rights will thwart the effectiveness of a system of law enforcement, then there is something very wrong with that system.

We hold, therefore, that where, as here, the investigation is no longer a general inquiry into an unsolved crime but has begun to focus on a particular suspect, the suspect has been taken into police custody, the police carry out a process of interrogations that lends itself to eliciting incriminating statements, the suspect has requested and been denied an opportunity to consult with his lawyer, and the police have not effectively warned him of his absolute constitutional right to remain silent, the accused has been denied "the Assistance of Counsel" in violation of the Sixth Amendment to the Constitution as "made obligatory upon the States by the Fourteenth Amendment," Gideon v. Wainwright, 372 U.S., at 342, and that no statement elicited by the police during the interrogation may be used against him at a criminal trial.

Nothing we have said today affects the powers of the police to investigate an unsolved crime by gathering information from witnesses and by other proper investigative efforts. We hold only that when the process shifts from investigatory to accusatory—when its focus is on the accused and its purpose is to elicit a confession—our adversary system begins to operate, and, under the circumstances here, the accused must be permitted to consult with his lawyer.

The facts of this case, the Court's holding, and the selected extracts from the majority opinion signify a new alertness on the part of the nation's high court to insure the preservation of the intrinsic value of the constitutional guarantee of the right to legal assistance: that it should be helpful to the person accused of a crime and not negated by pretrial procedures.

Counsel—When a Suspect is Interrogated

The many decisions of the U.S. Supreme Court that are known as "the confession cases"[9] (a long history of correcting individual violations of a suspect's rights during pretrial interrogation sessions), culminated in a decision with a definitive majority opinion that established the time of police interrogation as a time when a suspect was entitled not only to legal counsel, but also to a warning about his right to silence.

In each of these cases[10] the defendant, while in police custody, was questioned by police officers, detectives, or a prosecuting attorney in a room in which he was cut off from the outside world. None of the defendants was given a full and effective warning of his rights at the outset of the interrogation process. In all four cases the questioning elicited oral

9. Beginning with Brown v. Mississippi, 297 U.S. 278 (1936).
10. Miranda v. Arizona, Vignera v. New York, Westover v. United States, and California v. Stewart 387 U.S. 436 (1966), usually cited as Miranda v. Arizona, 387 U.S. 436 (1966).

admissions—and in three of them, signed statements as well—which were admitted at their trials. All defendants were convicted.

Ernesto Miranda was arrested at his home, taken in custody to a Phoenix police station, identified by the complaining witness, then taken to an interrogation room in the detective bureau. There he was questioned by two police officers. Miranda was not advised that he had a right to an attorney present. Two hours later, the officers emerged from the interrogation room with a written confession signed by Miranda. At the top of the statement was a typed paragraph stating that the confession was made voluntarily, without threats or promises of immunity and "with full knowledge of my legal rights, understanding any statement I make may be used against me."

At his jury trial, the written confession was admitted into evidence over the objection of defense counsel, and the two officers testified to the prior oral confession made by Miranda during the interrogation. Miranda was found guilty of kidnapping and rape. The U.S. Supreme Court reversed the trial court's action, ruling that Miranda's constitutional rights were violated. The statements of guilt were obtained under circumstances that did not meet constitutional standards for protection of the privilege against self-incrimination.

The following are selected extracts from the Court's majority opinion in *Miranda:*

> We start here, as we did in *Escobedo,* with the premise that our holding is not an innovation in our jurisprudence, but is an application of principles long recognized and applied in other settings. We have undertaken a thorough re-examination of the *Escobedo* decision and the principles it announced, and we reaffirm it. That case was but an explication of basic rights that are enshrined in our Constitution—that "No person . . . shall be compelled in any criminal case to be a witness against himself," and that "the accused shall . . . have the Assistance of Counsel"—rights which were put in jeopardy in that case through official overbearing. These precious rights were fixed in our Constitution only after centuries of persecution and struggle. And in the words of Chief Justice Marshall, they were secured "for ages to come, and . . . designed to approach immortality as nearly as human institutions can approach it," *Cohens* v. *Virginia,* 6 Wheat. 264, 387 (1821).

> Over 70 years ago, our predecessors on this Court eloquently stated:

> "The maxim *nemo tenetur seipsum accusare* * had its origin in a protest against the inquisitorial and manifestly unjust methods of interrogating accused persons, which (have) long obtained in the continental system, and, until the expulsion of the Stuarts from the British throne in 1688, and the erection of additional barriers for the protection of the people against the exercise of arbitrary power, (were) not uncommon even in England. While

*No one is bound to accuse himself.

the admissions or confessions of the prisoner, when voluntarily and freely made, have always ranked high in the scale of incriminating evidence, if an accused person be asked to explain his apparent connection with a crime under investigation, the ease with which the questions put to him may assume an inquisitorial character, the temptation to press the witness unduly, to browbeat him if he be timid or reluctant, to push him into a corner, and to entrap him into fatal contradictions, which is so painfully evident in many of the earlier state trials, notably in those of Sir Nicholas Throckmorton, and Udal, the Puritan minister, made the system so odious as to give rise to a demand for its total abolition. The change in the English criminal procedure in that particular seems to be founded upon no statute and no judicial opinion, but upon a general and silent acquiescence of the courts in a popular demand. But, however adopted, it has become firmly embedded in English, as well as in American jurisprudence. So deeply did the iniquities of the ancient system impress themselves upon the minds of the American colonists that the States, with one accord, made a denial of the right to question an accused person a part of their fundamental law, so that a maxim, which in England was a mere rule of evidence, became clothed in this country with the impregnability of a constitutional enactment. *Brown* v. *Walker,* 161 U.S. 591, 596–597 (1896)."

In these cases, we might not find the defendants' statements to have been involuntary in traditional terms. Our concern for adequate safeguards to protect precious Fifth Amendment rights is, of course, not lessened in the slightest. In each of the cases, the defendant was thrust into an unfamiliar atmosphere and run through menacing police interrogation procedures.

It is obvious that such an interrogation environment is created for no purpose other than to subjugate the individual to the will of his examiner. This atmosphere carries its own badge of intimidation. To be sure, this is not physical intimidation, but it is equally destructive of human dignity. The current practice of incommunicado interrogation is at odds with one of our Nation's most cherished principles—that the individual may not be compelled to incriminate himself. Unless adequate protective devices are employed to dispel the compulsion inherent in custodial surroundings, no statement obtained from the defendant can truly be the product of his free choice.

We have recently noted that the privilege against self-incrimination—the essential mainstay of our adversary system—is founded on a complex of values. All these policies point to one overriding thought: the constitutional foundation underlying the privilege is the respect a government—state or federal—must accord to the dignity and integrity of its citizens. To maintain a fair state-individual balance, to require the government to shoulder the entire load, to respect the inviolability of the human personality, our accusatory system of criminal justice demands that the government seeking to punish an individual produce the evidence against him by its own independent labors, rather than by the cruel, simple expedient of compelling it from his own mouth. In sum, the privilege is fulfilled only when the person is guaranteed the right "to remain silent unless he chooses to speak in the unfettered exercise of his own will."

The circumstances surrounding in-custody interrogation can operate very quickly to overbear the will of one merely made aware of his privilege by his interrogators. *Therefore, the right to have counsel present at the interrogation is indispensable to the protection of the Fifth Amendment privilege under the system we delineate today.* Our aim is to assure that the individual's right to choose between silence and speech remains unfettered throughout the interrogation process. A once-stated warning, delivered by those who will conduct the interrogation, cannot itself suffice to that end among those who most require knowledge of their rights. A mere warning given by the interrogators is not alone sufficient to accomplish that end.

Thus, the need for counsel to protect the Fifth Amendment privilege comprehends not merely a right to consult with counsel prior to questioning, but also to have counsel present during any questioning if the defendant so desires. Accordingly we hold that an individual held for interrogation must be clearly informed that he has *the right to consult with a lawyer and to have the lawyer with him during interrogation* under the system for protecting the privilege we delineate today.

On the important issue of guilt or innocence, a careful review of the two foregoing decisions dictates the conclusion that an accused's statement procured either after failure to give him an opportunity to consult with his counsel, failure to warn him of his right to remain silent, or in the absence of police attempts to advise the accused person of his constitutional rights, cannot be employed at trial.

Counsel—When a Suspect is Placed in Police Lineup

In the case of *United States* v. *Wade*,[11] the U.S. Supreme Court moved the right to counsel forward in the time clock of a criminal proceeding, to the time of a pretrial police lineup.

A federally insured bank was robbed by a man with a small strip of tape on each side of his face. He pointed a pistol at the female cashier and the vice-president, the only persons in the bank at the time, and forced them to fill a pillowcase with the bank's money. The robber then drove away with an accomplice who had been waiting in a stolen car outside the bank. After an investigation, during which the two eye witnesses selected Wade's mug-shot photograph from among others presented to them by FBI agents, an indictment was returned against Wade for conspiring to rob the bank, and for the robbery itself. Wade was arrested and counsel was appointed to represent him.

Fifteen days later an FBI agent, without notice to Wade's lawyer, arranged to have the two bank employees observe a lineup made up of

*Emphasis added.
11. United States v. Wade, 388 U.S. 218 (1967).

Wade and five or six other prisoners and conducted in a courtroom of the local county courthouse. Each person in the line wore strips of tape such as allegedly worn by the robber and upon direction each said something like "put the money in the bag," the words allegedly uttered by the robber. Both bank employees identified Wade in the lineup as the bank robber. At trial, the two employees, when asked on direct examination if the robber was in the courtroom, pointed to Wade. The prior lineup identification was then elicited from both employees on cross-examination. At the close of testimony, Wade's counsel moved for a judgment of acquittal or, alternatively, to strike the bank employees' courtroom identifications on the ground that conduct of the lineup, without notice to and in the absence of his appointed counsel, violated his Fifth Amendment privilege against self-incrimination and his Sixth Amendment right to the assistance of counsel. The motion was denied, and Wade was convicted.

The court's ruling in *Wade* was:

1. Neither the lineup itself nor anything required therein violated respondent's Fifth Amendment privilege against self-incrimination since merely exhibiting his person for observation by witnesses and using his voice as identifying physical characteristic involved no compulsion of the accused to give evidence of a testimonial nature against himself which is prohibited by that Amendment.

2. *The Sixth Amendment guarantees an accused the right to counsel not only at his trial but at any critical confrontation by the prosecution at pretrial proceedings where the results might well determine his fate and where the absence of counsel might derogate from his right to a fair trial.**

3. *The post-indictment lineup* (unlike such preparatory steps as analyzing fingerprints and blood samples) *was a critical prosecutive stage at which respondent was entitled to the aid of counsel.**

   a. There is a great possibility of unfairness to the accused at that point, (1) because of the manner in which confrontations for identification are frequently conducted, (2) because of dangers inherent in eyewitness identification and suggestibility inherent in the context of the confrontations, and (3) because of the likelihood that the accused will often be precluded from reconstructing what occurred and thereby obtaining a full hearing on the identification issue at trial.

   b. This case illustrates the potential for improper influence on witnesses through the lineup procedure, since the bank employees were allowed to see respondent in the custody of FBI agents before the lineup began.

   c. *The presence of counsel** at the lineup will significantly promote fairness at the confrontation and a full hearing at trial on the issue of identification.

4. In-court identification by a witness to whom the accused was exhibited before trial *in the absence of counsel** must be excluded unless it can be

*Emphasis added.

established that such evidence had an independent origin or that error in its admission was harmless. Since it is not clear that the Court of Appeals applied the prescribed rule of exclusion, and since the nature of the in-court identifications here was not an issue in the trial and cannot be determined on the record, the case must be remanded to the District Court for resolution of these issues.

Selected extracts from the majority opinion in *Wade* are:

The fact that the lineup involved no violation of Wade's privilege against self-incrimination does not, however, dispose of his contention that the courtroom identifications should have been excluded because the lineup was conducted without notice to and in the absence of his counsel.

When the Bill of Rights was adopted, there were no organized police forces as we know them today. The accused confronted the prosecutor and the witnesses against him, and the evidence was marshalled, largely at the trial itself. In contrast, today's law enforcement machinery involves critical confrontations of the accused by the prosecution at pretrial proceedings where the results might well settle the accused's fate and reduce the trial itself to a mere formality. In recognition of these realities of modern criminal prosecution, our cases have construed the Sixth Amendment guarantee to apply to "critical" stages of the proceedings. The guarantee reads: "In all criminal prosecutions, the accused shall enjoy the right . . . to have the Assistance of Counsel *for his defense.*"* The plain wording of this guarantee thus encompasses counsel's assistance whenever necessary to assure a meaningful "defense."

As early as *Powell* v. *Alabama*,[12] we recognized that the period from arraignment to trial was perhaps the most critical period of the proceedings, during which the accused requires the guiding hand of counsel, if the guarantee is not to prove an empty right. That principle has since been applied to require the assistance of counsel at the type of arraignment—for example, that provided by Alabama—where certain rights might be sacrificed or lost: "What happens there may affect the whole trial. Available defenses may be irretrievably lost, if not then and there asserted." *Hamilton* v. *Alabama*, 368 U.S. 52.

The principle was also applied in *Massiah* v. *United States*, 377 U.S. 201, where we held that incriminating statements of the defendant should have been excluded from evidence when it appeared that they were overheard by federal agents who, without notice to the defendant's lawyer, arranged a meeting between the defendant and an accomplice turned informant.

The Government characterized the lineup as a mere preparatory step in the gathering of the prosecution's evidence, not different—for Sixth Amendment purposes—from the various other preparatory steps, such as systematized or scientific analyzing of the accused's fingerprints, blood sample,

*Emphasis added.
12. Powell v. Alabama, 287 U.S. 45 (1932).

clothing, hair, and the like. We think there are differences which preclude such stages being characterized as critical stages at which the accused has the right to the presence of his counsel. Knowledge of the techniques of science and technology is sufficiently available, and the variables in techniques few enough, that the accused has the opportunity for a meaningful confrontation of the Government's case at trial through the ordinary processes of cross-examination of the Government's expert witnesses and the presentation of the evidence of his own experts. The denial of a right to have his counsel present at such analysis does not therefore violate the Sixth Amendment; they are not critical stages since there is minimal risk that his counsel's absence at such stages might derogate from his right to a fair trial. But the confrontation compelled by the State between the accused and the victim or eyewitnesses to a crime to elicit identification evidence is peculiarly riddled with innumerable dangers and variable factors which might seriously, even crucially, derogate from a fair trial.

The vagaries of eyewitness identification are well-known; the annals of criminal law are rife with instances of mistaken identification. A major factor contributing to the high incidence of miscarriage of justice from mistaken identification has been the degree of suggestion inherent in the manner in which the prosecution presents the suspect to witnesses for pretrial identification. Suggestion can be created intentionally or unintentionally in many subtle ways. And the dangers for the suspect are particularly grave when the witness' opportunity for observation was insubstantial, and thus his susceptibility to suggestion the greatest.

The impediments to an objective observation are increased when the victim is the witness. Lineups are prevalent in rape and robbery prosecutions and present a particular hazard that a victim's understandable outrage may excite vengeful or spiteful motives. In any event, neither witnesses nor lineup participants are apt to be alert for conditions prejudicial to the suspect. And if they were, it would likely be of scant benefit to the suspect since neither witnesses nor lineup participants are likely to be schooled in the detection of suggestive influences. Improper influences may go undetected by a suspect, guilty or not, who experiences the emotional tension which we might expect in one being confronted with potential accusers. Even when he does observe abuse, if he has a criminal record he may be reluctant to take the stand and open up the admission of prior convictions. Moreover, any protestations by the suspect of the fairness of the lineup made at trial are likely to be in vain. The jury's choice is between the accused's unsupported version and that of the police officers present. In short, the accused's inability effectively to reconstruct at trial any unfairness that occurred at the lineup may deprive him of his only opportunity meaningfully to attack the credibility of the witness' courtroom identification.

What facts have been disclosed in specific cases about the conduct of pretrial confrontations for identification illustrate both the potential for substantial prejudice to the accused at that stage and the need for its revelation at trial. In sum, the principle of *Powell* v. *Alabama* and succeeding cases requires that we scrutinize any pretrial confrontation of the accused to determine whether the presence of his counsel is necessary to preserve the defendant's basic right to a fair trial as affected by his right meaningfully to cross-examine the witnesses against him and to have effective assistance of counsel at the trial itself. It calls upon us to analyze whether potential substantial prejudice to defendant's rights inheres in the particular confrontation and the ability of counsel to help avoid that prejudice.

Of course, nothing decided or said in the opinions in the cited cases links the right to counsel only to protection of Fifth Amendment rights. Rather those decisions no more than reflect a constitutional principle established as long ago as *Powell* v. *Alabama*. It is central to that principle that in addition to counsel's presence at trial, the accused is guaranteed that he need not stand alone against the State at any stage of the prosecution, formal or informal, in court or out, where counsel's absence might derogate from the accused's right to a fair trial. The security of that right is as much the aim of the right to counsel as it is of the other guarantees of the Sixth Amendment—the right of the accused to a speedy and public trial by an impartial jury, his right to be informed of the nature and cause of the accusation, and his right to be confronted with the witnesses against him and to have compulsory process for obtaining witnesses in his favor. The presence of counsel at such critical confrontations, as at the trial itself, operates to assure that the accused's interests will be protected consistently with our adversary theory of criminal prosecution.

Jail House Lawyers and Habeas Corpus

A strange extension of the right to counsel has developed because of the lack of attorneys available to prisoners confined in state prisons or local jails. In a few areas, there is a regular system of assistance by public defenders, or law-school students. In most areas one or more inmates advise, aid, or assist other inmates to prepare writs and other legal matters. Partly in the interest of limiting the practice of law to licensed attorneys, and partly to preserve prison discipline, jailhouse lawyers are often disciplined by prison or jail authorities, and forbidden to continue helping other inmates as substitutes for legal counsel. However, in the reality that is institutional life in American prisons and jails, if illiterate or poorly educated prisoners cannot have the assistance of a jailhouse lawyer to file habeas corpus petitions their possibly valid constitutional claims will never be heard in any court.

It is reasonable to control any propensity of prisoners to abuse both the giving and seeking of assistance in the preparation of applications for legal remedies related to their imprisonment. On the other hand, unless and until the administrator of a prison or jail provides a reasonable alternative to jailhouse lawyers—such as public defenders or voluntary legal assistance—to assist inmates in the preparation of petitions for postconviction relief, it does not serve the ends of justice to enforce a regulation barring capable prisoners from furnishing such assistance to other less capable inmates.

The jailhouse lawyer who assists other prisoners in seeking habeas corpus and other legal remedies is no less than an extension of the Sixth Amendment's right to counsel in a rudimentary form.

Selected References

Books
Beaney, William M. *The Right to Counsel in American Courts.* Ann Arbor: University of Michigan Press, 1955.
Lewis, Anthony. *Gideon's Trumpet.* New York: Random House, 1964.

Cases
Brown v. Mississippi, 297 U.S. 278 (1936).
Escobedo v. Illinois, 378 U.S. 478 (1964).
Miranda v. Arizona, 387 U.S. 436 (1966).
United States v. Wade, 388 U.S. 218 (1967).

Chapter XII

The Burger Court and Individual Rights

The decade of the 1960s was indeed a decade of conflict. It defined the limits of governmental power, state and federal, more closely than at any time in our history. Court decisions of the 1960s were more concerned with individual liberty than at any time since the framing and adoption of the Constitution and its first amendments. All of this judicial review was done in an atmosphere of rising crime rates, increasing violence in the streets of our cities, and some deadly ambush attacks on the police.

Limiting the power of government as opposed to the rights of suspects and defendants in criminal cases was achieved despite the severest criticism of the courts by government officials and laymen, who were justifiably concerned about the crime and violence which was increasing in the nation. On the other hand, an extension of the power of government in that decade in reaction to crime and violence could have stripped citizens of the liberties preserved for nearly 200 years.

In the 1970s the decisions of a differently constituted United States Supreme Court began limiting the expansion of individual rights. On June 24, 1969, Chief Justice Warren E. Burger took office. What had been the Warren Court became the Burger Court as members resigned, retired, or died, and new justices were appointed. (See Figure 3, p. 187)

The first case indicating the Burger Court's swing away from the expansion of individual rights was decided in 1971. The Court's decision in *Harris* v. *New York*[1] allowed the introduction of the statement of the accused into the trial record, despite the fact that the statement was invalid

1. Harris v. New York, 401 U.S. 222 (1971).

under the *Miranda*[2] doctrine because the accused had not been warned by police of his constitutional rights to silence and legal counsel. Chief Justice Burger, in delivering the court's opinion, minimized the adulteration or erosion of the *Miranda* doctrine by noting that a *Miranda*-tainted confession, which is inadmissible as evidence against the accused in the prosecution's case in chief, is useable for the purposes of impeachment where the defendant testifies contrary to the facts of his *Miranda*-tainted statement. "The shield provided by *Miranda* cannot be perverted into a license to use perjury by way of a defense, free from the risk of confrontation with prior inconsistent statements," the Chief Justice wrote. However, Justice Brennan's comment in his dissenting opinion argues to preserve the full *Miranda* doctrine: "The majority opinion goes far toward undoing much of the progress made in conforming police methods to the Constitution."

Four cases during 1972 and 1973 illustrate the action of the Burger Court in extending governmental power into areas in which the Warren Court had previously limited such power. Two cases are in the area of police lineups and eyewitness identification of suspects, and the other two concern searches without warrants at the time of arrest by police officers.

These four cases also illustrate the impact of a membership change in the composition of the court. Chief Justice Burger and newly-appointed Associate Justices Blackmun, Powell, and Rehnquist favored the swing away from the Warren Court, while holdover members cast the votes in dissent and wrote dissenting opinions. (See Figure 3.)

Eyewitness Identification—Lineup Cases

The U.S. Supreme Court's decision in *Kirby* v. *Illinois*[3] held that the doctrine of *United States* v. *Wade*[4] and *Gilbert* v. *California*[5] as to the right to counsel did not apply at pre-indictment confrontations. *Kirby* redefines the "critical stage of the prosecution" as beginning at the time criminal charges are formally made against an accused and he becomes the subject of a criminal prosecution.

In 1973, the Court's decision in *United States* v. *Ash*[6] held that a pre-trial event constitutes a "critical stage of the proceedings prior to trial only when there is a physical confrontation with the accused and the accused requires aid in coping with legal problems or help in meeting his

2. Miranda v. Arizona, 387 U.S. 436 (1966).
3. Kirby v. Illinois, 406 U.S. 682 (1972).
4. United States v. Wade, 338 U.S. 218 (1967).
5. Gilbert v. California, 388 U.S. 263 (1967).
6. United States v. Ash, 413 U.S. 300 (1973).

adversaries" (police and prosecutor). The Court ruled that a post-indictment scanning of photographs for the purpose of allowing a witness to attempt an identification of the offender was not a situation entitling the accused to have legal counsel present.

The result of these two decisions is to move away from at least one of the purposes of the *Wade* decision: to insure there is no improper influence or suggestion made to the witness by having the accused's attorney present when a witness attempts an identification.

The following two case studies present the Court's opinion in the *Kirby* and *Ash* cases.[7] The words of these opinions offer insight into the Burger Court's approach to eyewitness identification and its implications in the fields of individual rights and gaining a fair trial.

Case Study No. 1—Kirby v. Illinois (1972)*

Mr. Justice Stewart announced the judgment of the Court and an opinion in which The Chief Justice, Mr. Justice Blackmun, and Mr. Justice Rehnquist join.

In *United States* v. *Wade*, 388 U.S. 218, and *Gilbert* v. *California*, 388 U.S. 263, this Court held "that a post-indictment pretrial lineup at which the accused is exhibited to identifying witnesses is a critical stage of the criminal prosecution; that police conduct of such a lineup without notice to and in the absence of his counsel denies the accused his Sixth [and Fourteenth] Amendment right to counsel and calls in question the admissibility at trial of the in-court identifications of the accused by witnesses who attended the lineup." *Gilbert* v. *California*. Those cases further held that no "in-court identifications" are admissible in evidence if their "source" is a lineup conducted in violation of this constitutional standard. "Only a *per se* exclusionary rule as to such testimony can be an effective sanction," the Court said, "to assure that law enforcement authorities will respect the accused's constitutional right to the presence of his counsel at the critical lineup." In the present case we are asked to extend the *Wade-Gilbert per se* exclusionary rule to identification testimony based upon a police station showup that took place *before* the defendant had been indicted or otherwise formally charged with any criminal offense.

On February 21, 1968, a man named Willie Shard reported to the Chicago police that the previous day two men had robbed him on a Chicago street of a wallet containing, among other things, traveler's checks and a Social Security card. On February 22, two police officers stopped the petitioner and a companion, Ralph Bean, on West Madison Street in Chicago. When asked for identification, the petitioner produced a wallet that contained three travelers checks and a Social Security card, all bearing the name of Willie Shard. Papers with Shard's name on them were also found in Bean's possession. When asked to explain his possession of Shard's property, the petitioner first

---

7. Kirby v. Illinois, 406 U.S. 682 (1972); United States v. Ash, 413 U.S. 300 (1973).
*Extracts only, footnotes and citations deleted.

THE IMPACT OF MEMBERSHIP CHANGE IN THE UNITED STATES SUPREME COURT (1960s–1970s)

	The Warren Court	The Burger Court	Kirby	Ash	Robinson	Gustafson
			DISSENTING VOTES			
Chief Justice *Earl Warren*	X					
Associate Justice *Felix Frankfurter*	X					
Associate Justice *John M. Harlan*	X	X*				
Associate Justice *William J. Brennan, Jr.*	X	X	X	X	X	X
Associate Justice *Hugo L. Black*	X	X*				
Associate Justice *Potter Stewart*	X	X				
Associate Justice *Thomas C. Clark*	X					
Associate Justice *Charles E. Whittaker*	X					
Associate Justice *William O. Douglas*	X	X	X	X	X	X
Associate Justice *Byron R. White*	X	X	X			
Associate Justice *Arthur J. Goldberg*	X					
Associate Justice *Abe Fortas*	X					
Associate Justice *Thurgood Marshall*	X	X	X	X	X	X
Chief Justice *Warren E. Burger*		X				
Associate Justice *Harry A. Blackmun*		X				
Associate Justice *Lewis F. Powell, Jr.*		X				
Associate Justice *William H. Rehnquist*		X				

*Resigned or retired prior to the decisions listed.

Figure 3. Impact of the Supreme Court's Change. Membership in the U.S. Supreme Court in the 1960s under Chief Justice Earl Warren, and in the 1970s under Chief Justice Warren E. Burger. The four cases listed are 1972 and 1973 decisions limiting individual rights and extending governmental (police) power. Note that all dissenting votes in these four cases were by carry-over members of the Warren Court.

said that the traveler's checks were "play money," and then told the officers that he had won them in a crap game. The officers then arrested the petitioner and Bean and took them to a police station.

Only after arriving at the police station, and checking the records there, did the arresting officers learn of the Shard robbery. A police car was then dispatched to Shard's place of employment, where it picked up Shard and brought him to the police station. Immediately upon entering the room in the police station where the petitioner and Bean were seated at a table, Shard positively identified them as the men who had robbed him two days earlier. No lawyer was present in the room, and neither the petitioner nor Bean had asked for legal assistance, or been advised of any right to the presence of counsel.

More than six weeks later, the petitioner and Bean were indicted for the robbery of Willie Shard. Upon arraignment, counsel was appointed to represent them, and they pleaded not guilty. A pretrial motion to suppress Shard's identification testimony was denied, and at the trial Shard testified as a witness for the prosecution. In his testimony he described his identification of the two men at the police station on February 22, and identified them again in the courtroom as the men who had robbed him on February 20. He was cross-examined at length regarding the circumstances of his identification of the two defendants. The jury found both defendants guilty, and the petitioner's conviction was affirmed on appeal. The Illinois appellate court held that the admission of Shard's testimony was not error, relying upon an earlier decision of the Illinois Supreme Court, holding that the *Wade-Gilbert per se* exclusionary rule is not applicable to pre-indictment confrontations. We granted certiorari, limited to this question.

We note at the outset that the constitutional privilege against compulsory self-incrimination is in no way implicated here. The Court emphatically rejected the claimed applicability of that constitutional guarantee in *Wade* itself:

"Neither the lineup itself nor anything shown by this record that Wade was required to do in the lineup violated his privilege against self-incrimination. We have only recently reaffirmed that the privilege 'protects an accused only from being compelled to testify against himself, or otherwise provide the State with evidence of a testimonial or communicative nature. . . .'"

* * *

"We have no doubt that compelling the accused merely to exhibit his person for observation by a prosecution witness prior to trial involves no compulsion of the accused to give evidence having testimonial significance. It is compulsion of the accused to exhibit his physical characteristics, not compulsion to disclose any knowledge he might have. . . .'"

It follows that the doctrine of *Miranda* v. *Arizona*, 384 U.S. 436, has no applicability whatever to the issue before us; for the *Miranda* decision was based exclusively upon the Fifth and Fourteenth Amendment privilege against compulsory self-incrimination, upon the theory that custodial *interrogation* is inherently coercive.

The *Wade-Gilbert* exclusionary rule, by contrast, stems from a quite different constitutional guarantee—the guarantee of the right to counsel contained in the Sixth and Fourteenth Amendments. Unless all semblance of principled constitutional adjudication is to be abandoned, therefore, it is to the decisions construing that guarantee that we must look in determining the present controversy.

In a line of constitutional cases in this Court stemming back to the Court's landmark opinion in *Powell* v. *Alabama*, 287 U.S. 45, it has been firmly established that a person's Sixth and Fourteenth Amendment right to counsel attaches only at or after the time that adversary judicial proceedings have been initiated against him.

This is not to say that a defendant in a criminal case has a constitutional right to counsel only at the trial itself. The *Powell* case makes clear that the right attaches at the time of arraignment, and the Court has recently held that it exists also at the time of a preliminary hearing. *Coleman* v. *Alabama*. But the point is that, while members of the Court have differed as to existence of the right to counsel in the contexts of some of the above cases, *all* of those cases have involved points of time at or after the initiation of adversary judicial criminal proceedings—whether by way of formal charge, preliminary hearing, indictment, information, or arraignment.

The only seeming deviation from this long line of constitutional decisions was *Escobedo* v. *Illinois*, 378 U.S. 478. But *Escobedo* is not apposite here for two distinct reasons. First, the Court in retrospect perceived that the "prime purpose" of *Escobedo* was not to vindicate the constitutional right to counsel as such, but, like *Miranda*, "to guarantee full effectuation of the privilege against self-incrimination . . . ." *Johnson* v. *New Jersey*, 384 U.S. 719,729. Secondly, and perhaps even more important for purely practical purposes, the Court has limited the holding of *Escobedo* to its own facts. *Johnson* v. *New Jersey*, and those facts are not remotely akin to the facts of the case before us.

The initiation of judicial criminal proceedings is far from a mere formalism. It is the starting point of our whole system of adversary criminal justice. For it is only then that the government has committed itself to prosecute, and only then that the adverse positions of government and defendant have solidified. It is then that a defendant finds himself faced with the prosecutorial forces of organized society, and immersed in the intricacies of substantive and procedural criminal law. It is this point, therefore, that marks the commencement of the "criminal prosecutions" to which alone the explicit guarantees of the Sixth Amendment are applicable.

In this case we are asked to import into a routine police investigation an absolute constitutional guarantee historically and rationally applicable only after the onset of formal prosecutorial proceedings. We decline to do so. Less than a year after *Wade* and *Gilbert* were decided, the Court explained the rule of those decisions as follows: "The rationale of those cases was that an accused is entitled to counsel at any 'critical stage of the *prosecution*,' and that a post-indictment lineup is such a 'critical stage.'" We decline to depart from that rationale today by imposing a *per se* exclusionary rule upon testimony concerning an identification that took place long before the commencement of any prosecution whatever.

What has been said is not to suggest that there may not be occasions during the course of a criminal investigation when the police do abuse identification procedures. Such abuses are not beyond the reach of the Constitution. As the Court pointed out in *Wade* itself, it is always necessary to "scrutinize *any* pretrial confrontation . . . ." The Due Process Clause of the Fifth and Fourteenth Amendments forbids a lineup that is unnecessarily suggestive and conducive to irreparable mistaken identification. *Stovall* v. *Denno*, 388 U.S. 293; *Foster* v. *California*, 394 U.S. 440. When a person has not been formally charged with a criminal offense, *Stovall* strikes the appropriate constitutional balance between the right of a suspect to be protected from prejudicial procedures and the interest of society in the prompt and purposeful investigation of an unsolved crime.

The judgment is affirmed.

* * *

Case Study No. 2—United States v. Ash (1973)*

Mr. Justice Blackmun delivered the opinion of the Court.

In this case the Court is called upon to decide whether the Sixth Amendment grants an accused the right to have counsel present whenever the Government conducts a post-indictment photographic display, containing a picture of the accused, for the purpose of allowing a witness to attempt an identification of the offender. The United States Court of Appeals for the District of Columbia Circuit, sitting *en banc*, held, by a 5-to-4 vote, that the accused possesses this right to counsel. The court's holding is inconsistent with decisions of the courts of appeals of nine other circuits.

We reverse and remand.

On the morning of August 26, 1965, a man with a stocking mask entered a bank in Washington, D.C., and began waving a pistol. He ordered an employee to hang up the telephone and instructed all others present not to move. Seconds later a second man, also wearing a stocking mask, entered the bank, scooped up money from tellers' drawers into a bag, and left. The gunman followed, and both men escaped through an alley. The robbery lasted three to four minutes.

A Government informer, Clarence McFarland, told authorities that he had discussed the robbery with Charles J. Ash, Jr., the respondent here. Acting on this information, an FBI agent, in February 1966, showed five black-and-white mug shots, of Negro males of generally the same age, height, and weight, one of which was of Ash, to four witnesses. All four made uncertain identifications of Ash's picture. At this time Ash was not in custody and had not been charged. On April 1, 1966, an indictment was returned charging Ash and a codefendant, John L. Bailey, in five counts related to this bank robbery.

Trial was finally set for May 1968, almost three years after the crime. In preparing for trial, the prosecutor decided to use a photographic display to determine whether the witnesses he planned to call would be able to make in-court identifications. Shortly before the trial, an FBI agent and the prosecutor showed five color photographs to the four witnesses who previously had tentatively identified the black-and-white photograph of Ash. Three of the witnesses selected the picture of Ash, but one was unable to make any

*Extracts only; footnotes and citations are omitted.

selection. None of the witnesses selected the picture of Bailey which was in the group. This post-indictment identification provides the basis for respondent Ash's claim that he was denied the right to counsel at a "critical stage" of the prosecution.

No motion for severance was made, and Ash and Bailey were tried jointly. The trial judge held a hearing on the suggestive nature of the pretrial photographic displays. The judge did not make a clear ruling on suggestive nature, but held that the Government had demonstrated by "clear and convincing" evidence that in-court identifications would be "based on observation of the suspect other than the intervening observation."

At trial, the three witnesses who had been inside the bank identified Ash as the gunman, but they were unwilling to state that they were certain of their identifications. None of these made an in-court identification of Bailey. The fourth witness, who had been in a car outside the bank and who had seen the fleeing robbers after they had removed their masks, made positive in-court identifications of both Ash and Bailey. Bailey's counsel then sought to impeach this in-court identification by calling the FBI agent who had shown the color photographs to the witnesses immediately before trial. Bailey's counsel demonstrated that the witness who had identified Bailey in court had failed to identify a color photograph of Bailey. During the course of the examination, Bailey's counsel also, before the jury, brought out the fact that this witness had selected another man as one of the robbers. At this point the prosecutor became concerned that the jury might believe that the witness had selected a third person when, in fact, the witness had selected a photograph of Ash. After a conference at the bench, the trial judge ruled that all five color photographs would be admitted into evidence. The Court of Appeals held that this constituted the introduction of a post-indictment identification at the prosecutor's request and over the objection of defense counsel.

McFarland testified as a Government witness. He said he had discussed plans for the robbery with Ash before the event and, later, had discussed the results of the robbery with Ash in the presence of Bailey. McFarland was shown to possess an extensive criminal record and a history as an informer.

The jury convicted Ash on all counts. It was unable to reach a verdict on the charges against Bailey, and his motion for acquittal was granted. Ash received concurrent sentences on the several counts, the two longest being 80 months to 12 years.

The five-member majority of the Court of Appeals held that Ash's right to counsel, guaranteed by the Sixth Amendment, was violated when his attorney was not given the opportunity to be present at the photographic displays conducted in May 1968 before the trial.

We now undertake the threshold analysis that must be addressed.

A substantial departure from the historical test would be necessary if the Sixth Amendment were interpreted to give Ash a right to counsel at the photographic identification in this case. Since the accused himself is not present at the time of the photographic display, and asserts no right to be present, no possibility arises that the accused might be misled by his lack of familiarity with the law or overpowered by his professional adversary. Similarly, the counsel guarantee would not be used to produce equality in a trial-like adversary confrontation. Rather, the guarantee was used by the Court of Appeals to produce confrontation at an event that previously was not analogous to an adversary trial.

Even if we were willing to view the counsel guarantee in broad terms as a generalized protection of the adversary process, we would be unwilling to go so far as to extend the right to a portion of the prosecutor's trial-preparation interviews with witnesses. Although photography is relatively new, the interviewing of witnesses before trial is a procedure that predates the Sixth Amendment. In England in the 16th and 17th centuries counsel regularly interviewed witnesses before trial. The traditional counterbalance in the American adversary system for these interviews arises from the equal ability of defense counsel to seek and interview witnesses himself.

That adversary mechanism remains as effective for a photographic display as for other parts of pretrial interviews. No greater limitations are placed on defense counsel in constructing displays, seeking witnesses, and conducting photographic identifications than those applicable to the prosecution. Selection of the picture of a person other than the accused, or the inability of a witness to make any selection, will be useful to the defense in precisely the same manner that the selection of a picture of the defendant would be useful to the prosecution.

Pretrial photographic identifications, however, are hardly unique in offering possibilities for the actions of the prosecutor unfairly to prejudice the accused. Evidence favorable to the accused may be withheld; testimony of witnesses may be manipulated; the results of laboratory tests may be contrived. In many ways the prosecutor, by accident or by design, may improperly subvert the trial. The primary safeguard against abuses of this kind is the ethical responsibility of the prosecutor, who, as so often has been said, may "strike hard blows" but not "foul ones." If that safeguard fails, review remains available under due process standards. These same safeguards apply to misuse of photographs.

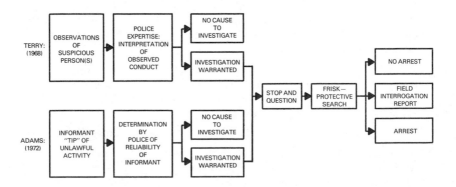

Figure 4. Stop-and-frisk doctrines of *Terry* v. *Ohio* and *Adams* v. *Williams*.

We are not persuaded that the risks inherent in the use of photographic displays are so pernicious that an extraordinary system of safeguards is required.

We hold, then, that the Sixth Amendment does not grant the right to counsel at photographic displays conducted by the Government for the purpose of allowing a witness to attempt an identification of the offender. This holding requires reversal of the judgment of the Court of Appeals.

Reversed and remanded.

Search and Seizure Cases

The first indication that the Burger Court might extend the power of police to engage in searches without warrants appeared in the 1972 case of *Adams* v. *Williams*.[8]

In this case the arresting officer was told by an informant, known to the officer, that an individual (Williams) seated in a nearby automobile was carrying narcotics and had a handgun tucked into his belt. The officer approached the car and when Williams rolled down the car's window, the officer reached in and removed a revolver from William's belt. In a search incidental to arrest for unlawful possession of a handgun (Connecticut law), Williams and his vehicle were searched and quantities of heroin found, along with a long-bladed weapon (machete) and a second handgun.

In *Terry* v. *Ohio*[9] (see Figure 4) the Warren Court had limited police action regarding suspicious persons to a brief stop (based on the viewing police officer's expertise and his personal observations of the suspect or suspects) and a pat-down, self-protective search for weapons. The Burger Court, in *Adams* v. *Williams* stated, "We reject respondent's argument that reasonable cause for a stop and frisk can only be based on the officer's personal observation, rather than on information supplied by another person."[10]

In 1973, the Burger Court's decisions in *United States* v. *Robinson*,[11] and *Gustafson* v. *Florida*[12] carried forward this extension of police power to carry out warrantless searches when an arrest is made for a traffic offense. Also the Burger Court upheld the legality of a full search without warrant *of a person* unrelated either to the cause for arrest or to the probability that weapons would in fact be found. In the case of a lawful custodial arrest a full search of the arrestee is not only an exception to the war-

8. Adams v. Williams, 407 U.S. 143 (1972).
9. Terry v. Ohio, 392 U.S. 1 (1968).
10. Adams v. Williams, 407 U.S. 143 (1972).
11. United States v. Robinson, 414 U.S. 218 (1973).
12. Gustafson v. Florida, 414 U.S. 260 (1973).

rant requirement of the Fourth Amendment, but is also a reasonable search under that Amendment.

The text of the Court's opinion in these two cases reveal the Burger Court's appraisal of the reasonableness of warrantless searches at the time of arrest as opposed to the Warren Court's prior doctrine.

Case Study No. 3—United States v. Robinson (1973)*

Mr. Justice Rehnquist delivered the opinion of the Court.

Respondent Robinson was convicted in United States District Court for the District of Columbia of the possession and facilitation of concealment of heroin. He was sentenced to concurrent terms of imprisonment for these offenses. On his appeal to the Court of Appeals for the District of Columbia Circuit, that court first remanded the case to the District Court for evidentiary hearing concerning the scope of the search of respondent's person which had occurred at the time of his arrest. The District Court made findings of fact and conclusions of law adverse to respondent, and he again appealed. This time the Court of Appeals *en banc* reversed the judgment of conviction, holding that the heroin introduced in evidence against respondent had been obtained as a result of a search which violated the Fourth Amendment to the United States Constitution.

On April 23, 1968, at approximately 11 o'clock P.M., Officer Richard Jenks, a 15-year veteran of the District of Columbia Metropolitan Police Department, observed the respondent driving a 1965 Cadillac near the intersection of 8th and C Streets, Southeast, in the District of Columbia. Jenks, as a result of previous investigation following a check of respondent's permit four days earlier, determined there was reason to believe that respondent was operating a motor vehicle after the revocation of his operator's permit. This is an offense defined by statute in the District of Columbia which carries a mandatory minimum jail term, a mandatory minimum fine, or both.

Jenks signaled respondent to stop the automobile, which respondent did, and all three of the occupants emerged from the car. At that point Jenks informed respondent that he was under arrest for "operating after revocation and obtaining a permit by misrepresentation." It was assumed by the majority of the Court of Appeals, and is conceded by the respondent here, that Jenks had probable cause to arrest respondent, and that he effected a full custody arrest.

In accordance with procedures prescribed in Police Department instructions, Jenks then began to search respondent. He explained at a subsequent hearing that he was "face to face" with the respondent, and "placed [his] hands on [the respondent], my right hand to his left breast like this (demonstrating) and proceeded to pat him down thus (with the right hand)." During this patdown, Jenks felt an object in the left breast pocket of the heavy coat respondent was wearing, but testified that he "couldn't tell what it was" and also that he "couldn't actually tell the size of it." Jenks then

*Extracts only; footnotes and citations are omitted.

reached into the pocket and pulled out the object, which turned out to be a "crumpled up cigarette package." Jenks testified that at this point he still did not know what was in the package:

"As I felt the package I could feel objects in the package but I couldn't tell what they were . . . . I knew they weren't cigarettes."

The officer then opened the cigarette pack and found 14 gelatin capsules of white powder which he thought to be, and which later analysis proved to be, heroin. Jenks then continued his search of respondent to completion, feeling around his waist and trouser legs, and examining the remaining pockets. The heroin seized from the respondent was admitted into evidence at the trial which resulted in his conviction in the District Court.

It is well settled that a search incident to a lawful arrest is a traditional exception to the warrant requirements of the Fourth Amendment. This general exception has historically been formulated into two distinct propositions. The first is that a search may be made of the *person* of the arrestee by virtue of the lawful arrest. The second is that a search may be made of the area within the control of the arrestee.

Examination of this Court's decisions in the area show that these two propositions have been treated quite differently. The validity of the search of a person incident to a lawful arrest has been regarded as settled from its first enunciation, and has remained virtually unchallenged until the present case. The validity of the second proposition, while likewise conceded in principle, has been subject to differing interpretations as to the extent of the area which may be searched.

Throughout the series of cases in which the Court has addressed the second proposition relating to a search incident to a lawful arrest—the permissible area beyond the person of the arrestee which such a search may cover—no doubt has been expressed as to the unqualified authority of the arresting authority to search the person of the arrestee.

In its decision of this case, the majority of the Court of Appeals decided that even after a police officer lawfully places a suspect under arrest for the purpose of taking him into custody, he may not ordinarily proceed to fully search the prisoner. He must instead conduct a limited frisk of the outer clothing and remove such weapons that he may, as a result of that limited frisk, reasonably believe the suspect has in his possession. While recognizing that *Terry* v. *Ohio* did not involve an arrest for probable cause, and it made quite clear that the "protective frisk" for weapons which it approved might be con-Appeals felt that the principles of that case should be carried over to this probable cause arrest for driving while one's license is revoked. Since there would be no further evidence of such a crime to be obtained in a search of the arrestee, the Court held that only a search for weapons could be justified.

Terry v. *Ohio*, did not involve an arrest for probable cause, and it made quite clear that the "protective frisk" for weapons which it approved might be conducted without probable cause. The Court's opinion explicitly recognized that there is a "distinction in purpose, character, and extent between a search incident to an arrest and a limited search for weapons":

"The former, although justified in part by the acknowledged necessity to protect the arresting officer from assault with a concealed weapon, is also justified on other grounds, and can therefore involve a relatively extensive exploration of the person. A search for weapons in the absence of probable cause to arrest, however, must like any other search, be strictly circumscribed by the exigencies which justify its initiation." Thus it must be limited to that which is necessary for the discovery of weapons which might be used to harm the officer or others nearby, and may realistically be characterized as something less than a "full" search even though it remains a serious intrusion.

" . . . An arrest is a wholly different type of intrusion upon the individual freedom from a limited search for weapons, and the interests each is designed to serve are likewise quite different. An arrest is the initial stage of a criminal prosecution. It is intended to vindicate society's interest in having its laws obeyed, and it is inevitably accompanied by future interference with the individual's freedom of movement, whether or not trial or conviction ultimately follows. The protective search for weapons, on the other hand, constitutes a brief, though far from inconsiderable, intrusion upon the sanctity of the person."

Terry, therefore, affords no basis to carry over to a probable cause arrest the limitations this Court placed on a stop-and-frisk search permissible without probable cause.

Chief Judge Cardozo of the New York Court of Appeals summarized his understanding of the historical basis for the authority to search incident to arrest in these words:

"The basic principle is this: Search of the person is unlawful when the seizure of the body is a trespass, and the purpose of the search is to discover grounds as yet unknown for arrest or accusation. Search of the person becomes lawful when grounds for arrest and accusation have been discovered, and the law is in the act of subjecting the body of the accused to its physical dominion.

"The distinction may seem subtle, but in truth it is founded in shrewd appreciation of the necessities of government. We are not to strain an immunity to the point at which human nature rebels against honoring it in conduct. The peace officer empowered to arrest must be empowered to disarm. If he may disarm, he may search, lest a weapon be concealed. The search being lawful, he retains what he finds if connected with the crime."

The Court of Appeals in effect determined that the *only* reason supporting the authority for a *full* search incident to lawful arrest was the possibility of discovery of evidence or fruits. Concluding that there could be no evidence or fruits in the case of an offense such as that with which respondent was charged, it held that any protective search would have to be limited by the conditions laid down in *Terry* for a search upon less than probable cause to arrest. Quite apart from the fact that *Terry* clearly recognized the distinction between the two types of searches, and that a different rule governed one than governed the other, we find additional reason to disagree with the Court of Appeals.

The justification or reason for the authority to search incident to a lawful arrest rests quite as much on the need to disarm the suspect in order to take him into custody as it does on the need to preserve evidence on his person for later use at trial.

The standards traditionally governing a search incident to lawful arrest are not, therefore, commuted to the stricter *Terry* standards by the absence of probable fruits or further evidence of the particular crime for which the arrest is made.

Nor are we inclined, on the basis of what seems to us to be a rather speculative judgment, to qualify the breadth of the general authority to search incident to a lawful custodial arrest on an assumption that persons arrested for the offense of driving while their license has been revoked are less likely to be possessed of dangerous weapons than are those arrested for other crimes. It is scarcely open to doubt that the danger to an officer is far greater in the case of the extended exposure which follows the taking of a suspect into custody and transporting him to the police station than in the case of the relatively fleeting contact resulting from the typical *Terry*-type stop. This is an adequate basis for treating all custodial arrests alike for purposes of search justification.

A police officer's determination as to how and where to search the person of a suspect whom he has arrested is necessarily a quick *ad hoc* judgment which the Fourth Amendment does not require to be broken down in each instance into an analysis of each step in the search. The authority to search the person incident to a lawful custodial arrest, while based upon the need to disarm and to discover evidence, does not depend on what a court may later decide was the probability in a particular arrest situation that weapons or evidence would in fact be found upon the person of the suspect. A custodial arrest of a suspect based on probable cause is a reasonable intrusion under the Fourth Amendment; that intrusion being lawful, a search incident to the arrest requires no additional justification. It is the fact of the lawful arrest which establishes the authority to search, and we hold that in the case of a lawful custodial arrest a full search of the person is not only an exception to the warrant requirement of the Fourth Amendment, but is also a "reasonable" search under that Amendment.

The search of respondent's person conducted by Officer Jenks in this case and the seizure from him of the heroin, were permissible under established Fourth Amendment law. While thorough, the search partook of none of the extreme or patently abusive characteristics which were held to violate the Due Process Clause of the Fourteenth Amendment in *Rochin* v. *California*, 342 U.S. 165, (1952). Since it is the fact of custodial arrest which gives rise to the authority to search, it is of no moment that Jenks did not indicate any subjective fear of the respondent or that he did not himself suspect that respondent was armed. Having in the course of a lawful search come upon the crumpled package of cigarettes, he was entitled to inspect it; and when his inspection revealed the heroin capsules, he was entitled to seize them as "fruits, instrumentalities, or contraband" probative of criminal conduct.

The judgment of the Court of Appeals holding otherwise is reversed.

Case Study No. 4—Gustafson v. Florida (1973)*

Mr. Justice Rehnquist delivered the opinion of the Court.

Petitioner James Gustafson was convicted in a Florida trial court for unlawful possession of marihuana. At his trial the State introduced into evidence marihuana which had been seized from him during a search incident to his arrest on a charge of driving without an operator's license. The District Court of Appeal of Florida, Fourth District, reversed petitioner's conviction, holding that the search which had led to the discovery of the marihuana was unreasonable under the Fourth and Fourteenth Amendments. The Supreme Court of Florida in turn reversed that decision. For the reasons set forth below, we affirm the judgment of the Supreme Court of Florida.

Petitioner urges that there could be no evidentiary purpose for the search conducted by Smith, and therefore the authority to search for weapons incident to a lawful arrest is controlled by the standards laid down in *Terry* v. *Ohio*, 392 U.S. 1, (1968). Petitioner contends that this case is different from *United States* v. *Robinson* in that petitioner had experienced no previous encounters with the officer in this case, and the offense for which he was arrested was "benign or trivial in nature," carrying with it no mandatory minimum sentence as did the offense for which Robinson was arrested. Petitioner points out that here, unlike *Robinson*, there were no police regulations which required the officer to take petitioner into custody, nor were there police department policies requiring full scale body searches upon arrest in the field. Petitioner also points to the fact that here, as in *Robinson* the officer expressed no fear for his own well-being or for that of others in dealing with the petitioner.

We have held today in *United States* v. *Robinson* that "it is the fact of the lawful arrest which establishes the authority to search, and . . . in the case of a lawful custodial arrest a full search of the person is not only an exception to the warrant requirement of the Fourth Amendment, but is also a 'reasonable' search under that Amendment." Our decision in *Robinson* indicates that the limitations placed by *Terry* v. *Ohio* on protective searches conducted in an investigatory stop situation based on less than probable cause are not to be carried over to searches made incident to lawful custodial arrests.

Though the officer here was not required to take the petitioner into custody by police regulations as he was in *Robinson*, and there did not exist a departmental policy establishing the conditions under which a full scale body search should be conducted, we do not find these differences determinative of the constitutional issue. It is sufficient that the officer had probable cause to arrest the petitioner and that he lawfully effectuated the arrest, and placed the petitioner in custody. In addition, as our decision in *Robinson* makes clear, the arguable absence of "evidentiary" purpose for a search incident to a lawful arrest is not controlling. "The authority to search a person incident to a lawful custodial arrest, while based upon the need to disarm and to dis-

---

*Extracts only; footnotes and citations are deleted.

cover evidence, does not depend on what a court may later decide was the probability in a particular arrest situation that weapons or evidence would in fact be found upon the person of the suspect."

We hold therefore that upon arresting petitioner for the offense of driving his automobile without a valid operator's license, and taking him into custody, Smith was entitled to make a full search of petitioner's person incident to that lawful arrest. Since it is the fact of custodial arrest which gives rise to the authority to search, it is of no moment that Smith did not indicate any subjective fear of the petitioner or that he did not himself suspect that the petitioner was armed. Having in the course of his lawful search come upon the box of cigarettes, Smith was entitled to inspect it; and when his inspection revealed the homemade cigarettes which he believed to contain an unlawful substance, he was entitled to seize them as "fruits, instrumentalities or contraband" probative of criminal conduct.

The judgment of the Supreme Court of Florida is therefore affirmed.

Police Power and Constitutional Limitations

The foregoing cases show that the present court has expanded permissible police intrusions. There is little doubt that the membership of the Burger Court acted in full recognition of the growth of violent crime in the United States and the many problems facing the police when they attempt to control criminal activities. This Court has struck a new balance between individual rights and police activity in the battle against crime.

How far present and future membership on the United States Supreme Court will move in overruling the doctrine of *Chimel* v. *California*,[13] which limits police search of the place of arrest without a search warrant, is yet to be determined. The doctrine of *Mapp* v. *Ohio*[14] and the entire issue of the "exclusionary rule" may be reevaluated and new concepts and doctrines devised to keep police behavior in conformance with constitutional limitations.

Edward Bennett Williams, attorney, author, and educator, believes we are in the midst of a social revolution, and offers his views as follows:

It is the revolution of the young, the poor, the blacks, the social aliens of our society. It has created a crisis of authority, a crisis in which the authority of all our institutions is under challenge: the family, the university, the church, the judicial system, the economic system, and the very government itself.[15]

13. Chimel v. California, 395 U.S. 752 (1969).
14. Mapp v. Ohio, 367 U.S. 643 (1961).
15. Edward Bennett Williams, address to the California Bar Association; Los Angeles, September 17, 1970, *Journal of the State Bar of California* 45, no. 6 (November–December 1970): p. 819.

The problem of crime is a serious and emotional one. Perhaps the answer is not the abridgment of liberty, but rather an analysis of the entire system of justice. It certainly is easier and less expensive to blame the courts for crime than to give the police the men, the training, and the equipment needed to make the criminal realize he will get caught. With many it certainly is more popular to advocate restricting the Bill of Rights in the name of 'law and order' than to advocate an increase of taxes, or a sincere and well-funded program to combat ignorance, poverty, illiteracy, and racial discrimination. It would be a terrible paradox if we lost our freedom in an attempt to restore order.

Selected References

Books

Kohlmeier, Louis M., Jr. *God Save This Honorable Court.* New York: Charles Scribner's Sons, 1972.
Sayler, Richard H.; Boyer, Barry E.; and Gooding, Robert E. Jr., editors. *The Warren Court.* New York: Chelsea House, 1968.

Periodicals

Swindler, William F. "The Politics of Advice and Consent," *American Bar Association Journal*, vol. 56, pp. 533–42.

Cases

Adams v. Williams, 407 U.S. 143 (1972).
Gilbert v. California, 388 U.S. 263 (1967).
Gustafson v. Florida, 414 U.S. 260 (1973).
Harris v. New York, 401 U.S. 222 (1971).
Kirby v. Illinois, 406 U.S. 682 (1972).
United States v. Ash, 413 U.S. 300 (1973).
United States v. Robinson, 414 U.S. 218 (1973).

Part IV
The Courts

Chapter XIII

Criminal Proceedings

The basic thrust of justice in the criminal courts of the United States is to accuse and prove at trial: *accusatorial*. The accusatorial method necessarily implies a conflict between the state (the people) and the person accused of crime. However, in this instance, conflict is not a destructive force; in the courts of America, conflict is a creative force. Our system of justice is called the *adversary* system, wherein the inherent conflict is a creative force for discovering truth. This is a system that pits one adversary against another to find the truth. It is a system in which the conflict is resolved at a trial: a criminal proceeding in which the accusation is tested on the issue of guilt or innocence.

This testing at trial of an accusation of crime involves a classic triumvirate in America's legal system: the prosecuting attorney, the counsel for the defense, and the trial judge. The prosecutor and counsel for the defendant are adversaries: the prosecutor advocating the side of the accuser, and the defense attorney advocating the side of the defendant. The judge's role is to insure that the issues are joined within the rules of the legal system for the trial of persons accused of crime. In the three-sided interaction of prosecutor, attorney for the defense, and the trial judge, the court becomes a place where a fair balance is struck between the rights of the state and the rights of the individual.

In the prosecution of persons accused of crime in American courts, the formality of the procedure depends upon the seriousness of the crime. Lesser offenses, such as traffic violations, are disposed of by a magistrate in summary proceedings, although the accused person has the right to seek a postponement and formalize the most minor hearing unless the minor offense has been classified as an infraction by legislation. Infractions are punishable by fine only. A variety of offenses, from violations of local laws about sweeping sidewalks to petty theft, are also disposed of by a magistrate in the majority of cases, after the defendant has waived a more formal prosecution. It is in the trial of major offenses that the adversary system comes into full flower. These are the crimes at the felony level: the serious crimes in which the victim may be killed or injured; and crimes against property such as burglary or thefts in which the value of the stolen property exceeds $50.00 (or other minimum value).

In the trial of such crimes the accused shall enjoy the right to a speedy and public trial, and he has the right to representation by counsel, as well as other rights designed to safeguard persons accused of crime from an arbitrary, abusive, or wrongful process of criminal justice. The major provision of the Constitution dealing with the rights of an accused person and the mode of criminal proceedings is the Sixth Amendment:

> In all criminal prosecutions, the accused shall enjoy the right to a speedy and public trial, by an impartial jury of the State and district wherein the crime shall have been committed, which district shall have been previously ascertained by law, and to be informed of the nature and cause of the accusation; to be confronted with the witnesses against him; to have compulsory process for obtaining witnesses in his favor, and to have the Assistance of Counsel for his defense.

In addition, there is the Fifth Amendment guarantee of notice and preliminary investigation ("No person shall be held to answer for capital or otherwise infamous crime unless on a presentment or indictment of a grand jury . . ."); protection against double jeopardy (". . . nor shall any person be subject for the same offense to be twice put in jeopardy of life or limb . . ."); and privilege against self-incrimination (". . . nor shall be compelled in any criminal case to be a witness against himself . . ."). These were enacted to insure the protection of an accused person from arbitrary charges of crime and criminal proceedings by state or federal agents.

The criminal proceeding is to be a fair trial before an impartial tribunal, and it is to be preceded by a preliminary investigation by the prosecutor to insure that the crime committed is one which should be prosecuted. Then, if warranted, appropriate action is taken by the prosecutor to bring the accusation of crime before or within the power of the proper tribunal. The accused person must be given adequate notice of the offense charged against him, and an opportunity to prepare for trial, procure witnesses, and make such investigation as deemed necessary—with legal counsel to assist him in this work. Lastly, there should be provision for a suitable appellate review of the case.[1]

1. William M. Beaney, *The Right to Counsel In American Courts* (Ann Arbor: University of Michigan Press, 1955), pp. 4–5.

The concept of a fair trial before an impartial tribunal has been further enhanced by recent U.S. Supreme Court decisions. These have made applicable to the states and their agents and courts the first ten amendments of the United States Constitution by the provisions of the Fourteenth Amendment which forbid abridging the privileges or immunities of citizens or depriving any person of life, liberty, or property without due process of law.

Many other legal systems reject the adversary system and depend upon one with an inquisitorial thrust, often unimpeded by any guarantees of individual rights or the assistance of legal counsel. The trial itself is merely an appeal from an extensive pretrial investigation, or an appeal from a custodial interrogation.[2] In such jurisdictions, a speedy trial or the right to representation by counsel at trial are very hollow things. For all practical purposes, conviction is assured by the pretrial procedure permitted the government agents, the police, and the prosecutor.

The Prosecuting Attorney

The prosecuting attorney may be called the public prosecutor, the district attorney, the county prosecutor, the county attorney, or the state's attorney. Regardless of the terminology used to identify this agent of criminal justice, his role is essentially the same across the United States. It is the role of a lawyer representing the people of the state in a criminal proceeding. Sometimes, the role overlaps with some functions and duties in regard to civil law and the best interest of the county government, but the chief function of the prosecuting attorney is enforcement of the law against criminals of every kind, and prosecution of offenders before appropriate courts.

Prosecution by a public official educated in law developed rapidly in America. While the colonists adopted the English attorney general concept, there was a definite and early trend to creating local political offices for persons charged with the duty of conducting criminal prosecutions. The statewide attorney general may have been handicapped by transportation problems in the early years, but there is evidence the colonists preferred local control of this important role in government. They proceeded in its development with enthusiasm because of a wish to decentralize the office of attorney general in regard to local prosecutions. In many states, the first step was the designation of an assistant or deputy attorney general with local or limited territorial jurisdiction. Later, the office became one in which the prosecuting attorney was elected by the people of the jurisdictional district.

2. Escobedo v. Illinois, 378 U.S. 478 (1963), pp. 487–488.

With the advent of county government, this area of jurisdiction became the county. The prosecutor has a role in county government as legal advisor to county and other local officials (possibly defending the interests of the county in civil litigation). To some degree he is under the control of county government because of the budgetary administration of the office of the prosecuting attorney. In this balkanization of the ancient role of attorney general, it was never intended that a board of supervisors, or other county legislative or executive agents, be permitted to interfere with, or control the management of criminal prosecutions by the prosecuting attorney. In his capacity as prosecutor, the prosecuting attorney is clearly the agent of the state government and its people. He is under no direct control as public prosecutor because he acts by the authority and in the name of the *people* of the state.

The prosecuting attorney is the key law enforcement officer in the particular area over which he has jurisdiction. In this area, the potentialities of the office are limited only by the intelligence, skill, and legal and political capacity of the incumbent. In the formidable list of duties often assigned to this public official, the interests of the state are almost entirely in his hands. He is a quasi-judicial officer who determines from his own investigation, or evidence submitted to him by police or others, whether a criminal offense has been committed, and upon grounds of public policy the prosecuting attorney enjoys an absolute immunity from civil liability for his official acts (similar to judges and grand juries). The public interest demands the prosecuting attorney speak and act freely and fearlessly in the discharge of his important official functions and duties. The prosecuting attorney is expected to be the mainspring of law enforcement. If evidence of a crime is not available—and there is good reason to believe it might be secured—he is supposed to go out and get it.[3] The specific functions of the prosecutor are:

1. To serve as an agent (agency) of the executive branch of government particularly charged with the duty to see that the laws are faithfully executed and enforced in order to maintain the rule of law

2. To accept the dual role of administrator of justice and advocate, and exercise sound discretion in the performance of this role

3. To seek justice, not merely convictions

4. To know and be guided by the standards of professional conduct as defined in codes and canons of the legal profession.[4]

3. Raymond Moley, *Politics and Criminal Prosecution* (New York: Minton, Balch and Co., 1929), pp. 48–62.
4. Advisory Committee on the Prosecution and Defense Functions, American Bar Association, *Standards Relating to the Prosecution Function and the Defense Function–Tentative Draft* (New York: Institute of Judicial Administration, 1970), p. 43.

In performing his functions, the prosecuting attorney has considerable discretion at many decision points in the administration of criminal justice. However, the most important area of this discretionary power is the power to charge—or not to charge—a person with a crime. The decision to charge requires the resolution of three related, but independent issues:

1. A determination as to whether there is sufficient probability of guilt to justify bringing the case to trial
2. Whether prosecution is in the community interest
3. Decision making as to the specific crime or crimes to charge in the accusatory pleading.[5]

Nonlegal aspects of a case may suggest a decision not to charge an individual. Many prosecuting attorneys avoid family disputes unless a trial is vitally necessary to force a husband to recognize his responsibilities for his children; others hesitate to prosecute in cases of crimes without victims, or to serve as a collection agency in insufficient funds fraud check cases. In addition, the nature of a crime (nonprofessional gambling, shoplifting, fraud checks) may indicate that a jury will not focus on the issue of guilt or innocence, but will exercise their decision-making power to acquit the defendant for reasons unrelated to evidence of his guilt.

Many aspects of the decision to charge rests on standard legal issues. For instance:

1. Has a crime been committed?
2. What crime has been committed, both by common name and statute designation, and by the circumstances of the crime?
3. Was the crime committed within the area served by the prosecuting attorney?
4. Does the presence of facts indicate all of the elements of this crime in the circumstances of its happening?
5. Has the suspect been connected to the crime by either direct or indirect (circumstantial) evidence, or by the suspect's own statement?
6. Are there any legal problems precluding the successful prosecution of the suspect: missing witnesses, tainted evidence, double jeopardy, and so forth?

In preparing a case for trial, the prosecuting attorney sifts the evidence, and plans his case along the following lines: (1) presentation of the

5. Frank W. Miller, *Prosecution—The Decision to Charge a Suspect With a Crime* (Boston: Little, Brown and Co., 1969), pp. 3–5.

case in court, (2) proper direct examination of the state's witnesses and cross-examination of defense witnesses, (3) preparation of instructions for the use of the trial judge in charging the jury, and (4) preparation of the oral argument of the prosecution.

The presentation of a case in court is based on preparation before trial. In filing an accusatory pleading, the prosecuting attorney reviews the crime (offense) report, the arrest record, the connect-up sheet revealing the suspect's tie-ins with other crimes, the evidence summary and report, and the criminal history sheet of the suspect. Often, he interviews the investigating officers and prosecution witnesses, examines evidence, and participates in querying the accused. Then, in presenting the case to the grand jury for an indictment, or participating in a preliminary hearing before a magistrate at which the issue is whether the accused should be held to answer (predates the filing of an information by the prosecuting attorney), there is a review of the circumstances of the crime, the criminal agency, and the linking of the suspect to the crime and criminal agency. All of this is preparation for trial, and in the larger offices of prosecuting attorneys one or more assistants may participate in the case at these pretrial levels, and still another actually prepare the case for trial and take over its prosecution in court.

Traditionally, the prosecutor may best present his case in court by creating, from the beginning of the proceedings, an atmosphere of sincerity, earnestness, and confidence in the righteousness of his cause. The prosecuting attorney is, like all lawyers, a partisan in litigation, but as a public official he cannot allow this partisanship to lead him to an unjust harassment of the person accused. He should be as concerned with giving the accused a fair trial as he is of obtaining a conviction. He is an officer of the court and should be fair, seeking a conviction only by legal means. However, he is still the attorney for the people (the state) and may properly use legal means to secure a conviction. The suppression of facts or the secreting of witnesses capable of establishing the innocence of the accused is highly reprehensible. However, he is not bound to use as witnesses for the people any person whom he believes is mistaken as to the facts or likely to commit perjury; or to call any witness whose testimony he does not believe to be relevant or which might confuse the issue in dispute.

In direct examination of his witnesses, the prosecuting attorney seeks to preserve their credibility by revealing their ability to observe and recall their positions when they viewed the crime or a related event, their business at this place at this particular time, and all the other factors that make witnesses credible and their stories worthy of belief. In cross-examination, the prosecuting attorney attempts to destroy belief in the stories of defense witnesses by attacks on the personal knowledge of the witnesses and their motivation to tell the truth.

In making his requests to charge to the trial judge, the prosecuting attorney seeks to bring the appropriate sections of law to the attention of the jury. The substance of these requests varies with the circumstances of a case, but inherent in the advocacy of the state's case is to bring before the jury at the end of the trial, instructions that will present law and legal theory favorable to the prosecution and its case.

The prosecuting attorney's closing argument presents his case and its strong points, and points out the weakness and lack of merit in the defense case. Then, when it becomes time to reply to defense counsel's argument, the prosecuting attorney must destroy the defense argument. In both instances, this oral argument by the prosecuting attorney must be a well-founded and logical presentation utilizing the type of argument that can be followed easily and which will lead to reasonable conclusions. It must reconcile evidence in conflict with the prosecution's theory of the crime and the evidence structure of the case, and must destroy any favorable impressions the defense case may have made upon the minds of the jurors.[6]

The Defense Counsel

In California, the duties of an attorney are specified in state statutes as follows:

1. To support the Constitution and laws of the United States and of this State

2. To maintain the respect due to the courts of justice and judicial officers

3. To counsel or maintain such actions, proceedings, or defenses only as appear to him legal or just, except the defense of a person charged with a public offense

4. To employ, for the purpose of maintaining the causes confided to him such means only as are consistent with truth, and never to seek to mislead the judge or any judicial officer by an artifice or false statement of fact or law

5. To maintain inviolate the confidence, and at every peril to himself to preserve the secrets, of his client

6. To abstain from all offensive personality, and to advance no fact prejudicial to the honor or reputation of a party or witness, unless required by the justice of the cause with which he is charged

6. Manley J. Bowler, "Oral Argument in Criminal Prosecution," *The Journal of Criminal Law, Criminology and Police Science* 52, No. 2 (July–August 1961): 203–9.

7. Not to encourage either the commencement or the continuance of an action or proceeding from any corrupt motive of passion or interest

8. Never to reject, for any consideration personal to himself, the cause of the defenseless or the oppressed.[7]

In contrast to the prosecutor who has an attorney's responsibility to the people of the state, the county, and the accused, the counsel for the defense is responsible to his client only, within the bounds of the ethics of his profession and state law. He is the classic opponent of the prosecutor, and the protection of his client's rights may require him to oppose the wishes of the judge on various matters. He does this respectfully at all times, even when he must appear unyielding and uncooperative. As an advocate of his client he performs his function within our adversary system. He does not impede the administration of justice because he challenges the prosecutor or resists the judge, but rather fulfills his role in the administration of criminal justice. Defense counsel's obligations are multiple and complex. His obligation to his client is that of counselor and advocate; toward the prosecuting attorney he is a professional adversary; and toward the court he is an advocate for his client and a counselor to the court.

The specific function and role of defense counsel are:

1. To serve as the accused's counselor and advocate with courage, devotion and to the utmost of his learning and ability, and according to law

2. To serve as the professional representative of the accused, not his alter ego. He has no duty to execute any directive of the accused which does not comport with law or professional standards of conduct, and it is unprofessional conduct for a lawyer intentionally to misrepresent matters of fact or law to the court.[8]

A defense attorney retains for himself an independence of action and control over the defense case. All tactical and strategical decisions, such as which jurors to keep or excuse, what witnesses to call, how to conduct cross-examination, and which trial motions to attempt, should be made by the defense attorney after consulting with his client. As the defendant, the client must finally decide, after consultation with his legal counsel, what pleas to enter, whether to waive jury trial, and whether to testify in his own behalf.

---

7. *California Business and Professional Code*, Chapter 4, Section 6068.
8. American Bar Association, *Standards Relating to the Prosecution and Defense Functions*, p. 153.

For effective representation, the defense counsel must achieve a lawyer-client relationship with the accused. He must get the complete candor of the accused about the crime charged and its circumstances, and full consent to control the legal aspects of the defense case. When the accused understands the defense attorney's obligation of confidentiality in relation to any disclosures (privileged communication), this confidential relationship between lawyer and client will foster candor, and candor plus control establishes the basis for an effective defense.

Accused persons as clients often withhold information from their lawyers, sometimes for reasons of their own, but quite frequently because they believe this is the lawyer's desire. To break down this reluctance to disclose all the known facts, it is not uncommon for an attorney serving as defense counsel to use the "hard sell" to induce candor: a warning that if the client fails to disclose all relevant facts he will find himself looking for a new lawyer, as withdrawal from the case would be logical upon discovery of this lack of trust. Possibly some comment will be added about the reality of a criminal trial. It may be pointed out that nothing the client can disclose is likely to be as embarrassing or incriminating as a handicapped defense counsel attempting to locate witnesses, interview them, and investigate the facts of their stories, only to have the defense case set back at trial by surprise testimony or other evidence. At the very least, defense counsel should know as much about the case as his client.

Every man accused of a crime is entitled to have a lawyer to present a legal defense. But in this client-lawyer relationship, the client is not entitled to have a lawyer who will permit the client or a witness to testify to something which the lawyer knows is untrue. If a defense attorney knows his client or a defense witness is not telling the truth, he should not be a party to the perjury. In the client-attorney preparation of a case for trial, the attorney should probe vigorously into the evidence which corroborates or refutes the proposed testimony which is to be offered in court, and thus prevent the introduction of false testimony.[9] However, it is not the attorney's duty to judge the weight of the evidence and determine where truth lies when the evidence is in conflict. This is the function of the trial jury, or judge in a trial without a jury.

The relationship between the defendant and defense counsel does not require the attorney to be a "mouthpiece" for his client: a mere mechanical reproduction of the thoughts, words, and alibi of his client. The lawyer's obligation to client, court, and community does not include the presentation of false or improper testimony, nor does it justify untruthfulness and insincerity, but it does include service as an advocate who will present all the relevant facts and circumstances in his client's defense. In fact, despite any belief in the guilt of the defendant, the defense

9. Emory Buckner, "The Trial of Cases," in *The Lawyer's Treasury*, ed. Eugene C. Gerhart (New York: Charter Books, Bobbs-Merrill Co. 1963), pp. 400–01.

attorney has a duty to present the extenuating facts and circumstances on behalf of his client.[10] The defense attorney must represent his client's side when his evidence and that of the prosecution are different. It is not for him to decide who is telling the truth when each side claims truth.

A defense attorney must advise his client against unlawful conduct, and must refuse to be a party to illegal conduct in his service. The problem becomes critical when a defendant desires to testify falsely and informs his attorney of his resolve to take the stand as a witness. However, the absolute prohibition against subornation applies where the defendant himself wishes to testify. Therefore, the defense attorney should withdraw from the case rather than place himself in the position of offering a perjurious witness.

Sometimes, such a critical situation is aggravated by the fact that withdrawal will leave the defendant without counsel, and the court is likely to deny a request to withdraw. There are conflicting views as to whether an attorney should disclose any part of this conflict to the court, but it seems that the lawyer's duty to maintain confidentiality between client and attorney will not permit such a disclosure.

In this conflict between the obligation of an attorney and the defendant's absolute right to testify in his own behalf, a suggested solution is to counsel against such a course of action by the defendant and advise him that he (defense counsel) will not use such testimony in any way in his oral argument. When this fails, the defense attorney may: (1) allow the defendant to testify in narrative form and in his own words, but without direct examination in the conventional manner, and (2) avoid any reference to the defendant's testimony in conducting the remainder of the defense case. In this fashion, the defense attorney avoids participation in a fraud on the court.

A defense attorney cannot presume a client is guilty before guilt is established in accordance with due process: a verdict and judgment of guilty after a fair trial in a court of competent jurisdiction. However, what if the accused admits guilt or the attorney discovers direct evidence of it? So far as the accused is concerned, he is entitled to plead not guilty (placing the burden of proof of guilt on the prosecution), and maintains right to counsel. When his reputation, livelihood, freedom, and even life, are hazarded, some lawyer must take his case. One of the controlling factors in the plea decision is often whether the accused realizes the fact that obviously guilty persons have little evidence upon which to build a defense, and that the most appropriate action may be an attempt to achieve some bargain with the prosecuting attorney in exchange for a plea of guilty.[11]

10. A. S. Cutler, "Is a Lawyer Bound to Support an Unjust Cause?" in *The Lawyer's Treasury*, pp. 420–27.
11. Arthur Lewis Wood, *Criminal Lawyer* (New Haven, Conn.: College and University Press, 1967), pp. 242–45.

The prosecution has the burden of proof on the issue of guilt. In the absence of a voluntary plea of guilty by the defendant, the defense attorney need present nothing, reveal no confidences of his client, nor furnish any other information to help the prosecution's case. The public interest not to convict innocent persons accused of crime permits the defense attorney to put the state and its prosecuting attorney to its proof. Regardless of what he may think as to the issue of guilt or innocence, it is his job to put the prosecution's case in the worst possible light.

It is common defense strategy to plan along the lines of one or more of the following common defenses. These are:

1. The defendant did not commit the crime—the accused is the victim of mistaken identification, poor investigation, or coincidence.

2. The defendant did commit the crime, but it was excusable (self-defense; provocation), an accident, or the result of insanity or other factors diminishing the accused's capacity to develop intent or plan the crime.

3. No crime was committed—one or more essential elements of the crime charged cannot be proved, or there is insufficient evidence to prove the *corpus delicti.* [12]*

As the preparation of the defense case proceeds, beginning with the first client-lawyer interview, the defense counsel must develop a theory upon which to base his preparation for trial. This is a marshaling of facts so that by appropriate emphasis and orderly assembly at trial, the defense counsel can present evidence capable of arousing doubt in the minds of the jurors as to the guilt of the accused.

Jurors usually accept their grave responsibility and realize they have taken an oath to try the accused on the evidence presented by the prosecution and the defense. However, the total impact of the defense case must convince the jury, as triers of fact, that the prosecution has failed to establish the accused's guilt beyond a reasonable doubt. As early in the trial as the jury selection period—and as late as the time for filing requests to charge pertinent aspects of law—the defense counsel must define with simplicity and clarity the issues before the jury: the elements of the crime charged and the fact that the prosecution must prove each element beyond a reasonable doubt.

After all the evidence has been presented, the defense counsel's right to a closing argument for the defense is an important method by

12. Paul B. Weston and Kenneth M. Wells, *Criminal Investigation–Basic Perspectives* 2d ed. (Englewood Cliffs, N.J.: Prentice-Hall, 1973), pp. 250–51.
*Literally in Latin "the body of the offense," a sufficient set of facts to show a particular crime has been committed.

which he relates basic laws to the evidence presented. Of course, this is a partisan exposition in which the prosecution's case is stated or summed up to highlight its *improbabilities*, and the defense case presented as favorably as possible. After all, it is an "argument for the defense" (the prosecuting attorney is allowed time for *his* closing argument).

One of the strongest arguments likely to develop the necessary doubt in the jurors' minds, is the one based on improbabilities. The average juror is not a person trained in law or experienced in its enforcement, and tends to believe that which is in accord with his own experience and the recorded experience of others. He is reluctant to believe that which he considers improbable. This avenue of persuasion may be linked to sub-arguments based on what the prosecution has *not* proved: (1) the lack of motive (a classic ploy in murder trials is that more victims are killed by persons with some motive for killing them than by those who have no motive), (2) the good character of the accused, (3) an attack on the value of circumstantial evidence and on the credibility of accomplice testimony as completely unreliable and untrustworthy (when appropriate), (4) a spirited defense of alibi witnesses who testify for the accused.[13]

Defense counsel often requests that specified instructions be given to the jury by the trial judge as he instructs them in the law, just prior to the jury's determination of the facts in their quest for a verdict.[14] (These "requests to charge" suggest the direction of major defense attacks on the prosecution's case.)

Jury instructions required by law or commonly requested by lawyers in criminal cases have developed some uniformity. The following illustrations are based on California case law, California statutory law, and Los Angeles County Superior Court instructions:

> *Presumption of Innocence, Reasonable Doubt, Burden of Proof*—A defendant in a criminal action is presumed to be innocent until the contrary is proved, and in case of a reasonable doubt whether his guilt is satisfactorily shown he is entitled to an acquittal, but the effect of this presumption is only to place upon the State the burden of proving him guilty beyond a reasonable doubt. Reasonable doubt is defined as follows: It is not a mere possible doubt; because everything relating to human affairs, and depending on moral evidence, is open to some possible or imaginary doubt. It is that state of the case which, after the entire comparison and consideration of all the evidence, leaves the minds of the jurors in that condition that they cannot say they feel an abiding conviction, to a moral certainty, of the truth of the charge.
>
> *Credibility of Witnesses*—The jury are the sole and exclusive judges of the effect and value of evidence addressed to them and of the credibility of the

13. G. Arthur Martin, "Closing Argument to the Jury for the Defense in Criminal Cases," *The Journal of Criminal Law, Criminology and Police Science* 58, no. 1 (March 1967): 2–17.
14. Henry B. Rothblatt, *Successful Techniques in the Trial of Criminal Cases* (Englewood Cliffs, N.J.: Prentice-Hall, 1961), pp. 189–225.

witnesses who have testified in the case. Every person who testifies under oath is a witness. You are the sole and exclusive judges of the credibility of the witnesses who have testified in this case.

In determining the credibility of a witness you may consider any matter that has a tendency in reason to prove or disprove the truthfulness of his testimony, including but not limited to the following:

His demeanor while testifying and the manner in which he testifies;

The character of his testimony;

The extent of his capacity to perceive, to recollect, or to communicate any matter about which he testifies;

The extent of his opportunity to perceive any matter about which he testifies;

His character for honesty or veracity or their opposites;

The existence or nonexistence of a bias, interest, or other motive;

A statement previously made by him that is consistent with his testimony;

A statement made by him that is inconsistent with any part of his testimony.

The existence or nonexistence of any fact testified to by him;

His attitude toward the action in which he testifies or toward the giving of testimony;

His admission of untruthfulness;

His prior conviction of a felony.

A witness willfully false in one material part of his testimony is to be distrusted in others. You may reject the whole testimony of a witness who willfully has testified falsely as to a material point, unless, from all the evidence, you shall believe the probability of truth favors his testimony in other particulars.

However, discrepancies in a witness' testimony or between his testimony and that of others, if there were any, do not necessarily mean that the witness should be discredited. Failure of recollection is a common experience; and innocent misrecollection is not uncommon. It is a fact, also, that two persons witnessing an incident or a transaction often will see or hear it differently. Whether a discrepancy pertains to a fact of importance or only to a trivial detail should be considered in weighing its significance.

You are not bound to decide in conformity with the testimony of a number of witnesses, which does not produce conviction in your mind, as against the testimony of a lesser number or other evidence, which appeals to your mind with more convincing force. [Testimony which you believe given by one witness is sufficient for the proof of any fact.] This does not mean that you are at liberty to disregard the testimony of the greater number of witnesses merely from caprice or prejudice, or from a desire to favor one side as against the other. It does mean that you are not to decide an issue by the simple process of counting the number of witnesses who have testified on the opposing sides. It means that the final test is not in the relative number of witnesses, but in the relative convincing force of the evidence.

Motive—Motive is not an element of the crime charged and need not be shown. However, you may consider motive or lack of motive as a circumstance in this case. Presence of motive may tend to establish guilt. Absence of motive may tend to establish innocence. You will therefore give its presence or absence, as the case may be, the weight to which you find it to be entitled.

Character—Evidence of the defendant's character as to those traits which ordinarily would be involved in the commission of a crime such as that charged in this case is relevant to the question of the defendant's guilt or innocence because it may be reasoned that a person of good character as to such traits would not be likely to commit the crime of which the defendant is charged.

Evidence of good character may be sufficient to raise a reasonable doubt whether the defendant is guilty, which doubt otherwise would not exist.

If the evidence establishes that the defendant's character as to certain traits has not been discussed among those who know him, you may infer from the absence of such discussion that his character in those respects is good.

But if, after weighing all the evidence, you are convinced beyond a reasonable doubt that the defendant is guilty of the (a) crime charged against him in the information, your duty will be to find him guilty (of that offense), notwithstanding the testimony that he was or is a person of good character.

Direct and Circumstantial Evidence—The testimony of a witness, a writing, a material object, or anything presented to the senses offered to prove the existence or nonexistence of a fact is either direct or circumstantial evidence.

Direct evidence means evidence that directly proves a fact, without an inference, and which in itself, if true, conclusively establishes that fact.

Circumstantial evidence means evidence that proves a fact from which an inference of the existence of another fact may be drawn.

An inference is a deduction of fact that may logically and reasonably be drawn from another fact or group of facts established by the evidence.

It is not necessary that facts be proved by direct evidence. They may be proved also by circumstantial evidence or by a combination of direct evidence and circumstantial evidence. Both direct evidence and circumstantial evidence are acceptable as a means of proof. Neither is entitled to any greater weight than the other.

You are not permitted to find the defendant guilty of the crime charged against him based on circumstantial evidence unless the proved circumstances are not only consistent with the theory that the defendant is guilty of the crime, but cannot be reconciled with any other rational conclusion and each fact which is essential to complete a set of circumstances necessary to establish the defendant's guilt has been proved beyond a reasonable doubt.

Also, if the evidence is susceptible of two reasonable interpretations, one of which points to the defendant's guilt and the other to his innocence, it is your duty to adopt that interpretation which points to the defendant's innocence, and reject the other which points to his guilt.

The specific intent with which an act is done may be manifested by the circumstances surrounding its commission. But you may not find the defendant guilty of the offense charged in this case unless the proved circumstances not only are consistent with the hypothesis that he had the specific intent to commit the crime charged but are irreconcilable with any other rational conclusion.

Also, if the evidence as to such specific intent is susceptible of two reasonable interpretations, one of which points to the existence thereof and the other to the absence thereof, you must adopt that interpretation which points to its absence. If, on the other hand, one interpretation of the evidence as to such specific intent appears to you to be reasonable and the other interpretation to be unreasonable, it would be your duty to accept the reasonable interpretation and to reject the unreasonable.

Accomplice—An accomplice is one who is liable to be prosecuted for the identical offense charged against the defendant on trial.

To be an accomplice, the person must have knowingly and with criminal intent aided, promoted, encouraged, or instigated by act or advice, the commission of such offense.

A conviction cannot be had upon the testimony of an accomplice unless it is corroborated by such other evidence as shall tend to connect the defendant with the commission of such offense.

Corroborative evidence is evidence of some act or fact related to the offense which, if believed, by itself and without any aid, interpretation or direction from the testimony of the accomplice, tends to connect the defendant with the commission of the offense charged.

However, it is not necessary that the corroborative evidence be sufficient in itself to establish every element of the offense charged, or that it corroborate every fact to which the accomplice testifies.

In determining whether an accomplice has been corroborated, you must first assume the testimony of the accomplice has been removed from the case. You must then determine whether there is any remaining evidence which tends to connect the defendant with the commission of the offense. If there is not such independent evidence which tends to connect defendant with the commission of the offense, the testimony of the accomplice is not corroborated.

If there is such independent evidence which you believe, then the testimony of the accomplice is corroborated.

The corroboration of the testimony of an accomplice required by law may not be supplied by the testimony of any or all of his accomplices, but must come from other evidence.

Merely assenting to or aiding or assisting in the commission of a crime without guilty knowledge or intent is not criminal, and a person so assenting to, or aiding, or assisting in, the commission of a crime without guilty knowledge or intent in respect thereto, is not an acomplice in the commission of such crime.

It is the law that the testimony of an accomplice ought to be viewed with distrust. This does not mean that you may arbitrarily disregard such testimony, but you should give to it the weight to which you find it to be entitled after examining it with care and caution and in the light of all the evidence in the case.

Alibi—The defendant in this case has introduced evidence tending to show that he was not present at the time and place of the commission of the alleged offense for which he is here on trial. If, after a consideration of all the evidence, you have a reasonable doubt that the defendant was present at the time the crime was committed, he is entitled to an acquittal.

The Judge

The judge is the person, educated in law, whose role in the administration of justice is to settle all kinds of legal controversy. These controversies may be civil questions of contracts, wills, or personal injury, involving a person's money; and they may be criminal issues, involving a person's life or liberty.

There is a continual search for ways and means to improve the quality of the judiciary through better selection and improved disciplinary procedures. While federal judges are appointed by the President with the "advice and consent" of the Senate, and in a few states the judiciary is largely appointed, the election of judges is the major method of selection. Pending an election, governors often make selections to fill vacancies. Such appointments are usually tantamount to permanent positions, because rarely does an incumbent judge have opposition, and even more rarely is an incumbent defeated. Discipline of judges is a delicate subject, and impeachment is much too cumbersome, expensive, and ineffective. Since the establishment of the federal courts, only eight judges have been impeached. Other disciplinary methods are by resolution,* recall,** and removal or discipline by the judiciary. New Jersey's supreme court has the power to discipline members of the state judiciary by its contempt power and its power to issue administrative orders.

A member of the judiciary can influence the actual enforcement of the laws by his own attitude toward particular crimes. If he regards an offense as so minor that it deserves no punishment, the prosecuting attorney becomes reluctant to prosecute, and policemen begin to close their eyes to this offense and concentrate available enforcement on other violations. While the prosecuting attorney has vast powers because of the discretion allowed him to make decisions to charge or not to charge an accused, the judge is influential because of the authority entrusted to him as the decision maker.

*Resolution of the legislature.
**Recall by popular vote.

In the administration of criminal justice the government has the power to take a person's life or liberty in order to preserve an orderly society. This power is given to the trial judge to exercise. The trial judge is the center of the process which includes the victim, the accused, the prosecutor, the defense attorney, jurors (when appropriate), spectators (public trial), and himself. The decisions and actions of the others are governed in a large measure by the immediate rulings of the trial judge.

The public impression of our legal system is largely shaped by the impact of the trial judge on victim, juror, and spectator. His dignity and demeanor, his even-handed control of the proceedings, his courtesy toward all involved, and his display of respect for the rules of evidence and other procedures and courts, are important factors in shaping the total image.

The judge is an arbiter, an umpire, and an advisor in the process of trying and determining the facts. If he is the trier of fact (trial without a jury), his is the final word on the credibility of witnesses and facts in dispute. His primary role, however, is to insure that the proceedings against the accused are conducted fairly and within the rules of the adjudicatory process: the judicial supervision over criminal proceedings requiring a decision by judge or jury. The trial of most serious offenses in the United States is by jury unless the defendant, and his counsel, waive a jury trial and place the entire adjudicatory process in the hands of the trial judge.

The trial judge also has supervision of the Sixth Amendment right to a speedy trial (enforceable against the states as one of the basic rights preserved by the constitution).[15] This constitutional guarantee is essential to protect the accused from: (1) undue and oppressive incarceration prior to trial, (2) anxiety and concern accompanying public accusation, and (3) long delays likely to impair the ability of the accused to defend himself. Initially, an accused who has not been released on bail because of the nature of the charge, or an inability to post the required bail, has a problem keeping in touch with his counsel and with potential defense witnesses. When long delays prolong the pretrial period, the accused—in or out of prison—has a problem mitigating the corrosive effects of time: the disappearance of witnesses and evidence, memory failure, and a loss of perspective concerning past events.

The prosecuting attorney is often the prime mover in securing a speedy trial. The accused's right dates from the time he was first accused or held to answer for the crime charged. Usually, the trial of defendants in custody has first priority, but in scheduling cases for a court's calendar, the prosecuting attorney must advise the presiding judge of the relevant facts used to determine the order of cases to be scheduled, and his reasons for not scheduling past-due cases. Continuances which postpone the trial of a case are only granted by a court for good cause based on a trilogy of interests: the prosecution, the defense, and the public.

15. Klopfer v. North Carolina, 386 U.S. 213 (1968).

The selection of a jury is the first step in a criminal trial in which the right to jury is not waived. Under the trial judge's supervision, the qualifications of jurors called to serve are examined under oath. Each of the advocates, the prosecuting attorney and the defense counsel, seek the right people for a trial jury. (This is within the concept of the adversary system of justice and part of the role of attorney.) Challenges for cause (without limit) are used to get rid of those prospective jurors who indicate an inability or unwillingness to participate in a verdict based on the law as it will be explained by the trial judge, and the facts of the case as they will be presented in the trial. Each side is allowed a certain number of peremptory challenges (which varies with state law, nature of charges, and number of defendants) to dismiss from the jury any person that attorney deems unsuitable, but whose responses did not establish grounds to challenge for cause.[16]

There is extensive judicial supervision of this jury selection process, despite the fact that the district attorney is an officer of the court and should be fair, seeking a conviction only by legal means. It is improper for a prosecutor to willfully try to pack a jury or to attempt to place on the jury persons who are biased against the defendant to such a degree as to make them unfair jurors under the law. *Ex parte** exclusion of potential jurors by a prosecutor (removing their names from the master jury list through the jury commissioner or other persons charged with the selection and formation of jury lists and panels) is also improper and calculated to thwart the objectives of justice. Trial by an impartial jury, not one composed from a list which consciously eliminated "pro-defense" jurors, is guaranteed. Juries are not to be hand picked by prosecutors so that they may merely ratify indictments and information with verdicts of guilty.[17] Trial judges do make inquiry into the entire process of selecting jurors, but they also recognize the fact that the prosecuting attorney is still the lawyer for the people, and may in a legitimate way ascertain the character, standing, and integrity of jurors before they are sworn.[18]

When the jury has been selected, the trial judge administers the oath to the selected jurors and alternates. The actual trial begins with an opening by both sides, usually brief statements of what each attorney intends to prove in court. This is followed by the state's case—all the witnesses and other evidence assembled by police and prosecutor. When the prosecution rests, the defense has the opportunity to present their witnesses and assembled evidence. When the defense rests, the prosecution responds to the defense case (rebuttal), and this is followed by a defense answer to the latest attempt by the prosecutor to prove the accusation

16. Paul B. Weston and Kenneth M. Wells, *The Administration of Justice*, 2d ed. (Englewood Cliffs, N.J.: Prentice-Hall, 1973), pp. 202–06.
*Of or from one side or party, without notice to the adverse party.
17. Noland v. State Bar, 63 Cal. 2d 298 (1965).
18. People v. Reuf, 14 Cal. App 576 (1910).

(surrebuttal). When the presentation of evidence is ended, opposing attorneys have a chance to request the trial judge to instruct the jury on various points of law, and each attorney has an opportunity to present a closing or oral argument to explain the case and its evidence to the jury.[19]

The adversary system for the conduct of trials in our legal system is rigorously institutionalized with rigidly defined roles for the prosecuting attorney and defense counsel. The purpose of this contentious system is clear, its rules are known, and it is the watchful trial judge who depersonalizes this battle by forcing participants to follow the rules and attempt to achieve the adversary system's goal: truth.

One judicial problem in relation to any jury trial on the issue of guilt or innocence is that only one side can win. Part of the judicial role is to convey this fact to the jurors in the case, and to point out the collateral fact that their decision as to the winner should be based on the merits of the case as they see it through their evaluation of the evidence presented in the courtroom.

Many persons fail to realize the fervent love for the administration of justice that exists in the hearts of judges, jurors, and the counsel for both sides who fulfill the adversary system roles of prosecuting attorney and counsel for the defense. It is as American as the traditional apple pie, and the court in which these people work cooperatively is preserved by a calm, unemotional, and dignified management of criminal proceedings by men of loyalty and sincerity who "call them as they see them coming over the plate."[20]

Disparities in Justice and Voir Dire

From the preliminary hearing to verdict, there are disparities in the quality and measure of justice because of a defendant's age, sex, education, economic status, and race.

The age of a defendant acts to secure a young person a lighter sentence (usually on first offender rules), but disadvantages the youth since he is less likely to receive the procedural safeguards insuring fair trial and due process. The processes of justice have a standard sex orientation (chivalry) in favoring the female, but the large number of male criminals may account for this disparity. The less educated defendant is more likely to go to prison, either because he is unaware of his rights, docile about the denial of them, or because he is not believed to be a good risk for probation. The indigent defendant is found guilty upon trial, either because the poor are usually passive in their defense, or are more likely to have a prior record, or be guilty as charged, or all three.

19. Weston and Wells, *The Administration of Justice*, 2d ed. p. 194.
20. Harold A. Medina, "Some Reflections on the Judicial Function," in *The Lawyer's Treasury*, pp. 481–89.

As a black or Spanish-speaking defendant, there is a greater likelihood of no release on bail, or representation by a court-appointed attorney, of trial without a jury, or conviction as a result of plea negotiations. This may not result from discrimination against minorities, but rather from the correlation between minority groups, poverty, and lack of education, plus a distrust of all-white or near-white juries.[21]

Disparity does not mean discrimination with its overt implication of being unfavored, nor does it mean any inequity because of gross unfairness. It does mean that the accused is disadvantaged in some way in the postarrest process. Since defendants from minority groups are likely to be disadvantaged because of their ethnic background, their poverty, their lack of education, and in some instances their youth, it is important that these defendants be protected against any disparity of justice.

In the final analysis the issue of guilt or innocence is in the care of the jury. If justice is to be obtained for a minority group defendant in our adversary system of trial, a good beginning must be in the careful selection of the jury. Therefore, to guard against any disparity of justice, defense counsel must be alert and work hard to screen out undesirable jurors at the pretrial *voir dire** examination.

A general question does not single out the bigot, or the prejudiced. Simply asking a prospective juror if he (or she) harbors prejudice (that cannot be set aside for the purpose of a fair trial) on the subject of race, religion, or national origin does not probe and pry adequately. A probing series of questions is required. For instance:

Q: Mr. Smith, I suppose that you, like most of us, have certain feelings about members of the Negro race, blacks, that are different from our feelings about members of our own race?

Q: Do you personally know many blacks?

Q: Have you ever had a black in your home as a social guest?

Q: Have you ever been in a black person's home as a social guest?

Q: Do your children have close friends who are blacks?

Q: If the daughter of one of your close friends married a black, do you feel that would create problems for that girl and her family?

Q: (If the answer is "Yes") Why do you think such a marriage would create problems?

Q: When you indicate in your answer that it is because most people are prejudiced, do you think that applies to this jury panel also?

Q: Do you feel that those feelings would bias most jurors against my client, who is a Negro, a black?

21. Stuart S. Nagel, *The Legal Process from a Behavioral Perspective* (Homewood, Ill.: Dorsey Press, 1969), pp. 88–112.
*Questioning to determine qualifications.

Q: Do you share those feelings yourself?

Q: Would you have a difficult time setting aside those biases in fairly considering my client's case?[22]

These questions point up the real extent of the problem in finding jurors truly unbiased in a black defendant's cause, no matter in what part of the nation the trial is held.

The problem of bias is further complicated by the fact that the trial courts are not agreed on whether they will even allow such probing questions. In those trial courts which do allow the defense attorney to ask probing questions, a basis can be developed for excusing a juror for cause, or the defense attorney may excuse the prospective juror on a peremptory challenge.

There are jurisdictions which leave the entire *voir dire* to the judge, allowing only limited questioning by the attorneys, or no questioning at all though permitting the submission of questions to the court. In these jurisdictions, the judge uses his own discretion as to which of the attorney's questions to ask the jurors.[23]

Attorneys on both sides of the system contend that the court does not have the same interest in discovering prejudices of jurors; they often are more concerned with the speed in which they can complete a case, thus keeping crowded calendars within manageable limits.

The courts counter this claim by pointing out their traditional concern in conducting a trial fair to both sides, and their duty to control tactics which only delay and do not contribute to the administration of justice.

There is a long journey yet to travel before bias and prejudice are finally and completely excluded from our system of justice. However, it is happening more often, and in more and more areas. The court of judge, prosecutor, and defense counsel is a forum for justice, and justice is based on the ideal of a fair trial before an impartial jury.

Selected References

Books

Advisory Committee on the Prosecution and Defense Functions, American Bar Association. *Standards Relating to the Prosecution Function and the Defense Function—Tentative Draft*. New York: Institute of Judicial Administration, 1970.

Miller, Frank W. *Prosecution—The Decision to Charge a Suspect with a Crime*. Boston: Little, Brown and Co., 1969.

22. Herbert Hafis, "Adequate *Voir Dire*," *Journal of the California State Bar* 44, no. 6 (November–December 1969): 858–60.
23. People v. Crowe, 8 Cal. 3d 815 (1973).

Rothblatt, Henry B. *Successful Techniques in the Trial of Criminal Cases*. En-
  glewood Cliffs, N.J.: Prentice-Hall, 1961.
Weston, Paul B. and Wells, Kenneth M. *The Administration of Justice*, 2d ed.
  Englewood Cliffs, N.J.: Prentice-Hall, 1973.
Wood, Arthur Lewis. *Criminal Lawyer*. New Haven, Conn.: College and Univer-
  sity Press, 1967.

Periodicals
Hafis, Herbert. "Adequate *Voir Dire.*" *Journal of the California State Bar* 44, no.
  6 (November–December 1969): 858–60.

Cases
Klopfer v. North Carolina 386 U.S. 213 (1968).
Noland v. State Bar, 63 Cal. 2d. 298 (1965).
People v. Crowe, 8 Cal. 3d 815 (1973).
People v. Ruef, 14 Cal. App 576 (1910).

Chapter XIV

Plea Negotiations

At least 90 percent of all persons convicted of crime in the United States are convicted by their plea of guilty. Less than 10 percent of the persons arrested and accused of crime are convicted as a result of trial by either a judge or a jury.[1] Plea negotiations (or "deal" as it is often termed) are the means for maintaining a constant percentage of guilty pleas necessary to keep from swamping the courts with work, creating greater delays in time between accusation and trial.

Trials take time and are costly. The courts throughout the country are usually staffed to offer trials to no more than 10 percent of the persons arrested and accused of crime. One may imagine what would happen to the machinery of justice if 20, 30, or 50 percent of the criminal cases went to trial. The courts which now are not in a workload chaos, live on the verge of one. Obviously, the present functioning of our courts is dependent upon this working arrangement: pleas of guilty save both the time of a court and the expense of a trial. Any legal system which must have a "back door" arrangement of plea negotiations to survive is in constant danger of sacrificing the accused for the goal of expediency; of trading fairness to the accused individual for perpetuation of a system that can only function efficiently because of plea negotiations.

The participants in plea negotiations are the prosecutor, the defendant, the defense counsel, and the judge. Because of the arcane methodology involved in plea negotiations, the defendant is an outsider to whom the nuances of plea negotiations and agreement are explained by his counsel. In a spin-off from the adversary system of trials in the American legal system, the antagonists in plea negotiations are the prosecuting

1. U.S., President's Commission on Law Enforcement and Administration of Justice, *The Challenge of Crime in a Free Society* (Washington, D.C.: Government Printing Office, 1967), p. 134.

attorney and the defense counsel. However, to make certain that cases come to trial without long delays, a judge of the trial court having jurisdiction over a case is an interested party. In fact, the sentencing judge has a strange role in plea negotiations. He has not only a vested interest in the number of cases that do *not* go to trial, but he also has to concur in the plea agreement—or there is no "deal."

The major potentials for injustice as a result of plea negotiations are: (1) innocent persons may plead guilty in fear of the consequences of a trial; (2) persons who plead guilty may be rewarded with a sentence unsuited to their correctional needs; and (3) the ends of justice may be defeated by one of the antagonists securing a greater "advantage" from the plea agreement than justified by the facts.

While plea negotiations result in conviction without trial, there is nothing improper in arriving at substantial justice which is agreeable to all parties to the litigation without the time and expense of a trial. Instead of a jury or judge determining what is justice in a specific case, the parties at interest and the judge arrive at the proper and final disposition.

The Advantage in Plea Bargaining

There is an initial pressure on prosecuting attorneys to conclude plea negotiations with a plea of guilty because this agency of criminal justice is universally understaffed. Just as the judiciary has a vested interest in reducing the number of accusations that move on to become court trials, so too has the prosecutor. In addition, as elective officials, prosecutors survive or perish in the community's evaluation of their professional competence. At the very least, successful plea negotiation will give a prosecutor a conviction ratio beginning at 90 percent. If an inept prosecutor, or one with a subpar staff, loses half the cases that go to trial, he can point with pride to a conviction ratio of about 95 percent. Plea negotiations in 90 percent of all cases has made a paper tiger out of many prosecutors who are failures as trial lawyers.

Because of the nature of the work and the frequency of contact with the criminal element of a community, there is also a potential for corruption in plea negotiation. There is the danger that the prosecutor will be offered monetary or political rewards for his cooperation—an advantage of sorts.

On the defense side, one of the basic advantages is the resolution of a pending case rapidly and without trial. In all jurisdictions the institutionalized legal services in public defender's offices are grossly overcrowded and there is a need for this shortcut. Privately retained counsel have more lucrative law work with clients other than those charged with crime. Most good trial attorneys have a heavy work load and must allocate

their time to the best advantage of their clients and the successful operation of their practice. They, too, find plea negotiations an excellent
shortcut.

The major advantage to the defense, however, is in planning a
client's strategy of defense. Plea negotiation sessions are informative. A
great deal can be learned of the prosecution's case when the defense
counsel is skilled at these negotiations and the prosecuting attorney is less
skilled or careless. In addition, the overview of a case may indicate to a
skilled attorney that the defendant will be convicted as charged if the case
goes to trial, and his best service to his client is to advise him to plead
guilty in return for concessions from the prosecutor.

Just as in trial proceedings, the prosecutor and the defense counsel
are in opposition. Plea negotiating is bargaining. In winning at the conclusion of a plea-negotiating session, one of the opposing attorneys must
gain some advantage. For this reason, neither antagonist is completely
open and honest about the chances of success for his side if the case goes
to trial. In fact, prosecuting attorneys assure defense counsel that their
client does not have a chance if the case goes to trial; and defense counsel
quite appropriately (and with equal regard for truth) responds with assur-
ances that the state just does not have sufficient evidence to go to trial on
the original accusation. It is difficult to say, in an individual case, who is
the buyer and who is the seller in these plea negotiations; but it is safe to
say that the prosecuting attorney is the merchant in the beginning stages
of plea negotiations.

There is a well-founded suspicion around most courthouses in
America that police and prosecuting attorneys select the most serious possible charge as the base of the original accusation against a suspect. From
this place of beginning, without any plea negotiations, it is not unusual for
the prosecuting attorney to reduce the charge to a lesser crime more
suited to the evidence collected in the case *if he has to go to trial.*
Likewise, an omnibus indictment may be filed in the first instance, alleging a series of crimes, but the defection of witnesses or the likely suppression of evidence may result in the consolidation of these charges into a
single accusation of crime if the case has to go to trial. Prosecutors sometimes press the most serious possible charge or multiple charges at the
time of an arrest because past experience has indicated the time period
between apprehension and trial is frequently sufficient to flush out unknown witnesses and discover other evidence of guilt. When this evidence is not forthcoming, the prosecutor must reduce the initial charges
to meet his evidentiary needs if he has to go to trial. Since the lack of the
necessary evidence to support the most serious charge is known only to
the prosecutor (usually the police are unsure), he is in an advantageous
position to begin talking to defense counsel about a plea agreement.

When a case fails to develop the evidence necessary for a conviction
if it goes to trial, the prosecutor is not only willing, but possibly eager, to

amend the accusation to a lesser charge, to dismiss other pending cases, and to seek judicial approval of leniency in the sentencing just so long as the accused will plead guilty and the case will not have to go to trial.

Under these circumstances, a defendant acting as his own counsel is not prepared to cope with an experienced prosecutor. Many otherwise skilled defense attorneys are poor advocates for their clients when faced with a prosecutor who is skilled in the give and take of plea negotiations and who knows the real situation as to the evidence in the case. The advent of a defendant's right to pretrial discovery* in many jurisdictions has tended to equalize the bargaining position of each side.

A thing of value to the prosecutor which may be turned to the advantage of a defendant is cooperation beyond the plea of guilty. This means an agreement to help the police and prosecutor by becoming a state's witness, if warranted by the circumstances of the case, or serving as an informant about other crimes (the facts of which are known to the defendant). Such cooperation is useful when the prosecutor must seek the approval of the sentencing judge for an assurance that the defendant will receive a reduced sentence as part of the plea agreement. Of course, the prosecutor can seek leniency on the mere plea of guilty, but additional cooperation is helpful in some plea negotiations.

Guilty or innocent, there is tremendous pressure on an accused awaiting trial. Life in a county jail is a miserable experience. Release on bail is no more than a marking-time period. There is a building up of pressure to get it over with. It is a situation which encourages a plea of guilty. To many accused persons any deal appears more attractive than the risk of a threatened trial.

To protect defendants who enter into plea negotiations and then reject the idea of pleading guilty, there is a confidentiality to this act. The fact that the defendant, or his counsel, and the prosecuting attorney engaged in plea discussions, or made a plea agreement which was later rejected by the defendant, should not be received in evidence against or in favor of the defendant in any subsequent criminal proceedings.

In review, the fact that the ultimate decision in plea negotiations must be the defendant's, may be a mechanism for injustice rather than justice because of the pressure of the pretrial situation. The seeming advantage gained in a plea agreement may, in the end, be a far greater penalty than that which would have been imposed by any sentence after trial.

Conviction Without Trial

A person who pleads guilty makes an in-court admission of every essential element involved in the crime charged. This is the equivalent of a

---

*The right of defendant to see and copy police reports of investigation and interviews of possible witnesses before the case goes to trial.

verdict of guilty after a trial. There is no trial on a plea of guilty; the plea formalizes and settles the issue of guilt or innocence. A plea of guilty must constitute an intelligent and understanding waiver of three basic rights: (1) the right against self-incrimination, (2) the right to trial by jury, and (3) the right to be confronted by witnesses.

In all jurisdictions, there must be a court arraignment for pleading after a formal accusation has been filed by the prosecutor. If a defendant does not have retained or assigned counsel at this time, he is advised of his right to counsel, and informed that the court will appoint counsel if he is indigent and cannot retain his own attorney. If the defendant or his counsel requires more time to consider a plea, it is common practice to allow a continuance for a reasonable period. This is a time of great importance to an accused person.

In the event the defendant enters a plea of guilty, there may be a judicial examination of the defendant's action as to whether the facts support or corroborate the guilty plea. The defendant must fully understand the nature and consequence of a plea of guilty, and it must be determined whether the plea is made voluntarily.[2]

Voluntariness of Plea

An accused's plea of guilty may be accepted by the court only if "voluntarily and understandingly made": the plea reflects the considered choice of the accused, free of any factor or inducement which has unfairly influenced or overcome his will. A guilty plea that is induced by coercion or promises, or which is otherwise unfairly obtained or given through ignorance, fear, or inadvertence, is involuntary and inconsistent with due process of law. Due process requires that before a guilty plea is accepted the court must determine that the defendant has a clear understanding of the charge, and is aware of possible defenses to it and circumstances in mitigation thereof, and that his admission of guilt is without reservation. A judge is not relieved of his duty to ascertain that a guilty plea was understandingly and knowingly made merely because the defendant is represented by counsel.[3]

The court's role in determining voluntariness is not so much to inquire as to whether the defendant made a wise decision in pleading guilty—although this is not out of order—but to make certain that the defendant is telling the truth when he states the decision was voluntary. Therefore, the assigned judge must inquire into the full circumstances under which the defendant made the decision to plead guilty. This is for the purpose of ascertaining whether the decision was voluntarily made,

2. Paul B. Weston and Kenneth M. Wells, *Criminal Evidence for Police* (Englewood Cliffs, N.J.: Prentice-Hall, 1971), pp. 197–99.
3. U.S. ex rel Elksnis v. Gilligan, 256 F. Supp. 244 (1966).

whether the defendant understands all the implications of his action, and that the defendant was not pressured into his plea and does not really understand what he is doing.

In times past, plea negotiation was as widespread as it is now, but there was a greater tendency to handle the details of the plea negotiations with some secrecy, and with a ritualized fiction for the court record. The court ritual required that for the public record, the defendant verbalize a denial that any promises were made to him in return for his plea of guilty, and that it was—in fact—voluntary. In truth, there had been tripartite discussions participated in by the prosecutor, the defense counsel, and the sentencing judge, and as a result an agreement had been reached to allow the defendant to plead to a lesser charge or to exchange a reduced sentence for a plea of guilty. No plea of guilty would have been made unless the defendant's attorney assured him that the prosecutor would amend the accusation, the judge would pronounce a reduced sentence, or both.

It is difficult to understand why many members of the judiciary tolerated this threat to the integrity of the entire process of justice. This ritual for the public record of court procedures never contributed in any fashion to the public image of the courts. So many persons involved in courts and court proceedings knew that, as a standard operating procedure in plea negotiations, promises had been made to the defendant. They also knew that judges were fully aware of the methodology of these negotiations.

There is little wonder then, that the court's procedure for determining the voluntariness of a plea of guilty has always been clouded by the fact that the defendant would be forced to lie when queried in court as to whether promises had been made to him to induce his plea of guilty.

Under such circumstances, it is not surprising that the judicial examination required in all guilty pleas failed to uncover instances in which innocent persons pled guilty to crimes in which they were not involved.

The Plea Agreement

The American Bar Association (ABA) has proposed standards for plea negotiation which are intended to formalize the plea agreement for the protection of the defendant and the public. The proposed standards are within the concept of open disclosure of the entire plea negotiations. They would allow the prosecuting attorney to enter into plea discussions and agreements when such action is in the interest of the public and the effective administration of justice. These negotiations should be made through the defendant's lawyer unless the defendant is acting as his own attorney by order and agreement of the court.

These standards for plea negotiations would establish three major areas of plea agreement:

1. Acceptance of a plea to another offense reasonably related to the defendant's criminal conduct (lesser offense)
2. The dismissal of other charges or accusations (pending)
3. The type of sentence (probation, prison, fine), and its length of term.[4]

To insure uniformity of plea agreements, these ABA standards admonish the prosecuting attorney to make equal opportunities available to similarly situated defendants in order to comply with the constitutional mandate of equal protection. There is also the equally desirable criminal justice objective of demonstrating to defendants that they have been fairly treated by agents of justice responsible for their defense, their prosecution, their judgment, and their sentence.

To make certain that the ultimate decision as to the plea agreement is made by the defendant, these standards further suggest the following safeguard:

Defense counsel should conclude a plea agreement only with the consent of the defendant, and should insure that the decision whether to enter a plea of guilty or *nolo contendre** is ultimately made by the defendant. To aid the defendant in reaching a decision, defense counsel—after appropriate investigation—should advise the defendant of the alternatives available and of considerations deemed important by him in reaching a decision.[5]

There is hope that these standards will provide the guidelines that will bring a new uniformity and openness to de facto procedures previously identified with secret deals and courtroom ritual in which the defendant was forced to state a basic untruth.

Judicial Participation in Plea Negotiations

There has always been a belief that active participation by a sentencing judge in plea negotiations threatens judicial integrity. Among the major reasons for such belief are the following:

4. American Bar Association Committee on Minimum Standards for Pleas of Guilty, *Standards Relating to Pleas of Guilty* (New York: Institute of Judicial Administration, 1970), pp. 6–12.
*No contest.
5. Ibid., pp. 69–70.

1. Judicial participation in plea negotiations can create the impression in the mind of the defendant that he would not receive a fair trial before this judge (after rejecting offers of a bargain plea).

2. Judicial participation may suggest to some defendants a risk in not going along with the disposition apparently desired by the judge, and this may create a pressure so great that the defendant will be induced to plead guilty even if innocent.

3. Judicial participation in these discussions make it difficult for the judge to objectively determine the voluntariness of the plea when it is offered.

4. Judicial participation to the extent of promising a certain sentence is inconsistent with the theory behind the use of presentence investigation reports, and the need of the sentence to serve as a general program of rehabilitation for offenders. [6]

The 1966 *Elksnis*[7] case is a good example of how any fundamental fairness of judicial procedures is jeopardized by a judge's active participation in plea negotiations. Almars Elksnis was arrested for the killing of his wife. He claimed his wife had attacked him first with a hammer and knife. The cause of death was stabbing wounds inflicted by the four-inch knife the defendant claimed he had wrested from his wife when attacked. He was promptly indicted for murder, pled not guilty, and retained counsel. After several conferences between defense counsel and the prosecuting attorney, the defendant and his counsel conferred with the assigned trial judge in his chambers about a change of plea (to guilty) and a sentence of no more than ten years. Considering all the circumstances of this case known to the judge at this time, the defendant and his counsel were assured that if the defendant would plead guilty to manslaughter (a lesser charge than murder), the sentence would be to a term in state prison not to exceed ten years.

Soon after this conference in the judicial chambers the defendant withdrew his plea of not guilty and pleaded guilty to manslaughter in the first degree. Sentence was deferred, and the prosecuting attorney filed an information charging the defendant as a second felony offender (that he had been previously convicted of assault, second degree). Defense counsel, based upon an official transcript which indicated the conviction was for assault in the third degree (a misdemeanor) challenged the accuracy of the information, whereupon the matter was put over. At a subsequent hearing the prosecution again charged that the defendant was a multiple

6. American Bar Association, *Pleas of Guilty*, p. 73.
7. U.S. ex rel Elksnis v. Gilligan, 256 F. Supp. 244 (1966).

offender, but this time presented a certified copy of the prior conviction. The judge then found as a matter of law that the prior conviction was a felony, and after an off-the-record "discussion between counsel and the Court" and a plea of mercy on behalf of the defendant, imposed a sentence of from 17 to 35 years—contrary to his promise that the maximum term would be ten years.

The circumstances in this case attendant upon the entry of the plea of guilty hardly supports a claim that it was understandingly and knowingly made. The defendant's answers in response to the questions by the court and the prosecutor immediately prior to the entry of the guilty plea do not clearly establish that he acknowledged guilt without reservation. Quite to the contrary, they reveal a challenge to the charge—an attempt to assert a plea of self-defense or insanity—and yet without further inquiry by the court, the plea of guilty was summarily accepted. The transcript of the hearing record reveals the following dialogue between the defendant, the judge, and the prosecutor:

Prosecuting Attorney:

The defendant became involved in an argument with his so-called common law wife. As a result of which I believe he spilled some hot water on her and she became annoyed. Thereafter the argument grew worse and I understand there was some question relative to a hammer being used by the wife, which, of course, as your Honor knows, would be a matter of proof—and thereafter he tried to defend himself, he was cut and became enraged, apparently, after which he disarmed her and thereafter stabbed her with a knife several times, after which, of course, the woman died.

The Court (to defendant):

Q: Did you use a knife in that fashion—did you stab her?

A: Not that I know that I stab her.

Q: But you were in a fight with her?

A: Yes, I remember I was in some kind of a fight; I know I was cut myself.

Q: You were the only one there?

A: I think so.

Q: Don't you know?

A: I don't know for sure, but I think so.

Q: You used the knife, didn't you?

A: Not to my knowledge.

Prosecuting Attorney:

Q: Now, Mr. Elksnis, you were engaged in an argument with your wife, is that right? You remember that? You had a fight with your wife?

A: I remember that, yes.

Q: And do you remember that she came at you with a hammer?

A: Yes, I was hit by the hammer.

Q: Was that hammer in your wife's hands?

A: Yes.

Q: After you were hit by the hammer, did you then try to protect yourself?

A: Yes, I did.

Q: And then there was a knife produced?

A: Yes, she cut me in my hand.

Q: After she cut you with the knife, did you do something with the knife?

A: I was trying to get the knife.

Q: We want you to be certain about this. Did you try to get the knife away from your wife?

A: Yes, I was dodging that knife; I recall that, and I recall I twisted her arm.

Q: And you got the knife?

A: I think I did.

Q: And thereafter did you remember that you moved it toward your wife or made a thrust at your wife?

A: I don't know; something exploded in my head and it was black all around, a complete black.

Q: Was there anybody else with you?

A: Not when the argument started.

Q: Mr. Elksnis, are you stating to the Court that you did not do this?

A: No, I mean it is not in my mind or in my knowledge that I did.

Q: Is it your belief that you did do it?

A: I believe later, after the evidence was shown—there was blood on my clothes and it could not have been anybody else and I have come to the conclusion it must have been me.

The Court:

We will accept the plea.

The New York Appellate Court reversed the judicial action of accepting this plea of guilty and the sentence imposed, and they ordered a trial on the merits of the case. Their conclusion was that the defendant had not pled guilty because he was in fact guilty, but because he was compromising his claimed defenses in exchange for the sentence he then believed would be imposed upon him as previously agreed. The forthwith acceptance of the guilty plea without a searching inquiry as to the merits of the alleged self-defense plea and the defendant's claim that "something exploded in my head," stamp the plea as one not understandingly and knowingly made and this ground, too, requires that it be declared void.

In its majority opinion in this case, the New York Appellate Court judges summed up the importance of the judiciary remaining aloof from the actual plea bargaining in these words:

Petitioner first considered surrendering his right to trial and his defenses when his counsel informed him of the proposed reduction in the charge from murder to manslaughter, and that if he pleaded thereto the judge was agreeable to a sentence not to exceed ten years. As against the proffered sentence his lawyer stressed a possible term of from forty years to life in the event of conviction on the second degree murder charge. Then followed the chambers conference at which the judge made the express promise to the defendant. That it induced the plea cannot be gainsaid. To deny the compelling force of the promise is to deny the reality of experience.

The unequal positions of the judge and the accused, one with the power to commit to prison and the other deeply concerned to avoid prison, at once raise a question of fundamental fairness. When a judge becomes a participant in plea bargaining he brings to bear the full force and majesty of his office. His awesome power to impose a substantially longer or even maximum sentence in excess of that proposed is present whether referred to or not. A defendant needs no reminder that if he rejects the proposal, stands upon his right to trial and is convicted, he faces a significantly longer sentence. One facing a prison term, whether of longer or shorter duration, is easily influenced to accept what appears the more preferable choice. Intentionally or otherwise, and no matter how well motivated the judge may be, the accused is subjected to a subtle but powerful influence. A guilty plea predicated upon a judge's promise of a definite sentence by its very nature does not qualify as a free and voluntary act. The plea is so interlaced with the promise that the one cannot be separated from the other; remove the promise and the basis for the plea falls.

A judge's prime responsibility is to maintain the integrity of the judicial system; to see that due process of law, equal protection of the laws and the basic safeguards of a fair trial are upheld. The judge stands as the symbol of even-handed justice, and none can seriously question that if this central figure in the administration of justice promises an accused that upon a plea of guilty a fixed sentence will follow, his commitment has an all-pervasive and compelling influence in inducing the accused to yield his right to trial. A plea entered upon a bargain agreement between a judge and an accused cannot be squared with due process requirements of the Fourteenth Amendment.

This case points up the hazards of judicial participation in negotiating pleas of guilty, and indicates that when plea negotiations do involve a sentencing judge all participants should be instructed by him that his final action will depend upon all the facts being as represented to him by the various participants. It will certainly protect judicial integrity if it is fully understood by all concerned, and particularly by the defendant, that if the facts are subsequently found to be different from those represented to him for his agreement, then the judge may reject the entire plea agreement. He may allow the defendant to withdraw his plea and then bring the case to trial. In spite of this prior bargaining to a plea of guilty, there will be no prejudice at trial or at a sentencing session in the event of a verdict of guilty.

The Doctrine of Fundamental Fairness and Plea Negotiations

One of the major myths of the American legal system is that there is little or no injustice. While the major thrust has been to guard against the conviction of innocent people, there is also a belief that the legal system should operate in such a manner as to provide all persons accused of crime with a fundamental fairness, from the time of arrest until the final disposition of the charges.

The negotiated plea of guilty has always been a threat to this fundamental fairness because of the prosecuting attorney's power to make the decision as to which crimes to charge, and how many to be brought to trial. His power extends to his capability of securing the sentencing judge's cooperation in setting a sentence; and the vulnerability of a defendant once he enters a plea of guilty.

A classic case in this area of guilty pleas as they relate to fundamental fairness is *Boykin* v. *Alabama*.[8] Boykin was arrested and indicted for a two-week crime spree in Mobile, Alabama, consisting of a series of armed robberies of grocery stores, in two of which shots were fired. In one robbery, a shot was discharged into the ceiling without personal injury; but in the second shooting, a bullet hit the floor and then struck a customer in the leg. Before trial, the court of arraignment determined that the defendant was indigent and appointed counsel to represent him. Three days later, in a court appearance to plead to five indictments charging robbery—a capital offense in Alabama—the defendant pled guilty to all

8. Boykin v. Alabama, 395 U.S. 238 (1968).

five crimes. The judge did not question the defendant, and the defendant did not address the court.

In accordance with Alabama law, a penalty trial was held, with the prosecution presenting its case largely through eyewitness testimony. While defense counsel went through the motions of cross-examination, it was very brief, and the defense presented no character evidence and the defendant did not take the stand in his own behalf.

The judge's instructions to this penalty jury stressed that the defendant had pleaded guilty to five cases of robbery, each carrying a penalty provision of from ten years in the penitentiary (minimum) to death by electrocution (maximum). The jury deliberated and returned with a sentence of death on each of the five indictments. The Alabama Supreme Court reviewed the sentences and affirmed them.

In a review by the U.S. Supreme Court on the question of the voluntariness of Boykin's plea of guilty to five capital crimes, the court held that acceptance of Boykin's guilty plea under the circumstances of this case constituted reversible error because the record did not disclose that Boykin voluntarily and understandingly entered his plea of guilty. The following extracts from the majority opinion in this case review the doctrine of fundamental fairness in relation to pleas of guilty:

> A plea of guilty is more than a confession which admits that the accused did various acts; it is itself a conviction; nothing remains but to give judgment and determine punishment. Admissibility of a confession must be based on a "reliable determination on the voluntariness issue which satisfies the constitutional rights of the defendant." *Jackson* v. *Denno*, 378 U.S. 368. The requirement that the prosecution spread on the record the prerequisites of a valid waiver is no constitutional innovation. In *Carnley* v. *Cochran*, 369 U.S. 506, we dealt with a problem of waiver of the right to counsel, a Sixth Amendment right. We held: "Presuming waiver from a silent record is impermissible. The record must show, or there must be an allegation and evidence which show, that an accused was offered counsel but intelligently and understandingly rejected the offer. Anything less is not waiver."

> We think that the same standard must be applied to determining whether a guilty plea is voluntarily made. For, as we have said, a plea of guilty is more than an admission of conduct; it is a conviction. Ignorance, incomprehension, coercion, terror, inducements, subtle or blatant threats might be a perfect cover-up of unconstitutionality. The question of an effective waiver of a federal constitutional right in a proceeding is of course governed by federal standards.

> Several federal constitutional rights are involved in a waiver that takes place when a plea of guilty is entered in a state criminal trial. *First*, is the privilege against compulsory self-incrimination guaranteed by the Fifth Amendment and applicable to the States by reason of the Fourteenth. *Second*, is the right to trial by jury. *Third*, is the right to confront one's accusers. We cannot presume a waiver of these three important federal rights from a silent record.

What is at stake for an accused facing death or imprisonment demands the utmost solicitude of which courts are capable in canvassing the matter with the accused to make sure he has a full understanding of what the plea connotes and of its consequences.

California has formalized and brought into the open its plea negotiation procedures by often instituting court-initiated plea negotiation sessions following three basic rules:

1. Counsel must disclose any plea bargain to the court and the terms of the bargain must be related in open court on the record with the defendant present.

2. A plea is not involuntary because it is the product of a plea bargain (promise) between the defendant and the state.

3. The court may accept a bargained plea to any lesser offense reasonably related to the offense charged in the accusation and to which the defendant is in fact guilty.[9]

When the process of plea negotiation becomes a visible, open, and public part of the administration of justice in all jurisdictions it is more likely that fundamental fairness will be commonplace in the courts of America in which guilty pleas are entered by persons accused of crime. Secrecy, mysterious circumstances surrounding plea agreements, and the subversion of judicial integrity as it concerns promises to defendants, are at odds with the concepts of equal treatment, fundamental fairness, and the belief that defendants should only plead guilty when they know the nature of the charges and the consequences of this plea—and are, in fact, guilty as charged.

Selected References

Books
American Bar Association Committee on Minimum Standards for Pleas of Guilty. *Standards Relating to Pleas of Guilty.* New York: Institute of Judicial Administration, 1970.

Newman, Donald J. *Conviction.* Boston: Little, Brown and Co., 1969.

President's Commission on Law Enforcement and Administration of Justice. *The Challenge of Crime in a Free Society.* Washington, D.C.: Government Printing Office, 1967.

Radin, Edward D. *The Innocents.* New York: William Morrow Co., 1964.

9. People v. West, 3 Cal. 3d 595 (1970).

Cases

Boykin v. Alabama, 395 U.S. 238 (1968).
People v. West, 3 Cal. 3d 595 (1970).
U.S. ex rel Elksnis v. Gilligan, 256 F. Supp. 244 (1966).

Chapter XV

Crime and Publicity

Justice cannot survive behind walls of silence. Justice requires a charge fairly made and fairly tried in a public tribunal free of prejudice, passion, excitement, and tyrannical power. These two basic concepts clash in our scheme of justice in the field of criminal proceedings.

Standards for the release of crime news, originating in court decisions or the action of authoritative organizations interested in criminal justice, will establish reasonable rules for news reporting of crime and criminals. News gatherers for the press, radio, and TV, however, are in a competitive business. The right of an accused person to a fair trial without prejudiced jurors is more or less jeopardized, depending on the newsworthiness of the case. Sensational crimes will test any standards for limiting news, and may require court action on an individual basis.

Secret Trial

The belief that justice for a person accused of a public offense is mutually exclusive from a secret trial (walls of silence) arose in the 1948 case of *In re Oliver*.[1] In this case a Michigan judge was conducting, in accordance with Michigan law, a secret one-man grand jury investigation of crime. A witness (Oliver) was held in contempt of court for alleged false and evasive testimony and sentenced to 60 days in jail. The proceedings were secret. The case was appealed to the U.S. Supreme Court, and their majority opinion contained these words on the hazards of secret tribunals:

> Here we are concerned, not with petitioner's rights as a witness in a secret grand jury session, but with his rights as a defendant in a contempt proceed-

1. In re Oliver, 333 U.S. 257 (1948).

ing. The powers of the judge-grand jury* who tried and convicted him (Oliver) in secret and sentenced him to jail on a charge of false and evasive swearing must likewise be measured, not by the limitations applicable to grand jury proceedings, but by the constitutional standards applicable to court proceedings in which an accused may be sentenced to fine or imprisonment or both.

Thus our first question is this: Can an accused be tried and convicted for contempt of court in grand jury secrecy?

First. Counsel have not cited and we have been unable to find a single instance of a criminal trial conducted *in camera*** in any federal, state, or municipal court during the history of this county. Nor have we found any record of even one such secret criminal trial in England since abolition of the Court of Star Chamber† in 1641, and whether that court ever convicted people secretly is in dispute. Summary trials for alleged misconduct called contempt of court have not been regarded as an exception to this universal rule against secret trials, unless some other Michigan one-man grand jury case may represent such an exception.

This nation's accepted practice of guaranteeing a public trial to an accused has its roots in our English common law heritage. The exact date of its origin is obscure, but it likely evolved long before the settlement of our land as an accompaniment of the ancient institution of jury trial. In this country the guarantee to an accused of the right to a public trial first appeared in a state constitution in 1776. ‡ Following the ratification in 1791 of the Federal Constitution's Sixth Amendment, which commands that "In all criminal prosecutions, the accused shall enjoy the right to a speedy and public trial . . ." most of the original states and those subsequently admitted to the Union adopted similar constitutional provisions. Today almost without exception every state by constitution, statute, or judicial decision, requires that all criminal trials be open to the public.

The traditional Anglo-American distrust for secret trials has been variously ascribed to the notorious use of this practice by the Spanish Inquisition, to the excesses of the English Court of Star Chamber, and to the French monarchy's abuse of the *lettre de cachet*. § All of these institutions obviously symbolized a menace to liberty. In the hands of despotic groups each of them had become an instrument for the suppression of political and religious heresies in ruthless disregard of the right of an accused to a fair trial.

*A one-man grand jury comprised of a circuit court judge; unusual, but in accordance with Michigan law.
**In chambers; in private; with spectators (public) excluded.
†Some authorities have said that trials in the Star Chamber were public, but that witnesses against the accused were examined privately with no opportunity for him to discredit them. Apparently all authorities agree that the accused himself was grilled in secret, often tortured, in an effort to obtain a confession and that the most objectionable of the Star Chamber's practices was its asserted prerogative to disregard the common law rules of criminal procedure when the occasion demanded.
‡Pennsylvania; North Carolina (criminal convictions only by jury verdict in open court).
§An order of the king that one of his subjects be forthwith imprisoned or exiled without a trial or an opportunity to defend himself.

Whatever other benefits the guarantee to an accused that his trial be conducted in public may confer upon our society,* the guarantee has always
been recognized as a safeguard against any attempt to employ our courts as
instruments of persecution. The knowledge that every criminal trial is subject to contemporaneous review in the forum of public opinion is an effective
restraint on possible abuse of judicial power. One need not wholly agree with
a statement made on the subject by Jeremy Bentham over 120 years ago to
appreciate the fear of secret trials felt by him, his predecessors and contem-
poraries. Bentham said: ". . . suppose the proceedings to be completely
secret, and the court, on the occasion, to consist of no more than a single
judge,—that judge will be at once indolent and arbitrary: how corrupt
soever his inclination may be, it will find no check, at any rate no tolerably
efficient check, to oppose it. Without publicity, all other checks are of small
account. Recordation, appeal, whatever other institutions might present
themselves in the character of checks, would be found to operate rather as
cloaks than checks; as cloaks in reality, as checks only in appearance."

In giving content to the constitutional and statutory commands that an accused be given a public trial, the state and federal courts have differed over
what groups of spectators, if any, could properly be excluded from a criminal
trial. But, unless in Michigan and in one-man grand jury contempt cases, no
court in this country has ever before held, so far as we can find, that an accused can be tried, convicted, and sent to jail, when everybody else is denied entrance to the court, except the judge and his attaches. And without
exception all courts have held that an accused is at the very best entitled to
have his friends, relatives and counsel present, no matter with what offense
he may be charged.

The Court's holding in *Oliver* was that the secrecy of the trial for
criminal contempt violated the due process clause of the Fourteenth
Amendment: (1) The facts of the case did not justify a secret trial of an offense punishable by fine or imprisonment. (2) An accused is entitled to a
public trial, at least to having counsel, relatives and friends present, no
matter what the offense. (3) As a minimum, due process requires that an
accused be given: (a) reasonable notice of the charge against him, (b) the
right to examine witnesses against him, (c) the right to testify in his own
behalf, (d) the right to be represented by counsel.

Fair Trial Without Prejudice

The standard of criminal justice in America—that an accusation be
fairly made and the accused fairly tried in a public tribunal free of prejudice or other disabling factors—is a constitutional right applicable to
state agents by the due process clause of the Fourteenth Amendment.

*Public trials come to the attention of key witnesses unknown to the parties. These wit-
nesses may then voluntarily come forward and give important testimony.

The U.S. Supreme Court, in *Chambers* v. *Florida*[2] summed up the dimensions of this right in the majority opinion, and the following extract from this opinion not only explains the rationale for unprejudiced trials, but also terms this right one of the "blessings of liberty":

> The scope and operation of the Fourteenth Amendment have been fruitful sources of controversy in our constitutional history. However, in view of its historical setting and the wrongs which called it into being, the due process provision of the Fourteenth Amendment—just as that in the Fifth—has led few to doubt that it was intended to guarantee procedural standards adequate and appropriate, then and thereafter, to protect, at all times, people charged with or suspected of crime by those holding positions of power and authority.
>
> Tyrannical governments had immemorially utilized dictatorial criminal procedure and punishment to make scapegoats of the weak, or of helpless political, religious, or racial minorities and those who differed, who would not conform and who resisted tyranny. The instruments of such governments were, in the main, two. Conduct, innocent when engaged in, was subsequently made by fiat criminally punishable without legislation. And a liberty loving people won the principle that criminal punishments could not be inflicted save for that which proper legislative action had already by "the law of the land" forbidden when done. But even more was needed. From the popular hatred and abhorrence of illegal confinement, torture and extortion of confessions of violations of the "law of the land" evolved the fundamental idea that no man's life, liberty or property be forfeited as criminal punishment for violation of that law until there had been a charge fairly made and fairly tried in a public tribunal free of prejudice, passion, excitement, and tyrannical power.
>
> Thus, as assurance against ancient evils, our country, in order to preserve "the blessings of liberty," wrote into its basic law the requirement, among others, that the forfeiture of the lives, liberties or property of people accused of crime can only follow if procedural safeguards of due process have been obeyed.
>
> The determination to preserve an accused's right to procedural due process sprang in large part from knowledge of the historical truth that the rights and liberties of people accused of crime could not be safely entrusted to secret inquisitorial processes. The testimony of centuries, in governments of varying kinds over populations of different races and beliefs, stood as proof that physical and mental torture and coercion had brought about the tragically unjust sacrifices of some who were the noblest and most useful of their generations.

A free press bulwarks all of a citizen's freedoms under the constitution, among them the right to a fair trial. Freedom of the press was so highly regarded by the framers of our constitution that it was included in

2. Chambers v. Florida, 309 U.S. 227 (1939).

the first amendment to the constitution. The legislative intent was that the liberty of the press should be as broad as was consistent with an orderly society. In probing all areas of government, however, there has emerged a well-founded belief that a free press would insure that criminal accusations and trials be open to public scrutiny. The possibility of public disclosure of any miscarriage of justice would prevent police, prosecutors, or the judiciary from any acts of oppression or other injustice.

On the other side of the coin is publicity, which by its nature and quantity, can be a threat to the integrity of the trial itself. Such publicity makes it impossible for an accused to receive a fair trial because of the prejudice generated by the news media among local residents likely to be jurors, witnesses, or other participants in the trial.

The Case of Sam Sheppard

The case of Dr. Sam Sheppard in Cleveland, Ohio, in 1954, is a classic example of the ability of the press to create a situation in which a fair trial is unlikely or impossible.[3] Dr. Sam Sheppard was accused, tried, and convicted of the murder of his wife. The facts are these: Sheppard's pregnant wife was beaten to death with an unknown instrument in her upstairs bedroom in their home in a suburb of Cleveland, Ohio, on July 4, 1954.

Immediately after discovery Sam Sheppard gave the following story: Sheppard and his wife had entertained friends that night. When the friends left, his wife went to bed and Sheppard dozed off on the couch in the living room. The next thing he remembers is hearing his wife cry out. He ran upstairs to the bedroom and saw a form standing next to his wife's bed. He fought with this person, but was struck and knocked unconscious. When he became conscious again, he looked at his wife, checked her pulse and decided she was dead. He ran downstairs and pursued a figure (who was leaving the house) to the beach, where another struggle took place, and Sheppard was again struck and knocked unconscious. He awoke on the beach, hurried home, went upstairs again to his wife and checked her pulse. He found no pulse, went to the telephone, and called a friend (the local mayor who lived nearby), who came over immediately.

Sam Sheppard became the prime suspect in the case. Police arrested Sheppard, and he was formally accused of murder and brought to trial in the city of Cleveland, county of Cuyahoga, state of Ohio.

This was a case that could not be dropped or delayed. A young and expectant mother had been brutally bludgeoned and had died in her bed.

3. Paul Holmes, *The Sheppard Murder Case* (New York: David McKay Co., 1961), pp. 303–06.

There was public pressure on police, coroner, and prosecutor to produce the killer. It was a case, however, in which the police-prosecutor team could only gather a limited amount of evidence against Dr. Sheppard. However, when the investigation of the case failed to disclose any other person as the murderer, or even as another suspect, the prosecutor's decision was to go ahead with the trial despite the less-than-conclusive evidence.

Up to this point the news media had a field day in reporting their theories of the crime, interviews with so-called experts in homicide, and police views and reports relating to the investigation and to Dr. Sheppard as the major suspect—all of it prejudicial to Sheppard. Some of the headlines and editorial headings were:

Doctor Sheppard Balks at Lie Test

Somebody is Getting Away with Murder

Why Isn't Sam Sheppard in Jail?

Quit Stalling—Bring In Sheppard

The trial itself was unbelievable. Twenty-five days before the trial the names and addresses of 75 selected prospective jurors were published in the papers. As a result, all of them received phone calls concerning the impending trial from friends as well as anonymous callers. In a courtroom 26 feet by 48 feet, 20 local newspaper representatives were assigned front row seats; and behind them television, radio, and out-of-town newsmen were assigned the next four rows of benches. Special telephone and broadcasting equipment was set up in the courthouse for the news media. All the participants were photographed, including the jurors and witnesses, and the testimony of each witness was printed verbatim in the newspapers on each day of the trial, together with all the court rulings and attorneys' motions. These extensive daily summaries were headed by, or contained, editorial comment that repeatedly expressed certainty of Dr. Sheppard's guilt and the expected verdict of guilty.

The publicity totaled such proportions that one reporter commented: "The question of Dr. Sheppard's guilt or innocence still is before the courts. Those who have examined the trial records carefully are divided as to the propriety of the verdict. But almost everyone who watched the performance of the Cleveland press agrees that a fair hearing for the defendant, in that area, would be a modern miracle."[4]

4. John M. Harrison, "The Press vs. the Courts," *Saturday Review*, 15 October 1955, pp. 9–10, 35.

Sheppard v. Maxwell—
Court Rule Making

To assure the public full information about government and its affairs, to protect an accused's right to a public trial, and to prevent the
suppression of other individual rights, the American press is free. Only
when the historic right to a fair trial is endangered is there a question
about whether there must be some limitation on the press to protect an
accused from prejudicial publicity which inflames public opinion against
him and creates a preverdict judgment of guilty as charged.

Basic limitations were established in the U.S. Supreme Court's review of Dr. Sam Sheppard's conviction in Ohio for the murder of his wife.
The case, *Sheppard* v. *Maxwell*[5] was decided in 1965.

The Court's majority opinion in the Sheppard case reveals its review
of the prejudicial publicity, its belief in the accountability of the trial
judge, and its response to the question as to limitation on a free press in
its crime reporting. The following extracts sum up the Court's views:

> Sheppard stood indicted for the murder of his wife; the State was demanding
> the death penalty. For months the virulent publicity about Sheppard and the
> murder had made the case notorious. Charges and countercharges were
> aired in the news media besides those for which Sheppard was called to trial.
> In addition, only three months before trial, Sheppard was examined for more
> than five hours without counsel during a three-day inquest which ended in a
> public brawl. The inquest was televised live from a high school gymnasium
> seating hundreds of people.
>
> While we cannot say that Sheppard was denied due process by the judge's
> refusal to take precautions against the influence of pretrial publicity alone,
> the court's later rulings must be considered against the setting in which the
> trial was held. In light of this background, we believe that the arrangements
> made by the judge with the news media caused Sheppard to be deprived of
> that judicial serenity and calm to which he was entitled. Bearing in mind the
> massive pretrial publicity, the judge should have adopted stricter rules gov-
> erning the use of the courtroom by newsmen, as Sheppard's counsel re-
> quested.
>
> *First*, the number of reporters in the courtroom itself could have been li-
> mited at the first sign that their presence would disrupt the trial. They cer-
> tainly should not have been placed inside the bar. Furthermore, the judge
> should have more closely regulated the conduct of newsmen in the court-
> room.
>
> *Secondly*, the court should have insulated the witnesses. All of the newspa-
> pers and radio stations apparently interviewed prospective witnesses at
> will, and in many instances disclosed their testimony. A typical example
> was the publication of numerous statements by Susan Hayes, before her
> appearance in court, regarding her love affair with Sheppard. Although the

5. Sheppard v. Maxwell, 384 U.S. 333 (1965).

witnesses were barred from the courtroom during the trial the full verbatim testimony was available to them in the press. This completely nullified the judge's imposition of the rule.

Thirdly, the court should have made some effort to control the release of leads, information, and gossip to the press by police officers, witnesses, and the counsel for both sides. Much of the information thus disclosed was inaccurate, leading to groundless rumors and confusion.

More specifically, the trial court might well have proscribed extrajudicial statements by any lawyer, party, witness, or court official which divulged prejudicial matters, such as the refusal of Sheppard to submit to interrogation or take any lie detector tests; any statement made by Sheppard to officials; the identity of prospective witnesses or their probable testimony; any belief in guilt or innocence; or like statements concerning the merits of the case.

Being advised of the great public interest in the case, the mass coverage of the press, and the potential prejudicial impact of publicity, the court could also have requested the appropriate city and county officials to promulgate a regulation with respect to dissemination of information about the case by their employees.

In addition, reporters who wrote or broadcast prejudicial stories, could have been warned as to the impropriety of publishing material not introduced in the proceedings. The judge was put on notice of such events by defense counsel's complaint about the WHK broadcast on the second day of trial.

In this manner, Sheppard's right to a trial free from outside interference would have been given added protection without corresponding curtailment of the news media. Had the judge, the other officers of the court, and the police placed the interest of justice first, the news media would have soon learned to be content with the task of reporting the case as it unfolded in the courtroom—not pieced together from extrajudicial statements.

From the cases coming here we note that unfair and prejudicial news comment on pending trials has become increasingly prevalent. Our process requires that the accused receive a trial by an impartial jury free from outside influences. Given the pervasiveness of modern communications and the difficulty of effacing prejudicial publicity from the minds of the jurors, the trial courts must take strong measures to ensure that the balance is never weighed against the accused.

Of course, there is nothing that proscribes the press from reporting events that transpire in the courtroom. But where there is a reasonable likelihood that prejudicial news prior to trial will prevent a fair trial, the judge should continue the case until the threat abates, or transfer it to another county not so permeated with publicity. In addition, sequestration of the jury was something the judge should have raised *sua sponte** with counsel.

If publicity during the proceedings threatens the fairness of the trial, a new trial should be ordered. But we must remember that reversals are but palliatives; the cure lies in those remedial measures that will prevent the prej-

*Upon his own responsibility; of his own motion.

udice at its inception. The courts must take such steps by rule and regulation that will protect their processes from prejudicial outside interferences.
Neither prosecutors, counsel for defense, the accused, witnesses, court staff
nor enforcement officers coming under the jurisdiction of the court should be
permitted to frustrate its function. Collaboration between counsel and the
press as to information affecting the fairness of a criminal trial is not only subject to regulations, but is highly censurable and worthy of disciplinary measures.

Since the state trial judge did not fulfill his duty to protect Sheppard from the
inherently prejudicial publicity which saturated the community and to control disruptive influences in the courtroom, we must reverse the denial of
the habeas petition. The case is remanded to the District Court with instructions to issue the writ and order that Sheppard be released from custody unless the State puts him to its charges again within a reasonable
time.

F. Lee Bailey, Dr. Sheppard's counsel in the above proceedings and
in the ensuing trial that exonerated Sheppard, commented that public
opinion can be a real source of strength to the proper administration of
justice only when it is not misinformed or deliberately misled, saying:
"There need never be another Sam Sheppard if enough people come to
know and understand this one, and understand what happened to him,
how it happened, and why it was all so unnecessary."[6]

Standards for the Release of Crime News

The accomodation of the First Amendment guarantee of a free press
with the Sixth Amendment right to a speedy and public trial before an
impartial jury must be solved without interfering with the press' invaluable function in discovering and disclosing public corruption and injustice. The solution to the problem of the publicity that surrounds crime
must also be responsive to the possible adverse impact of news coverage
on: (1) the investigation of the crime, (2) the opinions of potential or actual
jurors; (3) the conduct of police, prosecuting attorney, defense counsel,
and trial judge; and (4) the integrity and stature of the adjudicating process and our legal system. This accomodation between the First and Sixth
Amendments will require the adoption of limitations, both as to content
and timing, on the release of information by members of the bar and by
law enforcement agents about the apprehension and trial of criminal defendants. Appropriate remedies will have to be made available whenever
there is evidence to show that a fair trial has been jeopardized by adverse
publicity to the accused.[7]

6. Dr. Sam Sheppard, *Endure and Conquer* (Cleveland: World Publishing Company,
1966), pp. *vii-x* (Foreword by F. Lee Bailey).
7. Paul C. Reardon and Clifton Daniel, *Fair Trial and Free Press* (Washington, D.C.:
American Enterprise Institute for Public Policy Research, 1968), pp. 1–27.

There are excesses in publicity about crime and criminals which can be removed without real damage to the freedom of the press, or the right of the public to know, and which will increase the probability of a fair trial for the accused. Two problems are identified, and three areas are isolated as potential sources for solutions:

1. Problems
   a. What matters reported endanger the fairness of the criminal process?
   b. How can such matters be reduced or eliminated from reporting without abridging freedom of speech and press and open trials?
2. Solutions
   a. The conduct of attorney
   b. The conduct of law enforcement officers and judicial employees
   c. The conduct of judicial proceedings.

Identification of the basic problem, the persons whose conduct will be significant in its resolution, and guidelines for the release of information by such persons have been superimposed on the time clock of a criminal proceeding by a committee of the American Bar Association.[8] These standards do not directly offer any control over the press, but rather suggest procedures that will control the source of news in regard to crime and its publicity. The control of the source of crime news is suggested by these standards as follows:

> *At the time of arrest*—Law enforcement agents and officials should release no more information than the identity of the person arrested, the circumstances of the arrest, the crime charged, and the identity of the victim. Officials should not give out results of investigative examinations or tests; the existence or content of a "confession"; the information that an accused has refused to make a statement; or the accused's prior criminal record, if any. Officials should not state personal opinions about the guilt of the accused or about the credibility of witnesses or any other matter which might jeopardize a fair trial. In addition, as a general rule, no information should be released that is highly prejudicial, unless public disclosure serves a significant law enforcement function.[9]
>
> *Prior to trial*—Law enforcement personnel, prosecutor, and defense counsel may release information concerning the commission of the crime and its general scope, but may not release data which identifies the suspects prior to arrest, except for the purpose of assisting in discovery and apprehension of

---

8. American Bar Association Advisory Committee on Fair Trial and Free Press, *Standards Relating to Fair Trial and Free Press* (New York: Institute of Judicial Administration, 1966), pp. 7–14.
9. Ibid., pp. 98–109.

suspects, or in the furtherance of the investigation. The results of scientific or other tests should not be released, nor should those involved in the investigation express opinions which may prevent a fair trial. The court may either close the pretrial hearing or order that certain evidence presented not be disseminated by the news media if good cause is shown that such evidence produced at the hearing may be inadmissible at the trial, and thus its dissemination would or could jeopardize a fair trial.[10]

During the trial—It is ethically improper for a lawyer of either side to make out of court statements about the trial, the issues, the parties, or witnesses except to quote from the public record of the trial. The court may order others (parties, witnesses, and court personnel) not to make extrajudicial statements regarding the case or their part in the case. Where the court feels it proper he may exclude all except the parties and their attorneys in matters of law or fact which are taken up outside the presence of the jury, and should grant a change of venue if he believes, because of news coverage, the defendant cannot obtain a fair trial in his jurisdiction.[11]

Rules of the court have long been familiar to lawyers and police officers. Such rules are necessary for the orderly procedure vital to the operation of the courts. They can be extended to cover the enforcement of reasonable regulations limiting publicity, in accord with the "standards" cited above. This does not mean that law enforcement agencies, prosecutors' offices, and institutionalized legal services for the defense (public defender, legal aid groups), should not adopt similar regulations for their employees. The recommended rules of the court would support such action by local agencies and provide a statewide application. Certainly, such action is within the role of any court to assure fair trials.[12]

In prior years, newspapermen have been skeptical about any codes or standards because restricting the release of news is prior censorship. Since every newsman employed by any of the communications media is a participant in a competitive business of getting the news, there is likely to be some prying and probing to get data not released by criminal justice agents or agencies.

In Minot F. Jelke's first trial on charges of compulsory prostitution the press was excluded from the courtroom on the orders of the trial judge. The judicial rationale was concerned with public morals: the probable content of the testimony of the call girl prostitutes scheduled to appear as witnesses in this case. The reality of news reporting, however, failed to shield public morals, and all of the colorful testimony of the prostitutes was not kept secret. Newsmen used second-hand sources of information because of the judge's edict. In addition, Jelke's conviction was

10. American Bar Association, *Fair Trial and Free Press*, pp. 80–90.
11. Ibid., pp. 90–97.
12. Council of Judges of the National Council on Crime and Delinquency, *Model Rules of Court on Police Action from Arrest to Arraignment* (New York: National Council on Crime and Delinquency, 1969), pp. 27–28.

reversed on appeal because the press was barred from the courtroom. In the opinion that ordered a new trial for Jelke, the New York Appellate Court stated:

> Due regard for the defendant's rights to a public trial demanded, at the very least, that he not be deprived of the possible benefits of attendance by the press.[13]

News media will publish data when sensational crimes occur, whether it is obtained from secret sources, leaks in the criminal justice establishment, witnesses, or other persons concerned with the circumstances of the crime or suspects. However, the staff of an increasing number of newspapers, weekly news magazines, and radio and TV news bureaus are aware that the abuse of the freedom of the press jeopardizes the right to a fair trial and they have displayed a willingness to accept internal controls. Hopefully, it will be in alignment with the standards for releasing data on crime and suspects by agents of criminal justice.

Have You Formed or Expressed an Opinion?

The theory of trial by jury is that a body of citizens will be more likely to discover the truth on the issue of guilt or innocence than a single person—a judge or magistrate. In the early years of jury trials, local citizens who knew the circumstances of the crime or the facts of life about the defendant were sought for juries. Later, it was found that more equitable verdicts were returned by jurors without any knowledge of the crime or the defendant. In modern jurisprudence, the panel of citizens called for jury duty must be representative of local citizenry and no group of citizens can be systematically excluded because of race, color, creed, sex, or national origin. Individual prospective jurors are then examined in a *voir dire* session to make certain they are not bigoted or prejudiced, and can arrive at a verdict as a result of the evidence presented during the trial. What is being sought in this *voir dire* examination is a completely objective and impartial juror.

Publicity cannot be discounted as an influence on jury verdicts because on *voir dire*, in response to questions from the attorney or judge, jurors reply that they either haven't formed opinions, will not form opinions, or will not read about the case. While the court will instruct jurors to decide the case only on the evidence adduced in court and not to read news articles about the case, such instructions often go unheeded.

Too many cases have been recorded showing the influence of publicity on juries to consider verbal admonition by the trial judge an adequate safeguard. For instance:

13. Jelke v. New York, 308 N.Y. 85 (1954).

1. Out of 430 prospective jurors, 268 were excused for cause because they had fixed opinions as to guilt. Ninety percent admitted to some opinion.[14]

2. After extensive publicity accusing the defendants, every member of the trial jury admitted to a prior opinion of guilt.[15]

3. Of 68 prospective jurors questioned, eight were seated on *voir dire*, and four of these individuals said they had an opinion of guilt they could not set aside.[16]

4. After the defense counsel used all of the defense's peremptory challenges, there were four prospective jurors who admitted to an opinion based on what they had read, and who stated they would not want one of their loved ones tried by a jury with their attitudes.[17]

5. All of the prospective jurors said that they had heard or read of the case in which pretrial reporting included extensive details of the crime and the defendant's confession.[18]

6. Despite the court's instructions to the jury to decide the case only on the evidence adduced at the trial, there was mention in the jury deliberations of the indictment of the defendant on another crime of violence which was not a part of the evidence in the present case.[19]

7. A juror had read an inaccurate news report of the trial, discussed it with other jurors, and based his opinion of guilt upon it.[20]

8. Several jurors had read about confessions of the defendant in an unrelated case (the confessions were later discredited), and discussed them during their deliberations.[21]

When excessive publicity endangers a fair trial the standard remedy is a motion for a change of venue to a locality where publicity and citizen involvement is not a factor. However, there must be a show of threat, then a motion for change of venue will be granted when it is determined that because of the dissemination of potentially prejudicial material, there is a *reasonable likelihood* a fair trial cannot be held. A show of actual prejudice is not required. An alternate method is a request for a continuance to delay the actual trial and jury selection, until the impact of the excessive publicity has diminished. However, time and again, a de-

14. State v. Kociolek, 20 N.J. 92 (1955).
15. People v. Lessard, 58 Cal. 2d 447 (1962).
16. People v. Whitmore, 257 N.Y.S. 2d 787 (1965).
17. Irwin v. Dowd, 366 U.S. 717 (1961).
18. Juelich v. United States, 214 F. 2d 950 (1954).
19. Hagan v. State, 372 S.W. 2d 946 (1962 Texas).
20. People v. Duncan, 350 P. 2d 103 (1960).
21. People v. Odom, 369 S.W. 2d 173 (1963 Mo.).

fense counsel is forced to rely on the *voir dire* examination and his ability to challenge for cause, or his limited peremptory challenges to secure objective jurors.

When there is a likelihood that jurors will be ineligible because of exposure to adverse publicity to the defendant, the questioning *(voir dire)* must probe what the prospective juror has read and heard about the case and how his exposure has affected his attitude towards the trial and the defendant. A prospective juror who states he is unable to overcome his prejudgment or preconceptions is subject to challenge for cause. One who remembers a great deal of the content of the prejudicial news which is significant on the issue of guilt or innocence (confession; incriminating evidence), and may be inadmissible in evidence during the trial, is also subject to challenge for cause, despite claims of an impartial attitude. Other prospective jurors exposed to such publicity must be examined to determine whether the exposure—or their recall of the news content—creates a substantial risk that the juror's judgment has been prejudiced.[22]

An early case, *People* v. *Brown*,[23] sets out the kind of questioning which is proper to determine bias or prejudice from pretrial publicity.

During the examination of prospective jurors, M. P. Troxler was questioned as to his qualifications. He stated that he had heard some talk of the case, had read accounts of the affair in the local newspapers, thought he had read the evidence taken before the coroner, and had formed an opinion in reference to guilt or innocence of the defendant. He was then asked by defendant's counsel:

Q: Was that opinion favorable to the defendant?

(Objection by prosecutor; sustained by court.)

Q: What is your opinion *now* from what you read as to the guilt or innocence of the defendant?

(Objection by prosecutor; sustained by court.)

Q: What impression did the reading of these articles make on your mind?

(Objection by prosecutor; sustained by court.)

Q: Could you enter upon the trial of this case with the presumption that the defendant is innocent until he was proved guilty? Or would you enter upon the trial presuming that defendant is guilty, and desiring to see him vindicated by the testimony of the witnesses here?

A: I don't think I could.

Q: That is, you don't think you could enter upon the trial of the case with the belief that the defendant is innocent?

22. Alfred Friendly and Ronald L. Goldfarb, *Crime and Publicity—The Impact of News on the Administration of Justice* (New York: Twentieth Century Fund, 1967), pp. 95–106.
23. People v. Brown, 72 Cal. 390 (1887).

A: No sir.

Q: Do you think you could give the defendant a fair and impartial trial?

A: I think I could, notwithstanding I have an opinion from what I have heard and read. It would take good evidence to remove that opinion.

Q: In other words, you would be of opinion that defendant is guilty until he had proved himself innocent; isn't that the exact state of your mind?

(Objection by prosecutor; sustained by court.)

While the trial court refused to rule that this prospective juror was prejudiced (he was challenged for actual bias), and allowed him to remain on the jury, the California Appellate Court approved the questions of defense counsel and ruled that the juror should have been excused for bias when challenged.

The court's opinion in the *Brown* case sums up the important question of publicity as a threat to trial by jury in these words:

> The precise question before the court was as to the existence of a state of mind on the part of the juror which would or might prevent him from acting with entire impartiality, and without prejudice to the rights of defendant. It was evident the juror had a fixed opinion as to the guilt of defendant, which he said would require good evidence to remove. The purpose of the attempted examination was to ascertain so far as possible the extent of this opinion, its character, and whether it resulted to any extent from prejudice against defendant or his case. We think the examination was proper, and that the court erred in sustaining the objections of the prosecuting attorney.

Lack of impartiality and objectivity on the part of jurors may originate in circumstances other than excessive publicity, but publicity adverse to the defendant has been identified as one of the most common causes of bias and prejudice. To ruin any opportunity for a fair trial, entertaining a fixed opinion that the defendant is guilty is not necessary; all that is required is a preconception or suspicion of guilt.

It is to prevent such suspicions from developing in the minds of prospective jurors (and others who may be significant to the outcome of a trial, such as witnesses and criminal justice personnel) that reasonable standards are necessary to limit the freedom of the press, to prevent its abuse and the destruction of the right to a fair trial.

Sensational Crimes—The Corona Case

The major problems surrounding crime and publicity occur when a crime is sensational; one with great news value. It may be because of the newsworthiness of the participants (the Lindbergh kidnapping case in New Jersey) an unusualness or new dimension of monstrosity (the Sharon Tate case in Los Angeles), sex and murder (the Wylie-Hoffert case in New York City), or mass murder. A case of mass murder was, literally, unearthed when law enforcement agents in Yuba City, California, dug up the remains of 25 murder victims from orchards north of the city.

These were grisly murders; the farm labor victims had been hacked with a sharp-edged weapon. The total number of victims made this a record crime (newsworthy in itself), outranking the 16-victim mass murder in Texas by Charles Whitman (the "tower sniper" at the University of Texas); young psychopath Howard Unrah's shooting attack in New Jersey in which he killed 13 people in a few moments; and the eight nurses murdered by Richard Speck in Chicago.

To make this Yuba City case even more newsworthy, it appeared that the times of death spanned no more than a two-month period before the discovery of the victims, indicating a systematic execution modus operandi. The victims were all transients, homeless men and "winos" from the skid rows of Yuba City and neighboring Marysville; without friends or relatives who would miss them when they were murdered, and who would normally report their absence to police.

Reporters, photographers, and television crews swarmed into Yuba City: this might be the crime of the century. The sheriff and his deputies were restrained during the initial period, as were the prosecutor and the local judge who issued the search warrant when the first suspect developed. No one knows the mechanics of the breaking down of this restraint on the part of public officials, or the results of such restraint on newsmen already under tremendous pressures from employers and professional competition. What did happen between the discovery of the crime and the time the prime suspect was indicted and formally accused of murder is a fine example of how the search for news (in sensational crime cases) and its publication can rob an accused of his opportunity for a fair trial.

What happened in the reporting of this case of mass murder is indicative of how judges and law enforcement officials can err in their judgment and release data prejudicial to the accused. Men and women of the news media will find imaginative ways of reporting such gaffes, and when no further information is released, they will obtain some news from secret sources and present it as the truth.

Chronologically, this is a sampling of the reporting of the details of these murders and the interpretations concerning the guilt of the accused in the local press.*

---

*The *Sacramento Bee*. This is a daily paper with a mass circulation audience in Northern California, and it has wide circulation in Yuba City (45 miles from Sacramento) and in Sutter County.

On May 30, 1971, a front page story headlined the arrest of the only major suspect in this case: MASS MURDER AND THE SUSPECT. The story briefly reviewed the fact that Juan Corona was a Mexican-born labor contractor, 37, and the father of four children. Then, it went on to the main content of the story: a detailing of data released by the local judge who had ordered the suspect's home searched on the authority of a search warrant. The following extract of Sutter County Sheriff Roy Whiteaker's application for a search warrant was quoted in its entirety:

> The nature of the wounds and their savagery, the disposition of the bodies of the murder victims, and the sheer number of victims indicates that the perpetrator of these offenses is at least seriously mentally ill and probably a homicidal maniac.

One of the following paragraphs quoted the same source and stated that a police official had talked to a man (unnamed) who knew the Corona brothers (Juan's brother lived nearby) and their families. This man had informed the police officials that Juan Corona was known to have fits of temper that were so bad that the family had to take ropes and tie him down until he became quiet again. The article concluded with this statement from an unidentified source: "Corona had often indicated to friends that he had no use for white, transient farm laborers, particularly winos, who only had one desire and that was to earn enough for another bottle."

Also on May 30, 1971, but in a story on an interior page, alongside the carryover of the page-one story, there was an alleged report of contact with Juan Corona's mother in Mexico, headed: "SUSPECT'S MOTHER STUNNED." Two nearby stories also related to this crime. One was headed: "MASS MURDERS TALLY—YUBA CITY MULTIPLE SLAYINGS WILL BECOME CLASSIC IN ANNALS OF GRISLY CRIMES." It began with the Jack-the-Ripper case in London and progressed through seven or eight mass murder cases to the Boston Strangler's chain of murders. The other was headed: "WHY JUDGE RELEASED DOCUMENTS," and was a self-serving documentary detailing the judge's explanation for releasing 65 pages of police reports and investigative documents filed with him by the Sutter County sheriff for the purpose of justifying his application for a search warrant.

On May 31, 1971, the following headlined articles appeared on a single page:

Empty Skid Row, Killings Clean Out Area Where Men Loitered

Sutter Mass Killer Slew Many of Skid Row Mission's Flock

Lax Labor License Law Failed To Uncover Corona's Mental History

An earlier report had disclosed an interview with the foreman of the ranch on which most of the victims were found. In this interview, the foreman was quoted as saying that Corona was mentally ill. In a follow-up story, it was disclosed that fifteen years before (1956) Juan Corona had been committed for a few months to a nearby state hospital treating mental illness. Diagnosis, it was alleged, classified Juan's problem as schizophrenia.

On June 4, 1971, an article on the front page headlined: SUTTER COUNTY MURDER LIST OF VICTIMS IS REVEALED. Although the article conceded that the district attorney refused to confirm or deny the story, or even discuss such a list, it proceeded to detail the circumstances of this list and its contents in the following way:

> Sutter County officials are investigating what they believe is an itemized "mass murder list" found on May 26th in the home of the accused murderer, Juan Corona. The list contains thirty-four names, five of the names are the same as those of murder victims in the Yuba City case.

Then the article stated:

> It was first speculated that the men on the list owed Corona money or were men who might have contacted him for prospective farm labor jobs, but officials are completely convinced the list is a compilation of victims in the case, the dates the men disappeared, and in some cases times and sites of burial.

The list was then printed, apparently verbatim. After the list, the article then states without identifying its source of information, that one victim was shot, the bullet was recovered during the autopsy, and that cartridges of the same size were found in Corona's van (labor bus).

On June 8, 1971 the front-page lead article headlined BLOOD IS FOUND ON WEAPONS FROM THE HOME OF ACCUSED SUTTER MASS SLAYER CORONA. The story noted: "Reliable sources confirmed that human blood has been found on several weapons recovered during a predawn search on May 26 of the Juan Corona home." These same reliable sources were also given as the source of a following paragraph which stated that two Bank of America deposit receipts bearing Juan Corona's name were found when one of the bodies was unearthed earlier. The discovery of the receipts was related to previous disclosures from another unidentified source that two grocery receipts had been found buried six inches above the thigh of one of the victims. The story noted that both the sheriff and the district attorney refused to acknowledge any of the disclosures, but the article used this comment in a fashion that suggested this silence was strongly supportive of the merits of the story and its disclosures.

On June 7, 1971, the widely read news weekly, *Time*, allocated DEATH IN THE ORCHARDS almost a full page of copy. These are extracts from this story:

1. Police arrested a Mexican-born farm-labor contractor named Juan Corona, 37, married and the father of four daughters, but they were by no means sure that they had come to the end of the trail of bodies. They evidently discovered some of the corpses by checking out X marks on a crude map found in Corona's Bible. "I don't know where it's going to stop," said Sutter County Sheriff Roy Whiteaker. "We'll keep digging until we quit finding bodies."

2. Sheriff Whiteaker said of Corona, "We are sure that he committed the murders."

3. Although Corona had no criminal record in Sutter County, in 1956 he spent three months in DeWitt State Hospital, a nearby mental institution, after being committed by his brother, Natividad; two doctors tentatively diagnosed his illness as schizophrenia. He was released as cured.

The news reporting in this case was reflected in the news broadcasts of radio and television stations that blanket the Sutter County area. From the foregoing samples it can be readily noted that the murdered victims were tied in with the suspect, Juan Corona, by the disclosures about a murder list, bloodied weapons, X-marks on a map, and bank receipts; and the monstrosity of the case related to the alleged temper and mental illness of Corona. Collaterally, the silence of public officials was utilized to suggest that they also knew about these items of evidence, but could not in good conscience make any public admissions. Strangely, the silence of the public officials in this case appeared to give news reporters a license to print unvalidated material or speculative reports. The use of *reliable sources* is so vague that there is little or no chance of checking the source to make certain that the news is valid and not mere speculation.

In sensational crimes the conflict between free press and fair trial is unresolved. It is only the ordinary crime, the routine crime, the unimaginative crime that will benefit from the efforts thus far made to limit criminal trials to courtrooms: trials in which a jury is comprised of impartial jurors who have not formed opinions, nor been bombarded with the extrajudicial evidence of the news media. However, it isn't this latter type of criminal case which is threatened by an unfair trial. It has little newsworthy appeal and the publicity, if any, has always been buried in back pages and small print. The well-intentioned committees, commissions, and associations which suggest solutions for the problem of fair trial vs. free press have not as yet found the answer for the sensational criminal case which is so newsworthy that it makes headlines no matter where it happens. The Lindbergh kidnapping, the murder of Mrs. Sheppard, the Kennedy assassinations, and the Sharon Tate case are the types of stories which will be told in great detail, despite the likelihood that such publicity will ruin the accused's right to a fair trial.

Selected References

Books
American Bar Association Advisory Committee on Fair Trial and Free Press. *Standards Relating to Fair Trial and Free Press.* New York: Institute of Judicial Administration, 1966.

Holmes, Paul. *The Sheppard Murder Case.* New York: David McKay Co., 1961.

Sheppard, Dr. Sam. *Endure and Conquer.* Cleveland: World Publishing Company, 1966.

Periodicals
John M. Harrison. "The Press vs. the Courts." *Saturday Review*, 15 October 1955, pp. 9–10, 35.

Cases
Chambers v. Florida, 309 U.S. 227 (1939).

Hagan v. State, 372 S.W. 2d 946 (1962 Texas).

In re Oliver, 333 U.S. 257 (1947).

Irwin v. Dowd, 366 U.S. 717 (1961).

Jelke v. New York, 308 N.Y. 85 (1954).

Juelich v. U.S., 214 F. 2d 950 (1954).

People v. Brown, 72 Cal. 390 (1887).

People v. Lessard, 58 Cal. 2d 447 (1962).

People v. Odom, 369 S.W. 2d 173 (1963 Mo.).

People v. Whitmore, 257 N.Y.S. 2d 787 (1965).

Sheppard v. Maxwell, 384 U.S. 333 (1965).

State v. Kociolek, 20 N.J. 92 (1955).

Part V
Corrections

Chapter XVI

Justice for Juveniles

Children who engage in acts which would be criminal if committed by adults, or who are likely to become or are in danger of becoming delinquent, present a different problem for the community from the problem of adult criminal behavior. Sanction law specifies actions against persons or property which are criminal by statute, and assigns a range of appropriate penalties without regard to the age of the offender.

However, in our legal system the age of the offender is a factor in determining criminal responsibility. Children under seven years of age are free of criminal liability for an act which would be criminal if committed by an adult; children over the age of seven but under the age of 16 to 18 (varies in different states) are considered juvenile delinquents rather than criminals. In the lawmaker's actions, such legal provisions reflect the community belief in the immaturity of children and youths, and the fact that society has always viewed our youngsters as its resource for future growth and development.

The protective nature of such laws, however, are only justified when supported by measures which will provide for the rehabilitation of delinquent juveniles without injustice to them or their parents. Since public officials are held accountable in a democratic society, they must justify their decisions and the decision making apparatus.

The separate legal system which evolved in America to protect its resources of children and youth was informal and private so that the judge might act as the benevolent parent. The proceeding was not subject to the glare of publicity which could follow the child through the rest of his life. The major thrust of the law was to protect the juvenile from the stigma of criminal conviction for his offenses. It is presumed that these acts are committed at a time when the juvenile lacks the mature judgment to understand the possible consequences on the remainder of his life.

Systematic inquiry has disclosed that, through evolution, juvenile courts now are conducted under a system of extensive screening done by police officers and probation personnel, identifying young people who are delinquent and referring them to court for a hearing. This screening is often discriminatory and decisions crucial to the young person are made on improper criteria, such as the juvenile's attitude and parental accessibility. Often, in the screening process, juveniles are asked to place their trust and confidence in their interviewers, and then their self-incriminating statements are used against them.

The doctrine under which special courts for juveniles were established was the doctrine of *parens patriae.** The court's role as a substitute parent, however, was sometimes very authoritarian, with the presiding judge assuming an administrative rather than a judicial role. The proceedings often switched from the adversary process guaranteed to all adult accused persons in the American legal system to a semi-inquisitorial system which jeopardized the basic rights of juvenile offenders.

Juvenile Delinquency

The breadth of the court's jurisdiction is usually justified by its advocates as the means of placing before the court the child in need of its services. The principle difficulty with this position is that it has created a court of law with almost limitless power over children. The definitions are broad enough to label nearly every child a delinquent at some point in his life. The built-in danger of the nonspecific definitions of delinquency in many states is that it permits, if it does not compel, the court to apply subjective standards of morality and child care: whether the juvenile's conduct qualifies as delinquent depends in great measure on the judge's own code of human behavior.

In New York City, the children's court in each county (there are five) is given exclusive original jurisdiction within the county to hear and determine all cases or proceedings concerning children under the age of 16 who are, or who are alleged to be, delinquent. The Domestic Relations Court Act of the City of New York defines as a juvenile delinquent any child over seven and under 16 years of age who:

1. Violates any law of the United States or of this state or any ordinance of the City of New York, or who commits an act which if committed by an adult would be a crime (child of 15 years may

---

*In substitution for parent.

be tried as an adult in criminal courts if the act he committed is punishable by death or life imprisonment)

2. Is incorrigible, ungovernable or habitually disobedient and beyond the control of his parents, guardian, custodian or other lawful authority

3. Is habitually truant

4. Without just cause and without the consent of his parent, guardian or other custodian, deserts his home or place of abode.

5. Engages in any occupation which is in violation of law

6. Begs or who solicits alms or money in public places

7. Associates with immoral or vicious persons

8. Frequents any place the maintenance of which is in violation of law

9. So deports himself as willfully to injure or endanger the morals or health of himself or others.

Whether a juvenile is guilty of serious delinquency depends on:

1. Whether the alleged offense was committed in an aggressive, violent, premeditated or willful manner

2. Whether the alleged offense was against persons or against property, greater weight being given to offenses against persons especially if personal injury resulted.

The Screening Process—Parents and Schools

Many children are referred to juvenile court not because of any delinquent behavior, but because they do not get along with one or both parents. These are the incorrigibles, the youngsters beyond control of their parents, or minors in need of supervision. These parents use the juvenile court concept and its original jurisdiction over children in a weird combination of parental discipline and the sloughing off of responsibility for the conduct of their child. A juvenile who is not getting on with his parents should not need the informal probation supervision of a consent decree, nor should he be threatened with future referral to juvenile court if he doesn't respond to parental control, or institutional care as a result of a juvenile court hearing. Justice might be better served if the youngster's parents found a relative or friend to provide a substitute home for the child while they attended counseling sessions to gain the necessary know-how to resolve the problem, without stigmatizing their child as incorrigible.

Any examination of the records of a juvenile court will indicate that delinquent young people often have records of truancy. However, the court records are silent on whether truancy is a threshold to delinquency, or whether the label of truant is a jet assist to the life style of a juvenile delinquent. A child does not have to qualify as a chronic truant to warrant some kind of special in-school action which will discover the reason or reasons for the absences. In some jurisdictions, there is inquiry by responsible teachers and conferences with the parents, and possibly a referral to the school counseling unit, but in many areas there is just a report to the pupil personnel office. When little more than the recording of absences and notifying the parents fails to have the necessary magical qualities, the truancy is reported to the probation department for adjustment. In some cases, action by the probation department must overcome a long history of poor marks and suspension from a neighborhood school because the truancy problem was not vigorously resolved by concerned school personnel. When the youngster presents a problem on probation, the record of truancy and bad marks in school is cited in the petition to the juvenile court almost as a self-fulfilling prophecy of delinquency.[1]

Parents and teachers are better equipped to work with children than are the more distant probation officers or staffs of juvenile institutions. Incorrigibles and troublemakers often yield to an early solution of their problems, and the child or youth is not lost to his home or school. Concerned parents, teachers, and school counseling personnel can serve as diagnosticians and therapists when they make a sincere effort accompanied by some expertise. Interception of these youthful problem children before they really become delinquents, is a better quality of justice than labeling them as wards of the juvenile court and giving them a record that may be part of a criminal history when they become adults.

The Screening Process—Police Encounters with Juveniles

The label of "delinquent," for close to half of all the juveniles who are taken into custody, originates with the police screening process. This is a process in which police do not acknowledge the juvenile's right to privacy, silence, or representation by counsel, and which may result in an official record for the juvenile and possibly some interference with his liberty.

The police role in serving young people is essentially a negative one. Rarely are police encounters with juveniles used for any purpose except to admonish or take into custody. The protective laws planned to allow

1. David L. Bazelon, "Beyond Control of the Juvenile Court," *Juvenile Court Journal* 21, no 2 (Summer 1970): 2–6.

police to help juveniles seem restrictive to them and evoke resentment toward the police. Attempting to prevent or even control juvenile delinquency has led to a polarization between youth and the police. Reports that police discriminate against juveniles and harass them are fairly numerous. In urban areas, there is the "battle of the corner," and in rural areas there is the "battle of the highway," setting police beat officers and traffic patrolmen against young people in a deadly serious combat in which both parties see a challenge in the behavior of the other.

The stated police function in relation to children and youths is protective rather than repressive. But the states' laws defining delinquency provide so many conditions which may be the basis of police action, that young people fail to understand the wide range of police response possible during these encounters.

As a part of general law enforcement, police note young people who gather on street corners or in premises (such as pool halls and drive-ins) with a local reputation for disorders and criminal activities. Police frequently admonish, warn, or take into custody some of these youngsters when they violate curfew or other laws. They also conduct field interrogations when the behavior of juveniles strongly suggests criminal behavior. Such police tactics are without blemish when not misused. A sincere interest in juveniles no doubt motivates most police officers to engage in such encounters when no overt, actual criminal, or delinquent behavior is observed by the officer. However, many youngsters believe this is harassment unless they are caught "doing something."[2]

The officials of many police departments ask their officers on patrol to take action against juveniles in violation of local laws against loitering. This is within the concept of aggressive patrol, serving to prevent or deter crime and possibly discover conduct requiring appropriate police action. Officers are directed to apply the law only for a specific violation and not to use it as a status violation, and to enforce it without regard to location or persons involved (impartial as to neighborhood or juvenile). The recommended method of handling this type of enforcement is:

1. On first contact, where there is no problem between the juvenile and the officer, the juvenile should be sent home after a field interview (FI) card is prepared.
2. On second contact, where there is no juvenile-officer problem, cite juvenile for the violation to probation department.
3. On subsequent contacts, or where a problem develops between the officer and the juvenile, remove the juvenile to the police

2. U.S., The President's Commission on Law Enforcement and Administration of Justice, *Task Force Report: The Police* (Washington, D.C.: Government Printing Office, 1967), pp. 179–86.

office or station, notify parents to pick up the youth and cite juvenile, or deliver into custody of juvenile hall if parents cannot be located.

The violation itself generally plays an insignificant role in the police action. While a number of these juveniles are seen as serious delinquents deserving arrest, many others are perceived as good boys. Thus, in police-juvenile encounters the assessment of character—the distinction between serious delinquents, good boys, misguided youths, and so on—and the dispositions which follow from these assessments are based on the juvenile's personal characteristics and not the offense or suspicious conduct. In exercising this discretion policemen are strongly guided by the demeanor of the juvenile. This practice ultimately means that certain youths are treated more severely than other juveniles for comparable conduct.

To a substantial extent, this discretion of police officers is simply an extension of the juvenile court philosophy: in making legal decisions regarding juveniles, more weight should be given to the juvenile's character and life-situation than to his actual offending behavior. However, police officers during these encounters do not have the data about juveniles available to juvenile court judges. Therefore, they must use fairly simple cues. Juveniles who are contrite about their conduct, respectful to officers, and fearful of the authority that might be employed against them, are viewed as basically law-abiding and amenable to informal or formal reprimand to guarantee their future conformity. In contrast, juveniles who are argumentative or who appear nonchalant during their encounters are likely to be viewed as would-be tough guys or punks who fully deserve the most severe sanction: arrest.[3]

There is a rationale for police response to insolence and noncooperation by juveniles during these encounters. It is a belief in the importance of fostering a positive and cooperative attitude toward police, and it is their professional opinion that a negative attitude is indicative of delinquent tendencies. While police admit that a youth's attitude in an encounter with police is often significant to the outcome, they believe the police response is more than an emotional reaction.[4]

Unfortunately, the basic injustice of such police encounters is that there is too great a range for police action. Often the dynamics of the encounter rather than the juvenile's offense or misconduct becomes the probable cause for determining which juvenile is to be officially branded as delinquent, and brought to the attention of the juvenile probation office or the juvenile court. Certainly, it is not comparable to the proba-

3. Irving P. Liavin and Scott Briar, "Police Encounters with Juveniles," *American Journal of Sociology* 70 (September 1964): 206–14.
4. David R. Barrett et al, "Juvenile Delinquents: The Police, State Courts, and Individualized Justice," *Harvard Law Review* 79, no 4 (February 1966): 775–810.

ble cause for arresting and accusing an adult of a similar criminal act.

The accessibility of a juvenile's family is often a factor in the screening of juveniles by police. It is not infrequent that two boys will be picked up for some infraction such as joy-riding. (This is auto theft under the criminal law.) Both boys are taken to the police station for the routine reports and calls are made to their parents. One boy's parents cannot be located, he is detained overnight in the local juvenile hall; the other boy's father answers the telephone and responds promptly by coming to the police station and picking up his son. He is not detained; the police have no reason to do so. However, one boy's record will always show "detained," while the other boy's record will indicate "released." It may not work out unfairly in future screening; it depends on the police officer (or others) who review these prior records.

The Screening Process—Probation

The police are the major source of referrals to the probation unit. Most of the referrals are by citation, with the summons directing the juvenile to appear at the probation office on a specified time and day, usually within a few days from the day of issuance of the citation. In some cases, the referrals concern juveniles detained by police at the local juvenile hall. Others may originate with parents or school officials. In any event parents are notified of the situation and requested to appear with their child.

The discretionary powers of a probation officer, and the dynamics of his encounters with juveniles, are unlike the police officer in the police-juvenile encounter. The police officer can almost create delinquency and the necessity for referral by categorizing the behavior of the juvenile as such in his police report of the event. But the practitioner in probation has usually been trained in the nonlegalistic and nonpunitive approach of casework, and the rehabilitative objectives of his probation agency. In the actual screening of juveniles and the articulation of instructions given during training sessions, there are instances in which the application of referral standards may depend on the availability of resources rather than the immediate needs of the juvenile or the nature of his problem.

The basic choice of a probation officer at an initial interview is between various nonjudicial alternatives and the filing of a petition seeking judicial action. The initial probation interview is an informal meeting with the minor and his parents, at which the alternative dispositions to filing a petition are discussed:

1. *Dismissal*—this action is justified when the preinterview investigation, and the facts disclosed in discussing the case with the juvenile and his parents, indicates to the probation officer that

the case is unfounded, or the evidence is untrustworthy or insufficient and does not warrant or sustain the charges.

2. *Referred to Resident Jurisdiction*—this referral is appropriate when the juvenile resides elsewhere and the problem does not justify action where the act of misconduct occurred.

3. *Referral to Other Local Agencies*—this is proper action when the investigation and discussion indicates another local agency is better equipped to handle the juvenile and his problem (usual referrals are to the welfare or mental health agencies).

4. *Counseling and Dismissal*—this action goes beyond outright dismissal, but not beyond a simple counseling session in which all concerned discuss the problem and plan possible solutions.

5. *Informal (consent) Supervision*—this is the most serious non-judicial alternative. It involves the provision of probation supervision to the juvenile with the consent of the parents (parent or guardian), and is only justified when it is apparent that the juvenile requires professional assistance in solving his problem. When initiated, the case is then processed through the probation agency to determine the supervision and counseling services that will be necessary, and the juvenile becomes part of the informal supervision caseload of the probation agency.

In making a decision as to alternatives for a judicial processing of a juvenile, probation officers often attempt to isolate and identify the most important single factor. Was it the current offense, the prior record of delinquency, or the attitude of the juvenile and his parents? (At this initial probation interview the intensive social-history case study needed to file a petition for juvenile judicial appearance has not been made.) The decision may be a combination of all three factors. Injustice can occur when the offense alone (except at felony levels) justifies referral to juvenile court. The previous history data of an offender at this stage of the screening process is generally no more than brief references, and usually fails to indicate if the current offense is part of a general pattern of delinquency—really the only justifiable grounds for considering past misdeeds when making this decision.

Attitude is subject to appraisal at any time. One juvenile may accept an opening statement by the probation officer about the purpose of the interview (whether to refer to court or not), while another may strongly resent this screening. As the interview progresses, there are many moments when some juveniles will strongly disagree with the way it is progressing; others submit silently without protest. Often there is a language barrier, or a communications gap, when the interviewer uses college level conversational style or professional terminology with poorly educated juveniles and their parents. It is certainly a miscarriage of justice to allow derogatory judgment of attitude to become a major influence in the action taken.[5]

Among the factors that may operate against an innocent juvenile are: (1) dispositional decisions in these intitial interviews are often made from improper criteria because more relevant data is not visible and easily ascertainable at this stage of the screening process; (2) the juvenile court referral is used as a threat to enforce the authority of the interviewer; and (3) an interview is usually terminated if the juvenile persistently denies his guilt when there is some evidence of his involvement.

Questioning of Juveniles

The theme of protecting a child from a life of crime or imminent hazard to his health or morals carries over into the area of questioning juveniles as to their conduct. Police are intent on the extent of a youth's involvement in crime or other misbehavior, and probation personnel and the juvenile court judge seek the true facts of a situation in order to take appropriate official action. In defense of this questioning, and the failure to warn the juvenile of his right to silence in accord with the privilege against self-incrimination, these agents of criminal justice have always claimed that when a juvenile is taken into custody or given a citation to appear at an official hearing, it is not an arrest. All the processing of juveniles are civil rather than criminal actions, and this includes the juvenile court hearings. Further, it is argued that the entire structure of agents and agencies involved in juvenile justice is investigative, diagnostic, and prescriptive, rather than merely accusatory and adjudicative.

There are also some expressed opinions in the literature of child saving that confession is good for children and youths. This is within the concept of the protective laws spelling out delinquency and aligned with the therapy of the juvenile court process. It is a means of developing the necessary attitude of trust and confidence toward the agents of juvenile justice who have the basic responsibility for handling juvenile offenders. On the other hand, there is an emerging belief that the individualized treatment of juveniles does not warrant compelling a child or youth to answer questions, without warning, parental guidance, or legal counsel. Bitterness and hostility are the likely products of confessions secured by persons in a *parens patriae* relationship, and these attitudes are subsequently used against the juvenile. These reactions certainly handicap any rehabilitation program.

The original humanitarian philosophy of the juvenile justice process was centered around a wholly informal and flexible procedure of gentle

5. U.S. Department of Health, Education and Welfare, *The Handling of Juveniles from Offense to Disposition*, prepared by James T. Carey et al (Washington, D.C.: Government Printing Office, 1967), vols. 1 and 2, *passim;* vol 3, pp. 13–14, 24–25, 48–49, 57–58.

and friendly probing by officials in juvenile justice agencies to uncover the roots of the child's difficulties and to make informed decisions on how to best meet his problems. Informality in both procedure and disposition thus became a basic characteristic of handling juveniles. On the other hand, for police officers or any official of juvenile justice to use the social service approach to secure self-incriminating statements from juveniles is certainly open to critical appraisal.

In a recent case before the District of Columbia Juvenile Court the presiding judge rejected the proffer of oral statements made to police by four juveniles who had been taken into custody for alleged involvement in an assault and attempted robbery.[6] The court explicitly stated that it did not rest its decision on a showing that the statements were involuntary, but because they were untrustworthy:

> Simply stated, the Court's decision in this case rests upon the considered opinion—after nearly four busy years on the Juvenile Court bench during which the testimony of thousands of such juveniles has been heard—that the statements of adolescents under 18 years of age who are arrested and charged with violations of law are frequently untrustworthy and often distort the truth.

However, an in-depth examination of an earlier case provides an overview of this problem of questioning and taking statements from juveniles about their guilt in acts which would be crimes if committed by adults. The case is based on a trial held in an Ohio court. The facts and circumstances of the case are these. The robbery of a store resulted in the fatal shooting of its owner. The police and prosecutor's theory, supported by some evidence, was that a boy aged 15, and two others, aged 16 and 17, committed the crime. Five days after the crime—around midnight—a 15-year-old boy named Haley was arrested at his home and taken to police headquarters. Beginning shortly after midnight, Haley was questioned by the police for about five hours without friend or counsel present. Around 5 A.M.—after being shown alleged confessions of his 16 and 17-year-old crime partners—the Haley boy confessed. A confession was typed in question and answer form by the police beginning with a statement that the youth was therein being informed of his constitutional rights, and that the law gave him the right to make a statement or not as he saw fit, with the understanding that it may be used at a trial in court either for or against him or anyone else involved in the crime. Haley completed the statement. He was put in jail about 6:00 A.M. or 6:30 A.M. on Saturday, shortly after the confession was signed, and taken before a magistrate and formally charged with a crime on the following Monday.

6. *In the Matter of Four Youths* no. 28-776-J, 28-778-J, 28-783-J, 28-859-J, Juvenile Court of the District of Columbia, April 7, 1961.

At his trial for murder in criminal court, over defense objections, Haley's confession was adjudged sufficiently voluntary to admit into evidence for the jury to weigh its voluntariness. The judicial instructions directed the jury to disregard the confession if they did not believe that Haley had made the confession voluntarily. Haley was convicted and sentenced.

The Haley conviction was reversed by the U.S. Supreme Court[7] because of Haley's age; the early morning hours of the questioning and its length; the absence of friend, parent, or legal counsel; and the assumption by police that a warning as to constitutional rights just before making and signing a confession, was sufficient for a 15-year-old boy (without counsel) to be equipped with the freedom of choice necessary to a valid waiver of his right to keep silent. In fact, the court termed the questioning of Haley under these circumstances an inquisitorial session which mocked the Fourteenth Amendment's guarantee of due process of law to man or child:

What transpired would make us pause for careful inquiry if a mature man were involved. And when, as here, a mere child—an easy victim of the law—is before us, special care in scrutinizing the record must be used. Age 15 is a tender and difficult age for a boy of any race. He cannot be judged by the more exacting standards of maturity. That which would leave a man cold and unimpressed can overawe and overwhelm a lad in his early teens. This is the period of great instability which the crisis of adolescence produces. A 15-year-old lad, questioned through the dead of night by relays of police, is a ready victim of the inquisition. Mature men possibly might stand the ordeal from midnight to 5 A.M. But we cannot believe that a lad of tender years is a match for the police in such a contest. He needs counsel and support if he is not to become the victim first of fear, then of panic.

The constitutional privilege against self-incrimination is applicable in the case of juveniles as it is with respect to adults. We appreciate that special problems may arise with respect to waiver of the privilege by or on behalf of children, and that there may well be some differences in technique—but not in principle—depending upon the age of the child and the presence and competence of parents. The participation of counsel will, of course, assist the police, juvenile courts, and appellate tribunals in administering the privilege. If counsel was not present for some permissible reason when an admission was obtained, the greatest care must be taken to assure that the admission was voluntary, in the sense not only that it was not coerced or suggested, but also that it was not the product of ignorance of rights or of adolescent fantasy, fright or despair.

We do not think the methods used in obtaining this confession can be squared with that due process of law which the Fourteenth Amendment commands.

7. Haley v. Ohio, 332 U.S. 596 (1947).

The Juvenile Court

When all other dispositional alternatives have been exhausted in the screening process, a juvenile presenting major problems to police, probation agencies, his school, or parents is referred to juvenile court. The court reviews the allegations of delinquency, incorrigibility, truancy, or other misbehavior, and decides whether the youth is involved in the alleged misconduct and makes a disposition of the case responsive to the juvenile and his problem.

Each juvenile appearing in a juvenile court is processed as a case: a person with some unique qualities and characteristics in a problem situation. Judicial assessment requires more than a guilt or innocence decision, but rather a decision based on the multitude of facts collected and presented to the court as part of the petition (complaint) on which the juvenile is arraigned. From factual data such as a brief life history and details of the current offense, the judicial role is to assess the juvenile and the problem and decide if the youngster is in need of the array of services available to the court, from admonishment through probation and allowing the child to remain at home, to institutional care and treatment.

Police, probation officers, and the staff of local schools (usually guidance and counseling personnel) are the referring persons who petition the juvenile court to review the case of a young person. These professionally educated workers do not refer children and youth to this court until, in their opinion, the juvenile has a problem which cannot be resolved by other and lesser remedial action. Therefore, any delay, refusal to act, or action contrary to the desires of these referring persons are regarded as judicial action jeopardizing the legitimate expectations of the referring person, and the police agency, probation department, or school—as the case may be. Reaction to any judicial failure to live up to these expectations will range from frustration to antagonism, but one thing is certain, and this is that referring persons expect the juvenile court to act in line with their expectations or those of their organization. In fact, these individuals and their agencies impose these demands almost as if they were the customers or clients of the court, and the court's primary purpose was to serve them rather than the juvenile with a problem.[8]

One of the major problems of the juvenile courts is to weigh the life history data and current situation of a juvenile and make a decision as to the juvenile's correctional needs. Judges of these courts have the stated recommendation of the referring person and agency, and the basic implication in the referral itself: urgent, this juvenile needs shock therapy, forceful and energetic handling, and disposition. However, justice for

8. U.S., The President's Commission on Law Enforcement and Administration of Justice, *Task Force Report: Juvenile Delinquency and Crime—Report on Juvenile Justice and Consultant's Papers* (Washington, D.C.: Government Printing Office, 1967), Appendix C, Robert Vinter, "The Juvenile Court as an Institution," pp. 84–90.

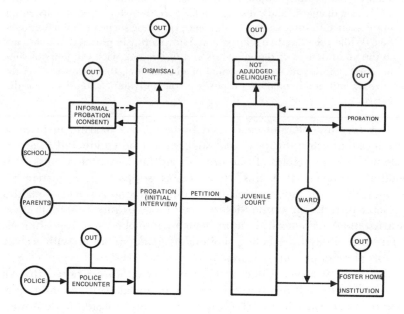

Figure 5. The Screening Process for Juveniles. Incorrigible or delinquent juveniles may be screened *out* of this process during the police encounter or initial probation interview; when adjudged *not* to be incorrigible or delinquent; or (when made a ward of the court), after a period of probation, in a foster home, or a juvenile-care institution.

juveniles may require rejection of prescriptive recommendations, and instead, an in-depth inquiry, and a judicial decision on the merits of the case.

When these judicial decisions emanate from the original philosophy of the juvenile court, a humanitarian compassion for offending children and youths, then juveniles, their parents, and the community can rest assured of the rehabilitation objectives of the judicial decision. However, when the screening process, the expectations of referring persons and their agencies, and other nonrehabilitative factors are allowed to influence these judicial decisions there is a great potential for injustice.

That these influences impinge on, and possibly ruin the role of juvenile court judge to effectively serve in any *parens patriae* capacity is suggested by a 1967 recommendation of the authoritative President's Commission on Law Enforcement and Administration of Justice. The following segment of a series of proposals aimed at restructuring juvenile justice contains this recommendation:

> The cases that fall within the narrowed jurisdiction of the court and filter through the screen of prejudicial, informal disposition modes would largely involve offenders for whom more vigorous measures seem necessary. Court

adjudication and disposition of those offenders should no longer be viewed solely as a diagnosis and prescription for cure, but should be frankly recognized as an authoritative court judgment expressing society's claim to protection. While rehabilitative efforts should be vigorously pursued in deference to the youthfulness of the offenders and in keeping with the general commitment to individualized treatment of all offenders, the incapacitative, deterrent, and condemnatory purposes of the judgment should not be disguised.

This recommendation concluded by terming a hearing in juvenile court an adjudicatory hearing, and suggested it be conducted in accordance with the principles of due process and fundamental fairness. It is doubtful, however, that this viewpoint is supportive of justice for juveniles, when the modern concept of adult corrections rejects penalties as a factor in reducing crime (deterrence); believes imprisonment alone (incapacitation) achieves little more than an annual crop of repeating offenders; and aligns any labeling of offenders (condemnation) with archaic concepts of revenge and punishment.

The U.S. Supreme Court in *Kent* v. *United States*[9] noted that all states had juvenile court systems rooted in social welfare philosophy rather than in *corpus juris*.* They are theoretically engaged in determining the needs of the juvenile and the community rather than adjudicating criminal conduct, and more concerned with the objectives of guidance and rehabilitation (for the child and the protection of the community) than the fixing of criminal responsibility, guilt, and penalty. In its majority opinion, the Court expressed concern for the gulf between theory and performance in juvenile court hearings, saying:

> While there can be no doubt of the original laudable purpose of juvenile courts, studies and critiques in recent years raise serious questions as to whether actual performance measures well enough against theoretical purpose to make tolerable the immunity of the process from the reach of constitutional guaranties applicable to adults. There is much evidence that some juvenile courts lack the personnel, facilities and techniques to perform adequately as representatives of the State in a *parens patriae* capacity, at least with respect to children charged with law violation. There is evidence, in fact, that there may be grounds for concern that the child receives the worst of both worlds: that he gets neither the protections accorded to adults nor the solicitous care and regenerative treatment postulated for children.

Legal Change in Juvenile Court

The danger of injustice in the philosophy of the juvenile court and police and probation screening practices is inherent in any situation in

9. Kent v. United States, 383 U.S. 541 (1966).
*The body of the law.

which well-intentioned persons are placed in positions of authority and allowed various sanctions to enforce their decisions. Justice Louis D. Brandeis pointed this out in his opinion in *Olmstead* v. *United States*[10] when he warned:

> Experience should teach us to be most on our guard to protect liberty when government purposes are beneficient. Men born to freedom are naturally alert to repel invasion of their liberty by evil minded rulers. The greatest dangers to liberty lurk in insidious encroachment by men of zeal, well meaning, but without understanding.

Almost a half century later, the decision of *In re Gault*[11] reflected the wisdom of Justice Brandeis. Gerald Gault was a 15-year-old boy. He was arrested (along with another boy) in June 1964, because of an oral complaint by a neighbor who complained of a lewd and indecent phone call. No notice was given to the parents, or message left at their home. No steps were taken to advise them of the arrest of their son. The parents only learned of the arrest through other neighbors after inquiry.

A deputy probation officer filed a petition against young Gault which only said: "Minor is under the age of eighteen years, and in need of the protection of this honorable court, and that said minor is a delinquent minor." At the hearing on a later date the complaining witness (victim) was not present to testify as to what was said or to make any voice identification as to which of the boys (if either) said the obscene words. There was a conflict of memory as to what young Gault said at the hearing. There was no transcript, recording, or other record made of the proceedings. The judge, at the conclusion of the hearing committed Gerald Gault to the State Industrial School for the period of his minority (until 21 years) unless sooner discharged by due process of law. No appeal was permitted by Arizona law.

The juvenile court judge stated at a subsequent habeas corpus proceeding that he committed Gerald under the law that states: "A delinquent child is one who has violated a law of the state or an ordinance or regulation of a political subdivision thereof," and that the law that Gerald was found to have violated was: "A person who, in the presence or hearing of any child uses vulgar, abusive, or obscene language is guilty of a misdemeanor." The penalty for this violation which would apply to an adult was a fine of $5 to $50, or imprisonment for not more than two months.

Contrary to the due process clause of the Fourteenth Amendment, Gerald Gault was denied in these proceedings the notice of charges, right to counsel, right to confrontation by witnesses (and cross-examination), and the privilege against self-incrimination. The United States Supreme

10. Olmstead v. United States, 277 U.S. 438 (1928).
11. In re Gault, 387 U.S. 1 (1967).

Court reviewed the philosophy of juvenile justice and its operation in this case, and they found it wanting, saying: "Neither the Fourteenth Amendment nor the Bill of Rights is for adults alone." In the majority opinion of the Court in this case, the Court examined the entire problem of juvenile justice:

> The juvenile court movement began in this country at the end of the last century. From the juvenile court statute adopted in Illinois in 1899 the system has spread to every state in the Union, the District of Columbia, and Puerto Rico. The early reformers were appalled by adult procedures and penalties, and by the fact that children could be given long prison sentences and mixed in jails with hardened criminals. They were profoundly convinced that society's duty to the child could not be confined by the concept of justice alone. They believed that society's role was not to ascertain whether the child was "guilty" or "innocent" but "what is he, how has he come to be what he is, and what had best be done in his interest and in the interest of the state to save him from a downward career." The child—essentially good as they saw it—was to be made "to feel that he is the object of (the State's) care and solicitude," not that he is under arrest or on trial. The rules of criminal procedure were therefore altogether inapplicable. The apparent rigidities, technicalities, and harshness which they observed in both substantive and procedural criminal law were therefore to be discarded. The idea of crime and punishment was to be abandoned.

From the point of view of the juvenile caught in the web of juvenile benevolence, the most confusing, disturbing, and disillusioning part of the process was the many-sided role of the probation officer. The first contact was paternal, helpful, and understanding and the juvenile was asked or instructed to trust and confide in this official. The next contact was in a court, and the probation officer was acting out his role as prosecutor, that is, persuading the judge that the child was a delinquent. The third contact after the juvenile was declared delinquent would be, "trust me again, and let me rehabilitate you." A confusion of roles incomprehensible to a child's mind, it is small wonder that many juveniles have a distorted and critical opinion of the American system of justice.

The decision in the case of Gerald Gault opened the way to a change in processing juvenile offenders. It allowed that juveniles are people and that the basic liberties must apply to them also. The court felt that the new direction must be somewhere between treatment as an adult, and the denial of all constitutional rights. Perhaps there is a middle ground which will allow the juvenile his constitutional liberties before the determination of guilt or innocence, and yet be concerned for the fact that he is a child and should not be held as fully accountable for his acts as a mature adult: that he should not be placed in an environment which will encourage and teach him criminal attitudes he did not already have.

The Court's directions in *Gault* were:

1. When proceedings may result in incarceration in an institution of confinement, "it would be extraordinary if our Constitution did not require the procedural regularity and exercise of care implied in the phrase 'due process.'"

2. Due process requires, in such proceedings, that adequate written notice be afforded the child and his parents or guardian. Such notice must inform them "of the specific issues that they must meet" and must be given "at the earliest practicable time, and in any event sufficiently in advance of the hearing to permit preparation."

3. In such proceedings the child and his parents must be advised of their right to be represented by counsel and, if they are unable to afford counsel, that counsel will be appointed to represent the child.

4. The constitutional privilege against self-incrimination is applicable in such proceedings: "an admission by the juvenile may not be used against him in the absence of clear and unequivocal evidence that the admission was made with knowledge that he was not obliged to speak and would not be penalized for remaining silent."

5. In the absence of a valid confession, a juvenile in such proceedings must be afforded the rights of confrontation and sworn testimony of witnesses available for cross-examination.

Parents, school officials in the area of guidance and counseling, police, and probation officers are the sources referring children and youths to juvenile court. In such referral, unhappily, there is a tagging or labeling process and the child or youth becomes, in the eyes of many people, a delinquent.

There is a screening process throughout the handling of juveniles, from the initial referral to the disposition of the case through probation procedures or court assessment of the juvenile and his problems. However, examination of the encounters between juveniles and police officers, the differentiating referral of probation officers, and the gap between theory and performance in juvenile courts have developed reasonable grounds to believe that justice for juveniles may be rank injustice.

The protective laws which relieved the young of criminal responsibility were enacted by lawmakers to protect juveniles from the stigma and consequences of being arrested, tried, convicted, and sentenced as adult criminals. But such laws should not be utilized to deprive the young of the rights of adults or to minimize in any fashion the critical importance of any action by the juvenile court or its referral sources which labels a boy or girl as delinquent.

Diversion of Juveniles from the Juvenile Justice Process

Programs planned to divert juveniles from the juvenile justice process are emerging throughout the United States. Disenchantment with the juvenile justice process in post-*Gault* years may have started the movement, but its growth has been nourished by the success of diversion programs, either managed by a police youth division, or by a community youth service bureau.

Several innovative police programs are based on coercive-voluntary participation by juveniles because many of these youths display an unwillingness to seek help, despite the fact that their delinquent behavior is an obvious signal for help. These programs are planned to divert first-offender juveniles from the juvenile justice process.

The diversion of first-offender juveniles from the traditional intake of juvenile hall, the children's court, probation supervision, and possibly institutional care and custody is designed to reduce the recidivism rate among juveniles and their ultimate progress to adult crime. Police activity in this area does not indicate any loss of faith in the professional competence of local probation personnel, or the loss of confidence in the adjudications and dispositions of children's court. It simply takes into account the fact that many juvenile offenders processed through the juvenile justice system are repeat offenders.

Police juvenile services officers recognize the neglected child, the child victim of family disturbances, the possibility of a juvenile's membership in a local gang, and the hazard of association with certain of the neighborhood youths or frequenting various "hot spots" on the local youth scene. In addition, being an associate of the arresting officer, the police juvenile specialist is in an advantageous position to deal diplomatically with various police reactions when the routine detention procedure leads into a period of background examination of the juvenile and his problems.

Police expertise joined with the training commonly given youth service personnel allows a background examination which considers all the factors likely to be involved in the juvenile's anti-social behavior, and identifies those factors concerned with the youth's environmental influences.

After the background examination is completed, the police juvenile specialist works with the family as the initial institution of social control to seek to bring about the necessary behavior change in the juvenile. The parent or parents are informed of how to recognize and deal with basic problems as a family unit. When parents are inadequate to the task, police juvenile officers arrange for long-term help from appropriate community service agencies outside the juvenile justice framework.

The diversion approach offers release to the juvenile, rather than detention and the lifetime stigma of being officially designated a juvenile delinquent. Diversion means the police will not "book" the youth, but will work with the offender and the offender's family to find acceptable solutions before a more serious crime is committed or a permanent orientation toward criminal behavior develops. Even if the signal for help is too subliminal for an offender's recognition and identification, there is a basic timeliness to intervention by police youth-services specialists with first-offender juveniles: a time when a juvenile is in trouble and police personnel offer help.

Tentative evaluation of first-offender juvenile diversion projects indicate that the recidivism rate can be materially reduced. The cost of police participation is not only warranted as innovative management of offenders, but also by the great promise of these programs to prevent repeated offenses by once-identified juveniles in trouble.

In another diversion program, many police agencies are working with the staff of local Youth Services Bureaus. These are independent agencies, outside of the criminal justice system. They are the result of a major recommendation in 1967 of the President's Commission on Law Enforcement and Administration of Justice, and have been partially financed by federal funds from the Law Enforcement Assistance Administration of the Department of Justice. (See Figure 6.)

The goals of Youth Service Bureaus are:

1. Diversion of juveniles from the juvenile justice system
2. Providing services to youth
3. Coordinating individual cases and young peoples programs
4. Modification of systems for delivering services to youth
5. Development of individual responsibility among juveniles participating in programs.[12]

Youth Service Bureaus are not patterned after the traditional organization of juvenile justice agencies. Many of the staff members are paraprofessionals rather than professionals with standard academic backgrounds. Often many staff members are juveniles in treatment status. There is a general attitude that there is no duty to account to police for the services provided youngsters. It is even required that the police close their case upon acceptance of a juvenile's referral by the Youth Service Bureau.

12. U.S., National Advisory Commission on Criminal Justice Standards and Goals, *Community Crime Prevention* (Washington, D.C.: Government Printing Office, 1973), pp. 51–57.

Diversion of juveniles from the juvenile justice system is a reaction to the problems related to processing delinquent juveniles through probation referral and children's court. The basic question has been and is whether the juvenile justice system is the most effective method of delinquency prevention and control. Each year so-called incorrigibles, truants, and runaways are labeled as delinquents by the juvenile justice system, and each year many juveniles apprehended by police for minor offenses that are not likely to recur or do not present a serious threat to community life are also processed within the juvenile justice system.

At the decision points of police-juvenile encounters, and at probation intake there has always been a selective reduction of young people prior to the next stage of the juvenile justice system. In the past these reductions have not been based on any clear-cut professional criteria or in accordance with any plan for such reduction.

Diversion is best described as pre-judicial processing which has clearly defined policies and in which decisions are based on predeter-

Source: Youth Development and Delinquency Prevention Administration, U.S. Department of Health, Education, and Welfare.

Figure 6. A Schematic Diagram of the Youth Services Bureau Approach.

mined criteria. It is a means whereby problems of youths, which would otherwise be dealt within the context of delinquency and official action, are defined and handled by non-justice system techniques. It encompasses only programs that have clearly stated objectives, those selected as rational and visible alternatives to further processing by the justice system. Diversion programs are operational rather than theoretical.[13]

Selected References

Books

U.S., Department of Health, Education and Welfare. *The Handling of Juveniles From Offense to Disposition.* Washington, D.C.: Government Printing Office, 1967.

U.S., The President's Commission on Law Enforcement and Administration of Justice. *Task Force Report: The Police.* Washington, D.C.: Government Printing Office, 1967.

————. *Task Force Report: Juvenile Delinquency and Crime–Report on Juvenile Justice and Consultant's Papers.* Washington, D.C.: Government Printing Office, 1967.

Periodicals

Barrett, David R. et al. "Juvenile Delinquents: The Police, State Courts, and Individualized Justice." *Harvard Law Review* 79, no 4 (February 1966): 775–810.

Bazelon, David L. "Beyond Control of the Juvenile Court." *Juvenile Court Journal* 21, no 2 (Summer 1970): 2–6.

Gemignani, Robert J. "Diversion of Juvenile Offenders from the Juvenile Justice System," U.S. Department of Health, Education, and Welfare, Social and Rehabilitation Service, Youth Development and Delinquency Prevention Administration, *New Approaches to Diversion and Treatment of Offenders.* Washington, D.C.: U.S. Government Printing Office, 1973.

Liavin, Irving P., and Briar, Scott. "Police Encounters with Juveniles." *American Journal of Sociology* 70 (September 1964): 206–14.

Cases

Haley v. Ohio 332 U.S. 596 (1947).

In re Gault, 387 U.S. 1 (1967).

In the Matter of Four Youths, Juvenile Court, D.C. (1961).

Kent v. United States 338 U.S. 541 (1966).

---

13. *Community Crime Prevention*, p. 59.

Chapter XVII

Crime and Punishment— Corrections and Rehabilitation

Crime deterrence and prevention has always relied upon legislative penalties (imprisonment, fines, probation) in various criminal or penal codes, or the morality of members of the community, and neither of these two forms of social control has ever been as successful as desired or expected. There is some evidence that a new awareness of the ineffectiveness of these traditional measures is leading to the funding of social justice programs to fight poverty, discrimination, and some of the other inequities in American communities which, to some degree, foster delinquency and crime. However, to date, the only supplement has been the reform role of corrections in the criminal justice system. In organizing for this role, local and state governments provide field agencies (probation, parole) and institutions (prisons, jails) for the care and rehabilitative treatment of offenders, with the aim of changing their criminal behavior to noncriminal behavior.

After a crime occurs, there is a major thrust to apprehend the offender. When an investigation does focus on a suspect, the case against the accused moves rapidly to the point at which the prosecutor must make his decision whether to charge. When the decision is to charge, the prosecutor pushes for trial, or a plea negotiation session. Sentencing is equally prompt after a trial or plea of guilty. Then, when the convicted person has been sent away, the process hesitates and slows to a stop.

Up to this point, the major thrust of the criminal-justice process is to investigate the crime as an event and to make a determination as to the guilt or innocence of the accused. Now, after the trial and its verdict, the police, prosecutor, and defense counsel are through. As for the trial judge, his only remaining duty is the sentencing session. After a verdict of guilty, the defendant becomes a convicted person, and after sentencing he is a prisoner to be committed to the care and custody of a corrections agency, as provided by law. His contacts are now with agents of the probation agency, or the staff of the institution in which he will serve his sentence. Outside of an abstract interest in justice, these agents are not concerned with the question of guilt or innocence. Institutionally, they assume guilt and work from this base toward the rehabilitation and eventual return of the offender to the community.

Imprisonment is the most common sentence for serious crimes in American courts. It was developed by humanitarians in the eighteenth century as an alternative to capital punishment, floggings, and other physical punishments. Summary physical punishment, as a direct reaction to the guilt of an offender, was a carryover from the precourt years in which the family or friends of a victim sought vengeance or revenge. Imprisonment was and is punitive; deprivation of liberty is painful. At the time of the transition from physical forms of punishment to imprisonment as a major tool of sentencing judges, a long term of years in confinement was believed to be a deterrent to the repetition of criminal acts upon release. It was a guarantee to the community that the law-abiding citizens would not be molested in any way by the offender while incapacitated in prison. Additionally, the example of imprisonment was seen as a deterrent to others to avoid criminal acts.

Over the years, however, a suspicion among nineteenth-century criminologists that imprisonment was ineffective in changing the behavior patterns of convicted offenders, became a twentieth-century belief among experts in law and its penalties. Mere restraint does not achieve the purposes for which a sentencing judge commits a convicted person to prison. Institutions for the custodial care of sentenced offenders tend to isolate them from the community, cutting them off from interaction with family, friends, and community services which provide the supportive influences necessary for any person to achieve minimum levels of social and material success. Prisons, with their procriminal subculture, do not prepare inmates for a law-abiding life upon their release. The cultural impact of a prison community for any extended period of time accustoms inmates to criminal lives.

The switch from suspicion to belief in the failure of prisons to correct convicted criminals may also be a switch from the old rule, "Let the punishment fit the crime," to a new creed of, "Let the treatment fit the needs of the individual offender." In this reform, the main focus of the postconviction period is not the deterrence of crime or the protection of the community by storing offenders in prisons, but rather a focus upon the individual offender for the purpose of rehabilitation. The community will be safer with this reform, by changing the behavior patterns of offenders so that they do not return to crime upon release from prison.[1]

Corrections in the United States have a federal, state, county, and sometimes, municipal level. In this probation-prison-parole complex a substantial number of persons are returnees, recidivists who have committed one or more crimes after release on a prior commitment. Of course, these backsliding individuals may have commited the new offense or offenses due to the causative factors which lead to crimes, despite supervision on probation or parole, or treatment during a term of imprisonment. Unfortunately, some of the most meaningful work done by agents and agencies in this field of corrections is negated by the complex influences acting upon the released inmate as soon as he returns to the free world and tries to rejoin the community. Most parolees or discharged prisoners return of necessity, not choice, to the same environment as that of the original criminal activity.

The Ethics of Punishment

Revenge as punishment belongs to the early years of community-approved sadism. Sanction law rejects the concept of retribution in assigning penalties for criminal acts.

The gibbet at the crossroads and the exhibition of severed heads in public places were techniques of terror associated with the doctrine that if whipping, severe flogging, and exposure in the pillory did not prevent crime, then capital punishment was justified. In the beginning of sanction law, there was a trial-and-error period. It was soon discovered, however, that severe punishment alone was a failure. In eighteenth century England, as the number of crimes for which the sentence could be death grew, the total number of crimes increased.

When Cesare Beccaria and Jeremy Bentham first probed crime and the rationale of punishment, they asked as to the efficacy of the death penalty: Is it really useful or necessary for the safety and good order of society? In Beccaria's view, the role of a legislator in assigning penalties to a crime was to set a punishment which would counteract the motives that led to such crime. Bentham had a mathematical concept of motives for crime and believed that an ascending schedule of punishment could serve as a deterrent to crime. This is the classical view that man is a calculating animal with free will, and not a person influenced by constitutional factors related to heredity; by compulsive drives, or unconscious motivations; or by the influences of environment and stress. In Beccaria's

1. U.S., The President's Commission on Law Enforcement and Administration of Justice, *The Challenge of Crime in a Free Society* (Washington, D.C.: Government Printing Office, 1967), pp. 159–65.

and Bentham's utilitarian concept, the principal end of a criminal punishment was to prevent like offenses.

Both of these early utilitarians also stressed the need for humanitarianism in setting penalties and passing sentences: punishment should be no greater in amount than the minimum necessary to deter men from the commission of crime. The amount of punishment should not be governed by the moral transgression of the offender or the intensity of public indignation over the crime, but rather by the social need to prevent such crimes. The utilitarian concepts of Beccaria and Bentham also extend the concept of humanitarianism to offenders who commit crimes due to extenuating circumstances. For instance, punishment would be less severe when the circumstances of a crime indicated extreme provocation, economic need, or reaction to sudden stress.[2]

In this classical view of crime and punishment, the main purpose of penalties set by legislators in sanction law is not in the punishment of convicted persons, but rather in the operation of the threat of punishment as a deterrent to crime among the far larger number of potential criminals. The eighteenth-century sentencing judge was assigned the role of putting its penalty into operation. Lawmakers and the judiciary served as agents of criminal justice in attempting to achieve the community objective of preventing crime.

The American view of punishment evolved from the penalties provided for various crimes in the English common law, the moralistic code of the Puritans who settled New England, and the administration of justice during the westward march of frontier settlements. Case law allowed the colonists to relate a specific crime to a range of punitive actions, and the Puritan mind provided a ready answer to any question as to the purpose of punishment: it was the spiritual welfare of the citizen and the good of the community. From these beginnings, punishments for crime in the United States were shaped by the close relationship between the rudimentary courts of justice and local citizens in frontier mining, lumber, and cow towns. Trials were frequently informal affairs attended by crowds of onlookers seeking satisfactory outcomes. The concept of criminal punishment in America may be summed up as originating in an accumulation of judicial decisions, the Puritan combination of ecclesiastical and secular authority, and the frontier citizen's demands for an observable and satisfactory justice.[3]

As part of the nineteenth-century evolution of punishment within the various criminal codes in the United States, the values of deterrence and incapacitation (public protection) were joined with the idea of corrections—restoring the offender to his basic role as a law-abiding citi-

2. Sir Walter Moberly, *The Ethics of Punishment* (Hamden, Conn.: Archon Books, Shoe String Press, 1968), pp. 43–59.
3. Louis B. Schwartz, "The American Penal System: Spirit and Technique," *Annals—Crime and the American Penal System* 339 (January 1962): 1–10.

zen in the community. Lawmaking allowed for greater judicial discretion in granting probation and introduced the concept of the indeterminate sentence (and its correlated parole release). Such discretion not only allows the sentencing judge to set an appropriate sentence for the individual offender, but also permits him to forego or shorten imprisonment in favor of a correctional treatment program which will minimize the offender's dislocation from the community and enhance his opportunity to readjust to community life.

Utilizing an objective analysis of available data as a prelude to the sentencing episode, the judiciary works with the practitioners in probation, prison, and parole agencies for the rehabilitation of offenders. In aligning the judiciary's interest in the offender as a person and the apparent intent to encourage rehabilitation in postconviction years, the practitioners in correctional agencies have developed a related correctional philosophy. This philosophy has five major aspects:

1. Convicted and sentenced offenders are social deviates requiring treatment.

2. The sentence imposed by the sentencing judge is the "criminal punishment" of sanction law.

3. It is the obligation of the correctional agency to administer its program so as to equip offenders to cope with life in the community upon release.

4. The treatment needs of individual offenders vary in accordance with what is "wrong" with them; the duration and circumstances of treatment for individual offenders have a corresponding variance.

5. There is an obligation by all correctional agencies to maintain control over offenders committed to their supervision, or care and custody.[4]

It should not be forgotten, however, that corrections have been and always will be handicapped by the basic assumption that crime can be reduced by increasing the severity of punishment.* A survey authorized by the California Assembly's Committee on Criminal Procedure studied penalties and deterrents. This study revealed that California's general public was almost unaware of the severity of criminal penalties, but the most delinquent group was quite aware of the severity of criminal penalties.** California's legislators had long assumed that more severe penal-

4. John P. Conrad, *Crime and Its Correction—An International Survey of Attitudes and Practices* (Berkeley and Los Angeles: University of California Press, 1967), pp. 11–14.
*Defined as increasing the amount of time served in prison.
**Inmates in California's youth centers and prisons answered 6.3 questions correctly out of a total of 11 queries; the general public's average was only 2.6.

ties would deter criminals and noncriminals from committing crimes, but it is apparent that a policy of severe penalties did not deter these offenders and would be unlikely to deter an unknowing member of the general public. The research team on this project concluded: "We can find no evidence that crime can be reduced by increasing the time served."[5]

In a follow-up study, a total of 7,925 California parolees were interviewed to determine whether time served in prison related to postrelease success on parole. The findings of these researchers were that recidivism rates for offenders who had served comparatively long terms of imprisonment (compared to others in the same offense category in the sample population) were higher than those who served short terms; and, in constructing mathematical models composed of significant characteristics to predict postrelease success, it was found that time served was *not* useful in predicting postrelease success.[6]

In regard to the philosophy of criminal punishment in America, it appears safe to assume that there has been a trend away from the classicist viewpoint: that fear of criminal punishment as a penalty for criminal acts is an effective deterrent. There is more acceptance of the concept that the sentencing of offenders should be oriented to their rehabilitation and not tied to any residual aspects of punishment.

In little more than a century criminal punishment (penalties based on sanction law), has changed from the crude philosophy of simple deterrence to a philosophy of correctional rehabilitation of offenders. There is still some recognition that the sanctions of criminal law serve as deterrents to many potential offenders. However, sentencing is more and more a judicial referral to the practitioners in corrections with the hope that professional care and treatment will lead to personal and legal rehabilitation.

Capital Punishment

The penalty of death by execution for a criminal act such as murder or kidnapping has long been a subject of controversy. In theory, its severity has been termed a deterrent to similar acts by others; its certainty pointed to as an asset (there can be no reduction in the sentence by parole); and its basic financial economy has even been lauded. On the other hand, there is persuasive evidence that capital punishment does not deter: murder rates are not affected by punishing people with death.

5. California, Assembly, Office of Research, *Crime and Penalties in California* (Sacramento: Assembly of the State of California, 1968), pp. 1–17.
6. California. Assembly, Select Committee on the Administration of Justice. *Parole Board Reform in California: Order Out of Chaos* (Sacramento: Assembly of the State of California, 1970), pp. 20–22.

The type of crimes for which death has been a penalty in the twentieth century are usually committed during an emotional episode—and murderous anger or rage leaves little room for intellectual consideration of the penalty. There is also significant evidence that the poor and members of minority groups are more likely to be given a death sentence, with less likelihood that it will be changed to life imprisonment prior to execution. While the pardoning authorities may strive to review the nature of the crime, the fairness of the trial, and the rehabilitation potential of the offender as a grounds for executive clemency, the reality of these decisions will often be based on the public pressure in the case and the executive's personal and political response to it.[7] Lastly, there is an awful finality to capital punishment. Post-mortem evidence of innocence does no more than restore the reputation of the executed offender.

The moral argument which questions the right of the state to take human life as punishment for behavior labeled as criminal by lawmakers is reinforced by the cold-blooded politeness of the execution. The person who is about to be put to death is expected to collaborate in a nice, sensible manner, as if it were to be an experience no worse than minor surgery; and if the victim is a woman she must put on waterproof underwear just prior to the execution.[8]

When a person accused of murder is convicted, the judgment and sentence decision is a solitary one. Since the *Furman* decision and the subsequent state legislation which attempts to reenact death penalty statutes which will overcome the criticism of the U.S. Supreme Court justices, the trial judge will do only that which the law mandates upon a given factual finding.[9]

Some years ago, the author encountered a precisely written judicial comment on the basic problem of the sentencing judge in deciding between the death penalty and life imprisonment. The case was murder, the two defendants were brothers, the trial was fair, and the verdict of guilty was warranted by multiple evidence of guilt.[10] This trial judge, with the awesome responsibility of determining whether two young men should live or die for a murder they had committed, decided on life imprisonment. He describes the matter of sentence and penalty in these words:

> I do want to state the reasons for my judgment . . . so that the two defendants may know the reasoning of the person who has held their lives in the balance . . . . The choice becomes a personal and internal one. Internal

7. Richard Quinney, *The Social Reality of Crime* (Boston: Little, Brown and Co., 1970), pp. 184–90.
8. Arthur Koestler, "Reflections on Hanging," in *Perspectives on Correction*, ed. Donald E. J. MacNamara and Edward Sagarin (New York: Thomas Y. Crowell Co., 1971), pp. 239–77.
9. Furman v. Georgia, 408 U.S. 238 (1972); California Penal Code, Section 190, *et. seq.*
10. People v. Lokey, Superior Court, Sacramento, California (No. 26156, 1962).

choices are secretly made and then publicly announced. It is possible to reach a judgment based entirely on subjective considerations. It is possible through anger to reach a harsh judgment and it is possible through pity to reach a soft judgment. Either judgment would find its critics, and its supporters who would marshall facts and arguments to criticize or praise a sentence which, while not intrinsically wrong, was reached by an emotional and, hence, erroneous process.

Judges and lawyers who have been instilled since the beginning of their training with zeal for equal justice intuitively dislike and avoid arbitrary judgments. Now, if in the course of what our State Supreme Court has called the "grim business" of selecting life or death, the law offers us an arbitrary choice, we must reject it and reach out strenuously for such objective standards as are available. Realistically, we know that subjective and, hence to that extent arbitrary, elements will insinuate themselves into the process. We must reduce and contain them so far as possible. We cannot reach a decision by mechanically perfect means, but it must be a rational decision.

Penologists have discerned four objectives of punishment; first, retribution; second, to protect society by executing or confining the wrongdoer; third, to deter others from crime; and fourth, to correct and rehabilitate. Were retribution a primary factor and were Bobby and Galen Lokey to be judged mainly by the terrible consequences of their action, they should certainly pay the heaviest penalty known to the law. If we were to judge these defendants by the law of the talon, an eye for an eye, and a tooth for a tooth, then the court might impose the death penalty upon them as the expression of an outraged community, and the outrage of the community is perfectly justified. Enlightenment, however, tells us that retribution is no longer a desirable object of punishment. A judgment grounded to any extent on social vengeance would degrade our progressive notions of criminal jurisprudence.

What about the objective of protecting society against future crimes by these defendants? Certainly, their death will accomplish that aim, but will life imprisonment do any less?

Now, deterrence. Certainly deterrence must be a prime objective of the sentence. To say that the death of Bobby and Galen would prevent other youthful delinquents from running amuck is patent error. To say that life imprisonment would encourage repetition of their crime is idiotic. The hard fact is that there are no facts which would sustain a choice between life and death for the purpose of deterrence. Each type of punishment is equally effectual and equally ineffectual. Since under California law there is no preference between the death penalty and life imprisonment, the fact of deterrence does not militate in either direction.

Now, we reach the fourth objective of penology, rehabilitation. From a temporal standpoint, death is utterly without rehabilitative value. At this point the scales tip significantly in the direction of life imprisonment. The Court was at some pains to ascertain whether either of these young men is afflicted with personality disorders tending toward incurable sadism; they are not so afflicted. In short, these defendants are good prospects for rehabilitation.

Galen Lokey will commence his life term at the age of twenty. He will become eligible for parole while still a young man. There is a prospect that at
some future day he will return to the world of freedom equipped with
sufficient maturity, self-command, and, above all, with a set of goals, which
will enable him to live decently, even happily.

Nor is rehabilitation irrelevant to the case of Bobby Lokey. It is ironic and
terribly sad that this young man, hardly more than a boy, this young man of
23 should be sitting before me with relief pumping through his veins at the
sour prospect of spending the rest of his life behind prison bars. The prison
community, I would say to Bobby, is like the outside world in this respect,
that it is populated by good, indifferent, and bad people. Bobby has had a
talent for trouble since his childhood, and there are a lot of people in prison
with a talent for trouble, and their talent manifests itself even in prison, and
they are troublemakers there. But, in prison there are also decent people,
there are opportunities for useful work, and, most important, for education.
Decency and usefulness and knowledge are there and available to Bobby
Lokey if he will reach out for them. At any rate, in his case, too, the rehabilitation factor calls for life imprisonment rather than death.

Data Base

To achieve both specific and overall objectives, an organization requires facts, and a data storage and retrieval system which will link these
facts together so that the interrelationships of data can be readily apparent when decisions must be made in the corrections process. A proper
data base should provide sufficient information about a person to indicate
whether probation is more desirable than prison, when a stay in prison
can be cut short for release on parole, or the dimensions of a specific
program of probation or parole supervision determined by the care and
treatment program in prison. In short, the data base should serve as a
guide to the solution most likely to effectively rehabilitate a specific offender.

The most adequate data base is a records system in the correctional
process which will connect up all the available information on a first
offender from police and court sources, and serve as a continuous inventory of the convicted offender from the time he is first placed under the
control of a correctional agency. The basic background study of all offenders is the presentence report, and this is followed up with a classification report when the offender is sentenced to prison. In either case, the
progress reports of correctional personnel while an offender is on probation, in prison, or on parole complete the data bank on each individual.
When an offender is returned to a correctional agency upon conviction for
a crime committed after his release from probation or prison, the data
base continues to function in its continuous inventory of a specific person.

Case or Career Management

The continuous-inventory concept of record keeping is aligned with case or career management, a new concept in corrections. Case management brings the full range of correctional care and treatment programs to each offender early in a criminal career. It is a means of developing a therapeutic program for each offender which will be oriented to solving specific individual problems as soon as possible. In addition, cases may be managed in groups when there is some relationship between criminal careers: correlated cases of crime partners such as wives, girl friends, or other family members; cases originating in a specific neighborhood; or cases involving other members identified with one or more subjects in the group (youth gangs, semicriminal groups such as the Hell's Angels, and the professional associations of organized crime).[11]

Case management based on factual data and innovative correctional practice holds great promise for achieving the objectives of rehabilitation as soon as possible in the career of an offender. In a report by The President's Commission on Law Enforcement and Administration of Justice, it was demonstrated that funds expended to nip a budding criminal career shortly after its known formal inception (first arrest and conviction) would be less costly to the community than allowing such careers to go unchecked until the repeating offender has returned to the criminal justice system time after time.[12]

Data Elements

The data base continuous-inventory records system is made up of elements providing factual information about the offender, his current offense, his prior crimes, and data likely to be significant in his rehabilitation.

Personal Information—data to identify the offender to the administrators of the courts and correctional agencies, and to provide police and prosecutor with a prior arrest history in case of rearrest. It consists of:

1. Age and place of birth
2. Physical characteristics (including data on spouse, if any)
3. Occupation
4. Race (color)

11. U.S., Institute for Defense Analyses, *Task Force Report: Science and Technology*, prepared for The President's Commission on Law Enforcement and Administration of Justice (Washington, D.C.: Government Printing Office, 1967), pp. 64–65.
12. Ibid., pp. 65–66.

5. Permanent home address
6. Residence (present)
7. Marital status
8. Children (sex, age, custody)
9. Parents (name, address, alive, deceased).

Current Offense Data—all known information as to the crime and its circumstances is placed in this portion of an offender's record. For instance, data about the following would aid in understanding the crime as an event:

1. Time and place of occurrence
2. Legal description of crime (common name, essential elements, grade of crime, and penalties)
3. Nature of offense and criminal agency used (directed against property or people; violence, unnecessary violence; entry into residence at night; weapon used)
4. Victim and crime situation (relationship between victim and offender; provocation or stress situation)
5. Progress of case (plea, plea negotiation, change of plea, insanity defense, trial, verdict).

Prior Criminal History—information on prior offenses, including data on crime partners should comprise this data element. It should be arranged to indicate that a thorough search of available sources of information has been made (FBI, state, local). Pertinent facts are usually:

1. Date and place of most recent felony arrest
   a. Name in which arrest was recorded; description of arrestee
   b. I.D. number given at time
   c. FBI number
   d. Charge (crime and final disposition)
   e. Circumstances of case
   f. Crime partner
   g. Connect-ups with other crimes
2. Data on other prior arrests in chronological order.

Basic Rehabilitation Data—block of information containing data useful to understand the specific individual problems of an offender, and to evaluate him as a person. This data element should include the following:

1. Family background (parental deprivation or rejection of offender as child; social-economic level)

2. Neighborhood (stable or transient, low rent, minority group, high crime area)

3. Education (grades, level attained, attitude toward school and teachers)

4. Employment history (job titles, average term of employment, salaries)

5. Religion (formal, informal; offender's attitude to preferred religion, if any)

6. Patterns of personal relationships (school, job, neighborhood, family)

7. Patterns of relationship to authority figures (police, courts; job supervisor)

8. Patterns of aggressiveness (disputes at school or with parents, wife, neighbors, fellow employees)

9. Leisure time activities (hobbies, school, travel)

10. Strengths and weaknesses (broad summary, including any evidence of drug abuse or mental illness).

Classification Work-up—data element containing information secured from an offender during a period of quarantine in a correctional institution. Usually termed a professional work-up by practitioners in corrections, it is primarily a report of tests and measurements and diagnostic interviews. This area of information usually provides relevant data on:

1. Attainments, abilities, interests and attitudes (educational, mechanical, vocational and motivational)

2. Results of psychological examination

3. Personal and social inventory, bringing the evaluation up to date—a summary of the present situation against the known background data

4. Interpretation or overview of his problems

5. Recommendation for appropriate correctional program.

Progress Reports—compilation and analysis of raw data on the behavior and progress of the offender while under the care and control of a correctional agency. Among the useful items of information are:

1. Adjustment to supervision, violations of conditions of probation

2. Adjustment to imprisonment

3. Disciplinary record and interpretation

4. Participation in correctional programs (assigned and volunteer), and vocational planning

5. Attitudes toward current offense, correctional rehabilitation, and release in the community

6. Continuing family and personal relationships in "free world" and reality level of support for offender upon release (review of correspondence and visits)

7. Violations of conditions of parole

8. New crimes (in prison or while on probation or parole).

Probation

By definition, probation is a device providing an individual correctional program for an offender who is:

1. Unlikely to get in trouble again

2. Likely to rehabilitate himself without institutionalization (prison)

3. Willing to comply with the conditions of probation

4. Amenable to supervision

5. Appreciative of the sentencing judge's power to promptly recommit him if he fails to meet the conditions of probation.

Not all offenders are entitled to probation. It is a concept used mainly for first offenders or as a penalty for lesser offenses. Except in unusual cases, most state laws forbid probation for offenders convicted of serious felonies such as armed robbery, assault with a deadly weapon, forcible rape, or certain offenses such as selling drugs to juveniles.

Most misdemeanants are given a suspended sentence (or sentence is set and its execution suspended), and placed on an informal probation status without professional supervision. Any return to crime would result in the possibility that the suspended sentence would be activated immediately on arrest, or added to the sentence for the most recent crime.

Persons convicted of felonies and some misdemeanants are placed on probation with supervision. The amount of supervision depends on the offender and his known problems. Progress reports prepared by a probation officer reveal whether he believes the offender is meeting the conditions of probation, adjusting adequately to the community, and not participating in any criminal behavior. Some conditions of probation set by the sentencing judge provide for imprisonment in the local jail (possibly over weekends), a fine, restitution, and—possibly—"keeping the peace." In any event, the role of the probation officer is to help the offender in his effort to meet the conditions of probation, and to supervise him while making sure he does so.

Criteria exists suggesting probation may relate to the crime, mitigating circumstances, the offender, and the existence of suitable resources in the community to assist in his rehabilitation. Criteria for probation includes:

1. The crime is a lesser offense, or resulted from misfortune rather than deliberate intent: the stress of provocation, overwhelming economic need, or did not cause or threaten seious injury to the victim.

2. The offender has been penalized by the humiliation of arrest and accusation; by a licensing agency (suspension; revocation); by substantial pretrial time in jail; by injury during the crime, pursuit or arrest; and by financial expenditures or losses (lawyer's fees, loss of salary).

3. The offender is willing to make restitution—when appropriate and warranted.

4. The offender is normally a good citizen, young, unsophisticated, with no past history of violence or disregard of the rights of others to their property; he is an offender with a criminal history of no more than minor and infrequent crimes, and no experience in jail, prison or youth corrections center (no previous failure while on probation); he is a person without bitterness because of past treatment by his family or agents of criminal justice, and an individual whose parents or spouse are law-abiding and willing or eager to help.

5. There is sufficient probation personnel available for the level of counseling and supervision needed to adequately control the offender, and there are sufficient educational, vocational training, guidance, and job placement facilities available locally to develop a program for the offender's rehabilitation.

Of course, in the final analysis, the probation officer's recommendation for probation in his presentence report, and the sentencing judge's final decision as to probation, is going to rest on an evaluation of the offender's intelligence and attitudes. An offender will be recommended for probation, and released on this alternative to imprisonment, when he appears to understand all of the implications of his crime, indicates a sincere willingness to be law-abiding, and genuinely accepts the controls of the conditions of probation.

When probation is recommended (or is a possible sentencing alternative), probation officers often suggest conditions of probation. Such conditions would be aligned with the specific rehabilitation objectives and solutions for an offender. They are similar to the correctional program recommended by classification personnel when offenders are committed to prison. In this instance, however, the probation officer serves as the diagnostic technician to evaluate the problems of the offender and recommends a program of conditions helpful in the solution of the individual's problems.

When an offender is placed on probation it is usually for a term less than the maximum sentence set forth in the penalty for the crime for which he was convicted. After a review of all the data in the case the supervisor of the probation agency determines the level of supervision required, notes any special conditions of probation in the sentencing judge's probation order, and assigns a probation officer to the offender. Supervision on probation is a combination of these relationships: (1) supervisor—supervised; (2) teacher—student; and (3) friend. Hopefully, the ideal situation will not deteriorate to either an overly supportive or a grossly authoritative relationship.

Imprisonment

Execution and physical punishment (as a means of controlling criminal behavior) were replaced by imprisonment because it was sufficiently punitive to be accepted as a deterrent to such behavior, and because it protected the community by providing a closed, custodial place for convicted offenders. In the beginning, prisons were funded from the public treasury and thought of as places of incarceration, nothing more.

It was many years until there was even conditional acceptance of the concept that mere restraint did not reform or rehabilitate offenders. In 1878 Boston became the first city in the United States to allow probation as an alternative to imprisonment in the sentencing of offenders. It was 1891 when the state of Massachusetts followed suit, and 1925 when the federal government enacted its law allowing probation for selected federal violators. Today, legislators and the general public only conditionally accept early release on parole as a successful alternative to long prison sentences. This acceptance is partly caused by the discovery in post-World War II years that early release of prisoners on parole is more economical than long imprisonment. Slow and grudging as it was, there is now firm recognition that prisons are places to keep people out of, or to release them from, as soon as possible.

The county jail is not a model of a prison. It is a way station for minor offenders serving short sentences. City jails are little more than drunk tanks in most areas. However, both city and county jails do house accused persons awaiting court action. At these local levels, jails are places in which little care, close custody, and no more is given to persons awaiting arraignment and trial or serving short sentences for minor violations or misdemeanors. Imprisonment in these institutions does not consider the goals of rehabilitation except for the impact of the time served. Very few of the thousands of local jails have any program of classification, education, vocational training, group counseling, or treatment.

It is at state levels, in a single prison or in a system of prisons, that these factors of classification, education, vocational training, group counseling, and treatment exemplify the new concept of imprisonment as providing a place and time for the care, custody, and treatment of offenders. Of course, the state prisons are closed and guarded; security-minded officials conduct roll calls and inspections; and there are lockups, off-limit areas, and a system of "ducats"* to control prison traffic. Stealing, violence, coerced and volunteered homosexuality, and tyranny occurs in a closed society when the prison staff controls the lives of the inmates, or when violent and aggressive inmates assume control over their cell partners and fellow inmates. To overcome these handicaps, state prisons now provide facilities with various levels of security, and there are prison systems which house inmates in cottage colonies, forestry camps, and honor farms. There are institutions without guard towers, firearms, constant surveillance by roll calls, inspections, the restriction of lockups, or a ducat system to restrict the mobility of inmates. These are prisons in which the treatment programs for offenders join in making imprisonment less of a jungle experience in which survival justifies in-prison criminal behavior.

Classifying incoming inmates becomes a base for determining the needs of new or returning prisoners and matching them with the various in-prison programs available. Incoming prisoners are segregated for the period of time needed for a staff of professional counselors, psychologists, and psychiatrists to examine them and to discuss and recommend various in-prison programs for their rehabilitation. Programs in education, vocational training, and group counseling are all part of the rehabilitation effort now sited in prisons. However, any effective treatment of inmates must join these programs of intellectual, occupational, and emotional self-improvement with an individual program for each inmate consisting of explicit tactics or procedures undertaken to change those conditions believed responsible for the inmate's criminal behavior. Treatment for any inmate implies a rationale that the criminal behavior of the individual is identified with particular causative factors, and the treatment program is designed to alter as many of these causative factors as possible.[13]

In the swing away from pure custody to custody and treatment, there has been greater employment of professional personnel capable of serving as correctional counselors or in-prison caseworkers. There are training programs which equip custodial staff personnel to help in innovative

*Ducat: prison slang for a pass.
13. Don C. Gibbons, *Changing the Lawbreaker—The Treatment of Delinquents and Criminals* (Englewood Cliffs, N.J.: Prentice-Hall, 1965), p. 130.

programs that are aligned with treatment objectives and the preparation of inmates for release on parole. This is a fortunate rearrangement of the services available to inmates because it makes prison a place to assess the prerelease needs of inmates. A new means is added to ongoing treatment programs that help inmates to get out of prison and to stay out of it.

There are also indications that modern correctional administrators accept the notion that collaboration between inmates and staff personnel can lead to better administration of a prison and to improved opportunities for achieving the goals of rehabilitation. When this new relationship is achieved, it may be a real breakthrough to the reintegration of offenders into the free community upon their release from prison. When rehabilitation becomes the joint responsibility of a prison's staff and its inmates, there is great hope that imprisonment will *not* continue to be a means of building up a greater and greater number of repeating criminals.

Parole

Parole is the release of a prisoner before a sentence of imprisonment has been completed, on condition that the parolee agrees to obey specific rules of conduct and assists in developing a postrelease plan of employment and adjustment to the community. The purpose of parole has been stated as the protection of the public by: (1) releasing a prisoner when he has the best opportunity of achieving a noncriminal life, and (2) allowing for the return of the parolee to prison whenever he breaks the specified rules of conduct or commits a new crime. In addition, as further protection for the public, prevailing correctional practices require: (1) use of the indeterminate sentence, to make certain all felons are not released without parole supervision; (2) supervision of parolees to include assistance, counseling and some surveillance; and (3) a policy that parolees are returned to prison after noncriminal conduct which threatens the parolee's chances of successfully completing his parole.[14]

The purposes of parole also include its role in the rehabilitation of the offender. While this is implied from the protection-of-society theme, it should be a stated purpose. One of the purposes of parole then, is to provide a sound correctional program after release, because all offenders (unless sentenced to death) do return to the open community. Imprisonment alone not only fails to reform but also operates to increase the risk of criminal acts following release.

Still another purpose of parole may be to save the state unnecessary expense. Since there is good evidence that primary reliance on closed,

14. Daniel Glaser, *The Effectiveness of a Prison and Parole System* (Indianapolis: Bobbs-Merrill Co., 1964), pp. 28–29.

custodial institutions is self-defeating for any program of corrections keyed to the rehabilitation of offenders, there is now a further recognition of the fact that prison cost savings can be made by earlier parole releases. Emphasis on the public protection function of a prison assumes that many prisoners are dangerous persons. However, research findings do not support this assumption; rather they indicate only a small percentage of prison inmates can be considered dangerous. Therefore, incarceration (especially lengthy incarceration) for many offenders is a misuse of public funds.[15]

A rational parole system supportive of the tripartite aims of public protection, rehabilitation of the offender, and effective use of public funds, must be based on a determination of the optimum minimum time any prisoner should serve before release on parole. The controlling element in this determination cannot be public safety, although the public mood often affects parole board decisions. The only way to guarantee no danger to a community would be no release at all, and this is costly and inhuman. Nor can this determination be affected by the costs of institutional care and custody, although institutional population pressures have long been rumored to be a major factor in parole releases. The controlling factor in determining parole release should be the offender's potential for "making it" on parole and in future life. Parole should serve the offender, and by effectively doing so, also serve the community.

Criteria for release on parole swing between eligibility and ineligibility factors. The concept of a data base for each offender in corrections will provide basic data about an offender, his progress while in prison, and some idea of his readiness to return to the community. However, it must be supplemented by a prerelease program, an analysis by a correctional counselor or an institutional caseworker, and a parole board hearing that examines all the collected facts and interviews the offender. The decisional process in parole release is partly intuitive and partly a logical projection from known facts, just as is the decision as to sentencing alternatives. However, the parole release decision makers are in possession of a better data base: the offender's continuous inventory which provides the parole officials not only with police and court data, but also with data about the offender while in prison. Additionally, they can interview the institutional counselor or caseworker and the offender, and seek their help in correlating known data to project future behavior patterns of the offender.

Criteria useful in making parole release decisions are:

1. The nature of the offender's response to correctional programs
2. The offender's adjustment to life in the prison community

15. California, Assembly, Committee on Criminal Procedure, *Deterrent Effects of Criminal Sanctions* (Sacramento, Assembly of the State of California, 1968), pp. 38–39.

3. The extent and kind of the offender's educational levels, and vocational preparation

4. The kind of personal stability and responsibility exhibited by the offender

5. The extent or degree of the offender's commitment to the criminal subculture and its values

6. The offender's personal psychological characteristics, and how he perceives the world and his relationship to it.[16]

When a parole release date is not set and the inmate is held in the institution, the reasons for the parole board's decision should become the basis of a work-up recommending particular programs for the rejected inmate to give him enough points on the local parole readiness index to improve his chances of release. At the least, they should attempt to remedy the deficiencies militating against his release.

If a parole release program is to acquire the necessary integrity among its inmate clients, the parole officials must be selected on the basis of professional competence and must be allowed to function with no more administrative control than an evaluation of the merits of the program: its achievements against the program goals and costs. This will allow these decision makers to develop an understanding of the interaction between the inmate and his confinement. It will allow them to collect factual data on the effects of prison programs of self-improvement and preparation for release, noting failure or successes in paroles.

Individualization of Corrections and Rehabilitation

Nothing less than an individual approach to the problems of each offender on probation, in prison, or released on parole, can possibly eradicate the causative factors and maladjustments responsible for the individual's criminal behavior patterns and lead to his rehabilitation and reentry into the community. To have any hope of achieving broad objectives, each person convicted of a crime and passed on to a correctional agency must be considered a specific problem. For instance, John Doe is sentenced to three years on probation. The specific problem is rehabilitating John Doe. Doe must live and work in the community without committing a criminal act while on probation, and remain "clean" after being released from the conditions of probation. In turn, solving the specific problem of rehabilitating John Doe contributes to the overall goal of corrections: rehabilitation.

16. Commission on Law Enforcement, *The Challenge of Crime*, pp. 179–80.

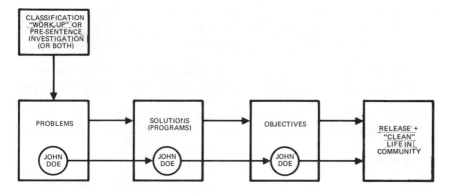

Figure 7. The Corrections-Rehabilitation Function. In criminal justice the general problems, solutions (programs) and objectives are aligned with the individual offender (John Doe) through diagnosis at a time prior to sentencing or when admitted to the prison system. Individualization of treatment and care programs attempts to solve the problems of the individual offender and to achieve the common objective of rehabilitation.

While imprisonment is only a prelude to parole release, both probation and parole are terminal programs in corrections. Probation is an after-care program in the postconviction period, and parole is an after-care program in the postprison period. Supervision of offenders in these terminal programs is not custodial. Probation and parole supervisors are not expected to control offenders assigned to their supervision, but they are expected to guide and assist them. Caseloads, except in some jurisdictions, are low enough to allow the contacts necessary for effective guidance and assistance.

This guidance and assistance in the after-care period is a means of educating the probationary offender or the parolee to develop resources within himself, so that when released from supervision he can adjust without support to life in the community.

To achieve overall objectives, the corrections function in criminal justice in America is concerned more with cure than punishment, more with care and treatment than custody, and more with postrelease success in the community than mere incapacitation.

Selected References

Books

Conrad, John P. *Crime and Its Correction—An International Survey of Attitudes and Practices.* Berkeley and Los Angeles: University of California Press, 1967, pp. 11–14.

Glaser, Daniel. *The Effectiveness of a Prison and Parole System.* Indianapolis: Bobbs-Merrill Co., 1964.

U.S., Institute for Defense Analyses. *Task Force Report: Science and Technology.* Prepared for The President's Commission on Law Enforcement and Administration of Justice. Washington, D.C.: Government Printing Office, 1967.

U.S., The President's Commission on Law Enforcement and Administration of Justice. *The Challenge of Crime in a Free Society.* Washington, D.C.: Government Printing Office, 1967.

Moberly, Sir Walter. *The Ethics of Punishment.* Hamden, Conn.: Archon Books, Shoe String Press, 1968.

Periodicals
Schwartz, Louis B. "The American Penal System: Spirit and Technique." *Annals—Crime and the American Penal System* 339 (January 1962): 1–10.

Cases
Furman v. Georgia, 408 U.S. 238 (1972).

People v. Lokey, Superior Court, Sacramento, Cal. (26156, 1962).

Chapter XVIII

Sentencing Offenders— the Least Drastic Alternative

It makes little sense for the police to invest substantial resources in the development of criminal prosecutions leading to convictions of persons accused of crime unless the sentencing judge has at his disposal a variety of adequate diagnostic services, treatment programs, and sentencing alternatives, and utilizes them in an appropriate response to the behavioral problem of the offender that warranted police action in the first instance.

There is a sentencing hierarchy in America, in which authority is divided among the lawmakers, the judiciary, and the correction officials (parole boards). Sanction law includes the lawmakers' views as to an appropriate penalty, either by the grade of crime (minor infraction, misdemeanor, or felony), or by some statutory provision affecting sentencing.

Lawmakers, in setting penalties in sanction law and in enacting provisions for mandatory sentencing procedures act in response to many influences ranging from research findings to public pressure and political advantage. In some instances, the statutory factors force the imposition of a severe sentence. For instance, courts must impose: (1) increasingly severe prison terms on recidivists; (2) a fixed minimum term of imprisonment on certain offenders to postpone any early eligibility for parole; and—in some jurisdictions—(3) consecutive sentences on offenders convicted of two or more offenses at one trial. Repeating offenders, and those who use weapons in crime, enter homes at night, or sell addicting drugs are the usual targets of these mandatory and severe sentencing laws.[1]

The sentencing judge bases his action on statutory requirements and data known to him at the time of sentencing, either from the trial or the presentence report conducted by an investigating probation officer and delivered to him prior to the appearance of the convicted offender for sentencing. Oftentimes, data is supplied by the prosecutor or the defense counsel, or incorporated in their arguments related to the sentencing. He may also gain data, in some jurisdictions, from the innovative practice of 60- to 90-day commitments to a corrections agency for diagnosis and report.

In their role as penologists, members of America's judiciary have developed sentencing practices which emphasize rehabilitation as an objective of sentencing, and the use of comprehensive personal data about the offender as a criteria for sentencing.

America's judiciary has not forgotten its obligation to the community in judgment-and-sentence decisions. The use of various alternatives to imprisonment indicates an awareness of the victim and the degree of violence in the offense. When the elements of physical force or coercion and the intent to injure or actual wounding are lacking, the severity of a sentence diminishes. A rank order usually is murder, felonious (aggravated) assault, armed robbery, narcotics violations, rape, fraud, burglary, larceny or theft, and auto theft.[2] The severity of a sentence reflects not only the judicial response to the offender as a potential threat to community safety but an evaluation of the offender as a habitual or professional criminal who is not a suitable candidate for alternatives such as probation or even early release by the parole board.

The rationale of any indeterminate sentence is that the period of controlled observation and supervision in the institutional setting affords an excellent opportunity to assess those attitudes and behavior of an individual that are relevant to the sentencing decision. While the sentencing judge has some data available to him at the moment of sentencing, the indeterminate sentence provides a secondary sentencing authority, the parole board, with up-to-the-minute data just before a decision is to be made on the prisoner's suitability for release on parole. This contemporary data includes all the clues about future behavior revealed by life in the prison community.

Under an indeterminate sentence, state laws delineating parole eligibility usually govern or influence in large measure the time an of-

1. U.S., The President's Commission on Law Enforcement and Administration of Justice, *Task Force Report: The Courts* (Washington, D.C.: Government Printing Office, 1967), pp. 14–18.
2. Edward Green, *Judicial Attitudes in Sentencing* (New York: St. Martin's Press, 1961), pp. 1–41.

fender will serve. Unfortunately, the actual practice of the various agencies granted discretionary power determines the effectiveness or abuses of the indeterminate sentence. Attack upon the indeterminate sentence, or the sentencing structures in which correctional administrators often determine to a greater extent than the sentencing judge the actual sentence to be served, is usually on two fronts: (1) the uncertainty of the indeterminate sentence affects the offender's morale and makes his planning for release difficult; and (2) the breadth of the discretion authorized by indeterminate sentencing subjects the offender to the use of power that is unchecked and often abused or misused by correctional staff and parole boards.[3]

The Trial Judge as Sentencing Agency

Jury sentencing should be phased out in those jurisdictions in which the jury's recommendation is binding or influential on the trial judge, and the trial judge should have full responsibility for sentence imposition.

In imposing sentence, the judge may consider the defendant's cooperation with authorities or his consideration for the victims of his criminal activity when a defendant has pleaded guilty. The fact of the guilty plea itself should not be considered as proof of either cooperation or consideration.

A sentencing judge may also consider time served prior to trial, during trial, and pending sentencing and give appropriate credit for it when sentencing. This is also true in resentencing offenders as a result of a second trial, or in any other circumstances where the ends of justice warrant giving credit to offenders for time served.

In seeking equality in sentencing, many difficulties confront the sentencing judge. The sentence should not be excessive or inappropriate, unjustifiably disparate in comparison with similar cases, or inconsistent with statutory criteria. Sentencing institutes, visits to prisons by the judiciary, and sentencing councils in courts with more than one judge, are all means by which sentencing judges can develop criteria for equality in sentencing which will assist them in arriving at the appropriate sentence despite the complex factors common to any sentencing decision.

Sentencing judges can also exercise supervision over sentenced offenders to insure that the correctional program is consistent with the purpose for which the sentence was imposed and that the offender is not being subjected to conditions that are unconstitutional, undesirable, or unrelated to sentencing objectives. An offender may have to raise the is-

3. U.S., National Advisory Commission on Criminal Justice Standards and Goals, *Report on Corrections* (Washington, D.C.: Government Printing Office, 1973), pp. 151–152.

sues involved, and many jurisdictions may have to modify their procedures to allow for appropriate hearings in open court, but the concept that new facts discovered since the initial sentencing now jeopardize fulfillment of the purpose of the original sentence, and therefore warrant modification of it, is no more than appropriate exercising of a continuing jurisdiction over sentenced offenders.[4]

Standards developed as guidelines by the National Advisory Commission on Criminal Justice Standards and Goals place the entire problem of sentencing and the structure of sentencing in the area of corrections. However, the sentencing standards developed by the national group and described in their *Report on Corrections* are designed to provide the judiciary with the resources, information, and guidance to make more effective sentencing decisions. In fact, the major thrust of the Commission's guidelines on sentencing is that the court should have continuing jurisdiction after the sentence has been determined and imposed, rejecting the doctrine that the judiciary should remain aloof from corrections. These new standards recommend that the correctional agency be required to execute the sentence the sentencing judge has imposed, and further judicial scrutiny is warranted as circumstance may require as within the inherent power of a court to continually supervise its own orders.[5]

Presentence Reports

The presentence report has the extraordinary potential of providing a sentencing judge with the kind and quantity of information necessary for equitable dispositions appropriate to the theories and practices of corrections and the needs of the individual offender. Presentence reports are especially indicated when the circumstances of the case reveal possible imprisonment upon sentence. It is usually standard in most jurisdictions in felony cases, and is being utilized more and more in cases involving minors and juveniles.

Disclosure of the contents of a presentence report is restricted. Copies of the report should be made available to defense counsel and the prosecutor a reasonable time prior to the date set for sentencing. Disclosure to correctional authorities, particularly when an offender has unusual problems, may be warranted. In this instance the presentence report becomes part of the offender's official file accompanying him or her to the place of commitment.

The National Advisory Commission on Criminal Justice Standards and Goals recommend that these reports develop the offender's

---

4. Commission on Criminal Justice, *Report on Corrections*, pp. 168–182.
5. Ibid., p. 173.

"background," prospects of reform, details of the crime involved and specific data such as:

1. Complete description of the situation surrounding the criminal activity with which the offender has been charged, including a full synopsis of the trial transcript, if any; the offender's version of the criminal act; and his explanation for the act

2. The offender's educational background

3. The offender's employment background, including any military record, his present employment status, and capabilities

4. The offender's social history, including family relationships, marital status, interests, and activities

5. Residence history of the offender

6. The offender's medical history and, if desirable, a psychological or psychiatric report

7. Information about environments to which the offender might return or to which he could be sent should a sentence of nonincarceration or community supervision be imposed

8. Information about any resources available to assist the offender, such as treatment centers, residential facilities, vocational training services, special educational facilities, rehabilitative programs of various institutions, and similar programs

9. Views of the person preparing the report as to the offender's motivations and ambitions, and an assessment of the offender's explanations for his criminal activity

10. A full description of defendant's criminal record, including his version of the offenses, and his explanations for them

11. A recommendation as to disposition.[6]

The integrity and validity of presentence reports are based on the belief that all information contained therein is factual and verified to the fullest extent possible. An additional supportive factor is that the preparer of the report is a trained probation officer who knows the importance of these reports to the sentencing judge. In many jurisdictions, the probation agency is administratively under the supervision of the local court or court system and its administrator. Being thus closely aligned with the local judiciary, the preparers of these reports are aware that they carry a certain burden of proof when any factual information reported is challenged, and are ready to explain all the circumstances involved. Anything less than these safeguards could result in justified refusal of the court to consider the presentence report at the time of sentencing, or could seriously erode their value to courts generally.

6. Ibid., pp. 184–85.

Sentencing Hearings

The formality of sentencing hearings depends upon local procedures established for the guidance of the judiciary. All evidence is usually received, subject to the exclusion of irrelevent, immaterial, or unduly repetitious evidence. Competent and reliable evidence is the basis for sentencing decisions. A continuance is in order when the court finds that available data should be supplemented by the services of physicians, psychiatrists, and other professionals, and the court may commit the defendant to a diagnostic center for a work-up of the defendant as a person and a subsequent report and recommendation.

A defendant is usually given the following rights at a sentencing hearing:

1. To be represented by counsel
2. To present evidence on his or her own behalf
3. To subpoena witnesses
4. To call or cross-examine the preparer of the presentence report, and persons serving as the prime source of derogatory and damaging data contained in the presentence report or other writings presented to the court
5. To present requests for probation and less severe sentence conditions, and to present arguments as to sentencing alternatives. [7]

Both the prosecutor and defense counsel should challenge and correct at a sentencing hearing any inaccuracies in the presentence report, and verify where warranted certain information contained in the report. In addition, counsel for both sides have an obligation to inform the sentencing judge of the details of any plea negotiations unknown to him. [8]

Sentencing Nondangerous Offenders

The least drastic alternative doctrine (a state must demonstrate a particular course to be the least drastic method of achieving a desired end) has developed as the key to sentencing nondangerous offenders. As long as the offender is not found to represent a substantial danger to others, judicial discretion should not be restricted by legislation as long as sentences imposed are consistent with public safety.

7. Commission on Criminal Justice, *Report on Corrections*, p. 190.
8. Ibid., p. 193

Alternatives in sentencing, from the least drastic to "total confinement" are:

1. Unconditional release
2. Conditional release
3. Fine
4. Release under supervision (probation) in the community
5. Sentence to a community correctional facility such as a half-way house
6. Sentence to local jail on a work- or education-release program: partial confinement with liberty to work or participate in training or educational programs
7. Total confinement in a correctional institution.[9]

Confinement would be appropriate if it is shown that the defendant is likely to continue his criminal behavior if not confined, or is in need of the services that can be provided in a prison setting and these services are available at the place of commitment.

On the other hand, a less drastic alternative is justified upon a showing that:

1. The offender's criminal conduct neither caused nor actually threatened serious harm.

2. The offender did not contemplate or intend that his criminal conduct would cause or threaten serious harm.

3. The offender acted under strong provocation.

4. There were substantial grounds tending to excuse or justify the offender's criminal conduct, though failing to establish defense.

5. The offender had led a law-abiding life for a substantial period of time before commission of the present crime.

6. The offender is likely to respond affirmatively to probationary or other community supervision.

7. The victim of the crime induced or facilitated its commission.

8. The offender has made or will make restitution or reparation to the victim of his crime'for the damage or injury which was sustained.

9. The offender's conduct was the result of circumstances unlikely to recur.

10. The character, history, and attitudes of the offender indicate that he is unlikely to commit another crime.

11. Imprisonment of the offender would entail undue hardship to dependents.

12. The offender is elderly or in poor health.

---

9. Ibid., p. 150.

13. The correctional programs within the institutions to which the offender would be sent are inappropriate to his particular needs or would not likely be of benefit to him.[10]

Probation has become a sentence itself, an alternative to more drastic sentences, rather than an act of leniency. It may become the standard sentence in cases involving nondangerous offenders. A sentence to probation should be for a specific term not exceeding the maximum sentence authorized, but probation for misdemeanants may be for periods less than one year.

The conditions of probation are part of the sentence. They should be shaped to meet the needs of the defendant and the community, and the defendant should not only be given written notice of these conditions, but also otherwise informed of the reasons for each of them.

Hearings should be available to people on probation to modify certain conditions imposed, and must be held when there is probable cause to believe the probationer has violated the conditions of his or her probation.*

Sentencing Dangerous Offenders

In the interest of public protection a sentencing judge may consider long terms of imprisonment as a means of incapacitating dangerous offenders. Such offenders are usually termed: (1) persistent felony offenders, (2) professional criminals, and (3) dangerous offenders. Definitions of these three classifications of offenders are:

1. A persistent felony offender is a person over 21 years of age who stands convicted of a felony for the third time. At least one of the prior felonies should have been committed within the 5 years preceding the commission of the offense for which the offender is being sentenced. At least two of the three felonies should be offenses involving the infliction, or attempted or threatened infliction, of serious bodily harm on another.

2. A professional criminal is a person over 21 years of age, who stands convicted of a felony that was committed as part of a continuing illegal business in which he acted in concert with other persons and occupied a position of management, or was an executor of violence. An offender should not be found to be a professional criminal unless the circumstances of the offense for which he stands convicted show that he has knowingly devoted himself to criminal activity as a major source of his livelihood or unless it appears that he has substantial income or resources that do not appear to be from a source other than criminal activity.

10. Commission on Criminal Justice, *Report on Corrections*, pp. 150–151.
*See Chapter XIX, Procedural Due Process for Prisoners and Parolees.

3. A dangerous offender is a person over 21 years of age whose criminal conduct is found by the court to be characterized by: (a) a pattern of repetitive behavior which poses a serious threat to the safety of others, (b) a pattern of persistent aggressive behavior with heedless indifference to the consequences, or (c) a particularly heinous offense involving the threat or infliction of serious bodily injury.[11]

Source: National Advisory Commission on Criminal Justice Standards and Goals.
*Includes persistent felony offenders, professional criminals, and dangerous offenders: repeating violent, aggressive offenders.
**The maximum as prescribed by law.

Figure 8. Sentencing process and alternatives: nondangerous and dangerous offenders.

Summary

Guidelines expressed in the foregoing standards of the National Advisory Commission on Criminal Justice Standards and Goals not only assign to the sentencing judge all of the responsibility of sentencing, but also erect a structure of presentence reports to inform the judge of all the circumstances likely to be of utility in determining whether the offender can be classed as nondangerous, a persistent felony offender, a professional criminal, or a dangerous offender. The rights of the defendant and

11. Commission on Criminal Justice, *Report on Corrections*, pp. 155–56.

the role of defense counsel are delineated. Lastly, probation takes on new dimensions as a sentence itself, rather than an act of leniency, and an alternative to imprisonment likely to become the standard sentence in many criminal cases.

Although these standards are not now the law, they are an expression of the ideas of a knowledgeable group of persons who studied the present systems and proposed solutions to the numerous problems of sentence, punishment, and reprimand. The proposed solutions are a step in the necessary reconsideration of the present system and its failings. Systems must be continually scrutinized because today's solution so often becomes a serious problem tomorrow.

The doctrine of the least drastic alternative appears clearly in the foregoing standards. There is an apparent intent that a sentencing judge should clearly show his rationale for imprisonment or a selected alternative. Under the foregoing guidelines the burden of proof to justify a particular sentence is on the sentencing judge, and the court record must demonstrate that all other less drastic alternatives had been considered and rejected as not suitable for a particular defendant.

Selected References

Books

Busher, Walter H. *Ordering Time to Serve Prisoners: A Manual for the Planning and Administering of Work Release*. Washington, D.C.: Government Printing Office, 1973.

Change, D. H. and Armstrong, Warren B. eds. *The Prison: Voices From the Inside*. Cambridge, Mass.: Schenkman Publishing Cò., 1972.

Orland, Leonard. *Justice, Punishment, Treatment: The Correctional Process*. New York: Free Press, Macmillan Publishing Co., 1972.

U.S., National Advisory Commission on Criminal Justice Standards and Goals. *Report on Corrections*. Washington, D.C.: Government Printing Office, 1973.

Periodicals

Singer, Richard G. "Sending Men to Prison: Constitutional Aspects of the Burden of Proof and the Doctrine of the Least Drastic Alternative as Applied to Sentencing Determinations," *Cornell Law Review*, 58, No. 1 (November 1972): 51–89.

Chapter XIX

Procedural Due Process for Prisoners and Parolees

For many years correctional administrators viewed prison disciplinary hearing as non-adversarial, but as being primarily for the purpose of determining if the accused inmate did what he was accused of, and whether such conduct was a violation of regulations. Any form of procedural due process for prisoners in a semi-judicial setting or structure was opposed for four basic reasons:

1. Inmates are not deprived of any rights in such proceedings since they are sent to prison to be disciplined.

2. Due process requirements are incompatible with the therapeutic goals of the correctional process.

3. Any adversary system in internal prison disciplinary proceedings undermines discipline by equalizing inmate and prison officer or official.

4. Courts lack the expertise of correctional administrators to regulate the internal affairs of prisons and should defer to prison officials.[1]

Not only have the foregoing arguments lost their persuasiveness in regard to prisoners, they have been the subject of radical revision by the

1. Robert C. Vanderet, "Procedural Due Process in California Prisons: A Comparative Look at the New Directions," *California State Bar Journal* 48, No. 6 (November/December 1973): 669–75, 738–47.

U.S. Supreme Court in *Morrissey* v. *Brewer*.[2] This is a 1972 case in which the court established safeguards and structure for a reliable guilt-determination process for parolees.

The two case studies in this chapter probe the application of due process guarantees to prison disciplinary proceedings, and to administrative hearings concerning parole revocation. In each case, the circumstances of imprisonment and parole supervision reveal that inmates and parolees are subject to potential "grievous loss": referral of the case to a local prosecutor for criminal action, good-time forfeiture, transfer to isolation or segregation units, or return to prison from conditional release on parole.

Case Study No. 1—Due Process and Prison*

The first case involves an inmate of the California prison system. John Wesley Clutchette brought an action under the Civil Rights Act (42 U.S.C. Section 1983) on behalf of all inmates in San Quentin Prison, alleging deprivation of rights secured by the Due Process and Equal Protection Clauses of the Fourteenth Amendment.

> This civil action is brought pursuant to 42 U.S.C. Section 1983 to seek relief for state prisoners from alleged deprivation of their constitutional rights secured by the due process and equal protection clauses of the 14th amendment by state prison officials in prison disciplinary hearings. More specifically, they allege that the procedures by which charges of violations of prison rules are adjudicated do not contain sufficient due process safeguards, consistent with the nature of the potential punishment, to meet the standards of the 14th amendment. Plaintiffs seek a declaratory judgment, preliminary and permanent injunctive relief and damages for plaintiff Clutchette.

DISCIPLINARY PROCEDURES AT SAN QUENTIN

Procedures Employed

The San Quention Prison Institution Plan for the Administration of Inmate Discipline (the "Institution Plan") establishes the procedures to be followed in all cases in which inmates are charged with violating prison rules. It provides that when an employee believes an inmate's conduct seriously violates some prison rule, the employee is required to report the facts in writing on Form CDC-115. In some cases, the Form 115 may be supplemented by additional reports, but these are not required. Accused inmates are not permitted to see either the Form 115 or any supplementary reports. In serious cases, prisoners may be moved to isolation cells immediately after the alleged infraction and may be held there for up to seven days before adjudication by a disciplinary committee.

Within a day after placement in isolation, the inmate will be seen by an officer of the "Unit Disciplinary Hearing Court." This officer is supposed to

2. Morrissey v. Brewer, 408 U.S. 471 (1972).
*Clutchette v. Procunier, 328 F. Supp. 767 (1971). Extracts only; footnotes and citations omitted.

"inform the inmate of the charges placed against him, receive his plea of guilty or not guilty, and . . . carefully weigh the evidence against him." As a result of this adjudication, the officer may himself impose a penalty, but "serious" cases must be referred to the Unit Disciplinary Subcommittee. If such a referral is made, the officer is required to serve the inmate with a CDC Form 263 Notice of Complaint. These notices are required to state simply the charge number and title (*e.g.*, "Inmate Behavior D1201") but need not describe the particular act of misbehavior which may be charged in the Form 115.

Section ID-III-08 of the Institution Plan establishes three categories of disciplinary infractions: "administrative," "disturbance" and "major." These categories are used as a guideline for the Hearing Officer in deciding whether referral to the disciplinary subcommittee should be made, but any "serious" case may be referred regardless of the category in which it falls. The list of infractions does not purport to be complete. The acts enumerated are merely "examples" of what might be punishable.

Each housing unit at San Quentin has a disciplinary committee which meets once a week. It may hear from five to 15 cases per week, but the average is about seven cases. Three officers sit on the committee. There is no rule prohibiting a staff member who was involved in the incident from serving on the committee, although the practice is to avoid this whenever possible. Generally, the unit Hearing Officer is also a member of the committee.

The instructions regarding 'adjudication" are identical to those given Hearing Officers. They merely state that the committee should "inform the inmate of the charges against him, receive his plea of guilty or not guilty, and carefully weigh the evidence. Effort will be made to uncover the basic cause(s) underlying the infraction." There are no other procedural directives of any kind in either the Classification Manual or the Director's Rules, or the San Quentin Institution Plan.

If a felony charge is involved, the inmate is advised of his constitutional right to remain silent and to have an attorney present during interrogation; he is specifically advised that anything he says "can and will" be used against him in a court of law. However, if the inmate requests an attorney, he is told he cannot see one until such time as the district attorney interviews him. If he chooses to exercise his right to remain silent lest he say anything which may be used against him in a criminal case, the committee nevertheless proceeds to adjudicate the disciplinary infraction, relying solely on the written reports filed against him.

The committee obtains the Form 115 and any supplementary material in advance of the meeting at which the charges are to be adjudicated. The prisoner is not permitted to see the Form 115 even when he appears before the disciplinary committee; but it is read to him by the committee chairman. In some cases, but not all, there may be supplemental reports on the incident, and the "gist" of these may be summarized for the inmate.

Neither the author of the Form 115 nor the writers of these reports nor any other witnesses are present. The inmates are not entitled to call witnesses or to confront the persons who prepared the reports against them. They are not entitled to the assistance of either a lawyer, a staff member, or another inmate who might help them to present a defense to the charges. Neither the Director's Rules nor the Institution Plan specifies whether inmates may or may not have these procedural rights, but as a matter of invariable practice these rights are denied. In addition to the written reports, the committee's decision may be influenced by oral information "passed on" by other inmates. There is no requirement that the decision be based on evidence adduced at the hearing.

At the hearing, after a brief discussion of the incident, the inmate leaves the room. Most of the time spent by the committee in deliberation is devoted to deciding what disposition to take rather than in ascertaining guilt or innocence.

Consequences of Disciplinary Proceedings

The Director's Rules and the Institution Plan enumerate the punishments which may be imposed by a Unit Hearing Officer and the punishments which may be imposed only be a disciplinary committee. There are no guidelines for deciding which punishment should be imposed for any particular offense. Regardless of which category the violation falls within, the Hearing Officer or the disciplinary committee may order that any or all of the authorized punishments be imposed.

Section ID-II-05 of the Institution Plan authorizes a Unit Hearing Officer acting alone to take one or more of the following actions: dismissal; warning; reprimand; temporary loss of one or more privileges; one or more weekend lock-ups; assignment to special work detail; confinement to quarters not to exceed 30 days; isolation suspended for a six-month period; removal from Honor Unit status; referral to disciplinary committee; and recommendation that no action be taken by the Adult Authority on Parole/Discharge date status.

Section ID-II-06 authorizes the disciplinary committee to take one or more of the following actions in any case it hears: dismissal; referral for further investigation; warning; reprimand; temporary or permanent loss of one or more privileges; confinement in an Isolation and/or Quiet Cell, usually with loss of privileges also assessed; special isolation diet; confinement to cell; removal from assignment; assignment to Segregation status; recommendation to Adult Authority for appropriate action; recommendation to the Director of Corrections regarding forfeiture of earnings; assessment for damages when destruction of state property is involved; and appropriate change in custody. The consequences and impact of most of these is apparent from the description itself.

Whatever the decision ultimately reached by this court or any appellate court on a prisoner's right to affirmatively defend himself in normal disciplinary hearings, it is clear that when he is charged with an offense for which state criminal proceedings may be instituted, and is warned that he has a right to remain silent and that anything he says may and will be used against him in such a proceedings, a prisoner cannot be compelled to sacrifice his only defense in order to exercise his equally compelling constitutional right to remain silent.

In any proceeding in which an accused party exercises his right to remain silent, he naturally sacrifices one means of defense. In the normal criminal prosecution, or civil-criminal combination, we are not troubled by this sacrifice, as the defendant is protected by many procedural safeguards, and retains the alternative of defending himself by means of calling and cross-examining witnesses. In a disciplinary proceeding, prisoners are not protected by these same procedural safeguards, i.e., a presumption of innocence with the burden of proof beyond a reasonable doubt on the state. Furthermore, should the charged prisoner choose to exercise his right to remain silent, he is stripped of any possible means of defense. The choice thus put to him of sacrificing one fundamental right as a price for exercising another is repugnant to our notions of due process. Therefore, irrespective of or in addition to any arguments regarding a prisoner's right to call witnesses in his own behalf and cross-examine witnesses against him in disciplinary hearings generally, when the offense charged may be referred to the district attorney for prosecution in state courts, prisoners must be afforded these rights so as to maintain the integrity of their fifth amendment right to remain silent.

Now, therefore, it is ordered, adjudged and decreed that:

Plaintiffs are hereby granted a declaratory judgment with respect to their first cause of action insofar as this opinion and order declare that the disciplinary procedures employed at San Quentin Prison violate the due process and equal protection clauses of the 14th amendment by failing to provide for adequate notice of charges, the calling of favorable witnesses and cross-examination of accusing witnesses, counsel or counsel-substitute, a decision by a fact-finder uninvolved with the alleged incident, a written finding of facts, or uniform notice of any right to appeal the decision, when such a disciplinary hearing may result in grievous loss to the prisoner; and that certain disciplinary punishment, including but not necessarily limited to (a) indefinite confinement in the adjustment center or segregation; (b) possible increase in a prisoner's sentence by reason of referral of the disciplinary action to the Adult Authority; (c) a fine or forfeiture of accumulated or future earnings; (d) isolation confinement longer than 10 days; or (e) referral to the district attorney for criminal prosecution, constitute such a grievous loss to the prisoner.

Case Study No. 2—Due Process and Parole*

The second case concerns two Iowa convicts whose paroles were revoked. John J. Morrissey and G. Donald Booher filed habeas corpus petitions in the United States District Court for the Southern District of Iowa, alleging that they were denied due process because their paroles were revoked without a hearing.

Petitioners in these habeas corpus proceedings claimed that their paroles were revoked without a hearing and that they were thereby deprived of due process. The Court of Appeals, in affirming the District Court's denial of re-

*Morrissey v. Brewer, 408 U.S. 471 (1972). Extracts only, footnotes and citations deleted.

lief, reasoned that under controlling authorities parole is only "a correctional device authorizing service of sentence outside a penitentiary," and concluded that a parolee, who is still "in custody," is not entitled to a full adversary hearing such as would be mandated in a criminal proceeding. *Held:*

1. Though parole revocation does not call for the full panoply of rights due a defendant in a criminal proceeding, a parolee's liberty involves significant values within the protection of the Due Process Clause of the Fourteenth Amendment, and termination of that liberty requires an informal hearing to give assurance that the finding of a parole violation is based on verified facts to support the revocation.

2. Due process requires a reasonably prompt informal inquiry conducted by an impartial hearing officer near the place of the alleged parole violation or arrest to determine if there is reasonable ground to believe that the arrested parolee has violated a parole condition. The parolee should receive prior notice of the inquiry, its purpose, and the alleged violations. The parolee may present relevant information and (absent security considerations) question adverse informants. The hearing officer shall digest the evidence on probable cause and state the reasons for holding the parolee for the parole board's decision.

3. At the revocation hearing, which must be conducted reasonably soon after the parolee's arrest, minimum due process requirements are: (a) written notice of the claimed violations of parole; (b) disclosure to the parolee of evidence against him; (c) opportunity to be heard in person and to present witnesses and documentary evidence; (d) the right to confront and cross-examine adverse witnesses (unless the hearing officer specifically finds good cause for not allowing confrontation); (e) a "neutral and detached" hearing body such as a traditional parole board, members of which need not be judicial officers or lawyers; and (f) a written statement by the factfinders as to the evidence relied on and reasons for revoking parole.

We granted certiorari in this case to determine whether the Due Process Clause of the Fourteenth Amendment requires that a State afford an individual some opportunity to be heard prior to revoking his parole.

The parolee is not the only one who has a stake in his conditional liberty. Society has a stake in whatever may be the chance of restoring him to normal and useful life within the law. Society thus has an interest in not having parole revoked because of erroneous information or becauseof an erroneous evaluation of the need to revoke parole, given the breach of parole conditions. And society has a further interest in treating the parolee with basic fairness: fair treatment in parole revocations will enhance the chance of rehabilitation by avoiding reactions to arbitrariness.

Given these factors, most States have recognized that there is no interest on the part of the State in revoking parole without any procedural guarantees at all. What is needed is an informal hearing structured to assure that the finding of a parole violation will be based on verified facts and that the exercise of discretion will be informed by an accurate knowledge of the parolee's behavior.

We now turn to the nature of the process that is due, bearing in mind that the interest of both State and parolee will be furthered by an effective but informal hearing. In analyzing what is due, we see two important stages in the typical process of parole revocation.

(a) *Arrest of Parolee and Preliminary Hearing.* The first stage occurs when the parolee is arrested and detained, usually at the direction of his parole officer. The second occurs when parole is formally revoked. There is typically a substantial time lag between the arrest and the eventual determination by the parole board whether parole should be revoked. Additionally, it may be that the parolee is arrested at a place distant from the state institution, to which he may be returned before the final decision is made concerning revocation. Given these factors, due process would seem to require that some minimal inquiry be conducted at or reasonably near the place of the alleged parole violation or arrest and as promptly as convenient after arrest while information is fresh and sources are available. Such an inquiry should be seen as in the nature of a "preliminary hearing" to determine whether there is probable cause or reasonable ground to believe that the arrested parolee has committed acts that would constitute a violation of parole conditions.

In our view, due process requires that after the arrest, the determination that reasonable ground exists for revocation of parole should be made by someone not directly involved in the case. It would be unfair to assume that the supervising parole officer bears hostility against the parolee that destroys his neutrality; realistically the failure of the parolee is in a sense a failure for his supervising officer. However, we need make no assumptions one way or the other to conclude that there should be an uninvolved person to make this preliminary evaluation of the basis for believing the conditions of parole have been violated. The officer directly involved in making recommendations cannot always have complete objectivity in evaluating them. *Goldberg* v. *Kelly* found it unnecessary to impugn the motives of the caseworker to find a need for an independent decisionmaker to examine the initial decision.

This independent officer need not be a judicial officer. The granting and revocation of parole are matters traditionally handled by administrative officers. In *Goldberg*, the Court pointedly did not require that the hearing on termination of benefits be conducted by a judicial officer or even before the traditional "neutral and detached" officer; it required only that the hearing be conducted by some person *other* than one initially dealing with the case. It will be sufficient, therefore, in the parole revocation context, if an evaluation of whether reasonable cause exists to believe that conditions of parole have been violated is made by someone such as a parole officer other than the one who has made the report of parole violations or has recommended revocation. A State could certainly choose some other independent decisionmaker to perform this preliminary function.

With respect to the preliminary hearing before this officer, the parolee should be given notice that the hearing will take place and that its purpose is to determine whether there is probable cause to believe he has committed a parole violation. The notice should state what parole violations have been alleged. At the hearing the parolee may appear and speak in his own behalf; he may bring letters, documents, or individuals who can give relevant information to the hearing officer. On request of the parolee, a person who has given adverse information on which parole revocation is to be based is to be made available for questioning in his presence. However, if the hearing officer determines that an informant would be subjected to risk of harm if his identity were disclosed, he need not be subjected to confrontation and cross-examination.

The hearing officer shall have the duty of making a summary, or digest, of what occurs at the hearing in terms of the responses of the parolee and the substance of the documents or evidence given in support of parole revocation and of the parolee's position. Based on the information before him, the officer should determine whether there is probable cause to hold the parolee for the final decision of the parole board on revocation. Such a determination would be sufficient to warrant the parolee's continued detention and return to the state correctional institution pending the final decision. As in *Goldberg*, "the decision maker should state the reasons for his determination and indicate the evidence he relied on . . ." but it should be remembered that this is not a final determination calling for "formal findings of fact and conclusions of law." No interest would be served by formalism in this process; informality will not lessen the utility of this inquiry in reducing the risk of error.

(b) The Revocation Hearing. There must also be an opportunity for a hearing, if it is desired by the parolee, prior to the final decision on revocation by the parole authority. This hearing must be the basis for more than determining probable cause; it must lead to a final evaluation of any contested relevant facts and consideration of whether the facts as determined warrant revocation. The parolee must have an opportunity to be heard and to show, if he can, that he did not violate the conditions, or, if he did, that circumstances in mitigation suggest that the violation does not warrant revocation. The revocation hearing must be tendered within a reasonable time after the parolee is taken into custody. A lapse of two months, as respondents suggest occurs in some cases, would not appear to be unreasonable.

We cannot write a code of procedure; that is the responsibility of each State. Most States have done so by legislation, others by judicial decision usually on due process grounds. Our task is limited to deciding the minimum requirements of due process.

We emphasize there is no thought to equate this second stage of parole revocation to a criminal prosecution in any sense. It is a narrow inquiry; the process should be flexible enough to consider evidence including letters, affidavits, and other material that would not be admissable in an adversary criminal trial.

We do not reach or decide the question whether the parolee is entitled to the assistance of retained counsel or to appointed counsel if he is indigent.

We have no thought to create an inflexible structure for parole revocation procedures. The few basic requirements set out above, which are applicable to future revocations of parole, should not impose a great burden on any State's parole system. Control over the required proceedings by the hearing officers can assure that delaying tactics and other abuses sometimes present in the traditional adversary trial situation do not occur. Obviously a parolee cannot relitigate issues determined against him in other forums, as in the situation presented when the revocation is based on conviction of another crime.

Clutchette has had its impact on the California prison system and procedures. Revised rules offer inmates considerable procedural due process. Other states appear to be revising their rules for disciplinary procedures, with inmates being given the opportunity to be heard on the charges against him. The impact and implications of *Morrissey* require correctional administrators to give parolees a meaningful hearing.

Here is a summary of what must be done to assure due process when a parolee is accused of parole violation:

1. He must be given written notice of the claimed parole violations.

2. Administrators are required to disclose to the parolee the evidence against him.

3. The parolee is to be given opportunity to be heard in person and to present witnesses and documentary evidence.

4. The parolee has the right to confront and cross-examine adverse witnesses (unless the hearing officer specifically finds good cause for not allowing confrontation).

5. The parolee has a right to a neutral and detached hearing body such as a traditional parole board, members of which need not be judicial officers or lawyers.

6. After the hearing the parolee has a right to a written statement by the factfinders setting forth the evidence relied on and the reasons for revoking parole.[3]

It should be noted, however, that a parolee does *not* have the guarantee of legal counsel to assist in his defense, and the state does not have the burden of proving its accusations beyond a reasonable doubt as it must do in a regular trial.

Civil Disabilities

Every state has some type of civil disability law which applies to felons either in prison or outside, or both. Most of these laws suspend all

---

3. Morrissey v. Brewer, 408 U.S. 471 (1972), pp. 487–490.

civil rights during imprisonment, and may include within those civil rights suspended the right to contract, and to inherit property or to bring civil law suits. The voting franchise has been the subject of disability both during and after imprisonment.

An example of a disability statute is Section 2600 of the California Penal Code:

> A sentence of imprisonment in a state prison for any term suspends all the civil rights of the person so sentenced, and forfeits all public offices and all private trusts, authority, or power during such imprisonment. But the Adult Authority may restore to said person during his imprisonment such civil rights as the authority may deem proper, except the right to act as a trustee, or hold public office or exercise the privilege of an elector or give a general power of attorney.

> Between the time of the imposition of a sentence of imprisonment in a state prison for any term and the time the said person commences serving such sentence, the judge who imposed such sentence may restore to said person for said period of time such civil rights as the judge may deem proper, except the right to act as a trustee, or hold public office or exercise the privilege of an elector or give a general power of attorney.

> This section shall be construed so as not to deprive such person of the following civil rights, in accordance with the laws of this state:

> (1) To inherit real or personal property.

> (2) To correspond, confidentially, with any member of the State Bar, or holder of public office, provided that the prison authorities may open and inspect such mail to search for contraband.

> (3) To own all written material produced by such person during the period of imprisonment.

> (4) To purchase, receive, and read any and all newspapers, periodicals, and books accepted for distribution by the United States Post Office. Pursuant to the provisions of this section, prison authorities shall have the authority to exclude obscene publications or writings, and mail containing information concerning where, how, or from whom such matter may be obtained; and any matter of a character tending to incite murder, arson, riot, violent racism, or any other form of violence; and any matter concerning gambling or a lottery. Nothing in this section shall be construed as limiting the right of prison authorities (i) to open and inspect any and all packages received by an inmate and (ii) to establish reasonable restrictions as to the number of newspapers, magazines, and books that the inmate may have in his cell or elsewhere in the prison at one time.

Two of the following sections of California's Penal Code (2603 and 2604) modify the foregoing section by specifying that Section 2600 must not be construed to render the persons named therein incompetent as witnesses by affidavit or deposition in a civil case or proceeding or by affidavit or deposition or personally in a criminal case or proceeding, or incapable of making a will, or incapable of making and acknowledging a sale or conveyance of property; and that no conviction of any person for a crime works any forfeiture of any property, except in cases in which a forfeiture is expressly imposed by law; and all forfeitures to the people of the State, in the nature of a deodand,* or where any person shall flee from justice, are abolished.

Disabilities are not all found in the statutes, but are *de facto* and flow directly from imprisonment. In the area of private employment, discrimination against convicted felons is the usual, not the unusual. Bonding companies refuse to bond ex-convicts and thus deny a large area of employment to them. Even the Civil Rights Act which prohibits discrimination based on age, sex, or race does not prohibit discrimination based upon prior imprisonment. The licensing provisions for certain occupations also limit the meaningful opportunities open to ex-convicts.

Public employment also shows discrimination against the applicant who has a prison record. This may be done on a basis that the ex-convict may not hold public office or positions of public trust. Even where the employment decisions are left to individual agencies the employer is prone to accept the non-convict rather than the ex-convict.

Without reasonable employment opportunities there is only one direction left for many of the ex-convicts on parole or discharged: re-entry into the criminal life of the community where he or she is readily accepted and where there is almost unlimited opportunity.

The released convict may find restrictions on his right to marry and have children, to participate in the political process, to hold public office, to exercise various judicial rights, and to exercise property and contract rights.[4]

Disabilities for ex-felons whether by statute or *de facto* discrimination continue, but they are under attack by articulate ex-convicts and imaginative attorneys who make a speciality of prisoner's rights.[5]

The National Alliance of Businessmen, private industry's special effort to hire disadvantaged workers, is now providing placement services for persons with criminal records in their offices in over a hundred cities.[6]

---

*Relates to pious uses; things given to God.

4. "The Collateral Consequences of a Criminal Conviction," *Vanderbilt Law Review* 23, No. 5 (October 1970): 1001–1018, 1160–1184.

5. Ibid., pp. 1184–1218.

6. *Offender Employment Review* (American Bar Association, National Clearinghouse on Offender Employment Restrictions), No. 8, April 1974. See also *Laws, Licenses and the Offender's Right to Work—A Study of State Laws Restricting the Occupational Licensing of Former Offenders*, prepared for the American Bar Association by James W. Hunt, James E. Bowers, and Neil Miller (Washington, D.C.: National Clearinghouse on Offender Employment Restrictions, 1973).

The most pressing and critical problem of rehabilitation, which has been the contemporary direction of penology, is re-entry of the released offender into the community. Yet, it is at this very point that society places its most severe roadblock. There is an existing community hostility and distrust of the ex-convict and this existing attitude is reinforced by the disability laws which express distrust by limiting the opportunities or abilities of ex-convicts.

Selected References

Books

Tobriner, Hon. Mathew O. "Due Process: Parolees and Prisoners," in *Challenging Criminal Corrections—Report of the Western American Assembly on Prisoners in America.* Berkeley, Calif.: The Institute for Local Self-Government, 1974.

Periodicals

Murphy, George F. "The Court Looks at Prisoner's Rights," *Criminology* 1, No. 4 (February 1973): 441–459.

Vanderet, Robert C. "Procedural Due Process in California Prisons: A Comparative Look at the New Directions." *California State Bar Journal* 48, No. 6 (November-December 1973): 669–75, 738–47.

"The Collateral Consequences of a Criminal Conviction," *Vanderbilt Law Review* 23, No. 5 (October 1970): 1001–1018, 1160–1218.

Cases

Clutchette v. Procunier, 328 F. Supp. 767 (N. D. Cal. 1971).

Morrissey v. Brewer, 408 U.S. 471 (1972).

Part VI
The Criminal Justice System

Chapter XX

Organized Crime

Organized crime is a reality that is almost beyond belief. It is a threat to the criminal justice system. It has corrupted police, parole agencies, and the courts. Its influence even touches law-makers in the criminal justice system. Long underground as part of the pattern of crime and delinquency in America, and a prime mover in the country's urban graft and politics, this criminal syndicate was not officially recognized until 1951. It was not named with certainty until 1962, not defined until 1968, and not combatted adequately until recent years when nationwide surveillance of the top executives of this national crime mob led to exposure and prosecution at levels not previously attained.

The 1950–51 United States Senate Crime Investigating Committee, commonly referred to by the name of its chairman, the late Senator Estes Kefauver, uncovered an elusive and furtive organization of criminals and established the existence of a national conspiracy of crime: of local mobs associated into a national crime syndicate known as the *Mafia*.[1]

The Cosa Nostra

In 1962, an insider, a knowledgeable member of the criminal syndicate, broke the syndicate's code of silence and disclosed to another U.S. Senate committee the name and the game of organized crime. Joseph Valachi, in the largest intelligence breakthrough in the history of crime and its investigation, said the name was not the Mafia, but *Cosa Nostra*.

1. Estes Kefauver, *Crime in America* (Garden City, N.Y.: Doubleday & Company, 1951), pp. 12–14.

Mafia was a label used by outsiders; *Cosa Nostra* was the term used by its members.

Joseph Valachi revealed that Cosa Nostra was divided into major territorial and functional (criminal activities) segments known as *families*. The ruler of each of these major segments was a *capo* or boss, and next in command was a *soto capo* or underboss; while the *troops, soldiers* or *buttons* at the level of criminal operations were supervised by several *caporegime* or lieutenants.[2]

The game was still crime on a national scale under the executive leadership and operational secrecy of a membership that was more clan than club, more "Murder, Inc." than big business, and more a confederation of criminals than the often arrested and imprisoned losers of the underworld. Cosa Nostra was crime on a scale never previously visualized. It was big and powerful, flouted law enforcement, corrupted police and public officials, and serviced a multiplying complex of criminal operations and rackets (honest businesses run dishonestly, or almost-legal enterprises). It was a national crime syndicate, with international ties and foreign resources, conducting daily illegal activities over a period of no less than half a century in an environment of relative safety; immune to arrest and successful prosecution.

Organized Crime and Its Activities

The Congress officially defined organized crime and its membership in 1968 as follows:

> "Organized Crime" means the unlawful activities of the members of a highly organized, disciplined association engaged in supplying illegal goods and services, including but not limited to, gambling, prostitution, loansharking, narcotics, labor racketeering, and other unlawful activities of members of such organizations. "Organized Crime Offender" means a person who, with intent that conduct constituting a series of crimes be performed, plans, counsels, promotes, finances, organizes, manages, advises, supervises, directs, or conducts a conspiratorial relationship, composed of five or more conspirators, involving a structured division of labor, and having as its objective the engaging in or causing of the performance of such conduct as a part of a continuing course of activity. A person shall not be considered an organized crime offender within the meaning of this definition unless conduct constituting more than one crime as part of a continuing course of activity is engaged in or caused by one or more of the conspirators to effect the objective in the relationship.[3]

The national crime syndicate caters to public demands for illegal goods and services, forbidden in various overreaches of sanction law, and

2. Peter Maas, *The Valachi Papers* (New York: G. P. Putnam's Sons, 1968), pp. 35–47.
3. Omnibus Crime Control and Safe Streets Act of 1968.

it participates in any illegal activity which offers a high return on its investment of time, money, and know-how. Its major operations include gambling, loan sharking, narcotics, labor racketeering, the infiltration of legitimate business, and such lesser areas as prostitution, stealing, and merchandising stolen property.

Gambling provides a basic source of daily revenue to all of the "families" of organized crime. In ghetto areas, the income source is the numbers game, or policy racket. It is a nickels-dimes-and-dollars game that cuts the normal odds of any lottery to insure that players cannot win any significant percentage of the day's action. In all except the most rural areas, there are card and dice games, and gambling on horse races or sporting events. Horse-race and sports betting is another major income source, with the bookmakers hedging against any severe daily losses by spreading their customer's wagers among fellow members of the crime syndicate.[4]

Loan sharking is usury. It has been described time and again as a wondrous money machine by leading members of the crime syndicate. Usury is a profession akin to prostitution in that it is as old as the invention of a money economy. Roman law set forth penalties against those practising it, as did medieval law, which in turn had its roots in biblical injunctions against the charging of interest. In the United States toward the end of the 19th-century loan "sharks" had become so entrenched among some immigrant groups and members of the working class that legislation setting up and controlling small loan agencies and credit unions was enacted. However, particularly in times of depression, there are always many who cannot qualify for loans from any legal institution. It is these that loan sharks prey upon. There are reasonable grounds to believe that the membership of the crime syndicate has found loan sharking to be an effective way of investing its money and watching it multiply. The boss loans a substantial amount of money to one or more of his lieutenants, who in turn use one or more of their button men or soldiers to supervise on-the-street lenders. The average rate of interest paid by borrowers for short-term loans is 260 percent annually. The terms are inflexible; weekly interest payments must be made, penalties are exacted for delays, and the principle is due on demand. Murder and severe beatings, one the outgrowth of the other in many instances, await borrowers unwilling or unable to meet these terms.[5]

The illicit traffic in narcotics has long been a source of income to the national crime syndicate. Less respectable than gambling or loan sharking, the narcotics trade is conducted in secret so as not to boggle the minds of some of the syndicate's allies in public office. It is difficult to buy

4. Frederick Egan, *The Plainclothesman—Handbook of Vice and Gambling Operations* (New York: Arco Publishing Co., 1958), pp. 43–44.
5. "Loan-sharking: The Untouched Domain of Organized Crime," *Columbia Journal of Law and Social Problems* 5, No. 1: 91–136.

332   The Criminal Justice System

immunity for a trade as heinous as narcotics selling. Today, the different families in Cosa Nostra insulate their membership as much as possible from arrest by the use of "share-croppers"—pushers who do the retail selling and take the greatest risk of arrest. The syndicate has an underground transportation system for bringing heroin and other hard drugs into the United States. The business of importing and wholesaling illegal narcotics is lucrative. It is a buy-low-and-sell-high business of enormous profits which would be impossible except for the relationships of trust, and the strong internal security among syndicate members.[6]

Labor racketeering began in the 1930s, when Prohibition was about to be repealed. It was a new way of making money from an illegitimate enterprise or a legitimate one that was operated illegitimately. It was the earliest years of labor racketeering that spawned the syndicate's first troops specializing in murder: the local mob in Brooklyn's Brownsville section led by Abe (Kid Twist) Reles and later named "Murder, Inc."[7] Labor rackets range from extortion to looting welfare and pension funds. There's a fee for labor peace as the syndicate members control many unions or union locals, and there are millions of dollars in the welfare and pension funds. Side benefits are the salaries paid to the syndicate's personnel who function as union organizers, business agents, and union officials. Sweetheart contracts, which are conspiracies between management and dishonest labor officials, pay union members low wages while dishonest officials obtain illegal lump sum payments.[8]

Business infiltration is marked by the use of venture capital from the huge profits of gambling, or foreclosure on a loan shark's usurious loan. The syndicate moves in its trusted personnel to control the operations of a business, and introduces its standard illegitimate operating procedure. These activities range from no-cost sweetheart contracts with syndicate unions, through fraud in bankruptcy proceedings, to the looting of money collected as tax revenues, and the skimming of cash income to avoid the payment of taxes. The syndicate favors restaurants, bars, taverns, and vending machine merchandising because the cash intake of these businesses has little relation to the actual costs of operation, and cash can easily be skimmed off the top. They have also prospered in the field of legal gambling enterprises in Nevada (a licensed business operation).[9]

In any review of the organization and activity of organized crime the most frightening aspect is the apparent ability of the syndicate to corrupt

6. Paul B. Weston et al., *Narcotics, U.S.A.* (New York: Greenberg—Publisher, 1952), pp. 129–40. *See also* Alvin Moscow, *Merchants of Heroin* (New York: Dial Press, 1968), pp. 169–180.
7. Burton B. Turkus and Sid Feder, *Murder, Inc., the Story of the Syndicate* (New York: Farrar, Straus & Giroux, 1951), pp. 74–106.
8. U.S., The President's Commission on Law Enforcement and Administration of Justice, *Task Force Report: Organized Crime* (Washington, D.C.: Government Printing Office, 1967), p. 5.
9. Wallace Turner, *Gambler's Money—The New Force in American Life* (Boston: Houghton Mifflin Co., 1965), pp. 27–30.

persons in public life, particularly agents of criminal justice. It may be that corruption begins in a meeting of the minds that nothing is really *wrong* with gambling; after all, it has been legalized in Nevada and legal state lotteries are now commonplace in some parts of the nation. However, beneath the cloak of syndicate gambling, are the associated ventures of loan sharking, narcotics, labor racketeering, and murder—as the syndicate kills and maims to enforce its operational rules. Because of basic contracts made between public officials and syndicate gambling operators, a connection is developed for immunity in other illegal operations. It is primarily for this reason that the private government of organized crime must be recognized as a force threatening democratic government and its concepts of law and justice. It must be combatted at both local and national levels with a new vigor and new directions which will expose its vast operations and curtail its criminal activities, because "if we do not on a national scale attack organized criminals with weapons and techniques as effective as their own, they will destroy us."[10]

The hierarchy of organized crime allows for this vital business of nullification of law enforcement by recognizing a position in each "family" of a counselor or *"corruptor,"* whose role is to bribe and negotiate with public officials. In some families, corruptors of some rank and esteem handle relations with the top elected officials and judiciary who can be reached through friendship or previous contracts on syndicate business. Others, at lesser organization levels, are assigned to deal with police at the local levels.[11]

The mechanics of corruption—favors, pressures, and bribes—were exposed in a New York case in which a public official was corrupted by a syndicate labor official. Bribes were passed to secure city contracts for controlling firms, and even the city's largest public utility was compromised. A former political czar of New York City, Carmine DeSapio, was sent to jail as a corruptor.[12]

The "Scam"

A popular and financially rewarding scheme of organized crime in recent years has been to move into a large company, gain control, use the firm's established credit to run up thousands and thousands of dollars in unpaid invoices, then sell the inventory and let the firm go into bankruptcy. While the bankruptcy is involuntary, it is a planned bankruptcy.

10. Daniel P. Moynihan, "The Private Government of Crime," *Reporter*, 6 July 1961, pp. 14–20.
11. Donald R. Cressey, *The Theft of a Nation—The Structure and Operations of Organized Crime in America* (New York: Harper and Row, Publishers, 1969), pp. 248–89.
12. Walter Goodman, *A Percentage of the Take* (New York: Farrar, Straus & Giroux, 1971), pp. 60–68, 150–189.

The *"scam"* operation is nonviolent thievery in which a legitimate and solvent company or corporation is milked of its assets.

Common types of scam operations are:

1. *One-Step Scam:*
   a. A successful business with a good credit rating is purchased or control is achieved by other means such as loansharking, where a businessman pays off a debt by turning over his business to the loan sharks.
   b. No notice of the management change is provided to creditors or credit-rating services thus insuring use of a prior good credit rating.
   c. Arrangements are made with manufacturers and jobbers for the purchase of merchandise, and large orders are placed. The ordered material may be items not previously purchased, for scam operators seek merchandise with rapid turnover and some inherent difficulty in tracing.
   d. After the ordered merchandise has been received, the merchandise is sold, the money is milked from the business and this continues until creditors force the firm into bankruptcy.

2. *Three-Step Scam:*
   a. A new company or corporation is formed, managed by a member of the crime syndicate without a criminal record or past suspicion of arson, or a bankruptcy record.
   b. An initial large bank deposit is made to establish credit.
   c. A large store is rented, orders placed for merchandise with as many suppliers as possible. Small orders are placed initially, and these bills are promptly paid to establish credit.
   d. In the second month of operation, orders are placed for greater amounts of merchandise. Usually partial payment is made on these deliveries to protect initial credit rating.
   e. During the third month, very large orders are placed, and—again—merchandise may be different than previously ordered to secure merchandise such as jewelry and appliances which can easily be converted into cash.
   f. When creditors press for payment, the merchandise is converted into cash by selling it to an associate in organized crime who can mix the "scam" merchandise with his normal inventory.
   g. The involuntary bankruptcy goes on as planned. [13]

13. U.S., Department of Justice, Law Enforcement Assistance Administration, *Anatomy of a Scam: A Case Study of a Planned Bankruptcy,* prepared for the National Institute of Law Enforcement and Criminal Justice by Edward J. DeFranco (Washington, D.C.: Government Printing Office, 1973), pp 5–6.

Action Program—Supression of Organized Crime

A program for effective control of organized crime should have five main components:

1. An "Organized Crime Unit"
2. Training
3. Intelligence
4. Research and strategy development
5. Development of legislation.

It is obvious that organized crime differs fundamentally from other crime by reason of its organization and esprit de corps. This organization and its method of operations is also different in its social disruption, its social impact, and its economics—both in terms of profits to organized crime and losses to the general economy.

In view of the potential of organized crime, it is not at all unreasonable to undertake long-term commitments supporting a special squad of police and other experts (attorneys and accountants). This group would receive special training in the conduct of comprehensive investigations, the essential elements of crimes common to the national syndicate, the evidence necessary in these cases, and the common defense strategy of organized crime, particularly their corruption of friends in positions of authority.

The collection of intelligence is nothing more than securing a data base for proceeding against a well-organized criminal group. Without it, there is little likelihood that any police group will understand the assortment of relationships in organized crime. Federal agents have made excellent use of informants, undercover agents, and court-approved electronic eavesdropping. These are standard methods of intelligence gathering, but the syndicate's membership is alert and skilled in counter-intelligence gathering and the spoiling of sources of information.

Innovative research and the development of attack strategy should be aimed at specialized investigative techniques, such as the following: the detection of revenue violations, the general financial investigation of conspiracy and corruption, the discovery of the availability of illegal goods and services at local levels, and specialized prosecutorial techniques. The legislation unit would study existing legislation that permits wiretapping, electronic surveillance, or other interception techniques; the constitutional compatibility of adequate monitoring; the legislation necessary to grant immunity and to provide for contempt convictions, if witnesses refuse to talk despite immunity; the legislation for special grand juries and for blue ribbon trial juries; and other legislation which may be necessary to combat organized crime.

The high cost of organized crime is not always measurable. People lose money gambling, pay high interest on loans, buy narcotics (sometimes dying of an overdose), and union members and businessmen are victimized. But the more critical cost to the people of a community can be measured in terms of fear and loss of confidence in the government's ability to protect it from murder and corruption: the imposition of a second government upon the community.

Federal government task forces, under the direction of special assistant attorneys in the Department of Justice, and made up of agents of various government investigative agencies are reducing this threat to legitimate government by developing cases against the middle managers and executives of the national crime syndicate. The route has been hearings before federal grand juries and prosecutions in federal courts. In recent years, many of the so-called higher-ups have been convicted and sentenced to prison, but the multiple lower levels and complex operations of syndicated criminal operations demand investigation and prosecution at local and state levels.

State Crime Commissions

Local official corruption and organized crime usually have low visibility. Because of the cooperative relationship between local prosecutors and local police, the prosecutor usually permits the police chief and the police internal affairs division and/or intelligence squad to assume the responsibility for detecting any corruption among police and its ramifications into the operations of organized crime. Prosecutors must depend on police to investigate and assist in preparing cases for presentation in court, and to testify for the state upon the trial of offenders. There is need for a friendly, cooperative relationship.

Unless corruption is widespread, local prosecutors are reluctant to disturb the existing good relations with local police. Unless special funds are made available, they are equally reluctant to investigate and prosecute the difficult cases common to any crusade against public corruption and organized crime.

The most logical prosecutorial mechanism is state action, both within and without the criminal justice system. State action is insulated from local politics related to the agencies or officials accused, and prosecutions are not as likely to be labeled political maneuvers.

A model state anti-corruption program can be seen in the Temporary Commission of Investigation of the State of New York. A four-member commission (appointed by the Governor), with no more than two members from the same political party, was created in 1958 and has served effectively to date. It has the power to confer immunity upon witnesses, and may subpoena books, records, and documents relevant to an investigation.

At the direction of New York's Governor, the Commission conducts investigations in connection with:

1. Removing public officers
2. Formulating the Governor's recommendations related to the removal of public officers
3. Making recommendations to the Governor regarding changes in existing provisions of law necessary for more effective enforcement.[14]

The New York Commission has investigated harness racing, syndicated gambling, fraud in the construction industry, illegal awarding of municipal and state contracts for supplies and services, and infiltration into legitimate businesses by agents of the national crime syndicate. Its primary responsibility is the duty and power to conduct investigations in connection with:

1. The faithful execution and effective enforcement of the laws of the state, with particular reference to but not limited to organized crime and racketeering
2. The conduct of public officers and public employees, and of officers and employees of public corporations and authorities
3. Any matter concerning the public peace, public safety and public justice.[15]

The Commission holds hearings to bring to public view the inefficiency and misconduct of public officials or the operations of criminal syndicates. Evidence of criminal activity is referred to the local prosecutors for action. Inherent in these referrals is the threat that inadequate prosecutors at local levels can be replaced by special prosecutors appointed by the Governor.

Legalized Gambling

Legalizing gambling is an innovative means of attacking organized crime. It is a reasonable alternative to the law enforcement approach of detecting and apprehending individual members of organized crime

14. U.S. National Advisory Commission on Criminal Justice Standards and Goals, *Report on Police* (Washington, D.C.: Government Printing Office, 1973), pp. 267–269.
15. Ibid., p. 268.

groups. Legalization of gambling can deprive organized crime of a major portion of its economic base: the huge profits from illegal gambling.[16]

Illegal gambling is a crime without a victim. Gamblers seek out persons willing to accept their bets on horse races, sporting events, and "numbers" games, or to allow them to participate in illegal games of chance. Citizens demand such illegal services.

Repressive laws cannot be enforced broadly enough to stop or even reduce illegal gambling. Arrests are made and convictions secured where police attempt enforcement, but the business of illegal gambling goes on. Many police administrators prefer to assign police personnel to work preventing and investigating more serious crimes than illegal gambling. In addition, there are areas in which the police are corrupt and make little or no attempt to enforce anti-gambling laws.

The enactment of laws making gambling illegal originates in the Puritan or Protestant ethic in American society. It holds that there is a basic immorality to gambling; and in their role of protecting citizens from exploitation, local governments can rightfully deny citizens the opportunity to gamble. Every community has a history of incidents in which fathers and husbands have lost money they could not afford to lose. More recently, the compulsion to gamble has been recognized as a form of emotional disturbance, an almost irresistible impulse.

The reality of American life, however, is that these laws do not seriously restrict the opportunity to gamble. In fact, the demand for illegal gambling services had such a steady growth that the national crime syndicate recognized their potential as a money-maker early in its post-Prohibition struggle to replace income and jobs in boot-legging that were lost when the sale of alcoholic beverages was legalized.

Nationally, organized crime linked together its horse-racing and sports-betting enterprises with a nationwide wire service and a chain of master gamblers who provided such book-making services as these: (1) odds on horse races, (2) the time and winners of each race, (3) the early "line" (odds) on sports events, (4) the pre-game line, and (5) "lay-off" betting service—acceptance by master gamblers of bets upon races or sports events having heavy local "action" (betting) on favored participants. "Laying off" is a form of insurance for local illegal gambling enterprises. In the event the favored participant wins, their lay-off betting protects them from heavy financial losses.

Locally, organized crime took over the many urban area lotteries in which ghetto residents and others low on the socio-economic scale wagered small sums day after day. These are the "numbers" or "policy" games of New York, Washington, D.C., Chicago, and other large cities, and they produce great profits for their illegal operators, and many jobs for low-level members of organized crime.

16. Cressey, *Theft of a Nation*, pp. 292–296.

Betting at race tracks was legalized on the grounds that the poor did not go to the races. Supporting this fiction was a club-house for the wealthy and well-to-do, and a grandstand admission charge of several dollars. All this within the greater fiction that the horse races were being conducted for the "improvement of the breed," and not primarily to offer an opportunity to gamble.

When betting on horse races became legal at race tracks the publication of race results with the odds paid on win, show and place horses became part of the sports pages of newspapers, and later the subject of reports by radio and television stations. Baseball, football, basketball, and other sporting events also enjoy this publicity, with many papers carrying comment on the odds on each competing team or individual. The operators of many "numbers" games took advantage of this universal publicity to base the selection of winning numbers upon the money wagered upon various races each day. Baseball, football and basketball "pools" were developed as massive lotteries in which participants were sold weekly tickets, and the daily publicity allowed them to keep track of their progress as possible winners throughout the week.

It is true that the news media's basic justification for publishing data on horse races and sporting events is the public interest in the competition itself and the facts about the participants, and no one has ever justified any restriction of such news reporting. However, it is this competition and publicity that sets the stage for illegal gambling. Most of the money wagered goes to illegal bookmakers who offer some form of odds. Only a small percentage of betting is between two individuals, the so-called "friendly" bet.

Weighed against the legislative rationale for anti-gambling laws, the most valid argument against legalized gambling is that it will expand the opportunity to gamble. Weighed against the reality of publicity and public involvement in the outcome of horse races and sporting events, there is no valid argument against legalized gambling, particularly when the desire to gamble is served by illegal organizations of a nationwide crime syndicate. Profits from illegal gambling are often termed the *treasure chest* of organized crime.

The most valid argument for legalized gambling is that a well-run government operation can take over these profitable gambling operations from organized crime groups who now use their profits to finance other types of crime and to corrupt public officials. State operation of legal gambling may not be able to take over all the many and varied gambling operations of organized crime, but they can take over the most profitable enterprises and those in which the specific area of gambling requires extensive personnel. This would take away millions of dollars in profit now going to the bosses and under-bosses of organized crime, and would also deprive them of many jobs which support their criminal organization by providing regular incomes for gang members.

The objective of legalized gambling should be the elimination of its illegal counterpart; success should be measured by police intelligence surveys and reports on the extent of illegal gambling. Legalized gambling should be a technique *of* law enforcement, *not* a substitute for it.[17] Initially, police and the courts would have to be more diligent to suppress illegal gambling operations. After all, the concept of legalization as a means of attacking the economy of organized crime is based on the legal games attracting current customers. To deprive organized crime of a large and steady source of income is as much within the role of government as the enactment of laws attempting to suppress illegal gambling. Unless the legal game largely replaces illegal betting, it fails as an attack upon organized crime—the dollars earned by the legal gambling enterprise must have the added value of being denied to organized crime.[18]

Legalized off-track horse race betting, sports gambling, "pool" card betting, and "numbers" games are all ways to attack the economic structure of organized crime. Before off-track betting was legalized in New York City, police estimated that 150 to 200 million dollars were bet annually on horse races. A survey of that city's residents revealed 428 million dollars a year bet on sports events with illegal book-makers; 35 million dollars bet annually on "pool" card or sheet betting; and that 24 percent of all adults (1,352,718) in New York City play the "numbers" for a projected amount bet each year of over half a billion dollars.[19]

Of course, all of the money wagered is not profit, there are costs to illegal gambling as well as to legal games. However, the foregoing sums of money bet in these four forms of gambling indicate the potential profit of organized crime, the amount that would be lost to them if such games were legalized, and the fact that legalization could serve to raise revenue for the state.

Legal gambling will need safeguards. Revenue raising must be subordinated to the major purpose of eliminating illegal gambling. Infiltration of organized crime into legal games must be prevented. Police and courts must cooperate to block any attempt by organized crime to compete with the legal games.

It is necessary to keep in mind that organized crime has a unique capability for survival. If the nation's crime syndicate finds its profits reduced by legal gambling, it is likely it will attempt to open up some new field of illegal goods and services, or to expand fields such as drug-selling or the receipt and sale of stolen property, or even to step up their extortionist business.[20]

17. Joan Ransohoff and Clifford Goldman, *Legal Gambling in New York: A Discussion of Numbers and Sports Betting* (New York: Fund for the City of New York, 1972), p. 7.
18. Ibid., p. 6.
19. Ibid., pp. 24 and 31, p. 35, Appendix.
20. Cressey, *Theft of a Nation*, p. 295.

Selected References

Books

Cressey, Donald R. *The Theft of a Nation—The Structure and Operations of Organized Crime in America.* New York: Harper & Row, Publishers, 1969.

Egan, Frederick. *The Plainclothesman—Handbook of Vice and Gambling Operations.* New York: Arco Publishing Co., 1958.

Goodman, Walter. *A Percentage of the Take.* New York: Farrar, Strauss & Giroux, 1971.

Maas, Peter. *The Valachi Papers.* New York: G. P. Putnam's Sons, 1968.

Mollenhoff, Clark R. *Strike Force.* Englewood Cliffs, N.J.: Prentice-Hall, 1972.

U.S., The President's Commission on Law Enforcement and Administration of Justice. *Task Force Report: Organized Crime.* Washington, D.C.: Government Printing Office, 1967.

Periodicals

"Loan-sharking: The Untouched Domain of Organized Crime." *Columbia Journal of Law and Social Problems* 5, No. 1: 91–136.

Moynihan, Daniel P. "The Private Government of Crime." *Reporter*, 6 July 1961, pp. 14–20.

Chapter XXI

Careers in Criminal Justice Agencies

The history of criminal justice agencies in the United States reveals a continuing expansion of employment opportunities. Men and women planning on entering the field of criminal justice will find many opportunities for rewarding and meaningful work, at fair wages, and with career advancement more than equal to the upward occupational mobility in commerce or business.

Inducing, attracting, and motivating qualified individuals to seek such employment is of major importance to the administration of justice in America. Recruitment aims to enhance the public image of the various occupations embraced by police, courts, and corrections, and to present the incentives necessary to induce the most able young men and women in the community to select a career in the administration of justice.

The inherent challenge of recruitment is competition with business and commerce, as well as other public agencies, for the same talent in the labor market. Criminal justice recruitment must offer sufficient status, wages, career opportunities, and other benefits, to influence vocational choice.

The outstanding development in recent years in criminal justice agencies is recruitment for career service rather than for specific jobs alone. Career patterns have been developing which allow employees who prefer to serve at the *operational* level to qualify for salary advances on the basis of job performance. In time these salaries become comparable to those of supervisory and managerial positions. In the past, employees had no hope of higher wages if they did not wish to seek promotion to supervisory and management positions. Now, employees who receive adequate job satisfaction from daily operational responsibilities, and who perform at above average levels, can be rewarded by professional advancement to higher grades and higher wages.

Planned career advancement seeks to attract qualified persons who look for meaning in the hours on a job and significance in the preparation for such employment and advancement. The aim is to foster maximum employee contributions to the employing organization's objectives.

Job applicants in the criminal justice area can expect to be tested and retested. Testing to determine if applicants meet minimum standards and to array successful applicants in a rank order list for appointment is the policy in most areas of the United States. Applicants are usually notified at each step of the selection process, and most agencies make every effort to cut down the time between the filing of applications and the establishing of a list of eligible candidates.

Police Employment

The general field of policing ranges from service with town and village police units to large municipal police departments, and from employment with a county-wide sheriff's office or county police department to duty with a state police or a highway patrol. In addition there are the federal law enforcement agencies.

Until recent times, police agencies rejected applicants below specific height levels, with poor eyesight, or who did not meet standards for weight, hearing, and other physical requirements. A criminal history, inability to work under supervision, and emotional instability were also causes for rejection. On the other hand, prior police experience or many years of formal education beyond grade school were not required as entrance qualifications.

A growing realization that minimum height and visual ability requirements denied to the police many applicants with above-average promise has led to changes in many basic requirements. Height appears to be losing its importance as a police entrance requirement, and eyesight is no longer a problem for applicants if it is correctable to acceptable standards by glasses or contact lenses. In fact, the entire gamut of police requirements is in the process of change as more and more police executives realize the need for a broad recruitment base, including as many women and members of racial and ethnic minorities as possible.

It is now seen that women have a unique and vital role to play in American law enforcement. The under-utilization of minorities has switched to an active program of searching out black and Spanish-speaking candidates. In many departments minority hiring has gone beyond the requirements of social justice in terms of the percentage of minority representation. Such hiring is often based on the contribution minority employees can make to law enforcement because of their unique cultural knowledge, appreciation of the impact of ghetto life, and, in the case of Spanish-speaking persons, their bilingual ability.

Acceptable applicants are tested for strength, physical endurance, and agility; and those who are found qualified have to pass a written examination, and survive a comprehensive "background" investigation into their employment history and life style. In addition, many law enforcement agencies screen otherwise acceptable applicants by pre-employment interviews, and some agencies use psychological testing procedures and lie detection apparatus and experts to screen candidates.

A probationary period (six months to two years) is standard. Employees are protected from arbitrary dismissal during this period, but employers can terminate an employee who does not measure up to the standards for on-the-job performance.

Educational standards for police applicants as a condition of employment have been slow in developing, but are presently becoming more common. Police agencies are being encouraged to require as a condition of initial employment:

1. At least one year of education (30 semester units) at an accredited college or university; or completion of this requirement within three years from date of employment (for present candidates with a high school diploma or its equivalent)
2. From 1975 to 1978—at least two years of education (60 semester units) at an accredited college or university
3. From 1979 to 1982—at least three years of education (90 semester units) at an accredited college or university
4. Beginning in 1982 to 1983—at least four years of education (120 semester units or a baccalaureate degree) at an accredited college or university.[1]

For many years, sheriffs and police chiefs who came up through the ranks via the seniority system did not subscribe to the need for college-educated police officers and many, no doubt, felt threatened by such personnel. The growth of American police systems since mid-century has forced executive development programs upon law enforcement agencies which prepare men and women for advancement through the management hierarchy on the basis of performance and achievement rather than on seniority and experience. As a result, today's police leaders are seeking men and women educated in the behavioral and social sciences, and they are using the knowledge of such employees to improve police services.

1. U.S., National Advisory Commission on Criminal Justice Standards and Goals, *Report on Police* (Washington, D.C.: Government Printing Office, 1973), p. 369.

In addition, rank and file police personnel did not welcome college-educated police in past years. This attitude has also changed. This is probably due to the premium our American society has placed on educational attainments, rather than to any proven above-average job performance by college-level police. The fast-breaking community college movement upgraded the educational level of society generally, and the rank and file members of police departments began to accept college-level education as no more than normal for all new recruits.

Educational incentive programs are being used to encourage police officers to achieve a college education. They enhance the social acceptance of college-educated police recruits by offering rank and file police without formal education the opportunity to study and a specific motivation to do so. These educational incentive programs are fringe benefits to salary schedules. Incentive pay may add from two to five percent, or more, to an employee's salary.

Substantial pension programs, shorter hours of work, and liberal sick leave and hospitalization benefits are factors in attracting job applicants qualified for and adapted to the special requirements of policing. However, an attractive salary plan is most important. The rate of pay which will attract, and retain, persons competent in providing police services varies with the locality and the nation's economic state, but one of the problems has been that police salaries were not comparable to other professional employment. In 1954, a well-informed police survey analyst, Bruce Smith, Jr., reported:

> Substantial progress is being made toward a professional police service. A growing recognition by states, counties, and municipalities that capable men should be adequately paid is aiding the trend.[2]

Adequate salaries are now the rule rather than the exception. Public employers are not responsive to the basic concept that a community can only have quality police services if they are willing to pay for them, and police employee groups have fostered the theme that professionalization of police is linked to adequate salaries.

Career advancement in law enforcement agencies is developing into a planned, methodological approach to occupational professionalism with two career types or paths. One is advancement within the area of the agency's professional expertise at operational levels (functional), the second is advancement to managerial positions.

This dual career plan permits an employee to consider a professional career as a highly-skilled patrolman working in the uniformed force, or as an investigator or other specialist, as opposed to a supervisory and managerial career, with professional career advancement having salary poten-

2. Bruce Smith, Jr., "The Policeman's Hire," *The Annals of the American Academy of Political and Social Science* (New Goals in Police Management) 291 (January 1954): 119–126.

tials equivalent to those in the various levels of supervision and management.

Position classification plans are being developed by police and other law enforcement agencies which delineate the available career paths within an agency, and forecast the agency's requirements on all functional and managerial levels. Two core areas of these plans are: (1) guidelines for educational achievement likely to enhance advancement, and (2) a fair and impartial promotion process.

A long sought goal aligned with professionalization of police has been lateral entry: moving from one employing agency to another when career advancement is blocked; or when another agency appears more attractive for self-improvement and advancement, or offers the opportunity for more meaningful work assignments. However, the closed system of most police agencies (open hiring primarily at the entrance level) has always been attractive to agency employees as it offers upward mobility without threat of outside competition. The complications of residence requirements and non-transferable pensions are other factors blocking lateral entry.

Lateral mobility has been successful at the police executive level throughout the country. The International Association of Chiefs of Police regularly conducts nationwide tests for police departments with vacancies at this level. When it develops at lower levels, lateral entry offers:

1. Individual police officers intent on professionalizing their careers an opportunity to reach their full potential

2. Individual police agencies the opportunity to satisfy manpower needs above entrance levels

3. The police establishment an opportunity to maximize the efficient use of manpower resources.[3]

Police requirements expanding the potential universe of job applicants, testing as a screening process to forecast performance, probation as a further testing device, new educational standards and "social acceptance" of college-educated police by police leaders and rank and file members, educational incentive programs; adequate salaries, dual career paths (professional and supervisory-managerial), and the possibility of lateral transfer all contribute to police employment as a desirable and rewarding career.

The challenge of police service and the management of police organizations are great enough to test the skills, intellect, and competence of any qualified candidate. Policing is no longer keyed to the ability or willingness to use a gun or a police night stick. It still has its risk-taking and

3. Commission on Criminal Justice, *Report on Police*, pp. 437–439.

hazards, but law enforcement agents have become people with the human touch, with creativity, innovation, spontaneity, and empathy. Police employment offers opportunities for personal and professional satisfaction.

Court Administration

Professional court administration is becoming an essential part of the operation of American courts. It is the management of the nonjudicial business of a court or a system of courts.

Court administrators are usually appointed by the judges of the court or court system the administrator will serve. Most of the present court administrators have had legal training and prior court-related employment, usually as judges or court clerks. The average annual salary for state court administrators is about twenty-five thousand dollars, while trial court administrators average between twenty-three and twenty-four thousand dollars.[4]

Career advancement plans among court employees will probably follow the functional lines of the skills of nonjudicial employees (reporters, clerks, secretaries, bailiffs, etc.) for a nonmanagement career track; and a management career track for supervisors and middle managers.

Since many court administrators who were recruited and selected for this management position had court-related experience, these positions can be reached through career advancement, and by lateral transfer such administrators can seek better paying or more rewarding administration positions with other courts or court systems.

Correctional Manpower

Correctional manpower covers a broader spectrum of personnel categories than do the police or courts. There are two major settings for employment in corrections—institutions, and probation and parole agencies. Personnel categories are usually defined by the function to be performed, and there are four broad occupational categories in corrections: (1) administrators, (2) supervisors, (3) functional specialists, and (4) line workers.

An overview of the many personnel categories, with their functions implied by job title and job setting has been published by the Joint Commission on Correctional Manpower and Training:

4. U.S., National Advisory Commission on Criminal Justice Standards and Goals, *Report on Courts*, (Washington, D.C.: Government Printing Office, 1973), pp. 171–175.

DEFINITIONS OF PERSONNEL CATEGORIES

I. Job Categories in Institutions

Administrators
Warden and Superintendent
Assistant/Associate Warden and Superintendent
Business Manager
Education Department Head
Line Correctional Staff Department Head
Director of Inmate Classification
Farm and Food Services Department Head
Maintenance Department Head
Prison Industries Superintendent
Director of Clinical/Treatment Services
Child Care Staff Department Head
Supervisors
Educational Supervisor
Line Correctional Staff Supervisor
Prison Industries Shop and Factory Head
Child Care Staff Supervisor
Supervisor of Casework Services
Functional Specialists
Academic Teacher
Vocational Teacher or Instructor
Vocational and Educational Counselor
Classification Officer
Social Worker
Sociologist
Vocational Rehabilitation Counselor
Psychologist
Physical Education Teacher
Counselor
Institution Parole Officer
Line Workers
Line Correctional Non-Supervisory Staff
Cottage Parent/Counselor
Group Supervisor
Child Care Staff
Non-Supervisory Staff
Food and Farm Services
Maintenance
Prison Industries

II. Job Categories in Probation and Parole Agencies

Administration
Director of Court Services
Chief Probation Officer/Director

Director of Parole Supervision
Assistant/Associate Chief Probation Officer/Director
District Director
Supervisors
Staff Supervisor
District Supervisor
Assistant Supervisor
Functional Specialists
Field Probation Officer
Psychologist
Job Placement Officer
Field Parole Officer

III. "Other" Category Includes:

Chaplain
Attorney
Librarian
Medical and Dental Personnel
Training Personnel
Research Personnel
Parole Board
Parole/Probation Aid
Business and Personnel Technical Assistant
Others as defined by the institution or agency.[5]

Corrections is essentially a closed system. Promotion is usually confined to the employees of a single agency or department. A barrier to lateral entry not encountered in police agencies or the courts is the lack of uniformity of job titles in corrections, and the differing functions performed in various jurisdictions under the same or similar job titles. As a result, most incumbents in the personnel categories of administrator and supervisor have won these positions in competition with other employees of a department or agency. Only in the very top executive positions has outside recruitment of administrators broken this overall practice of internal promotion to high level positions.

In what may be described as the specialized manpower area, the management of correctional agencies is forced to seek applicants outside the agency or department. Specialized manpower encompasses such occupational and professional categories as psychiatrists, psychologists, social workers, rehabilitation counselors, recreation counselors, academic and vocational teachers, lawyers, librarians, nurses, dentists, physicians, chaplains, and vocational counselors. Graduate study achievements are a prerequisite to such employment; completion of doctoral work and even

5. U.S., Joint Commission on Correctional Manpower and Training, *A Time to Act* (Washington, D.C.: Government Printing Office 1969), p. 81.

post doctoral study is common among candidates for these occupational categories.[6]

The greatest employment opportunity in corrections for applicants with a four-year college or university education is in that segment of correctional manpower who work primarily with individual offenders: case managers, institutional counselors, parole agents, and probation officers. The undergraduate degree has become the standard educational requirement for entry-level work in this field, despite the fact that many agencies and departments publish job requirements calling for graduate study or a graduate degree. Preferred educational areas are psychology, sociology, social work, education, and public administration. Criminology/corrections and criminal justice are relatively new fields, but are disciplines that have achieved a high order of acceptance in recent years among employers of correctional manpower.

A growth in the potential pool of correctional manpower is inherent in the development of criminal justice and criminology/corrections core curriculums in two-year and four-year colleges and universities. Although relatively new, these programs promote understanding and appreciation of the entire criminal justice process, and students can become generalists or specialists, depending upon their own interests and selected areas of study.

Line workers in corrections are primarily concerned with restraint rather than treatment, with the majority working in some area of custody. Entry is still possible in this area with a high school education or less. However, a career ladder has been developing in most jurisdictions which affords an opportunity for those with high school education or less to enter the correctional manpower field and make their way to more skilled employment levels through a combined work and study program. This career mobility is in addition to the position classification plan providing for upward mobility through staff development; the work-study program allows an employee in corrections to add to whatever education he or she had at the time of entry-level hiring, and joins the academic work with on-the-job training. (See Figure 9, p. 352)

The variety of jobs complicates the recruitment of correctional manpower. However, this broad spectrum means that applicants with many different backgrounds have splendid opportunities for employment and rewarding careers in this area of criminal justice.

The Private Sector

The nature and extent of the private police industry (privately employed guards, investigators, patrolmen, alarm and armored-car per-

6. U.S., Joint Commission on Correctional Manpower and Training, *Perspectives on Correctional Manpower and Training* (Washington, D.C.: Government Printing Office, 1970), pp. 89–98.

sonnel) offers many opportunities for employment, either while studying in preparation for a career in the public sector of criminal justice, or as a career in itself.

Private investigators are usually state licensed and supervised with the licensee responsible for all of his employees. They may be self-employed, work for a small firm specializing in one geographic or investigative area, or be employed by one of the nationwide agencies (Pinkerton's, Inc.; William J. Burns International Detective Agency, Inc.; Wackenhut Corporation). Many of these agencies offer career opportunities equal to those offered by large state or municipal police, urbanized sheriff's departments, or federal law-enforcement agencies such as the Federal Bureau of Investigation.

Private investigation is the work performed by a privately employed person to collect information as to:

1. Crimes or wrongs

2. Persons, groups, or business organizations: identity, behavior, associates, reputation, history

3. Lost or stolen property

4. Fires, libel, slander, losses, accidents, injuries

5. Business and financial standing and credit responsibility of persons or business organizations.[7]

Guards, security officers, or patrolmen protect, or attempt to protect, persons and property from criminal depredations, damage, injury, or other loss (fire, flood, etc.). They operate within the boundaries of private property, but travel on public roads in protecting more than one location (as the "merchant" patrols in moving from one shopping center or business area to another). Aligned with these protective services are central station alarm agencies whose personnel wire premises with an intrusion alarm system with each alarm alerting monitoring personnel at a central monitoring station. These firms often have stand-by personnel who respond promptly to the premises in which the alarm system signals an intrusion; others work with local police, notifying them of an entry alarm. Armored car personnel use guards to protect property, usually cash, while being transported from business premises to a bank, or vice versa. Employment as a guard in any of these enterprises offers limited challenge and opportunity. However, ownership or executive management of guard forces offers opportunities for real career development.

Polygraph examination or lie detection is another field with professional career dimensions, as is service as a consultant or research

7. James S. Kakalik and Sorrel Wildhorn, *Current Regulation of Private Police: Regulatory Agency Experience and Views*, Vol. 3; R-871/DOJ (Santa Monica, Calif.: The Rand Corporation, 1971), pp. 2–3.

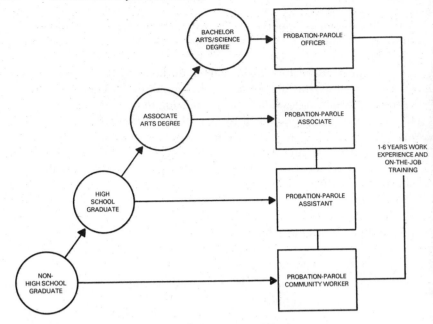

Source: Joint Commission on Correctional Manpower and Training.

Figure 9. A Career Ladder in Corrections. This approach creates a series of job classifications in relation to education through which corrections employees can progress through education, work experience, and on-the-job training.

specialist. Skilled experts in lie detection by machine have the competency to conduct examinations testing the responses of the person being questioned by measuring blood pressure, pulse, breathing, and electrical changes of the skin. These physiological measures are used to evaluate the truthfulness of responses. Experts in other professional fields warrant employment as consultants, but this usually requires years of prior work experience and study in the area in which expertise is claimed. Research technicians are in demand by organizations conducting criminal justice research. Many major state and federal research projects have been awarded to business firms or research groups associated with a college or university.

A field that is developing rapidly is pretrial investigation in civil practice. This is not an area of criminal justice, but the methods of investigation are the same as in criminal justice. However, medical malpractice, design failure, professional errors and omissions, and other areas of liability require more than mere investigative skill. There is a need for paraprofessional legal skills. In future years, educational and on-the-job requirements will be formalized. At present there are indications that this will become a field with both financial rewards and job satisfaction.

Prelaw Preparation

Criminal justice educational programs and employment in the public or private sector of criminal justice has developed as a de facto prelaw preparation program.

Traditionally, prelaw preparation has been associated with four-year college or university programs in the liberal arts, or in majors associated with government or political science. Graduates of these programs usually went right into law schools, without any break in their education.

It may be that legal training is a natural extension of an individual's motivation for a career in police or corrections. Contacts with judges, prosecutors, and defense attorneys may have their influence. The challenge in attempting the study of law and in the occupation of advocacy may be the prime mover.

In any event, four-year college and university programs in criminal justice offer interested students many opportunities to take liberal arts, government, and political science courses common to prelaw preparation, and many schools require such courses to satisfy the major's degree requirements. Work in criminal justice agencies after graduation offers time for reflection, a potential for financing the cost of law school, and the possibility of continuing employment in the public or private sectors while attending night law school classes.

Selected References

Books

American Bar Association Advisory Committee on the Police Function, Project on Standards for Criminal Justice, *Standards Relating to the Urban Police Function.* New York: American Bar Association, 1972.

U.S., National Advisory Commission on Criminal Justice Standards and Goals. *Report on Corrections.* Washington, D.C.: Government Printing Office, 1973.

————, *Report on Police.* Washington, D.C.: Government Printing Office, 1973.

Chapter XXII

Criminal Justice as a System

Criminal justice is a system comprised of four major functional parts: sanction law, police, courts, and corrections. Or, to rephrase, it is a system of lawmakers, law enforcement agents, the judiciary, and the personnel of corrections and rehabilitation agencies.

America's lawmakers enact new laws and amend old ones to provide at state, federal, and oftentimes municipal levels, the criminal codes of our country which punish violations by the application of penalties.

Police and other agents of law enforcement serve as the front line of criminal justice, discovering and apprehending violators; and in their role as peace officers the police have a function in which they adjust various differences and disputes without arrest.

The prosecuting attorney, the defense counsel, and the presiding judge make up a court for the prosecution of offenders. The prosecutor and the defense lawyer are both officers of the court, despite being opposing counsel as part of our adversary method of seeking truth in court proceedings.

At the conclusion of the criminal proceedings against an accused the probation-prison-parole complex (organized to rehabilitate offenders) takes over. This complex uses the sentencing power of the trial judge, the field supervision of probation and parole officers, and the professional competence of correctional counselors, caseworkers, psychologists, sociologists, and psychiatrists in a bifurcated program aimed at alternatives to imprisonment, and release on parole rather than lengthy incarceration. This complex of people, facilities, theory, and practice strive for the goals of rehabilitation: clean lives by persons previously convicted of crime and a diminishing in the number of persons who return to criminal acts after arrest, prosecution, conviction, sentence, and rehabilitation.

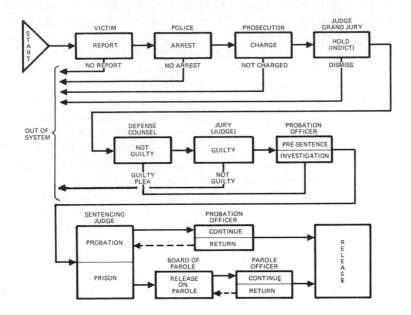

Figure 10. The Criminal Justice System. A model of criminal justice as a "system" based on the *offender* and the network of decision points which determine the offender's fate in the system.

At this time there is a balance in dealing with crime and delinquency: (1) control through sanction law enforcement with its individualized treatment of offenders oriented to their individual rehabilitation, and (2) control through removal of the causes of criminal behavior. Therefore, social control is a method of reducing crime and delinquency by maintenance of an effective criminal justice system. Through the integration of various social science and social justice programs in clinics and the community, crime can be prevented by removing causative factors related to poverty (deficiencies in education, vocational preparation, and job and career opportunities), and emotional problems related to constitutional defects or acquired in early childhood.

In social control there is a coexistence of two major thrusts, the one by agents and agencies of criminal justice, and the other by family, church, school, and government. The common goal of social control in any free society is to make life in a community of people manageable and sufficiently permissive so that each individual has a maximum amount of liberty and freedom to grow and develop—and in America, to pursue life, liberty, and happiness. The founding fathers were not unmindful of the controls and limits to liberty which are necessary to allow people to live together with a minimum of conflict. Each man could not be a law unto himself deciding what is right and wrong and enforcing his own moral or social concepts on others, acting as policeman, prosecutor, judge, jury, and executioner, all rolled into one. If society were so constituted it would have destroyed itself long ago.

On the other hand, each person must be able to live as an individual, have some area of decision as to how he lives his own life, and some privacy from the protective eye of government. The first eight amendments to the Constitution recognized that a person is an individual and that the individual must be protected from oppression by the government. Those amendments were not only meant for the protection of all, but also for the protection of any minority from the oppression of the majority. There are many diverse ways in which a person may live his life without infringing unnecessarily or substantially on the lives of others. The American system allows for—and even encourages—such divergence, and cautions government against unnecessary or unreasonable interference. The mere fact that there may be some benefit which accrues to a person who has committed a crime is unimportant when weighed against the specter of unlimited and uncontrolled government interference in the personal and private lives of its citizens. There are many examples of such unlimited government power over the citizen in both ancient and recent history to warn us of the dangers of power. Benjamin Franklin put it nicely: "Those who are willing to give up an essential liberty for the sake of a little security are deserving of neither liberty nor security."

While the zeal and expertise of many individuals in criminal justice and social science have contributed to a systems strategy for combatting crime and delinquency, there is still a need for new management resources. Agencies of criminal justice have been splintered by geography and function, and social science research programs and demonstration projects have been equally fragmented. Such management resources may be nondirective so as to protect the prerogative of local government, and yet through funding and fiduciaries exercise sufficient control to insure a new uniformity in planning, decision making, and field direction of the day-to-day work of social control. Under program budgeting procedures the attainment of objectives at reasonable costs can be emphasized.

Necessary Objectives in Crime Control

Absolutely necessary for the control of crime and delinquency is an approach keyed to the following objectives:

1. A data base information system containing not only the factual data on offenders, but also the relationship of this data to the efficacy of arrest-to-release programs to which these offenders have been exposed

2. Systematic studies of criminals and crime-prone groups, the social dependency of problem families, and the criminal-creating impact of the labels "juvenile delinquent" and "ex-convict"

3. A law of crimes that does not overreach, but rather confines itself to legislation concerning crimes that injure persons or cause financial loss, and a system of sanctions in the law which are not vengeance directed (punitive in nature); plus a system of penalties which will allow for dealing with an individual rather than mandating an inflexible punishment for a particular crime

4. A cost analysis of the costs of crime and delinquency in relation to the impact of crime on the offender and victim, the loss of productivity while offenders are in prison or pursuing a lifetime crime career, the welfare costs of supporting the families of offenders, and the victim's loss of property, injury, or death

5. The development of action programs keyed to social control projects organized for crime prevention and *management* of offenders, development and training of manpower to carry out such action programs, and projects which will reveal innovative methods of utilizing communications media to notify the public and secure their support and cooperation

6. A continuing overall systems research survey-and-report project which will speak out in public to the police, the prosecutors, the lawyers for the defense, the judiciary, the personnel of correctional agencies, and the scientists of the social sciences and other disciplines and technologies. They must be informed about the effectiveness or ineffectiveness of the criminal justice system and its goal of controlling crime and delinquency with justice rather than injustice.

There is a costs-to-benefits theme in the above planning by objectives. There is also a base of knowledge for the action programs, for revised laws, and for overall supervision and report by research technicians which is tied in with the ratio of costs to benefits. Action programs not based on factual knowledge are like shooting without aiming (a waste of ammunition). There is also a base point for developing and training adequate manpower, and this too reveals a costs-to-benefits consciousness. Untrained or poorly selected personnel is wasteful. Lastly, if the *real* costs of crime, rather than the costs of supporting the criminal justice agencies, are known, there is a better basis for funding programs with the objective of managing offenders, and turning them away from their criminal behavior patterns.

Action programs would be situated in four major functional areas: (1) prevention of crime and delinquency, (2) discovery of crime and the apprehension and prosecution of offenders, (3) fair trial and due process in criminal proceedings, and (4) case management of offenders. Measurements for evaluation can be established which will indicate whether the operations of these programs are meeting with success. Based on population, the rate of crime has always indicated the general failure of socialization and special programs to prevent crime. Offense and arrest data, correlated with statistics on conviction and final disposition of arrestees, has served to roughly measure the functioning of the apprehension process (from discovery to prosecution). Judicial review and circumstances disclosed by a series of cases or individual landmark cases are indicative of the prevailing practices threatening the concept of fair trial and due process. The criminal offender population, with its recidivism and escalation in the seriousness of crimes, is a fair indication as to the actual success or failure in the rehabilitation processes.

Criminal Justice Education

The law schools of America are reacting constructively to the challenge of crime, enforcement, prosecution, and postconviction problems. Courses offered range from criminal and constitutional law to evidence. In addition many law schools now list "clinical courses," special preparation in trial practice and advocacy. A few of these schools offer work experience courses in which students work with the inmates of a prison or juvenile hall in resolving legal problems.

College level police science education, dating back to 1916 at the University of California at Berkeley, has discarded many of the courses that duplicated the basic course given to police recruits at police academies during entrance level or vestibule training. Course offerings at community colleges, or the first two years of a four-year college or university program, offer courses with content which ranges from evidence and investigation to criminal justice and its administration. Requirements for a degree in the community colleges, or to attain third-year scholastic levels in a four-year college or university, require approximately two-thirds of the courses taken to be in the area of general education: science, art, humanities, mathematics, writing and speaking, psychology, political science, philosophy, and sociology. Police science programs at third and fourth year levels now range from criminalistics and police administration to current problems in criminal justice.

Closely aligned with the police science programs of education at academic institutions is the development of a similar public service program in the area of corrections. This is a breakaway from the traditional social work programs in the past, and it will provide greater educational opportunities in this field for many more individuals. Among the recommended courses in corrections education are:

1. Crime and delinquency
2. Correctional services in the community
3. Introduction to corrections
4. The court system
5. Probation, pardons, and parole
6. Group and individual counseling
7. Institutional procedures
8. Principles of correctional administration
9. The prison society
10. Administration of criminal justice
11. Crime and the criminal
12. Contemporary practices in corrections.[1]

There is a continuum in the criminal justice process: from a greater to a lesser involvement—with the victim and with the offender. At one end is law enforcement, with its agents exposed to the violence of crime, the agony of injured victims, and the hazards of fighting crime. Just beyond this sphere are the prosecutor and defense counsel who are more remotely aware of the many brutal aspects of crime and its impact on victims and offenders. The judiciary occupies a central or neutral position. It is aloof from both victim and offender and is mainly concerned with the facts in dispute and the just and accurate application of the law. Sentencing neutralizes the judiciary: it must weigh the seriousness of the crime (victim) against the offender's need for rehabilitation. Correctional personnel are remote from the victims of crime and in direct and frequent contact with offenders. Except for considering the potential victims of future crimes when evaluating parole readiness or continuance on probation, their role is one of almost total involvement with the offender. (See Figure 11.)

The central tendency of educational programs in law, police science, and corrections to form around the theme of criminal justice is indicative of new horizons in the administration of criminal justice as a system. In addition, these educational programs are being regrouped into departments of Criminal Justice or Administration of Justice at many community colleges and four-year colleges and universities.

1. Vernon B. Fox, *Guidelines for Corrections Programs in Community and Junior Colleges* (Washington, D.C.: American Association of Junior Colleges, 1971), pp. 29–30.

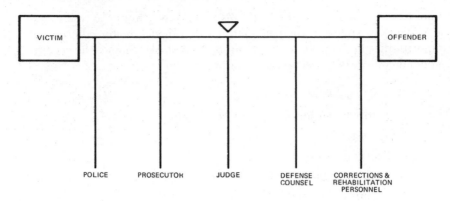

Figure 11. The Victim-Offender Continuum. The continuum between victim and offender and the relative positions of the agents of criminal justice.

The control of crime and delinquency will certainly be enhanced when the agents and agencies of criminal justice shorten the continuum between police and corrections, and work together to reduce crime and rehabilitate offenders.

List of Cases

To locate where a case is discussed go to the chapter or chapters as noted here and check the footnotes. Cases are identified there both by name and citations.

Adams v. Williams, XII
Barron v. Baltimore, X
Benton v. Maryland, X
Betts v. Brady, X
Boyd v. United States, X
Boykin v. Alabama, XIV
Brown v. Mississippi, VIII
California v. Green, X
Chambers v. Florida, XV
Chimel v. California, VIII, X, XII
Clutchette v. Procunier, XIX
Dred Scott v. Sanford, X
Escobedo v. Illinois, XI, XIII
Elkins v. United States, X
Furman v. Georgia, XVII
Gideon v. Wainwright, X, XI
Gilbert v. California, XII
Gitlow v. New York, X
Gustafson v. Florida, VIII, XII
Hagen v. State, XV
Haley v. Ohio, XVI
Harris v. New York, XII
In re Foss, I
In re Gault, XVI
In re Lynch, I
In re Nagle, V
In re Oliver, XV
In the Matter of Four Youths, XVI
Irwin v. Dowd, XV
Jelke v. New York, XV
Juelich v. United States, XV

Katz v. United States, VIII
Kent v. United States, XVI
Ker v. California, X
Kirby v. Illinois, VIII, XII
Klopfer v. North Carolina, XIII
McCray v. Illinois, VIII
McNabb v. United States, X
Malloy v. Hogan, X
Mapp v. Ohio, VIII, X, XII
Miranda v. Arizona, VIII, XI, XII
Morrissey v. Brewer, XIX
Noland v. State Bar, XIII
Olmstead v. United States, I, XVI
Palko v. Connecticut, X
People v. Belous, I
People v. Brown, XV
People v. Crowe, XIII
People v. Duncan, XV
People v. Lessard, XV
People v. Lokey, XVII
People v. Odum, XV
People v. Ruef, XIII
People v. West, XIV
People v. Whitmore, XV
Pointer v. Texas, X
Powell v. Alabama, X, XI
Robinson v. California, X
Sheppard v. Maxwell, XV
Snyder v. Massachusetts, II
State v. Kociolek, XV
Stromberg v. California, X
Twining v. New Jersey, X
Terry v. Ohio, VII, X, XII
United States v. Ash, VIII, XII
United States ex rel Elksnis v. Gilligan, XIV
United States v. Robinson, VIII, XII
United States v. Wade, VIII, XI, XII
Weeks v. United States, X
West v. Louisiana, X
Wolf v. Colorado, X

Index